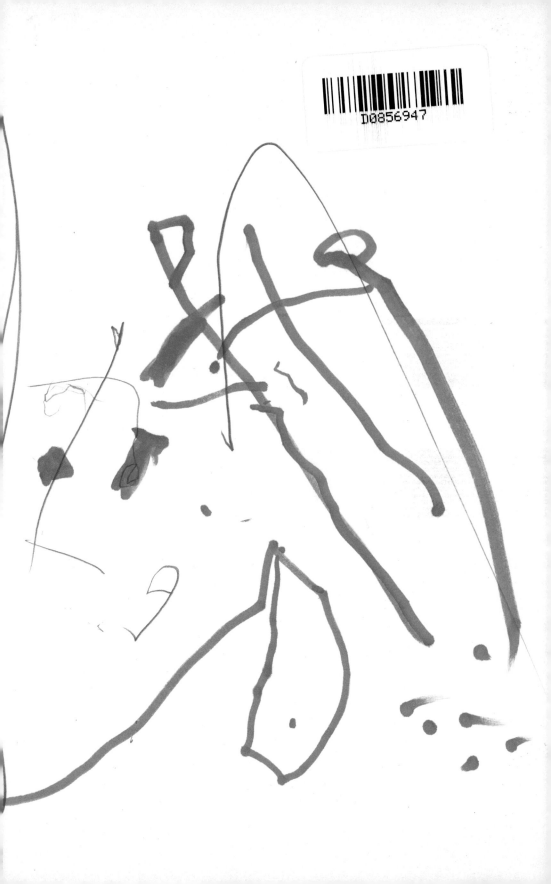

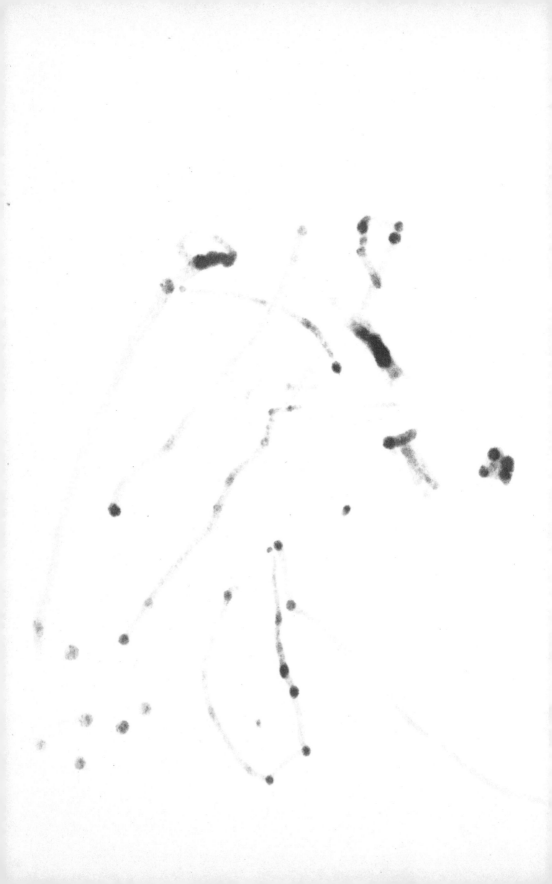

TOM MORRIS
OF ST ANDREWS

TOM MORRIS
OF ST ANDREWS
The Colossus of Golf

DAVID MALCOLM   **PETER E. CRABTREE**

BIRLINN

First published in 2008 in a limited edition
by Rhod McEwan at Glengarden Press
This edition published in 2010 by
Birlinn Limited
West Newington House
10 Newington Road
Edinburgh
EH9 1QS

www.birlinn.co.uk

ISBN 13: 978 1 84158 818 6

British Library Cataloguing-in-Publication Data
A catalogue record for this book is available from the
British Library

This book is also available as a limited edition. The large-format
limited edition contains 325 colour illustrations, many of them rare
and previously unpublished. For details and ordering information,
please see *www.rhodmcewan.com/tom_morris/index.htm*.

Typeset in Adobe Garamond at Birlinn

Printed and bound in Great Britain by
MPG Books, Bodmin, Cornwall

Contents

Plates

Tom Morris by Thomas Rodger in *c*. 1850
Allan Robertson by Thomas Rodger in *c*. 1850
Willie and Jamie, the Dunn twins from Musselburgh
James Ogilvie Fairlie with Tom Morris
Young Tom Morris at the age of 12
Young Tom Morris after his first tournament win, aged 16
The Challenge Belt presented to the Open Champion from 1860 to 1870
Plan of the Old Course at St Andrews in 1875
Davie Strath aged 28 years
Tommy Morris's 1870 Open Championship scorecard
Tommy Morris wearing the Challenge Belt after he had gained it as his own
Circular raising a memorial to young Tom Morris by subscription
Jof, Tom Morris's second son
The Links Road along the 18th fairway at St Andrews
Painting of the Road War by W. A. Dick
The Autumn Meeting of The Royal and Ancient in 1862 by Thomas Hodge
Tom Morris's daughter Elizabeth and her husband, James Hunter
Timber ships at the Hunter Wharfs, Darien, Georgia
The elderly Willie Park by John A. T. Bonner
The elderly Tom Morris by Thomas Hodge
Tom Morris with Jof at the Troon Tournament in 1886
Tom Morris with his workforce outside his shop
Tom Morris with his grandchildren and their dog 'Silver'
Tom Morris acting as starter in 1902
Tom Morris with ladies from the Tait family in 1902
Tom Morris's funeral procession in St Andrews in 1908

Acknowledgements

Many people have provided help and advice during the preparation of this work, and without their assistance this book could not have been completed.

We have benefited from the knowledge and support of David Hamilton and have called upon the knowledge and experience of Philip Truett. We appreciate their input, enthusiasm and encouragement. We also thank those who have been constructive in criticising the text, helped with historical accuracy and interpretation, guided in medical matters or have given encouragement: Gordon Christie, Margaret Grubb, Duncan Lawrie, Robert Smart, Robert Burnett, Malcolm Foggo, Jim Barclay, Sir Roddy MacSween, David Dobson, John Di Falco, Paul Dhillon, Kevin Costello, John Pyne, Steve McPherson, Ian Bunch and Roger Taylor. From Yorkshire, we are indebted to Christine Dewar, Ben Downs, Sir Harry Ognall and John Pearson for their editorial assistance and advice. Special mention must be made of the researches of Noel Terry in Melbourne, Australia, regarding David Strath.

Specialists in many libraries have been supportive and helpful. In St Andrews University Library Archives, Dr Norman Reid, Rachel Hart, Cilla Jackson and Moira Mackenzie have been tireless in their efforts. In the West Lothian Local History Library, Sybil Cavanagh sourced images and information and described the Whitburn township in mid-nineteenth century in words that no photograph could convey. In Darien, Georgia, Buddy Sullivan was encouraging and his writings were essential for an understanding of the life of the lumberman on the Georgia Tidewater. The help of the staff of Darien's Ida Hilton Public Library, the services of the staff of the Probate Court and Library in Mobile, Alabama, and the archivists of the University of South Alabama are appreciated.

Many libraries, museums and galleries have been visited. Among these, special thanks are given to the staff of the British Library Newspapers at Colindale, the British Library at St Pancras and Kew in London, the National Portrait Gallery, London, the National Archives of Scotland, the

National Galleries of Scotland and the National Library of Scotland, Edinburgh Public Library, Glasgow's Mitchell Library, the Carnegie Library in Ayr, South Ayrshire Council's Rozelle House Galleries, North Ayrshire Council Museums Service, the McManus Galleries and Museum in Dundee, Aberdeen University, the National Trust for Scotland Photographic Library, the St Andrews Preservation Trust and the Royal Collection at Windsor.

Golf club secretaries, councils and management committees have been unhesitating in providing records and images. Special thanks are due to the St Andrews, Thistle and New Golf Clubs of St Andrews, the Prestwick and Prestwick St Nicholas Golf Clubs, North Berwick, Gullane, New Luffness, Carnoustie, Bruntsfield, Earlsferry Thistle, Irvine, Glasgow, Royal Troon, Royal Liverpool, Royal North Devon, Royal Blackheath, Valderrama, Shinnecock Hills Golf Club and the National Golf Links of America.

We appreciate the help received from The Royal and Ancient Golf Club of St Andrews. Peter Dawson, the Secretary, and Aubyn Stewart-Wilson, the Members' Secretary, have been most supportive. Peter Lewis, Director of the British Golf Museum, and Angela Howe, the Assistant Director, have been unstinting with their help and guidance.

The help and input from the descendants of Tom Morris has been invaluable. Mrs Sheila Walker has allowed us access to family archives and records. Lady Morrow generously made available documents and images held by her family. Likewise, Andrew Rusack has been of the utmost help. Susan Tucker has added to our knowledge of the early Hunter family life in Darien and Mobile.

In the course of the preparation of this book, some of our friends who made significant contributions have died. We hope that our work contributes to their memory. John Behrend and Tom Jarrett were both inspirational and informative in their writings and conversations. Alistair Johnston of St Andrews was the last of the great club-makers and his knowledge and guidance was invaluable. Joseph Tiscornia made his extensive collection of clubs, balls, documents and photographs available to us and Dr Ronald Cant generously shared his wide knowledge of nineteenth-century St Andrews with us. We are particularly indebted to them.

Finally, we are especially grateful to our wives, Ruth and Peggy, and our families, for their tolerance, understanding and, above all else, patience, throughout the progress of this work.

Introduction

Over 58 million people play golf worldwide. The game has generated more economic activity and employment than any other sport and, despite the huge sums competed for by professional players, golf remains synonymous with good conduct, honesty and integrity.

This book is about how one man, Tom Morris of St Andrews, presided over the greatest period in the development of golf. It is about how he, more than anyone before or since in any game, stamped his individual character upon his sport and how, in large measure, he made golf what it is today.

Born in a linen weaver's cottage in St Andrews in 1821, he was un-educated even by the standards of his day but, by the time of his death in 1908, he had become a figure of international renown. He was the friend of dukes and earls, prime ministers and politicians, judges and felons, golfers of every calibre and caddies of every kind. When he was buried with all the pomp and ceremony befitting an eminent Victorian, *The Times* eulogised him in a long obituary. Newspapers throughout the world reported his funeral, followed by his interment below the effigy of his son, Tommy, amidst the ruins of St Andrews Cathedral.

In the course of his long life, he witnessed huge social and scientific changes in the world, none more so than in the game of golf that he had, in many respects, overseen and directed.

When Tom Morris was born, golf was little more than a parochial Scottish pastime played by a few hundred Scots on some twenty rudimentary courses, where conditions were almost entirely left to nature. By the time of his death, the game had expanded to become the most popular and geographically widespread of all sports. North America, much of Europe and the colonies of the British Empire had enthusiastically embraced golf, and the name of Tom Morris was synonymous with it. He was painted by artists, honoured by poets, patronised by royalty, revered by The Royal and Ancient Golf Club and showered with praise and affection by golfers everywhere. Tom Morris was a sporting hero in an age of heroes, as well as golf's first iconic figure.

Time, place and circumstance clearly helped Tom make his mark in golf. In his formative years, the Links of St Andrews and The Royal and Ancient Golf Club were already at the centre of the game and the Town was considered 'The Home of Golf'. When the gutta ball came to replace the feathery and the railway network reached every corner of the land, golf was on the threshold of rapid expansion. Tom Morris found himself in the right place at the right time.

From his start in the game as an apprentice feather ball-maker with Allan Robertson to his very reluctant retirement as 'Custodian of the Links' of St Andrews more than 60 years later, his is a remarkable and very human story, blessed with great triumphs but blighted by even greater tragedies.

Tom Morris was, of course, a great golfer. The record of Tom and Tommy, father and son, in the Open Championship stands as an enduring memorial to their golfing superiority. Between them they won eight of the first twelve Opens and are still respectively the oldest and youngest players to have won the Championship. Tom relinquished his Open title to 18-year-old Tommy in 1868, taking second place that year – a family performance unlikely ever to be repeated. Tom's 13-stroke victory in 1862 remains the largest winning margin and Tommy's four Open Championship wins in succession are unequalled – his was the first name to be engraved on the Claret Jug, the new Open Golf Championship Trophy, when it was first presented in 1872.

This book is not a catalogue of the golfing achievements of Tom Morris. While it is important to understand that it was his big money matches with Willie Park, and subsequently those of Tommy and Davie Strath, that established golf as a popular spectator sport, in order to appreciate Tom's total contribution to golf, it is necessary to look beyond his merely playing the game.

Tom Morris was the first golf professional engaged by a club to provide a golfing service to its members. He was arguably the first professional to design and build a course from scratch, and his first, at Prestwick, testified to his insight and creativity and set standards for all to follow. His development of St Andrews into the 'Old Course' that we know today has stood the test of time, and remains the most popular Open Championship venue and the most famous golf course in the world.

To understand the man and his character we must look at his family life: his marriage, the birth and death of his first son and the birth and upbringing of his second son, Tommy; the family's move to Prestwick, the birth of his sons and daughters there and the friendships they forged there; the marriages his children made and how they impinged on his life; Tommy's unlikely match with Margaret Drinnen who tragically died giving birth; his only daughter Lizzie's marriage to James Hunter, who amassed the family's fortune before his bizarre death in the Bay of Mobile in America – half a world away from his wife and children in St Andrews – and Tom's younger sons, the enigmatic James and the paraplegic John.

This book chronicles the life of a family man who outlived his wife, all of his children and their spouses, who was left alone with his grandchildren but who bore the cruel blows of fate with fortitude. It is about the people, the places and the events in Tom Morris's life that shaped his character, a character that he transferred to the game of golf.

It is over 100 years since the only other biography of Tom Morris was published. It is perhaps uncharitable to suggest that the Reverend W. W. Tulloch put little effort into his work, but he clearly laboured under the constraints of Victorian sensitivity and the fact that his subject was still living. We have been under no such burdens. After many years of research, we have related Tom's life as it was, his strengths as well as weaknesses, and have laid to rest some of the myths perpetuated and embellished over the years. We hope that in some small way we have brought Tom Morris to life in these pages.

Authors' Note

Every effort has been made to trace copyright holders of works quoted in this book. We ask the indulgence of any copyright holder whom we have been unable to identify.

Errors are inevitable in a work of this scope and scale and we apologise for them. We have verified the facts from source documents wherever possible, but there will always be different interpretations of events in the life of such a significant historical character. It is our earnest hope that topics raised within this book will encourage further research.

1 Roots in the Links

Tom Morris's ancestry can be traced back in St Andrews, as far as the earliest records permit, to a seventeenth-century namesake.[1] All the Morris families were handloom weavers who, for five generations, played a central role in the affairs of the Weavers' Craft Guild, having continuously at least one family member amongst its office-holders until the demise of the trades guilds in the mid-nineteenth century. Tom's earliest ancestors knew St Andrews at its greatest and through the generations witnessed its descent into penury as, first, the Reformation stripped it of its ecclesiastical wealth, and then the Union of the Crowns of Scotland and England in 1603 diminished its political status and importance as a centre of learning.[2] The Union of the Parliaments of England and Scotland in 1707 reduced St Andrews to an insignificant, decaying, provincial Scottish township, a relic of its great past.

Despite the ravages of ecclesiastical and political change in St Andrews, golf remained at the core of this small university town on the east coast of Scotland. As early as 1552, Archbishop Hamilton, on being granted the rights of harvesting rabbits from the Links for food and skins, was reminded that the townspeople reserved their hereditary rights to pasture animals, dig turf and play golf. Golf was sufficiently commonplace in the Town for the Kirk Session records to mention it as a distraction from Sunday worship. In one such record in 1583, Alexander Miller and his two disobedient sons along with two other miscreants were warned about playing golf when they should have been in the Kirk.

Golf, as we know it today, first flourished on the east coast of Scotland and St Andrews has long been the most important venue of the game. The golfing ground within the ancient links land of whin-covered dunes, bordered by the North Sea to the east and the estuary of the River Eden to the north, was a natural place to play golf. It is not surprising that it became the best and most testing arena for the early game and the premier place of play for the golfing gentry.

Although it is not known if Tom Morris's earliest ancestors played, there is circumstantial evidence that his great-grandfather did. John Morris was born in 1722 and married Janet Robertson in 1744, sister of Patrick and William, members of a golf ball making family already two generations established in the craft, with premises both in Leith and St Andrews.[3] John and Janet had four surviving children and their eldest, John, born in 1752, was undoubtedly associated with golf on the Links of St Andrews.

It was during the early childhood of this John Morris, Tom's grandfather, that an event of crucial significance took place that profoundly affected the future importance and prosperity of the Town. In 1754 twenty-two 'Noblemen and Gentlemen of Fife' gave a silver club to be played for over the Links and the Society of St Andrews Golfers was effectively formed, ultimately becoming The Royal and Ancient Golf Club in 1834 upon being granted Royal Patronage by King William IV.[4] Today, it is the premier club in the world, governing the game in all countries except the United States of America and Mexico.

That Tom's grandfather John and his great-uncle Robert were golfers is indisputable, for both figured prominently in a ten-year legal dispute known as the 'Dempster Case', or colloquially, as the 'Rabbit Wars', a bitter battle over the breeding of rabbits on the Links of St Andrews. In November 1797, a penurious St Andrews Town Council had sold the Links to Thomas Erskine who was Provost of the Town and Captain of the Golfing Society. The Links consisted of about 50 acres of arable land and 250 acres of sandy dunes covered with thick gorse and scrub. Within this area of dunes was a narrow strip of undulating grassland with humps and hollows interspersed with areas of flat plains. It was this small crook-shaped area of about 12 acres that constituted the golf course. Whether or not the Town Council had a right to sell the Links is a topic debated to this day, but sell the Links they did, with the reservation in the terms of the sale that, 'always no damage or hurt be done to the golf links'.

Two years later Erskine, now Sir Thomas, the Earl of Kellie, sold the lands on to a prominent St Andrews business family, father and son Charles and Cathcart Dempster.[5] The Earl and Stuart Grace, who was the Town Clerk and Secretary of the Golfing Society, both understood that the purpose of the transaction was for the Dempsters to farm the rabbit population on the Links for commercial purposes, effectively turning the golf course and surrounding lands into a warren.

While Rear-Admiral Horatio Nelson was turning his blind eye to the signal from the Fleet Commander to withdraw his ships at the Battle of Copenhagen in 1801, the Golfing Society of St Andrews was keeping a vigilant one on the state of the golfing ground. It would appear that the golf course quickly came under serious threat from the holes, scrapes and burrows that the much increased rabbit population made and, in that year, George Cheape, Captain of the Golfing Society, wrote to the Town Council complaining of the damage caused. The ancient rights of the citizens of the Town, he said, were not being upheld. By 1803 the conflicts brought matters into the courts and in 1805 the Council joined forces with the Society in claiming that the ancient right of playing golf on the Links was being seriously impaired; that the conditions regarding golf in the terms of the sale of the Links were being violated and that the townspeople had the right to take rabbits. War on the warrens was essentially declared. Marches of the citizenry on the Links were organised, the people were summoned by 'tuck of drum', rabbits were taken and warrens destroyed: the Dempsters were forced to bring a warrant against the Town, the Provost, magistrates and baillies, to prevent further destruction of their property.

When the case came to the Edinburgh Court of Session in 1805, the judge ordered that local evidence should be taken at St Andrews and in all some 39 witnesses were heard. Amongst the experts called to testify regarding the deterioration of the Links for golfing were the brothers John and Robert Morris. John was described as a 'weaver and golf cady in St Andrews' and Robert as 'weaver' who 'plays at golf frequently... and has acted as a cady occasionally'. Robert had for some years been paid by the Golfing Society to maintain the Course. With them in the witness box stood their cousins, the brothers Patrick and William Robertson, golf ball makers whose trade had clearly not benefited from the clearance of whins and who were adamant that 'rabbit scrapes are more abundant now than they were in the past'.

Tom's grandfather, John Morris, then aged 53, stated that he had been a caddy for 30 years and was frequently on the Links, and testified that 'these [rabbit] scrapes have become very numerous since Mr Dempster got the links'. In his opinion, 'these holes or scrapes are a great prejudice to playing the game of golf and that if the number of rabbits continue the same as at present, it will become very difficult playing the golf, if there be any playing at all'.

Robert Morris, John's brother, aged 49, surprisingly appeared for the Dempsters. He stated that he had known the Links for 40 years, played golf frequently himself and acted as a caddy occasionally for the last 20 years. Robert doubted that the Links had suffered from the rabbit farming enterprise. His testimony reflected the deep division in the Town over the Dempsters' activities. The legal case dragged on for years and the result was deadlock. In the end, the rabbits themselves solved the case by contracting an infectious disease that all but wiped them out.

From the 'Rabbit Wars' papers we learn something about the state of the Links between 1760 and 1805. We also learn much about the extent to which golf was played. The social spectrum of the people called to give evidence testified to the broad appeal of the game in the Town. For too long the notion has prevailed that only gentlemen at their leisure played golf, with men from the working class – the caddies – carrying their clubs. In truth, golf was played by every class of society in St Andrews in the eighteenth and nineteenth centuries and was an integral part of the way of life of the Town.

Looking back over two hundred years today, it is clear that the situation which arose on the Links of St Andrews in the first few years of the nineteenth century threatened the very existence of golf. Indeed, if the Society of St Andrews Golfers had not initiated legal proceedings to protect the Course, or if the outcome of those proceedings had been different, golf, if it had survived at all, would have in all probability remained a parochial Scottish pastime. With the game all but dying out at the time in Edinburgh and other golfing centres, the demise of the game at St Andrews would have been catastrophic. St Andrews literally kept the game alive for the next 30 or 40 years.

An altogether different outcome of the 'Rabbit Wars' was the debt incurred through legal costs by an already impoverished Town Council, who decided that a sale of land was the only solution to easing this position. Thus the triangle of land bordering the Town side of the eighteenth hole, known as Pilmuir Links, was sold in 1821 as a series of feus.[6] This land was an integral part of the Course of the day and the Society of Golfers immediately threatened legal action against the Council. With the great expense of the Dempster case still fresh in everyone's mind, a deal was struck. The Society withdrew its objections to the Council's sale in exchange for an option to obtain land on which to build a clubhouse at the top of the Links. Some 30 years later, in 1854, this option was exercised and the clubhouse was built on its present site. It is delightful to reflect that The Royal and Ancient's imposing building, so well known today throughout the world, came about as a consequence of an early nineteenth-century legal case concerning the breeding of rabbits.

2 The Way of a Weaver

Although John and Robert Morris were clearly much engaged in golf on the Links at the turn of the eighteenth century, they were first and foremost hand-loom linen weavers. Both were members of the Weavers' Guild and both played prominent parts in its affairs.

The relationship between hand-loom linen weaving and the development of golf in St Andrews cannot be over-stated. All of the leading artisan players in early golf in the Town were linen weavers; all of the great players whose names have come down to us were from weaving families. The Morrises certainly, the Kirks, Andersons, Herds and Robertsons; all were weavers and all played their part in the evolution of the game. It is not difficult to see why this should be the case.

The weavers were self-employed and the linen merchants' agents paid them by the yard for the cloth that they wove in their homes. In St Andrews, the Dempster family contracted the weavers for the production of tough, coarse, Osnaburg linen for its ship sail manufactory. They supplied the spun flax yarn that the women and children of the weavers' households wound onto the pirns for the shuttle. The more the weaver wove, the more he was paid. The weaver's time was his own to do with as he pleased and if indeed he wished to take a turn on the Links, or supplement his income by caddying, that is precisely what he would do. That was the way of a weaver.

The linen industry in Scotland is long dead, but in the early nineteenth century it made up a large part of the Scottish economy, even giving rise to the British Linen Bank, now absorbed into the Bank of Scotland. Fife was the jewel in the industry's crown. Not only did the county have the rich fertile land and the agricultural expertise to grow the flax, but also the water and manpower to heckle, spin and weave it.

Like the weavers, the hecklers, who stroked the flax fibres from the rotted plants, were well informed and erudite. Working in teams, they would club together to purchase newspapers that they had read to them while they worked. The reader might be a local schoolmaster or an impoverished minister of the breakaway Free Church. There were many such men eager to get their hands on the *Edinburgh Courant* or *The Times* for free and be paid for reading it to boot. In the weavers' cottages, anyone available would be called upon to read to the menfolk as they treadled the looms.

Hecklers and weavers took great delight in attending public meetings where they could show off their knowledge through pointed and often detailed questioning of the speaker. Not surprisingly, some notices of political meetings of the time were appended in bold black letters with the words, 'no hecklers or weavers allowed'. If the hecklers of Fife have an enduring name in 'heckling' on the political hustings, the linen weavers of St Andrews made a much more subtle impression on society by introducing an independent, obstinate attitude into the nature of the game of golf.

The weaving of plain coarse linen cloth did not require the constant attention needed for weaving a more complex pattern. Once the loom had been set up for the coarse weave, operating it was child's play. Indeed, it was more often than not deemed to be wife and daughter's play. A St Andrews weaver could be away to the Links and have a full round played without his loom having missed a single swing of the treadle. To do this and keep his family in hearth and home meant marriage from within the trade, so it is not surprising that few weavers married outside the craft.

In 1777 John Morris married Grizzel Gatherum from Anstruther, the daughter of a weaver, guildsman and burgess. Although it cannot be stated with certainty where previous generations of the Morris family had dwelt, John lived and worked at the loom in North Street, St Andrews. His cottage was near the Northgait or North Port as it came to be called. His brothers, Robert and William, lived in their weaving households only yards away along the row of weavers' cottages. Robert would marry Margaret Allan and move to Huxters Wynd, or South Castle Street as it is named today, but William would remain unwed and stay working at his loom until well into his eighties.

John and Grizzel raised their family in the weaver's cottage in North Street through very hard times. The general Scottish economic climate was not good but the linen weavers of St Andrews were hit particularly hard as the nineteenth century dawned against the background of the Industrial Revolution. After a disastrous failure of their sail canvas fitted to two British Navy men-of-war, the Dempsters closed their factory, reducing the local demand for coarse linen. The weaving trade was in terminal decline. By mid-century it was extinct.

Golf was also in decline and had been for a period of some twenty or thirty years. The golfing gentry of old resorted in fewer numbers and less frequently to the Links. The game was all but dead in Edinburgh and the Lothians. The Militia, practising manoeuvres for Napoleon's anticipated onslaught, as well as building works, had all but destroyed the links at Leith. Inflation and profligacy had financially crippled many of the great landed golfing families and those unscathed were too caught up in the new work ethic of the Industrial Revolution to give their time to golf as their fathers had done.

The Burgess Golfing Society in Edinburgh came close to extinction and the Honourable Company of Edinburgh Golfers suffered the indignity of having the Sheriff sell, by public auction, on 29 August 1833, the contents of their clubhouse including, 'The Household furniture, Paintings, Silver Plate etc.——'. This sale realised £106 9s 10d that was applied to discharging their debts, as was the proceeds from the sale of the clubhouse the following year. Happily, the Honourable Company recovered and reestablished itself at Musselburgh in 1836. These Edinburgh clubs had been brought to this sorry pass once the wining and dining that had been the true reason for their being were eschewed for the salons and the halls of the literary and philosophical societies of the Age of Enlightenment. The mind and not the swing preoccupied the gentry's young, and golf became a recreational indulgence, rather than an essential part of a Scottish gentleman's life.

A flickering flame was nevertheless kept alight by the old guard of the gentry, the 'Bonnet Lairds' of the countryside and the weavers of St Andrews. But a small clique of sporting landed gentlemen who were inveterate gamblers also kept the game alive and in the public eye. It mattered not to these men whether it was horse racing, hare coursing, curling, prize fighting or golf. They had the resources to indulge their passion for gambling, and matchplay golf was an ideal vehicle. The fortunes of any game of golf can ebb and flow and the expectations, and consequently the odds, can change dramatically from hole to hole. These men wagered heavily amongst themselves during their own matches, but they also set up high-stake contests between the leading 'professional' artisan golfers, who invariably also often acted as caddies. The betting during these challenge matches was heavy and continuous, with the odds and wagers changing from hole to hole. Although the contestants themselves were not risking any money, the winners would receive a generous reward from their backers. This scenario captured the interest of the press and consequently the imagination of the general public. Thousands flocked to the links to be part of the excitement.

It was this gambling set who provided regular employment to the better artisan players, as well as caddies and club and ball makers, when the game was at a low ebb. Just as these gentlemen golfers owned racehorses and employed jockeys and stable hands, so they added caddies and first-rate players to their entourage. These men they backed in money matches and partnered in foursomes' games. Some enduring partnerships evolved between patron and golfing servant, particularly in St Andrews. These arrangements were not nearly so strong at Leith or Musselburgh and this played no small part in the emerging pre-eminence of St Andrews. As the Edinburgh clubs declined in both number and influence, St Andrews became relatively stronger and more influential. Thus were laid the foundations of the authority of The Royal and Ancient Golf Club and the town of St Andrews.

Another outcome of this gambling craze was that it raised the standards of play. As the rewards for winning these big money matches increased, the quality of the golf improved. In this way the seeds were sown for the high earning professional tournament players of today.

The game was also being played abroad in the Empire, where soldiers of Scottish regiments not only made money, but also made time and golf courses for their national game. These men would return from their postings in the far-flung outposts of the Empire with their vigour and new-found wealth to fan the flames of the game at home.

The face of Scotland was changing with industrialisation. Improvement became the keyword and St Andrews became caught up in a frenzy of change. The foundation of the Madras College in 1832, together with a cheap supply of housing and land, led to more, and ever more affluent, families finding St Andrews an attractive place to live. The locals called them 'Indians', for the majority were families either still in active service in the Empire or newly retired from it. Golf became the healthy outdoor pursuit of choice for gentlemen and the game that had slowly evolved for centuries on the Links quickly became the *raison d'être* for men of leisure and the key factor for many of them taking up residence in the Town.

The Morris family of weavers was ideally placed to accommodate the changes. They were virtually an integral part of the Links and the golf and the independence that weaving made possible, meant that they were readily available for play. For another generation, however, the loom would remain central to their existence.

While John and Robert Morris, with their Robertson cousins, were caught up in the Rabbit Wars in the law courts, family life continued. John and Grizzel Morris's eldest son, yet another John, born in 1778, married Jean Bruce in 1806, the daughter of a Kilrenny weaver then in the process of moving his loom to better accommodation and representation in Crail. Tom Morris, born fifteen years later, was their sixth child.

Helen, born in 1807, was first, then Janet, named after her daft Auntie Janet at Kincaple, two years later. In 1811 came her first son, inevitably to be christened John like every Morris first son for five generations back. Four years elapsed before Margaret appeared in 1816, named after her maternal grandmother, then living in Crail. Jean had another three-year gap before George was born, and two years later, on 16 June 1821, Tom Morris came into the world. Jean's fecundity did not end with Tom, for after another two years, she had Jean and the Morris brood was finally complete. That she had seven children in sixteen years and all survived into adulthood attests to good care, good food and an innately solid constitution. John Morris chose well for himself when he married Jean Bruce from Kilrenny and Jean had much to be proud of in her choice of a husband, for John was a much-respected and well-connected man in the Town.

3 The Kirk, the School and Apprenticeship

Tom Morris was born in St Andrews on 16 June 1821, only a few weeks after Napoleon had died on the island of St Helena. Tom's birthplace was a two-roomed weaver's cottage in the middle of a row of such dwellings that stood near the point where North Street ended and the scrub land of the Links began.

The St Andrews that Tom Morris was brought up in would be broadly recognisable to a modern-day visitor. The three main streets, with the vennels and closes joining them, were much the same as today. The Links differed only in the density of whins and rough, sandy, gaping holes destined to become bunkers. By the close of the eighteenth century, buildings of stone had largely replaced the fragile timber houses and tenements of an earlier time, but this reconstruction constituted the limits of improvement and was all that was reflected in St Andrews of the Scottish Age of Enlightenment. Edinburgh had been transformed with the construction of its New Town, with architecture and planning that was the talk of Europe; what developments there had been in St Andrews were for the promotion of individual interests alone, and attempts at general civic improvements had mostly failed for lack of funds. The St Andrews of 1821 was in penury.

The Reverend Dr Buist christened Tom Morris 'Thomas Mitchell' on Sunday 24 June in the Church of St Salvator's in North Street.[1] It is reported that in attendance was the Very Reverend Principal Haldane, who was first Minister of Holy Trinity Church and Principal and Primarius Professor of Divinity at St Mary's College, one of the two colleges then comprising St Andrews University. Some twenty-five years later, in 1846, Haldane was to baptise Tom's first-born son.

It is not immediately clear why Dr Buist christened John Morris's children, for records show that he was not a frequent preacher in that pulpit, which is just as well because it was said that his sermons were 'very tedious'.[2] But the fact that Buist himself was a golfer of some considerable repute, both in St Andrews and on the Inch of his native Perth, may have had something to do with it.

Tom's father was certainly well known to both Buist and Principal Haldane, enjoying many a match with them on the Links. It is not unlikely, therefore, that through the golfing bond of their friendship, Buist performed Tom's christening, with Haldane present. Attending and indeed performing the christening of John Morris's son may not only have been a gesture of friendship and respect, but also an enjoyable experience for both. It was the custom, and still is, to 'wet the baby's head' after the christening, and a dram in John Morris's cottage with all his golfing cronies was something both would have enjoyed.

Principal Haldane was also a golfer and a character on the Links. Although a long way from being a great player, he was an enthusiast who was written about by his contemporaries with much affection and respect. It is said that the problems which the Principal had circumnavigating the great bunker that stands sentinel to this day in the middle of the sixteenth fairway on the Old Course is acknowledged in its name, 'The Principal's Nose'. If that is so, it is a lasting monument to a middling player and his dominant facial feature and an irony that the Principal's name endures on the Links while that of Buist, the better golfer, does not.

In 1826, when Tom was five years old, he would have joined his sister Margaret and brother George in the daily grind of the school. Attendance at school was not mandatory. The cost was one penny a week, although special rates were available for families with two or more scholars. Margaret, aged ten, was about to conclude her schooling while John, fifteen years old, was apprenticed to his father and worked the second loom in the house. Janet, at seventeen, was at home with her mother, serving the looms and helping out with the three-year-old baby, Jean.

St Andrews, with the Grammar and English Schools as the public educational establishments in 1821, was relatively enlightened in the provision of education, as one might expect of a university town. Many towns of comparable size at the time were dependent upon the Church or a wealthy benefactor for the provision of education for working-class children. That there was a demand from all classes of the townspeople of St Andrews is reflected in the fact that twelve schools were registered in the Town in 1779. As in most townships throughout Scotland, the majority of these schools were Dame Schools, 'ane-widow-woman-schools', where the sum total of the schoolmistress' learning was exceeded only by her ignorance.

The Grammar School stood where the lawn of the Madras College now extends to the ruins of the Blackfriars Chapel. The English School was sited in the building that is now the Public Library; it is almost certain that John Morris's family attended this school, set behind the Town Kirk, because this was where the children of tradesmen and the less affluent were educated.[3] Coming from a respectable craft family whose male members had long served as office-holders in the Weavers Guild, Tom would have received at least an elementary education which included reading and writing.

With no Burgh education records surviving, nothing is known of Tom's educational attainment. We do know, however, that he was no scholar, as he himself insisted, and there is the locally-held view passed down through families, even his own, that he was not altogether proficient with book or pen.

The Kirk played a central role in the life of the Morris family and, for Tom, it would continue to do so for the rest of his life. He would be introduced early to its ways and routines, particularly on Sundays, which was the day of rest for all but the Minister. John and Jean Morris probably had a long 'lie-in', with the bairns being pleaded with to stay in bed awhile. The fire would be lit but the loom dormant on a Sunday. The Town remained as silent as the grave until nearly eight o'clock when the church parade began.

From every door families emerged dressed in their Sunday best. Preceded by Helen and John, then Margaret fussing close behind with George and Tom, Jean and John Morris would take their brood in stately procession up North Street past the row of weavers' cottages. John's old Uncle William, as well as Robert Morris and his family a few doors further up the street, doubtless joined them. From all along North Street, from the Northgait at the west end to the Cathedral burial ground and beyond in the east, the parishioners of St Leonards would gather, summoned by the sonorous tolling of St Salvator's bell. Admonished and warned about their behaviour as they entered the Kirk, with perhaps a nudge to remind them as they made their way to their pew, the children would be cautioned again as they surreptitiously waved to friends already seated. There, for the next two hours while the children fidgeted through the minister's sermon and they all followed the precentor in singing the psalms, the townspeople were at one with the world and with each other. There may have been one or two who felt that, on a morning that was just too good to miss, a few holes of golf were worth the wrath of the Elders. But there would not be many and those few would be well discussed, much condemned and certainly decried from the pulpit the following Sunday. The Kirk-going habit that Tom acquired as a child would remain with him for the rest of his life.

The homeward parade was no doubt more leisurely, although the children would scamper like dogs let off the leash. John and Jean would walk home arm in arm, 'oxter'n-in', together with neighbours and friends who might 'stop by' for a cup of tea before making their way home to Sunday lunch, the best of the week. Grandparents or elderly single relatives, like John's eighty-year-old Uncle William, still at his loom two doors away, perhaps came in, or the children were sent round with a plate of something and doubtless the hope of a sweet, or farthing reward, for their effort. By the age of ten, Thomas Mitchell Morris's routine would be as regular as a clock wound up with the health and vigour of youth and ordered by the rigours of a Scots Presbyterian household.

In later life, Tom recorded little about his early childhood years, but the weaver's cottage in which he was brought up must have been a stimulating environment. As well as the to-and-fro of his father's cronies and friends of his older brothers and sisters, his grandfather also lived in the house and still took his turn at the loom. Old John would doubtless have many an entertaining tale of the Links, the crack players, the gambling set and the Rabbit Wars. An era came to an end with the death of Old John in 1830. Another one began a year later with the end of Tom's schooldays.

When Tom left school and later started his apprenticeship with Allan Robertson, his brother John, sisters Margaret and Jean, and both parents, were all still living in the weaver's cottage in which he was born. How they were all accommodated in the box beds in two rooms defies the modern imagination.

Tom's exposure to 'reading, writing and the arithmetic' may have been interrupted, like so many others in St Andrews born before and after him, through his easy access to the Links. As he himself related of his early years: 'I began to play when I was six or seven, maybe younger. A' St Andrews bairns are born wi' web feet an' wi' a gowf club in their hands. I wad be driving the chuckie stanne wi' a bit stick about as sune's I could walk.'

Golf became the central part of Tom's early life, as it did of every other boy of his generation in the Town, whether proficient or otherwise. Carrying a gentleman's clubs was an easy income for any able-bodied lad who made himself available on the bank in front of the Union Parlour at the top of the Links. If you were known – and John Morris's boy would certainly have been – you could be called upon to run messages and get a penny for the going and maybe another one when you got there.

There is no doubt that the Morris brothers' lives revolved around golf. When George, Tom's elder brother, left school, it was not to become apprenticed to a tradesman like the rest of his friends, but to a place in the household of Robert Chambers, a keen golfer and partner with his brother in the respected firm of W. & R. Chambers of Edinburgh, already then renowned as authors and publishers. With a family of six daughters, a son and a wife in poor health, Robert Chambers moved to St Andrews purportedly for family reasons and for respite from the stress of work.[4]

George Morris rose to the position of butler, the most senior of the servants, and maintained this post in St Andrews as well as in Edinburgh when the Chambers family returned there. When Mr Chambers moved to London, George was retained in the household of his son Robert who gained golfing immortality by winning the first Grand National Tournament at St Andrews in 1858.

George's service extended beyond the duties of butler, however, for he was also the family's caddy and partnered each of them in foursomes matches on the Links. Mr Chambers exercised his business acumen well when he employed George in the first instance. Not only did he get a diligent and presentable butler, but his family also acquired an outstanding golfer, through whom they could enjoy the vicarious excitement of the tournaments of the day, when George would pit his prowess against the best.

There is no information available about Tom's life between him leaving school around 1831 and becoming an apprentice ball-maker with Allan Robertson sometime in the second half of the 1830s. While word has come down through the generations in St Andrews that he was first apprenticed as a joiner or carpenter, there is no evidence of this and there are other possibilities. One is that he would learn the family craft of hand-loom linen weaving, like his eldest brother John. In a commentary on his life, published in 1907 under his signature, he stated, 'My father was a weaver to his trade, and I am pretty sure I was intended to be a weaver too, but that never came off.'

His father and brother were both listed as hand-loom weavers in the 1841 census, but by the mid-1830s it must have been obvious that the trade was in terminal decline and there would be no long-term future in it for Tom. The free and easy independent lifestyle of the hand-loom weaver was not an option for Tom or anyone else of his generation in St Andrews and there is some evidence that around 1836/7 a change of career was being sought for him.

H.S.C. Everard wrote in 1890 that '. . . his career was marked out for him, and arrangements all but completed, under which he was to have been apprenticed to a carpenter; but a casual question of old Sandy Herd, as to why he did not get apprenticed to Allan Robertson as a club-maker, put the idea into his head. Allan considered the matter, the upshot of which was that he agreed to take Tom, who served under him four years as apprentice and five as journeyman, and from that period began his golfing life.'

In support of this, Sandy Herd, writing in his autobiography, *My Golf-ing Life*, published in 1923, said, 'By the way, it was my grandfather who started Tom Morris in the club-making business by advising him to turn his attention to golf when Tom was looking in all directions for work'. There is conflicting evidence about when Tom entered the employment of Allan and the exact time is not known, but it appears it was between 1836 and 1839. The arrangements for him to become an apprentice carpenter clearly were made immediately before he joined Allan. That still leaves a gap of several years between him leaving school and joining Allan, of which we have no knowledge at all.

There is one difficulty about the above statement by Mr Everard. He refers to Allan as 'a club-maker'. He was renowned as a feather ball-maker, the most celebrated of his day. Apart from this reference, he has never been referred to as a 'club-maker'. There are no known clubs in existence today that were made by him but it is quite possible that, as an adjunct to his main business of ball-making, he did repair wooden-headed golf clubs. He was, like his father before him, agent in St Andrews for the renowned McEwan club-making firm of Edinburgh and would have been called upon to attend to McEwan clubs purchased from him that required repairs. Further evidence of Allan's ability to fashion club-heads is provided by J. G. McPherson, writing in 1891, 'Old Philp had polished at an apple-tree head for a whole afternoon, when modern makers would have considered it quite finished; and this Allan seized, reduced its weight to suit the thin handle, until it looked like a toy'. Additionally, Tom is quoted as saying in 1905, 'I went to work at making clubs and balls, principally the latter, with Allan Robertson'. Could it be that it was during his years working with Allan that Tom learned how to repair clubs, even though it is unlikely that this included making the complete article?

The 1841 Census confirms that at that date Tom's occupation was a 'Golf Ball Maker App.' and the conclusion must be, from the available evi-dence, that Tom Morris joined Allan Robertson as an apprentice sometime in the late 1830s where he principally learned the art of making feather balls. There can be no doubt, however, that it was Tom's association with Allan Robertson at this time that launched his career in golf.

The first notice we have of Tom enjoying a cash income from golf was recorded in the *Fifeshire Journal* in October 1841 when, at the age of 20, he won the 'Put-ins' (also known as the 'In-puts'). This was a caddies' com-petition played after the Autumn Meeting of The Royal and Ancient. The term derives from the fact that gentlemen players of the Club were required to 'put-in' or 'in-put' a sum of cash to a kitty for which the caddies would compete over one round of the Course. The 'put-ins' must have amounted to quite a substantial sum, for it was sufficient to raise controversy among the ranks of caddies. While Allan Robertson is recorded by the *Fifeshire Journal* of October 1839 as having won the 'In-puts' that year, which was the first mention of him in a newspaper, in 1841 a protest was made by the rank-and-file about him playing in the event because of the near inevitability of his winning. Their protest gained some support from the membership of The Royal and Ancient and Allan was excluded from the competition. It may be because of Allan's apparent invincibility that we have this earliest record of Tom's golfing success.[5]

Tom won this 1841 event with a round of 92 strokes, which was the lowest score recorded to date. He was named as Thomas Morris Junior, because in second place came Thomas Morris Senior. This has caused much confusion through the years. The two were, of course, distantly related, but it is doubtful if either of them would have been particularly knowledgeable about the relationship. Thomas Morris Senior was some ten years older than Tom and was the son of Thomas Morris, a friend and Weavers Guild brother of Tom's father. This Thomas Morris Senior was a spirit dealer, which meant that he ran a public house. This was sited at the west end of North Street where he and his wife Jean supplied the fisher folk and impoverished students with their tipple. His presence in the lists of the 'Put-ins' testifies to the extent to which golf supplemented incomes across the work spectrum of the townspeople. It is noteworthy, but not altogether surprising, that the list does not include tradesmen other than weavers or ball makers. Other employers would not readily release their journeymen and apprentices for the Autumn Meeting.

The *Fifeshire Journal* had hitherto only occasionally mentioned the 'Put-ins' event, without naming all the participants or giving the full results. When Tom won again in 1842, however, the complete list of entrants was published together with the leading scores. The best score until then was in 1838 when it was reported that Mr Geddes from Musselburgh won the 'In-puts', taking 93 strokes with 'very fine playing and the other scores were decidedly professional'. Could it be that the 1842 event was more fully reported because Tom Morris, a local St Andrean born and bred, had not only won but had also returned the best score to date for the second year running?

What we can be sure of is that the 21-year-old Tom must have aspired to make a life for himself in golf and that these wins would have boosted his ambition. The sum of money he pocketed would have been greater than he had ever handled before, and although there may be satisfaction in glory, cash would have been the great driving force. There is no doubt that Tom would have received every help and encouragement from Allan Robertson, his employer and mentor. Tom's golfing talent, however, must have been apparent to Allan before this time, otherwise he would surely not have encouraged him to start out in a golf ball-making apprenticeship, a move that was to prove defining for the game of golf.

St Andrews, albeit belatedly, found itself at the start of a building boom in the third decade of the nineteenth century, although why it took so long in reaching this stage is puzzling. Lassitude and the self-satisfaction of the townspeople and its merchant classes, coupled with an indifferent and uninterested university where professorships were retained within families, may be the reason. But with a Town Council deeply in debt and with land and property prices a fraction of what they were in even small townships as nearby as Cupar and Anstruther, it is difficult to see why St Andrews took so long to launch itself into the booming Scottish economy. Cupar, as the county town and rural marketplace, and Anstruther as the focal centre of the rapidly developing fishing industry, had obvious advantages, but St Andrews, for its part, seems to have made no effort whatsoever.

With the coming of the railways in the 1830s, Victorian tourism was gradually becoming established and St Andrews emerged as a resort of some importance. The Town's almost complete escape from the devastating measles, typhus and whooping cough epidemic of 1818 was widely known and, when it completely avoided the first great outbreak of cholera that killed 10,000 people in Scotland, the healthiness and longevity of its citizens was much discussed. In addition, good schools, an ample supply of reliable domestic servants and doubtless the Links with its golf conspired to make St Andrews a desirable place to reside.

4 'A Kind of King Amongst Them'

In 1815, Europe entered a new age with the defeat of Napoleon at Waterloo and in that same year golf entered a new era with the birth of Allan Robertson. His influence on the early development of golf cannot be overstated. He was indisputably the finest player of his day and commanded the respect of everyone who played the game in the mid-nineteenth century. In retrospect, he can well be considered the first true golf professional; he was certainly the first golfer of renown.

Like his father before him, Allan held no official position on the Links or within The Royal and Ancient Golf Club, but he nevertheless oversaw and to a large extent controlled, the play on the Links of St Andrews. He was simply Allan Robertson and he was in charge.[1]

After his death in 1859, at the relatively early age of 44, his character, humour and aura lived on through Tom Morris, for Allan taught Tom all he knew. He showed him how best to play the great game and deport himself on the Links, but he also taught him about life itself. It was surely from Allan that Tom acquired the resolution and fortitude, as well as the quirks of personality, which would bring him national and ultimately international fame as 'The Grand Old Man of Golf'.

Allan Robertson's house was situated at the corner where, today, Golf Place joins the Links Road, a place then called Sandyhill. It stood in isolation, a few yards up from where Hugh Philp had turned William Fairful's cart shed into his club-making workshop, ideally placed diagonally opposite the Union Parlour, the first clubhouse of the Society of St Andrews Golfers.[2] Opposite, on the other side of the short Links Road that ended in front of Philp's shop, a rough grass-covered sandy bank ran down to the seashore some hundred or so yards away, over the place where the Royal and Ancient Clubhouse stands today.

Allan was 21 years old when his father David died in 1836. Already an established golf ball-maker who had learned the trade from his father and uncles, he was also the pre-eminent player of his generation. He was considered as such even before he had overcome the 'old guard' of the early 1800s, Tom Alexander of Burntisland and Musselburgh, and the brothers David and Sandy Pirie of St Andrews.[3] It would not be long, however, before Allan did defeat them and the situation is summed up in an article written by Robert Chambers and published in *Chambers Edinburgh Journal* in October 1842:

> There is a ball-maker, Allan Robertson by name, who, besides having the highest character for his wares, is reputed to be the best player at St Andrews, and consequently in Scotland – I may as well add, in the world! This is an eminence which golfers must needs admire, and in the little world of the links, men of estate and title will be heard speaking of worthy Allan as if he were a kind of king amongst them.

As well as being the leading player, it is today generally accepted that Allan transformed golf in his lifetime, principally by perfecting the approach shot with the iron club, leading to a much greater and more extensive use of irons in general play. With his iron club play, Allan set the standard for others to follow. If his grandfather was the progenitor of the professional player, Allan was the founding exponent of modern golf.[4]

Allan's reputation was not confined to St Andrews, for his praise was early sung in the news presses of Edinburgh and Aberdeen. He was consulted on laying out the first recorded courses in Carnoustie and Cupar while playing the leading role in innovations at St Andrews. The Royal and Ancient Golf Club's records show that he was paid the considerable sum of £20 for 'double greens' over the winter of 1856/57 and subsequently £13 for attending to repairs on the Links between September 1857 and March 1859. Such sums reflect extensive work. The winter work of 1856/57 must have been for the construction and extension of the double greens, for the sum would have covered the costs of employing several men over that period.

Coming as he did from a long line of St Andrews feather ball-makers and weavers, Allan seems to have had a keen sense not only of history but also of his own place in it. He was certainly a proud man, well aware of his abilities and of his place and stature on the Links. He felt no need, for instance, to identify the feather balls made in his workshop other than stamping them simply 'Allan'. He similarly marked the heads of his personal clubs. He clearly felt that further identification, such as his surname, was superfluous.[5]

There can be no doubting that Allan Robertson was an intelligent, self-confident and purposeful man, determined to better himself in the class-conscious world of limited opportunity that was early nineteenth-century Scotland.[6] Much of Allan's character and habits rubbed off on Tom Morris and it would be interesting to know which of them instigated their relationship. Did Tom perceive in Allan the mentor through whom he could develop as a player and a man? Or did Allan see in Tom a man worthy of his talent and time, a partner with whom he could win and a companion whom he could enjoy? No matter how it came about, their association was crucial to the evolution of the character of modern golf.

Tom Morris learned a great deal more from Allan Robertson than how to make feather golf balls. What Allan also taught Tom was a much greater skill that would serve him to the greatest advantage for the rest of his life. He learned Allan's congenial ways so well that, as H.S.C. Everard wrote many years later, 'Tom Morris [is] a name known and revered it may be said without contradiction, in each of the four continents of the globe'. In the charm stakes, Tom Morris started where Allan Robertson left off.

Tom joined Allan at the most propitious time for golf and St Andrews. The Town was on the brink of a building boom that would result in it being restored to something of its pre-Reformation glory, thanks to the energy and efforts of one man, Major Hugh Lyon Playfair, who had returned in 1832 after military service in India. That St Andrews was to find salvation through golf was due in no small part to the irrepressible Playfair.

Playfair was born in 1786 at Meigle in Angus and educated at St Andrews. In 1805 he went to India as an officer in the Bengal Horse Artillery and, like so many before and after him, returned with a fortune to settle in St Andrews. Playfair reformed the Town in two decades, transforming it from a condition 'like a Bengali village' with cows and pigs roaming the streets, to a place of broad avenues and grand houses, his own being pre-eminent with a pagoda in its extensive garden. As a result, St Andrews became one of the most attractive residential Victorian towns in the British Isles with wide streets and broad pavements, fine terraced houses, a restored harbour, a greatly improved university and having the Madras College as a nationally acclaimed school. In two decades Playfair turned a decaying town into a choice resort, thereby laying the foundations for its future prosperity.[7] For his efforts he was showered with praise and honours, culminating in 1856 with a knighthood from Queen Victoria and an honorary Doctorate of Law from St Andrews University.

His earliest attentions, however, were applied to the Links and the organisation of the game at which he was adept. Brought up in St Andrews where his father was Principal of the United College (the larger part of the then collegiate of St Andrews University), Playfair was a golfer of some standing. He was also a promoter of the game as he played the leading role in establishing a golf club at Dum-Dum in India, recognised as a progenitor of the Royal Calcutta Golf Club. It was perhaps with this model in mind that he set about renovating golf in St Andrews.

About the time of Playfair's return to St Andrews, it was reported that 'the Links then lay almost an untrodden waste' and that 'little system was observed in promoting either the amusement of members or the facilities for playing the game'. In 1832 he was the driving force behind, at the Golfing Society's expense, the renovation of the Links. The Course was made somewhat longer and broader, with an early attempt being made to form a separate green for each of the already established eighteen holes. Prior to Playfair's initiative, there is no evidence that any effort had ever been made to materially improve the Course.

Playfair also formed the Union Club for the gentlemen of the Town, particularly those of the Company of Archers and the Golfing Society. He had a small building at the north end of Golf Place fitted out on similar lines to an Officers' Mess with 'convenient dressing-rooms, a billiard-room, reading-room etc., the whole put under the charge of a steward, and opened by the Provost 26th January 1835'. Under his control, the Union Club prospered with membership increasing to such an extent that, in 1853, 'it was considered judicious to erect a commodious and permanent Club-House'. The foundation stone of The Royal and Ancient Clubhouse was laid, with due Masonic ceremony, on 13 July 1853 by John Whyte-Melville, a year before the Light Brigade charged to its famous fate in the Crimean War. During his speech he said, 'It will form an ornament to this beautiful locality . . . and prove a source of much comfort and convenience to every member of the club'. He also paid tribute to Hugh Lyon Playfair saying, 'the Union Club is indebted for his indefatigable exertions for its benefit, for the great trouble he took in husbanding its resources, without which we would not have been here upon the present occasion'. This was praise well deserved, for Playfair had handed over some £800 to the building fund – a sum amassed over the years by his careful and able husbandry of the Union Club's income. There can be no doubt that his energy and foresight in founding the Union Club and in guiding the emergent Royal and Ancient Golf Club, laid the foundation for St Andrews' pre-eminence in golf.

It is not simply with the benefit of a century and a half of hindsight that we come to an appreciation of the combined importance of Allan

Robertson and Hugh Lyon Playfair. The contribution that they made was acknowledged in their own time. Allan's obituary in the *Dundee Advertiser* of 1859 reads:

> What Sir Hugh Lyon Playfair has been to the city proper, has Allan Robertson been to the links of St Andrews. They have been unwittingly in close partnership. Sir Hugh renovated the rough ruined streets; Allan had an eye the while to the improvement of the links. Sir Hugh attracted citizens, Allan, golfers; Ah! It was a magnificent partnership and has done wonders.

Others were also leaving their indelible mark on golf and St Andrews, few more so than Major John Murray Belshes. Described as a 'stately, pompous but very gentlemanly man', it was he who was responsible for the Society of Golfers gaining Royal patronage. The noblemen and gentlemen of the Society were clearly taken aback when, in 1833, William IV conferred his royal patronage upon the Perth Golfing Society which had been formed only nine years earlier. Major Belshes soon petitioned the King, as the Sovereign and also Duke of St Andrews, for a similar honour for the St Andrews Society with an additional request that the Society should henceforth be styled 'The Royal and Ancient Golf Club of St Andrews'. The King gave permission for the change of name but declined to become patron of the Club, 'as he had been under the necessity since his accession to the throne to decline similar requests'. This was not good enough for the forceful Major who humbly pointed out that the King had only recently extended his patronage to the Perth Golfing Society. A response was quickly received informing Belshes that the King was pleased to become patron of the Club in view of the Perth precedent. Reigning monarchs and other royalty of the United Kingdom have been patrons of The Royal and Ancient Golf Club ever since.

It is not surprising that at this time the celebrated Scottish artist Charles Lees produced his monumental painting, *The Golfers*, for the great and the good of the day were to be found at their leisure on the Links of St Andrews. This large oil painting, completed in 1847, embraces every aspect of the game as well as capturing the atmosphere and ethos of mid-nineteenth-century golf at St Andrews. Every golfing dignitary of any import is in it and the cream of the professional golfers and caddies of the day play a central part, reflecting their status and importance. Allan Robertson is identified, as are the Pirie brothers and Willie Dunn from Musselburgh, but Tom Morris is not, as he had not achieved prominence at the time the painting was being conceived in the early 1840s. He may be, however, the crouching figure in the pale-coloured coat, central and to the left of the seated elderly gentleman, Mr Paton. The figure bears some resemblance to a near contemporary photograph.

Tom Morris certainly found himself in the right place at the right time. While Allan Robertson was laying the foundations of the modern game, Major Hugh Lyon Playfair and his cohorts in the Union Parlour and the Town Council chamber were making the Town a fit and proper place to become the epicentre of golf.

5 Foundations for the Popularity of the Game

The Robertson and Morris families had been close for at least three generations. Allan and Tom had a great-grandmother in common and their grandfathers were first cousins and notorious in the Town for the part they had played in the Rabbit Wars. Their fathers were well-known, established players and caddies of choice to the gentlemen of the Society of Golfers, and although John Morris's praise is unsung, of David Robertson it was written, 'few were better on the golfing green'.[1]

Tom's apprenticeship to feather ball-making coincided with the start of the big money matches. The earliest of these matches to reach the newspapers, described as a 'grand match', was played in October 1840 between Tom Alexander, a ball-maker from Musselburgh, and Allan Robertson over two rounds of the St Andrews Links. Allan had a comfortable four-hole victory.

We know little of what went on before this date as the newspapers of the day recorded only matches involving the gentry. We do know that these matches were played for high stakes involving very complex bets and we also know the players were accompanied, partnered, aided and abetted by their favourite caddies. For some, gambling was the reason for playing the game: gambling and the camaraderie of the Union Parlour after a match with friends of the same persuasion.

In his *Circuit Journeys* of 1844, the great judge Lord Cockburn wrote of St Andrews being completely given over to golf:

> There is a pretty large set who do nothing else, who begin in the morning and stop only for dinner; and who, after practising the game, in the sea breeze, all day, discuss it all night. Their talk is of holes. The intermixture of these men, or rather the intermixture of this occupation, with its interests and hazards and matches, considerably whets the social appetite. And the result is, that

their meetings are very numerous, and that, on the whole they are rather a guttling population.

Cockburn was describing the resident gentry and the Bonnet Lairds; men described elsewhere as 'having a pickle land, large debt and a doocot'.[2] The 'big players' and gambling men of the 1830s and '40s were altogether different. It was this gambling cabal who turned out for the meetings of the leading clubs and were just as likely to be found on the links at Perth, Leith or North Berwick if there was a money match in the offing. St Andrews was described as 'the Doncaster of golfing', and this is an apposite metaphor, for many of these gentlemen kept racehorses and one at least, Colonel J. O. Fairlie, came close to winning the St Leger, the oldest Classic horse race in the world.

Fairlie's brother-in-law, John Campbell of Saddell and his friend Mac-Donald, Chief of Clanranald, were both notorious gamblers and members of what has been described as 'a very wild set of young men, who played high, hunted, kept racehorses, and so on'. Robert Clark commented that Campbell 'was a noble-looking man, pompous in his manners, and very irascible.' It is said that he resided in St Andrews because he could no longer afford to live anywhere else, while George Fullerton Carnegie, the sportsman and poet, is also condemned as having frittered away a fortune that provided him with an income of £5,000 a year (equivalent to half a million pounds today), ending up living in St Andrews with his estate in the hands of creditors and under trust. It was such men who put together the big 'professional' money matches of the 1840s that ignited the interest of the press and public and formed the foundations for the popularity of the game.

Possibly the most significant grand match took place in 1843, some time after Tom had started out as a feather ball-maker in Allan's house. Doubtless there were many money matches organised by the gentlemen players pitting their caddies, one against the other, for sizeable stakes. But this match was a big one and involved the most renowned player from each side of the Firth of Forth, Willie Dunn of Musselburgh versus Allan Robertson of St Andrews: a match of twenty rounds, making three hundred and sixty holes, home and away. Allan triumphed over his Lothian adversary by two rounds and one to play. We know nothing about the stakes or the backers but it clearly captured the public interest for the progress of the match was widely reported. It is interesting to note that in the first mention of the match in the local paper, Willie Dunn is referred to as William Dunny; Dunny was his nickname and the paper got his name right for the second round.

Allan Robertson and Willie Dunn crossed swords again in 1846. The newspaper reported on another, 'Great Match at Golf', noting that: 'A great number of gentlemen, interested in the game of golf, besides those interested in the match and who had taken bets upon it, were present from both sides of the Forth.'

Allan again won and the paper eulogised him:

We can have no hesitation in asserting what everyone conversant in this difficult game admits, that Allan has proved himself the best player extant, and we are glad to add that we understand that a number of gentlemen have made arrangements to present him with a handsome medal as champion, and well he deserves it, for he is not only the best golf player, but is quite a capital ball-maker, and withall a quiet, hard-boned, wiry little fellow, always as cool as a cucumber, and may be depended upon as doing his best at all times.

All the while these matches were taking place and golf was consequently being brought to the attention of the public through the newspapers, Tom Morris was employed by Allan Robertson as a feather ball-maker. David Anderson, known as Da', also came to work for Allan Robertson. It was sometime after 1841 that Da' joined Allan and Tom Morris in the craft of feather ball-making, for in the census of that year, he is recorded as a weaver. Da', two years older than Tom, was Allan's caddy of choice and as he himself emphatically stated, 'not a golfer'.

The workplace that Tom and Da' came to every day at the top of the Links was a peculiar mixture of many things. The house that Allan's father, David Robertson, had lived in since 1828 had been added to and altered as circumstances changed within the family and business on and off the Links. By the late 1830s it had become two-storied and a golf ball-making establishment, while remaining a home for Allan, his wife Helen, his widowed mother and younger brother David, who had found an apprenticeship with a linen cloth merchant. The house was also a boarding establishment and the residence of David Campbell, a fifty-year-old man of independent means.

But the home was also something of a 'Links Office', as it was there that the caddies assembled. Allan recommended them to gentlemen from the Club, fixed rates of pay and more or less regulated play on the Course. More importantly, he also often 'gave the odds' or fixed the handicaps in matches about to begin play on the Links.

Golf may have been the *raison d'être*, but the daily chore that Tom and Da' entered into in the downstairs front room of Allan's house overlooking the road down to Philp's shop, was the making of feather balls. One wonders how frequently the manufacturing process would be interrupted for a game of golf. Work must certainly have stopped altogether for the Spring and Autumn Meetings of The Royal and Ancient Golf Club and, not infrequently, throughout the rest of the year if gentlemen appeared in the Town determined upon a game. H. Thomas Peter described one such match that reflects the spirit of the day:

> I claim to have played with three others in a foursome, a greater number of rounds over St Andrews than had ever been done before – though whether since, I, of course, do not know. The players were my brother O'Brian and Tom Morris against Allan Robertson and myself. We played for two days consecutively, five rounds each day: and the match ended in a draw. When we finished, Allan said he had never had, 'sic a belly fu' o' gowf a' his days.' Neither I take it had the rest of us. We were young and agile then – and what can be compared to a game of golf in the heyday of youth over the magnificent turf of St Andrews with such partners as Allan and Tom? It was only after dark we could strike our colours. At the short holes I have seen play going on, with lanterns set at the holes to guide the putt.

Only the results of games of outstanding merit or of remarkable novelty have been passed down to the present day. Contemporary newspaper accounts of the 1830s and '40s were sporadic and appear to have been dependent upon the editor's personal involvement with golf or the participation of a significant social figure. The golfing townspeople themselves were not of sufficient social note to warrant mention. Allan's wife Helen, died in September 1843, the year of his triumph over Willie Dunn. The match was recorded because of the betting and the gentry's interest in it, while Helen's death passed unmentioned in the press. The death of Allan's dog, Tell, some years later, however, did merit a separate paragraph of its own. The *Fifeshire Journal* of 13 October 1853 noted:

> Died at St Andrews on Monday last, 'Tell', the sagacious and handsome Newfoundland dog belonging to Mr Allan Robertson. 'Tell' was well known for his quiet behaviour, sagacity, and dignified deportment, and his familiar face will be missed by frequenters of the links.

A year after Helen's death, Allan married again in June 1844. His new wife was Jane Kyles of St Cuthbert's parish in Edinburgh.

If the task of making feather balls was a hard one, it was surely not a dull one in the front room of Allan's house.[3] With the weather fair, there would be a collection of caddies on the bank in front of the house and the likelihood of a match. But even in inclement winter weather with the window shut tight against the wind off Lucklaw Hill, it must have been entertaining.

Da' has been described as 'extremely droll' and there is his court testimony in the Road Case of 1878 to support this. Tom affectionately referred to Allan as 'a droll wee body wi' just a wealth of sly, pawky fun about him'. Tom himself was described in Prestwick as 'a wonderful raconteur'. It is not hard to imagine these three characters swapping anecdotes – and what anecdotes they would have had to tell!

Doubtless, Allan's leg would be pulled mercilessly about his match with George Condie, a member of The Royal and Ancient and an amateur player from Perth of some considerable ability. Condie, who was receiving strokes, persuaded Allan to play for a club a hole, a 'pluck' match in which the winner of a hole could 'pluck' a club from his opponent. It is said that Allan lost all his clubs. If this story is true, then it was one of the few occasions that the pawky Allan lost anything. The number of times that Allan just 'managed' to beat his protagonist on the 17th green was legendary. The wins were masterfully wrought to save his opponent's face, and more importantly, to reduce the likelihood of him having to give increased odds on future encounters.

Allan has been described as 'unbeaten' by nineteenth-century local scribes. It has also been written that Allan never met Tom in a head-to-head on the Links and even that one or other of them avoided such matches. There were, however, a number of encounters recorded between the two, the first being in 1842, which Allan won by two holes. In May 1853 a private match of one round took place, '– a rare occurrence – some little cash depended on the issue', as the *Fifeshire Journal* put it. Played in rain, hail and a fierce northerly wind, Tom succeeded by three holes. It was this match that provoked colourful comment and correspondence in the *Fifeshire Journal* between Prestwick golfers supporting Tom and those of St Andrews championing Allan. After this match the Prestwick camp proclaimed Tom 'King of Clubs throughout Scotland', and challenged Allan to a further match, issuing a 'Proclamation of War'. The *Fifeshire Journal* ridiculed these assertions and claims.

There must have been other occasions when Allan and Tom were matched on the Links, as it is hard to believe that the big betting men of the day failed to induce them to play for a purse from time to time. What is absolutely certain is that they regularly played against one another with amateur partners in foursomes matches and that they played for money.

After The Royal and Ancient's Meetings, the gentlemen amateurs would partner their caddies in foursomes that frequently carried substantial bets. Allan's partner was invariably Sir Thomas Moncrieffe while Tom's was Colonel Fairlie of Coodham, Ayrshire. These matches became fixtures of the Meetings in St Andrews and generated considerable local interest, enough to merit the attentions of the press in Fife as well as in Ayrshire. Indeed, Everard described these matches as 'something of a standing dish at Prestwick and St Andrews'. The two amateurs were very evenly matched, competitive and determined sportsmen. Their foursomes matches with Allan and Tom often continued over three or four days with the honours most frequently evenly drawn.

The connection that Tom established with James Ogilvie Fairlie of Coodham during those weeks of the Royal and Ancient's Meetings throughout the 1840s was to have a momentous effect on his life and, more importantly, on the evolution of golf. Fairlie was a remarkable gentleman in many respects. Some twelve years older than Tom, he was an excellent shot, rider, curler, archer and golfer. Tom doubtless benefited a great deal from his associations with Fairlie; he certainly acquired the habit of pipe smoking that he enjoyed for the rest of his life.

Hobnobbing with the rapidly expanding golfing gentry on the Links of St Andrews may have encouraged the local golfers to set about their own golfing destiny. Whether inspired by Allan's matches with Willie Dunn or simply copying their social betters will never be known, but the St Andrews golfers of the artisan and tradesman classes formed their own golf club.

By 1843, several golf clubs had already come into being in the East Neuk of Fife, including Crail (1786), Leven (1817) and Kingsbarns (1793). These, however, were clubs largely for the local gentry, albeit what was accepted as gentry elsewhere was a bit broader than it was in St Andrews at that time.

Local merchants and businessmen had already established the St Andrews Thistle Golf Club in 1817. These were men of insufficient social status to feel comfortable in, or find an easy admission to, the Society of St Andrews Golfers. The Thistle was something of a casual affair with the members meeting in local pubs to organise themselves. But it was somewhat exclusive, embracing only 'men of business', and from the outset did not include ball-makers and weavers and certainly not caddies or others who made their living from the game.

The foundation of the St Andrews Mechanics' Golf Club in 1843 appears to have bridged this social divide because the founding members covered a broad spectrum of life in the Town. Tom's brother George, a manservant – sometimes rather grandly called a butler – was a founding member, as were joiners, plasterers, slaters and other such tradesmen. Although they were residents of St Andrews and could have played at any time, they held their meetings twice yearly in June and October, similar to The Royal and Ancient, whose traditions they followed in many respects. Prior to play in their seasons' meetings, they would march through the Town and, at the conclusion of play, solemnly walk in procession to their inn of choice for dinner. The meal was followed with songs and recitations of poems and many toasts drunk to present and absent friends. Tom Morris appears to have had a reputation as something of a singer, as well as a raconteur. Tom's rendition of 'Shire o' Argyle' was sufficiently popular to merit mention by George Bruce in his poem 'A Piece of Rhyme upon Golf'.

> Tom Morris, too wi' his 'Shire o' Argyle,'
> And Lister's 'Baby was sleeping;'
> And King's loud 'Sitting on the stile,'
> A' helped to enliven our meeting.

6 The Gutta Affair

Neither Tom nor Allan was a founding member of the St Andrews Mechanics' Golf Club in 1843. When they did become members they supported the Club in a number of ways, including, 'giving the odds', or fixing members' handicaps.[1] They did not compete in the Club's competitions and this clearly reflected not only their status as 'professionals', but also the level at which Allan and Tom were then considered to be playing relative to the other members of the Club.[2] As well as an acceptance of their golfing supremacy, it also illustrates the extent to which their joint word was law. The fact that Tom was included with Allan on an equal basis means that by 1844 Tom was considered by the Town's players to be Allan's equal on the Links. The formation of the Mechanics' Golf Club signified change on the Links and the ascendancy of Tom to a status matching that of Allan signalled change in the game.

Momentous changes were taking place in St Andrews and in golf. Playfair's improvements were well under way, and together with the introduction of the railway system providing the population with much greater mobility, the place was starting to become something of a resort. The increasing success and popularity of the Madras College was also helping to propel a building boom. Play on the Links was increasing rapidly and the newspapers were starting to recount the results of local clubs' medals and matches.

Then there was talk – there must always have been talk – of a new kind of ball. As the Victorian Age got into full swing, however, the vigour that the intellectually restless had applied to every other human endeavour, finally lighted upon golf and the gutta percha ball came into being. The effect of its introduction in 1846 was abrupt and seismic on the game, the Town and, emphatically, on the life of Tom Morris. It was by far the most important single development in golf to date, providing the conduit for the transformation of what was then essentially an obscure, parochial Scottish pastime, into the worldwide game that we know today.

Gutta percha was a juice obtained from a variety of trees growing in the Malaysian Peninsula and, when refined and enhanced, the resulting gum displayed what was then seen as remarkable properties. It could be easily worked and moulded by heating and, when set, was hard and extremely durable. Needless to say it found many uses in the newly emerging industrialised world. In 1846 golf suddenly had a solid and hard rubber-type all-weather ball that was easy to produce and, most importantly, was virtually indestructible. Its cost was also only a fraction of that of the feather ball, making it affordable to the general population. Moreover, as the gutta came to be developed over the years, its playing performance improved dramatically. In retrospect it is surprising that the ball took so long in coming.

Irrespective of the origins of the new ball, its impact was stupendous, despite the fact that in dry conditions the early gutta balls did not fly any further, and certainly no better, than the feathery. But they flew in the wet while the feather ball did not fly at all and was quite likely to burst, spewing its feathers over the wet grass.[3]

The fact that the earliest smooth guttas did not fly well is confirmed by contemporary writers and can be easily demonstrated today. The science of aerodynamics was unknown to the early players with the new ball, but they were sufficiently astute to appreciate that the ball's flight improved with use. Indeed, the more hacks it suffered the better it appeared to play. It was soon found that preliminary marking with a slater's hammer or a cleaver improved the flight. Eventually, moulds were made that carried patterned indentations and the gutta ball had indubitably arrived. The transition was not universally immediate. Because of the reluctance by some of the older players to give up 'leather and feather', it took some three or four years for the gutta to oust the feather ball completely, but the feathery's fate was absolutely certain.

H. B. Farnie explained the situation in 1857 in his *The Golfer's Manual*:

> The first flight of 'Guttas' was hailed with a burst of joy financial by every-one except the old monopolists of the feather manufacture. They saw no reason to rejoice; their occupation was, like Othello's, gone, at least in all seeming; and day after day, the demand for feathers dwindled, and gutta percha was the order of the time. A few prejudiced oldsters, indeed, remained staunch liegemen of the old system; but only for a time, and at last the ball-makers themselves, who had firmly nailed their colours to the mast, surrendered before the increasing volleys of guttas.

The decline of the feathery was indeed swift and dramatic. John Gourlay, the renowned feather ball-maker from Musselburgh, was supplying Douglas McEwan, club-maker of Musselburgh and Bruntsfield Links, with balls for re-sale during the changeover years. On Gourlay's death in 1869, Douglas and his son Peter, rendered accounts of their indebtedness to Gourlay's representatives for balls they had been supplied with over a period, surprisingly, of some 35 years. These accounts can be interpreted as evidence of the state of the golf-ball market at the time. In 1847, the first year the gutta became generally available to golfers, John Gourlay's sales of feather balls to Douglas McEwan plummeted by 75 per cent, and were nil in 1850 and 1851.

From these accounts we learn that Gourlay did start making 'Percha' balls in 1852, and by 1858 was supplying guttas in quantities a third greater than in the feather ball era. Indeed, in 1860, his volume was twice that of his heyday of the feather and leather period. He had adapted to the changed market and reaped the benefits of the new ball, which significantly, by virtue of its improved performance and much reduced cost, made the game of golf more popular.[4]

The coming of the gutta ball is also said to have led to Allan Robertson and Tom severing their personal, as well as business relationship in feather ball-making. There are several contemporary accounts of how this came about, but Tom's reminiscences, as told to H. S. C. Everard in 1905, would appear to be the most authentic:

> I can remember the circumstances well. It all happened in this way. Allan could not reconcile himself to the new ball at first at all, just in the same way as Mr John Low and many other golfers could not take to the Haskell when it first appeared. But the gutta became the fashion very quickly, as the rubber-cored has done, so what could we do? One day, and it is one that will always be clearly stamped upon my memory, I had been playing golf with a Mr Campbell of Saddell, and I had the misfortune to lose all my supply of balls, which were, you can understand, very much easier lost in those days, as the fairway of the course was ever so much narrower then than it is now, and with thick, bushy whins close in at the side. But to return to my story. I had, as I said, run short of balls, and Mr Campbell kindly gave me a gutta to try. I took to it at once, and, as we were playing in, it so happened that we met Allan Robertson coming out, and someone told him that

I was playing a very good game with one of the new gutta balls, and I could see fine from the expression on his face, that he did not like it at all, and, when we met afterwards in his shop, we had some high words about the matter, and there and then we parted company, I leaving his employment.[5]

Some have taken this to mean that Allan and Tom had fallen out, not only regarding Tom's employment, but also personally. If Allan had experienced the same dramatic reduction in sales of his featheries as had John Gourlay, then one can only imagine the highly emotional state he might have been in when confronted with the fact that his employee, Tom Morris, was playing with the very ball that seriously threatened his livelihood. If Allan terminated Tom's employment immediately, under the circumstances, that could be viewed as a not unreasonable reaction. The fact, however, that the two continued with their highly successful foursomes partnership in money matches, and also jointly allocated the handicaps at the Mechanics Golf Club, attests to their personal relationship not being impaired, and it is clear that the two remained friends until Allan's death in 1859.

The Old Course scorecards which Tom later gave to his customers and which the shop continued to issue into the twentieth century, show that Tom saw himself as being in business from 1848, for that is the date given on the cards as the establishment of his business. It is from that date too that he started to present balls as prizes to the Mechanics' Golf Club independently of Allan. These may have been feather balls, for there are several in mint condition stamped 'T. Morris' in existence today.[6]

The Mechanics' Golf Club, perhaps with Allan's prompting, took a somewhat Luddite stance at its Autumn Meeting in 1849 by spreading a 'flag on the green' bearing the words 'no gutta perchas allowed on the Green', painted on it. The press notice also remarked that 'A golfer, well known on the Links, who has been using the Perchas, on seeing the flag, took the hint to himself, and to show his contempt, turned it upside down.' The local press reported that 'A large consumption of gutta percha takes place here in the manufacture of golf balls, for which a maker in the city is becoming famous, having, besides the home trade, an extensive demand from other places which he supplies by hundreds at a time.'

There can be little doubt that the person being referred to was Tom Morris and that the editor of the *Fifeshire Journal* was mischievously enjoying generating friction. In the following issue, he concluded a lengthy piece on the demise of the feathery with a blatant chastisement of Allan's reluctance to change. Allan's business died, as did every other making feather balls. It ended in the way that all commercial enterprises end when there is no demand for the product they make. Tom Morris clearly not only saw the advantages of the gutta ball but also a great business opportunity. Unlike Allan, he was not burdened by a family tradition of feather ball-making going back several generations, and could immediately make the transition without emotions or qualms. Allan did eventually switch to making the new ball and it would be hard to imagine him not playing some part in its continuing development.

Tom and Allan took on the Dunn brothers from Musselburgh every year from 1847 to 1850 over the links of Musselburgh, North Berwick, Leven's Dubbieside and St Andrews. We have only scant details of most of these matches but the account of one match in particular, that of 1849, was made by contemporary writers because of the stupendous sum of £400 involved. Presumably there were wealthy backers on both sides who put up the stake money but neither the press accounts nor the gentlemen scribes of the day named them. This match consisted of three games of 36 holes each played over Musselburgh, St Andrews and North Berwick, the winner being the side that won the most games.

Over their home green of Musselburgh the Dunns made a terrible example of Tom and Allan, winning the game by 13 holes and 12 to play. In St Andrews however, the situation was reversed. The Links was then a much better and smoother course than Musselburgh and the standard of play was higher with the outcome uncertain until the last four holes, Allan and Tom eventually winning by three holes. The match stood 'all square' with only the North Berwick course left to play.

North Berwick then consisted of seven holes, requiring the players to play five rounds, with an extra hole added in the final round. H. Thomas Peter, in his *Reminiscences of Golf and Golfers,* recorded the encounter at North Berwick as a dramatic event:

> The match started amidst the greatest enthusiasm. The weather had cleared up, but the wind blew pretty strong from the South-west. Each party had its own tail of supporters, those for the Musselburgh men predominating. They were led by Gourlay, the ball-maker. I never saw a match where such vehement party spirit was displayed. So great was the keenness and the anxiety to see whose ball had the best lie, that no sooner were the shots played than off the whole crowd ran, helter-skelter: and as one or the other lay best, so demonstrations were made by each party.

Sir David Baird was umpire, and a splendid one he made. He was very tall, and so commanded a good view of the field; but it took all his firmness to keep tolerable order.

The early part of the match went greatly in favour of the Dunns, whose play was magnificent. Their driving, in fact, completely overpowered their opponents. They went sweeping over hazards which the St Andrews men had to play short of. At lunch time the Dunns were four up, and long odds were offered on them.

On resuming the match, the advantage went still further to the credit of the Musselburgh men and everyone thought that victory was theirs; but one never knows when the tide at golf will turn – and turn it did.

Details of the position at the start of the last round were provided by Howie Smith in his *The Golfer's Year Book for 1866*:

At the commencement of the last round of all the Dunns were four holes ahead and eight to play. However, Allan and Tom, by a magnificent game, gained the first hole, then the second, halved the third, gained the fourth, halved the fifth, and gained the sixth, thus making the poll all even and two to play.

H. Thomas Peter continued:

How different the attitude of the Dunns' supporters now from their jubilant and vaunting manner at lunchtime! Silence reigned, concern was on every brow, the elasticity had completely gone from Gourlay's step, and the profoundest anxiety marked every line of his countenance. The very Dunns themselves were demoralized.

On the other hand, Allan and Tom were serene, and their supporters as lively as they had been depressed before. We felt victory ours!

When the tee shots were played for the second last hole, off we flew as usual to see whose ball lay best! To our intense dismay Allan's lay very badly, while the Dunns' lay further on beautifully. Should the Dunns win this hole they would be dormy – they might win the match! Our revulsion of feeling was great, and as play proceeded was intensified, for Allan and Tom had played three more with their ball in a bunker close to and in front of the putting-green!

But, on the other hand, the Dunns' ball was lying close at the back of a kerb-stone on a cart-track off the green to the right! First of all they wished the stone removed, and called to someone to go for a spade; but Sir David Baird would not sanction its removal, because it was off the course and a fixture. One of the Dunns (I forget which) struck at the ball with his iron but hit the top of the stone. The other did the same; and again the same operation was performed and 'the like' played. All this time the barometer of our expectations had been steadily rising and had now almost reached 'Set Fair'. The odd had now to be played, and this was done by striking the ball with the back of the iron on to grass beyond the track. Had that been done at first the hole might have been won and the match also; but both men had by this time lost all judgement and nerve, and played most recklessly. The consequence was the loss of the hole, and Allan and Tom 'dormy'.

We felt the victory was now secure: and so in fact it turned out, and Allan and Tom remained the victors by two holes.

I think it only just to say that, in my opinion, the winning of the above match was due to Tom Morris. Allan was decidedly off his game at the start and played weakly, and badly for a long time – almost justifying the jeers thrown at him such as, 'That wee body in the red jacket canna play golf', and suchlike. Tom on the other hand played with pluck and determination throughout.

Howie Smith rather magnanimously summed the match up:

Thus ended one of the most interesting and keenly-contested matches of golf ever played in Scotland, which, though credit-able to Allan and Tom, is no less so to the brothers Dunn who, throughout the three greens, played a brilliant game, which it would be difficult to surpass.

This was certainly the first golfing spectacle recorded in the press of the day and it continued to be discussed for over 50 years. Lord Moncrieff re-lated his recollections of it in *Golf Illustrated* in 1908 and William Doleman responded with his own memories of 'the heated discussion between Allan Robertson and Jamie Dunn about the lifting of the stones'. Clearly, at the time, the outcome was not without controversy.

After six rounds on three different courses, the St Andrews pair had triumphed by one hole. We can only speculate on the amount of money privately wagered on the outcome. It was reported that odds of twenty to one were freely available against Tom and Allan at the start of the final round. As the fortunes of the game so abruptly changed the 'on course' betting must have been frenetic during this last round. The drama of golf was emphatically encapsulated in the happenings on the links of North Berwick that day and much money would have changed hands, doubtless to the satisfaction of the St Andrews brigade.

Allan must have had a spring in his step down to the harbour to board the boat back across the Forth to St Andrews and Tom would doubtless have had a very satisfactory pull on his pipe. One has no reason to doubt the account of the sum played for but no mention is made of the division of the pot. Whatever it was, it would have been substantial enough and very welcome to Tom, for he was now a married man with a family.[7]

7 Marriage and Movement

Agnes Bayne was born on 30 August 1818 in Middlefoodie, a place something less than a hamlet that sits at the back of the village of Dairsie.[1] Dairsie itself was no more than a row of houses straddling the road midway between St Andrews and Cupar. The house in which she was born was one in a cluster of cottages occupied by hecklers and weavers working the flax fibres into coarse Osnaburg linen cloth.

Agnes probably attended the Church Board School in Dairsie about a mile from her home and, like Tom, would leave the school when she was about ten years old. For the first few years she would be at home helping her mother service the loom and seeing to the chores of the weaver's household, identical in every respect to that of the Morris family at North Street in St Andrews at the same time. By 1841 Agnes was in St Andrews working in the home of Captain and Mrs Broughton in North Street, not fifty yards from where Tom Morris lived.

Domestic service was just about the only option open to a weaver's daughter: it was that or marriage. Agnes found a place as a domestic servant with the Broughtons where she joined Agnes Thorburn, Ellice Farnie and Ann Hay. Their collective duty was to maintain and service the household and to care for the five Broughton children.

Captain Broughton was a regular serving officer in Her Majesty's forces and, like many wives of officers of the day, Mrs Broughton would accompany her husband to his posting, leaving the household in the care of a housekeeper and her children in the care of a governess. The Broughtons had no obvious connection with St Andrews. Like an increasing number of regular officers, Broughton chose St Andrews as his family's domicile for reasons of costs, health, education and the availability of good, reliable domestic staff.

The 1841 census lists all four women in the Broughton house as domestic servants but it is not difficult to deduce the roles that they played. Miss

Farnie's role, with her Edinburgh background and education, was certainly that of teacher and governess. Miss Thorburn was the daughter of a shop-keeper in the Town and like Miss Farnie, was in her mid-thirties. She was almost certainly the housekeeper.

Ann Hay and Agnes Bayne both gave their ages as twenty-one to the census taker in 1841. Ann was in fact twenty-two and Agnes twenty-three years old: Ann also came from a weaver family. Their role in the Broughton household was straightforward enough, for they would be required to do whatever was asked of them. Agnes and Ann would have cooked, cleaned, shopped and looked after the Broughton children.

Captain Broughton was an urbane and intelligent man. He was a golfer of no great distinction or repute, a member of The Royal and Ancient as well as the Literary and Philosophical Society of St Andrews. He was also a pillar of the Episcopalian Church and a man of sufficient means to respond to Provost Playfair's appeal to the citizens to advance money to the Town to finance his improvements. Captain Broughton lent £500 at 5 per cent interest per annum, one of the very few to lend a three-figure sum.

Tom Morris was familiar with Captain Broughton. The story of his ex-perience with the Captain at the High Hole has been repeated many times as a testimony to Tom's decency. Tom, it was reported, found his ball in a difficult lie just off the green. The Captain remarked that he would put £50 on him not holing out from where he lay. Tom luckily holed his ball and the game continued. The next day, Captain Broughton was said to have sought out Tom with cash in hand, but Tom refused the money, saying that the wager was made in fun and he would not hold the Captain to it. If Captain Broughton's blessing was required for the hand of Agnes Bayne, he would surely have been quick to give it after this incident.

Tom would have known Agnes, or Nancy as she was called, if only as a neighbour. He would have met her in the street and seen her in the kirk on Sunday with the other domestic staff of the Broughton household. He probably also saw her at the *soirées* and social evenings in the Town Hall for there were entertainments aplenty in the summer months. The upper classes of Edinburgh and Glasgow were starting to resort to the Town for sea bathing, which was becoming something of an exercise and fad with the intelligentsia. Mr Mori, 'a pupil of Thalberg', took up residence, advertis-ing himself to be, 'in attendance for sea bathing'. With the resorters came the entertainments. In August 1842, Van Amburgh's Circus came to Town and made a grand entrance through the West Port with the first elephants that the townspeople had ever seen. An even greater, although inadvertent, spectacle was created when Mr Cyngell, a maker of fireworks at the north east corner of Bakers Wynd, blew himself up while in the process of making the pyrotechnics display for Queen Victoria's visit to Perth. Mr Beckett's Theatricals stayed for a week, as did the Collins Family, playing 'many and various musical instruments', and, for 'definitely one night only', Mr and Mrs Franks of the Nobility Concerts, London, appeared in the Town Hall.

There was certainly enough for a couple 'walking out' in St Andrews to see in the early 1840s, and nature offered even more spectacle with two great storms. Both wreaked havoc and as a result of the first, the pagoda in Provost Playfair's botanical garden was blown down and, in the second, a huge whale was washed up on the West Sands. This was immediately claimed for the Crown and sold by auction. A consortium of butchers bought the blubber and the Literary and Philosophical Society paid £10 for the remains and 'vital organs'. The sea, however, produced a high surging tide that removed the carcass entirely and nobody got anything.

The constant battles between the students and the Town's youths were concerning but certainly entertaining. Then there was the ongoing theological debate as the schismatics of the Free Kirk laid the foundations of their church in North Street and, to the indignation of the Establishmentarians, did so directly opposite St Salvator's ancient chapel.[2]

The fisher lassies who carried the mussels from the Eden estuary to bait the fishing lines caused a stir when they refused to comply with the Council's wish that they cover their knees when they came within sight of the Town. The Chartists, forbears of the trade union movement, caused some consternation when they held their first meeting in the Town Hall with the support of some members of the Town Council. They caused an even greater rumpus when they tore down the palings outside the gentlemen golfers' Union Parlour and threw the Town's artillery into the Swilken Burn. Life in St Andrews for Tom and Nancy may have been parochial but it certainly was not dull.

Nancy Bayne would have been familiar with Tom's parents, Old John and Jean Morris as well as with Janet and John, his sister and brother, both still at home and working the looms in 1841. Tom's eldest sister, Helen, had married Robert Hay in 1829 and moved into his weaver's cottage in the nearby village of Leuchars from where she would doubtless be a regular visitor. Margaret was already married to Thomas Black, a fisherman, and living in Castle Wynd. Nancy would have seen Janet Morris and William Wallace 'walking out' before their banns were cried in the Town Kirk for their marriage in February 1842, and she would have been at least aware of Tom's mother's illness and have mourned her death in December of that year.

At about this time, soon after his wife's death, Old John dismantled the looms and is said to have become a letter carrier for the fledgling Post Office. Young John persisted as a weaver before his early death in December 1846. The disappearance of Jean from all public records at this time suggests that she emigrated.

Just four weeks after Samuel Morse had transmitted the world's first telegraph message, Tom married Nancy Bayne on 21 June 1844. Their banns would have been cried in the Town Kirk on the two Sundays that preceded their wedding and few in the Town would have been unaware of the event. They were married in the newly built St Mary's Kirk in Market Street with Rev. Dr Ferrie in charge of the proceedings.

It is odd that Dr William Ferrie should officiate at Tom and Nancy's betrothal. He held the chair of Civil History in the University for eighteen years and was distinguished in that he gave only two lectures in that time. Ferrie was minister of the Kirk in the nearby village of Kilconquhar and an avid, popular and enthusiastic golfer in St Andrews where, for thirty-eight years, he was Chaplain to the Society of Golfers and The Royal and Ancient Golf Club. Indeed, he would appear to have been an all-round sportsman, for he was also a member of the Hercules Club at Colinsburgh which, as well as golfing, also ran general athletic contests.[3] One can only assume that Tom and Dr Ferrie knew each other well enough for Tom to ask him to conduct the service of his wedding.

There has been much speculation through the years about where Tom and Nancy lived after their marriage. The Town's property valuation rolls (Stent Rolls) register only the owners of property until the late 1850s so it is impossible to determine where and from whom Tom and Nancy initially rented their home. It is from the 1851 census that we find that they lived at 4 Pilmour Links, only a few doors from Hugh Philp and just round the corner from Allan Robertson.[4]

The year of 1846 was one of sadness and celebration for Tom and Nancy. Celebration when George, the last of the family to marry, had wed Agnes Peattie in the Town Kirk on 23 May.[5] There was more celebration when Nancy gave birth to a son, the fourth generation of the Morris line to be born in the weaver's cottage in North Street. But sadness too, for Old John died on 22 December and was buried on Christmas Eve 1846. He was in his seventy-sixth year and had not only lived long enough to see all his family married, but he also had the satisfaction of holding his son's child in his arms.

Nancy and Tom's son, Tommy, was born on 15 May and christened on 1 June 1846. It was surely a big occasion. Tom, already a significant figure on the Links, was from an old Town family with many friends and relatives, but Nancy too had her friends from the Broughton household in North Street and her family from not far out the Cupar road at Middlefoodie.

For Tom and Nancy life was good and it continued that way. Tom met Major James Ogilvy Fairlie at the Autumn Meeting of The Royal and Ancient in 1846 and would appear to have struck up an instant rapport. In that year they began a golfing partnership that enjoyed more success than failure; a partnership from which Tom must have earned a considerable income. Allan Robertson and Sir Thomas Moncrieffe were a challenge but in the main, against whoever opposed them in foursomes play, Tom and Major Fairlie took the laurels.

Tom's renown on the Links grew by the year and, by the time of the big match in 1849 when Allan and Tom took on the Dunn twins in the marathon match watched by thousands in St Andrews, Musselburgh and North Berwick, his place in the game was assured. The coming of the gutta ball may have caused some anxiety for a while, but Tom would have been well advised and quick to see the opportunities it presented.

There is a reasonable amount of evidence that Tom started ball-making on his own account around 1848. If he did, he would not only have made the old style feathery but also the new revolutionary gutta percha ball. Tom certainly had room enough and all of the facilities necessary to make balls in his house in Pilmour Links. He was independent and sufficiently well off to present balls for prizes to the Mechanics Golf Club and it is at least interesting that his brother George was a recipient of the prizes, as were Andrew Strath and Bob Kirk, other recognised players of the day.

The initial blissful years of Tom and Nancy's life together did not last long. On 17 April 1850 their four-year-old son Tommy died and was buried two days later in the Cathedral Cemetery beside his grandparents, John and Jean. This was a terrible blow to Tom and Nancy, for although infant mortality was high, by the age of four they must have felt confident that their boy was through the dangerous and difficult years. The bereavement that they suffered at this early stage in their married life must have contributed to the great fortitude they would show for the rest of their lives.

Distress at the loss may have ignited their determination to move and make a new life for themselves elsewhere, although there were doubtless other factors. Willie Dunn was about to leave his native Musselburgh to become Keeper of the Green and Professional at Blackheath in London. Tom may have also started to feel that living in Allan Robertson's shadow was restrictive and not all that it might be. Although independent in business he was nevertheless at risk with the vagaries of play on the Links.

Others were taking up gutta ball-making and he must have viewed the future with some uncertainty. The Scots population as a whole had become more mobile and alert to the possibilities of self-improvement.

With constant talk of much-travelled and prosperous men on the Links, it would be surprising if Tom and Nancy had not given some thought to improving their own position. The coming of the railway to Leuchars and the North British Railway establishing the world's first train ferry, across the Firth of Forth between Burntisland and Granton, had broadened the horizons of many in St Andrews. Edinburgh, Glasgow and even London were suddenly easily accessible. Scotland was on the move and self-improvement was being preached from the pulpit as well as talked about in the street.

Major Fairlie had intimated to Tom that gentlemen in the vicinity of Ayr were of a mind to expand their rudimentary course at Prestwick and have it properly established, developed and maintained. Tom and Nancy must have talked through the possibilities and the enthusiasm and support of Fairlie would have been crucial. Nancy was pregnant again and would give birth in May. It would be propitious for them to move to Prestwick in the summer of 1851 in order to make a new life for themselves and their new baby.

But before they did and just before Willie Dunn himself departed for Blackheath, Dunn's Musselburgh backers challenged Tom to a match over the Links of St Andrews. Particular interest was attached to it, not only because of the large wagers riding on the outcome, but also because both contestants were about to leave their native towns for pastures new. The odds were clearly on Tom and when he was unexpectedly beaten, the *Montrose Standard* of May 1851 lamented:

> Tom's performance at the outset was inauspicious . . .
> At the last hole Tom's ball rolled first down the east side and then over the west. Seeing that he could not halve the match Tom gave his ball a kick in disgust while Dunn took a snuff with great gusto.

Tom had much on his mind. Not only was there the new baby in the house as well as his sister-in-law Margaret Bayne, but also all of the work pressures of a self-employed man. With his departure for Prestwick imminent, it is not surprising that from time to time he gave vent to his emotions.

Emulating Allan Robertson, Tom started a scrapbook of newspaper cuttings just before he left St Andrews for Prestwick: it is interesting to note that his first cutting, dated October 1850, was an account of his patron, J.O. Fairlie, being installed as Captain of The Royal and Ancient. His second was the full newspaper account of his defeat by Willie Dunn in May 1851, which also reported that: 'Tom departs from St Andrews for Ayrshire in the end of this month, to a place in the vicinity of Ayr, called Prestwick, where they have links, and upon which Tom will likely soon astonish the natives of those parts; he will no doubt reign supreme as a golfer.'

The Reverend A.K.H. Boyd christened Tommy Morris in the Holy Trinity Kirk of St Andrews on the 10 May 1851. By the end of July the family was settled into their new home in Prestwick. Tommy's arrival, both in St Andrews and Prestwick, heralded a new era for golf in more ways than anybody at the time could have imagined.

8 Sowing Seeds in the West

As the Great Exhibition of 1851 was being held at London's Crystal Palace, Tom Morris was moving his family from St Andrews to the west coast of Scotland. Today Prestwick is no more than a three-hour drive by car from St Andrews. In 1851 it must have seemed to Nancy and her friends an entire world away. Tom may well already have visited at the invitation of the newly promoted Colonel Fairlie and his friends to have a look at what might be done with the place, for the coming of the railways had rendered such relatively distant places accessible.[1] A pregnant Nancy, however, is not likely to have made any preliminary trip there and surely would have required some reassurance from Tom that they would have a house and home and that there was a good life and future to be made for them in Prestwick.

With a two-month-old child and all of the goods and chattels necessary to set up a house, their move to Prestwick could not have been easy. As well as the tools of his trade, his own clubs sewn up in coarse linen, there would also be the equipment necessary for Tom to make and repair clubs as well as the materials to make balls.

They would need transport to Leuchars Junction station early in the morning.[2] This would have been straightforward enough for there were many carters known to them in the Town; it was nevertheless at least a one-hour journey by horse and cart. Then there was the train to Burntisland, after everything was loaded into the guard's van and Nancy and her baby installed in a carriage. This may well have been Nancy's first train journey and the thought of feeding her baby and keeping it clean during the hours of travelling must have weighed heavily upon her.

At Burntisland they would have had to move everything into the new train ferry to make the crossing to Granton, where it would all have to be loaded back on to the train for the short run into Edinburgh's North Bridge Station. A conservative estimate of the time for the journey from St

Andrews to Edinburgh based upon the railway timetables of the day would be about four hours.

At Edinburgh another train had to be boarded for Glasgow where it was necessary to change stations. This required a handcart at least, but there were carters plying their trade between the stations. From Glasgow to the Prestwick Station on the line to Ayr is a journey of only thirty miles. If they reached Prestwick eight hours after leaving North Street in St Andrews it would have been due to the fortuity of connecting train times. No matter how long it took to make the journey, Nancy must have thought it interminable and have been exhausted by the experience.

In Prestwick the walk from the station to the house that had been secured for them up at the Town Cross is some three hundred yards. Given the probable late hour of their arrival, it is most likely that arrangements had been made for them to spend their first night in a room at the Red Lion Inn across the road. But even if arrangements had not been made, one can be sure that the Hunter family of the Red Lion would have been over the road to offer them a bed for the night.

Prestwick is spread along the road to Ayr and in 1851 was a village with a population of two thousand. It extends today from the village parish of Monkton in the north and straddles what was then the main turnpike road to the busy township of Ayr to the south. A long, continuous shingle beach edges the Atlantic Ocean parallel to the road, on the other side of which lies the fertile farmland that supplied Glasgow with its kale, cabbages, meal and milk.

The focal centre of the Prestwick township is the Cross. In 1851 it was a market cross, set in an open area where three roads converged in a cluster of dwellings and shops. The Burgh Hall and the Red Lion Inn were the principal buildings about the Cross.

The railway line runs along the sea-side of the road to Ayr. The station at Prestwick is sited just below the Cross, some three hundred yards down the Wrack Road, so called because it was the road used by the farmers to cart the wrack, the seaweed, from the beach to fertilise their fields.

Beyond the railway, the links land sweeps down to the beach. In 1851 this land spread almost as far as the eye could see all the way south to Ayr and up to Troon in the north. The piece of land that had been secured for Prestwick Golf Course was bordered on the south side by the Wrack Road and to the north by the Pow Burn. To the west lay the sea, edged by a strip of silver sand and to the east the railway line separated the links from the village.

The home obtained for Tom and his family was close to the Cross, on the side of the busy Ayr road. It was not a large house, comprising only two rooms. To the rear was a living room with two boxed-in beds. The front room with its door onto the street was to be Tom's workshop with an area designated for storing the gentlemen's clubs. The house was not spacious and it was not grand, but it was no better or worse than what they had left in St Andrews and doubtless neither more nor less than Tom and Nancy had expected it to be.

On one side of their new house was Mr Hutchison's shop. Hutchison was a silk weaver who ran the general store that served much of the local needs. On the other side was Mr Wiseman, a wine and spirit merchant. Opposite, across the busy High Street and main road to Ayr, stood the Red Lion.

The inn stands to this day and from the outside, at least, has changed little. It was at one time a stopping place for the Ayr to Glasgow stagecoach and was then, after the coming of the railway in 1843, the hostelry that boarded travellers and served as the 'howf' for the local worthies. It would come to be the watering place and the 'nineteenth hole' of all the Prestwick golfers.

In 1851 the Red Lion was owned and run by the Hunters, a family that would come to play a central part in the lives of the Morris family through friendship and marriage. The Hunters would also come to play a key role in developing and expanding golf in Prestwick. William Hunter, 'mine host' of the Red Lion, was some fourteen years older than Tom. He farmed fifteen acres of land on the Monkton side of the parish to the south, as well as running the busy inn with his wife Elizabeth Gray, aged thirty-eight, and their four children.

William Hunter came from a large local family. His sister Mary Hunter, aged thirty-two and a spinster, worked in the inn and his brother James farmed twenty-five acres of land about half a mile up the road towards Ayr. In Ayr itself, William had two cousins in business. One was a timber merchant and it was this business which was ultimately to be the catalyst that created the Morris family fortune; the other cousin was Dean of Guild in the town. William's widowed sister-in law Jane, would come to live only a few yards along the road with her daughter Mary, a dressmaker, and her 22-year-old son Charlie Hunter, then a clerk in Boswell's law office and later in the Customs and Excise.

Tom Morris did not go to Prestwick to start the game in the West of Scotland; golf had been played there sporadically for some three hundred years. There had been a golf club in Glasgow in the early nineteenth century that played on Glasgow Green by the side of the river Clyde. The earliest records of the Glasgow Golf Club date from 1787 but it seems to have faltered somewhat from 1794 to 1809 when it again had a burst of activity. By 1835 however, it was once more in abeyance and it was not to be until some thirty-five years later that the Club was reconstituted. At this time, as James Colville in his *History of the Glasgow Golf Club*, points out, 'The well-to-do were finding ease and ostentation in setting up country houses, in building and planting, and in field sport. The old pastimes of city life were more left to the "wee corks" and merchants in a sma' way.'

Golf had been played at Prestwick in one form or another since at least the end of the eighteenth century and there is solid evidence, contained in *The History of the Kennedys*, that the game was played in Ayr in the sixteenth century. In the early eighteenth century, Macfarlane's *Geographical Collections* also relates that there were '. . . pleasant greens to the east and west where hare courses were run and golf playing and other amusements practiced on the town's lands.'

A recent discovery of a letter in the Kennedy family archives reveals that the local land owning gentry of Ayrshire played golf at least on a fortnightly basis in 1751. Like other loose golfing fraternities of the time, this apparently regular meeting would have long fallen by the wayside. With no records surviving, we can have no knowledge of how long play continued, but it is safe to assume that some of the golfing diehards of Girvan would have persisted into the nineteenth century.

Tom would find that, as with the local people of St Andrews, New Year's Day was the main day of the year for competition play amongst the artisan classes, but on many a good day in the winter there would be a game to be seen out on the links. Unlike St Andrews, however, there was no set course at Prestwick. A party of players would simply cut a number of holes and play without formality over any part of the links land.

The gentlemen players were determined that all of this should change, and Tom was charged with the laying out of a course, while they would form a Prestwick Golf Club along the lines of the established clubs in the east. It was not just the gentlemen players of Ayrshire, however, who wanted to see Prestwick links formed for regular play. There were also the ordinary local men from Prestwick and Ayr who were quick to support the laying out of a proper golf course on the links.

It is not surprising that Prestwick, only a short train journey from Glasgow, should become a centre for what Colville calls 'the "Tory Lairds", retired "nabobs" and planters, successful lawyers – and a very few "Moderate" clericals', people, in fact, not dissimilar from those that Tom had served in St Andrews and who were also to be found on the links of Aberdeen, Montrose, Musselburgh and North Berwick.

Contemporary writers or friends did not record Tom's first impressions of Prestwick and its links. It must have been a sobering experience for him to find himself alone on the Prestwick links land after the bustle of activity on the Links at St Andrews. He would surely have reflected on his friends and the farewell dinner that they had given him in the Cross Keys Hotel in St Andrews before he left. He must have also thought of the great matches that he had enjoyed with the gentlemen of The Royal and Ancient, for they had been many and rewarding that summer. The Earl and Countess of Eglinton had been at the dinner and would doubtless have been introduced to Tom and wished him well in his efforts on the links at Prestwick. The Earl, as Allan Robertson would have said, was, 'less of a player than a tryer', but nevertheless he was a great patron of the game, enjoying his golf at North Berwick as well as at St Andrews.

On 2 July 1851 the Prestwick Golf club was founded, and Tom was officially the Club's servant and greenkeeper. Everything had been organised in advance by the indefatigable Fairlie and his cohorts. The links had been leased from the Town Council as well as from the twelve Freemen with rights to the land. Special arrangements for play were made for the local artisan players, who were also permitted to use the facilities of Tom's workshop as a repository for their clubs. The two distinct groups of players, the gentlemen and artisans, were however, never likely to remain in mutual accord. The traditions of St Andrews, where the gentlemen and the townspeople's interests ran in parallel, were alien to the west. Deference and self-interest were soon in conflict and it must have been a trying time for Tom when altercations between the two groups occurred.

Tom was instrumental in starting a separate club for the tradesmen and artisans of the district, less than six months after his arrival in Prestwick. Prestwick Mechanics Golf Club was formed in November 1851 with twenty-eight founding members, somewhat fewer than its senior, the Prestwick Golf Club, and about half the number of the Mechanics Club in St Andrews. From the outset, however, it was a vigorous and enthusiastic institution.

A solution was soon found to the latent friction between the two clubs when Mr Hutchison, the grocer next door to Tom, provided a room at the back of his shop for the members of the Mechanics Club to store their golfing gear. Their social facilities were also improved when they were allowed to put up a shed on the links to dispense refreshments between rounds. Within two years, the Mechanics was a well-established club with a membership from beyond Ayr and its environs as far afield as Glasgow. Some of them, like the Doleman brothers whose origins were in Musselburgh, were outstanding players with a 'bob or two' to back themselves.

Reading the Founding Member's list of the Prestwick Golf Club, how-ever, is like reading a selection from the lists of The Royal and Ancient, the Burgess Club, the Honourable Company of Edinburgh Golfers and that of North Berwick put together. These men were interrelated through marriage and common interests. Some were brother officers in the British Army and in particular from the regiments serving in India. They were landowners, men of property and wealth, with sporting interests that ex-tended beyond golf and they were spread like couch grass across the links lands of Scotland.

The golfing fraternity of gentlemen players in the west of Scotland was not large but it was dedicated and at its core was a devotee with vigour and drive who had a clear vision for Prestwick. This man was Lieutenant Colonel James Ogilvy Fairlie of Coodham by Prestwick, Tom's benefactor and foursomes partner on the Links of St Andrews.

Fairlie was born in Calcutta in 1809, the son of William Fairlie, a merchant and banker of Calcutta and London, and his wife Agnes, the daughter of Mungo Mire of Bruntwood. William Fairlie died before he had the chance to develop his new estate of Cowdam, about three miles inland from Prestwick. His wife did develop the estate in 1831 and upon it she spent £20,000 building a mansion house which she called Williamsfield in memory of her late husband. The original name stuck in the local con-sciousness, however, and it was not long before the family estate reverted to it, spelled in Scots phonetic vernacular, Coodham. The widowed Agnes Fairlie settled there with her daughter and two sons, John and James.

John Fairlie and his younger brother James became regular army offic-ers. James served in India with Major Playfair with whom he formed a close friendship that brought him to St Andrews in 1840 and his introduction to golf. He had already acquired a sporting reputation as a steeplechaser riding to hounds in Leicestershire, as well as with the Duke of Beaufort and the Earl of Eglinton. He was also an outstanding billiards player and a successful curler. He kept racehorses at Coodham and amongst many local and North of England successes, took second place in the St Leger at Doncaster. Shooting and fishing were his principal distractions until he fell upon the golf at which he quickly excelled.

In Howie Smith's *The Golfer's Yearbook for 1866*, the Earl of Dalhousie acclaimed James Ogilvy Fairlie as the 'Champion Amateur of Scotland', for he was in one season the holder of the medals of The Royal and Ancient, North Berwick and Prestwick, the 'Grand Slam' of the time.

James Ogilvy Fairlie's athletic talents appear to have been bound-less. When his close friend and sporting associate, the Earl of Eglinton, attempted to resurrect medieval jousting by staging a Grand Tournament at Eglinton Castle in 1839, Fairlie was first in the lists. He commissioned a set of armour to be made and had a lance fashioned to suit. Kerr, in his book on Kilwinning, relates how Fairlie went through the field, finally ending up against Sir Francis Hopkins in the final joust. In weather conditions that would have kept even the most foolhardy golfer indoors, the two splashed their steeds through heavy mud at one another in three passes. Although Fairlie broke his lance at the second pass, Hopkins was unseated and Fairlie declared the winner.

Two of the fair maids at this incredible event were the sisters Anne-Eliza and Jane, the daughters of the MacLeod of MacLeod. In 1840, Fairlie married Anne-Eliza while Campbell of Saddel, whose residence was the Priory, St Andrews, married Jane.

At Coodham, Anne-Eliza produced two sons before her untimely death in 1844. In 1845 Fairlie married again, this time to Elizabeth Constantina, the only daughter of William Houison Craufurd of Craufurdland and Borehead. Elizabeth bore Fairlie a further four sons, one of whom was the distinguished architect, Reginald Fairlie.

All of the Fairlie boys were taught to play golf on the links of Prestwick and in the parks of Coodham by Tom Morris. All of them distinguished themselves at the game. The eldest, named after his father, was Chamberlain to His Holiness Pope Leo XII and became Captain of Prestwick as well as The Royal and Ancient in St Andrews.

Clearly James Ogilvy Fairlie was an able and energetic all-round sportsman but he was also a tireless organiser and innovator. In Tom Morris he had the perfect servant and supporter, playing partner and friend.

That Tom and Fairlie had a close friendship, as well as a master and servant relationship, is revealed through Tom's own expressions about Fairlie, as well as the Fairlie sons' closeness to Tom long after their father's death in 1870. Shortly after his father died, James, the eldest son, sold the Coodham estate to Sir William Houldsworth, an industrialist and enthusiastic golfer, before purchasing Myres Castle near Auchtermuchty in Fife, some eighteen miles from St Andrews.

Tom Morris and James Ogilvy Fairlie would trigger the events that were to change the face of golf and set the game off on a course that would spread it throughout the world and make it the richest and most widely played of all games.

9 A New Beginning as an Era Ends

With Nancy and young Tommy installed in their new house, Tom's next task would be to take stock of the links and the position in which he found himself. In the 1850s the links of Prestwick would have appeared to stretch forever. The three miles of the bay-shore south to Ayr and the same distance north to Troon were a sea of whins and sand dunes on a scale that dwarfed St Andrews' Links peninsula. Tom must have looked at it and despaired. In St Andrews there was hardly a minute in the day when you would fail to see somebody about on the Links and many of them at their golf. In Prestwick there would be very few people to be seen and barely a soul playing the game.

Tom himself said some fourteen years later that when he first came to the village he was 'dull enough, for there was very little play', and he thought he had made a mistake in accepting his position at Prestwick. But if Tom was downhearted, he certainly did not show it, and the enthusiasm he had for the game quickly infected his new friends. As he himself said: 'But by and by one after another of my neighbours was tempted to try his hand. Gentlemen came out from Ayr and they, with the visitors at Eglinton Castle and Coodham, gave the game a good start and kept me pretty busy.'

Making clubs and balls, as well as teaching and encouraging all who came to 'try their hand' at the golf, would have kept him busy enough, but he was also building a golf course. There were whins to be cleared and grass to be scythed to make greens on the soft, springy turf. The links lands of the west coast are different in character from those of the east. Prestwick links are geologically older than those of St Andrews, with a higher content of organic matter which retains more water and supports a lusher growth of grass. The west coast has a higher average rainfall than the east and is altogether milder, generating a thicker sward with greater texture. Tom would have felt the turf in the places where the rabbits had kept the grasses grazed tight and marvelled at it. Indeed, he must have been inspired by it to produce what he did in the years that followed.

Place and vista are contributing factors in the pleasure of golf. Prestwick's great dunes induce both a sense of wonder and isolation. The vistas of Arran and Lady Isle, the Carrick Hills and the Bay of Ayr present wonderful backdrops to holes that vary as much, if not more, than on any of the other famous links courses.

Tom clearly had an eye not only for the hole that would test the best golfer but also for beauty. His twelve holes were being lauded and applauded back in St Andrews in the columns of the *Fifeshire Journal* as well as the national press, within a year of his arrival in Prestwick.[1] *Golf,* from the Badminton Library series, later described the course:

> For years Prestwick was celebrated as a twelve-hole course. It went dodging in and out among lofty sand hills. The holes were, for the most part, out of sight when one took the iron in hand for the approach; for they lay in deep dells among these sand hills, and you lofted over the intervening mountain of sand, and there was all the fascinating excitement, as you climbed to the top of it of seeing how near to the hole your ball might have happened to roll.

Just how much of a hand Colonel Fairlie had in laying out the course will never be known, for there are no records. It is likely that Tom would discuss and consult with him at length when they played together on their new course. Fairlie, as a soldier and Victorian 'man of parts', would bring considerable expertise to the exercise, and the scale of the work was such, as the records of the Prestwick Club show, that Tom was required to hire additional labour for some of his undertakings. Throughout his entire tenure at Prestwick, the work of improving the course was continuous and progressive. After the layout of the holes was completed and the gorse cleared for play, greens were expanded and improved, bunkers formed and the Pow Burn banked and controlled. The lessons he learned and the experience he gained developing the Prestwick green would stand him in good stead and place him in demand for the laying out of many new golf courses for the rest of his life.

His social experiences were also crucial to the emergence of the game in Prestwick. Although the Prestwick Club eventually came to own its land, the links were there for anyone and everyone who wanted to take up a club and a ball. The breadth of the social spectrum of the early players on Prestwick links was such that Tom might find himself partnering the Earl of Eglinton in foursome play one day and encouraging the local grocer the next.

Competition is the driving force of all games and none more so than in golf. Competitions require planning, organization, knowledge and understanding, as well as application. Tom had the knowledge and understanding in abundance and the men of Prestwick proved eager to apply themselves to the game.

The Earl of Eglinton was the first Captain of the Prestwick Club in 1851 and would become Captain of The Royal and Ancient in 1853. The Earl, with a party of friends, had, prior to Tom's arrival, been accustomed to having a few holes cut on the links while they took a train from Eglinton Castle to Prestwick. The railway had been opened in 1843 and his lordship had the privilege of stopping any train he wanted. Colonel Gillan of Walhouse, Colonel Hamilton of Cairnhill and, of course, Colonel Fairlie of Coodham, were also accustomed to playing at Prestwick. They, together with Mr Cuthbert and Mr Kirkland of Ayr and Dr Pollock of Kingston Parish Church in Glasgow, formed the nucleus of the Prestwick Club.

Mr Hutchison, the grocer and Tom's neighbour, was also a player of long standing. He had played for some time with Dr Pollock and his son who made sojourns, sometimes for days at a time, to golf on the links at Prestwick. It is interesting that Dr Pollock was a minister of the church who had left the Free Presbyterian Church for the Established Church when the movement in the opposite direction was more common. Mr Hutchison had done just that. Together with the Reverend Thomas Burns, the son of Gilbert, the celebrated poet Robert Burns's elder brother, he had left the Established Church to serve for fifty-three years as an elder in the Prestwick Free Church. Needless to say, Mr Hutchison was popularly known as 'the elder', and was a driving force in the Mechanics Club.

Tom would have been glad to see the Prestwick Mechanics Golf Club founded for the local men in November 1851. His income, aside from his regular wage from keeping the links, would depend on it. The locals would play at all times and require a constant supply of gutta balls and clubs. For every golfer, a new club is the panacea for all ills – or if not all, then certainly for the current problem of getting away from the tee or placing the approach shot into the green just right. To an uncertain player, a new putter is often the promise of greater things to come. Tom learned well from Allan Robertson: he would be encouraging and supportive but he would also be quick to make up a club and sell it.

The gentlemen of the senior club would need balls, too, but they were more likely to covet a McEwan or a Philp club. Their play would be irregular, with the calls of the regiment, business or social engagements taking precedence. Their social calendars would contain notice of the season's meetings, but outside of these, play would mostly be intermittent.

It is not surprising, then, that Tom Morris's name should head the list of the members of the Mechanics Club, followed by that of Mr Manson. Manson, a brother-in law of William Hunter of the Red Lion Inn, was a writer's clerk in a law office in Ayr, and just the man for the job of secretary and treasurer. William Hunter himself was the next to be recruited. Every Club needs a watering hole and the Red Lion was virtually adjacent to the links. Then there were William's cousin, Dean of Guild Hunter from Ayr, a local man of affairs, and Robert Howie Smith, the editor of the *Ayr Express,* who would faithfully report on the embryonic club's activities, so keeping it in the public eye. Howie Smith was to produce the first golf annual or yearbook in 1867, entitled *The Golfer's Year Book for 1866.*[2] If Tom could have hand-picked his founder members, he could not have made a better job. It comes as no surprise that the membership doubled within a year and pressure was brought to bear on the members by the senior club to limit their numbers.

The Hunter clan figured prominently in the early years of the Prestwick Mechanics Golf Club. William Hunter of the Red Lion, one of three golfing brothers, together with his wife's cousin, John Gray, and his nephew Charlie Hunter, were leading lights of the young club.[3] Charlie was amongst the first of Tom's converts to golf in Prestwick: he was the ablest and the most devoted to the game and would become Custodian of the Links and professional to Prestwick Golf Club for over fifty years.

The house that Tom and Nancy moved into on the High Street was known as the Golf House and referred to by this name in all official records. It acted as both a meeting place for the members of Prestwick Golf Club as well as a storage place for their clubs. It was the penultimate dwelling in the street before the Wrack Road turned down towards the railway station and onto the links. Families with children surrounded them. The Wisemans, with a grown-up son and three daughters under the age of twelve, occupied the last house, No. 39, in the High Street. On the other side, at No. 41, the Hutchisons had two young daughters, Mary, thirteen and Janis, ten. Next door to the Hutchisons was an old lady, Mary Patrick, a silk stocking weaver, aged seventy-nine, who lived with her granddaughter, Margaret Tennant, a farm servant. Conveniently sited next door to old Mary was the Burgh School. Young Tommy would have had nursemaids enough and not far to go when his time for schooling came.

Across the road at the Red Lion, William and Elizabeth Hunter had a fair brood of children when Tom and Nancy arrived. John was thirteen,

Mary eight, Jane five and James aged two. Robert was born within two months of the Morris's settling in so it is hardly surprising that Nancy Morris and Elizabeth Hunter should become close friends and remain so as their families grew up together. Elizabeth would have a further two sons, William born in 1853 and Andrew born in 1858.

On the twentieth of June 1853, Nancy gave birth to a daughter, Elizabeth. Her christening in Monkton Parish Church was witnessed by William and Elizabeth Hunter and the fact that Tom and Nancy should name their daughter after the latter testifies to the closeness of the friendship that, even after only two years, had been forged between the Morris and Hunter families. It was a friendship that would become closer as the years passed, with the children growing up together, and which would ultimately become sealed through marriage.

Four years elapsed before Nancy gave birth to another son on 8 January 1856. He was named James and his birth was registered the next day. He was registered again on the 10th when he was named James Ogilvy Fairlie Morris, doubtless after Tom had seen Colonel Fairlie and sought permission to name his son after him. Family and friends would, for the rest of his life, refer to James as 'Jof'.

Just a month after the first momentous discovery of oil in Pennsylvania had given the world an important new source of energy, the Morris family was completed with the birth of John on 25 September 1859. It must have been a day of gladness and sadness, for it was clear from the day of his birth that he had a hip deformity. John would never be able to walk.

John's condition would have been a terrible blow to Tom and Nancy. Only a week earlier, Tom had returned from St Andrews where he had attended the funeral of his old friend, mentor and playing partner, Allan Robertson. Allan had died as a result of jaundice that had debilitated him for many months. Tom had been with him in the spring when he was still fit to play but already afflicted with the sickness, although Allan had played so well with Mr Bethune of Blebo in September of the previous year that the seventy-nine strokes he recorded was considered to be the best round ever played on the St Andrews Links. They had met again in the summer when Tom found Allan all but confined to his bed. Allan's death would nevertheless have come as a shock when it was announced in the *Herald* and the *Scotsman* on 2 September 1859. The *Scotsman* carried an article on Allan's death which read:

Death of Allan Robertson the Golfer – Yesterday afternoon, Allan Robertson the celebrated golfer, expired at his residence in St Andrews. For five or six months Allan had suffered from a severe attack of jaundice, and under that disease it was obvious for some time that he was sinking. His performances as a golfer were, it is admitted, without parallel; and being a man of the most amiable and obliging disposition, he was highly esteemed by every frequenter of the Links. Allan was, we believe, 45 years of age and only this year played his best round with Mr Bethune of Blebo.

Allan's funeral was held on Monday 5 September and, as the *Fifeshire Journal* reported, 'was attended by more than 400 mourners, among them Noblemen and Gentlemen from all parts of the Country.'

The esteem in which Allan was held is best summarised in a remark from Robert Clark who wrote: 'after laying poor Allan in his grave, we walked down the Scores to the Club, with a late dear friend, Mr Sutherland, who suddenly broke from his reverie by exclaiming: "they may toll the bells and shut up their shops in St Andrews for their greatest is gone".'

For Tom, an era ended with the passing of Allan Robertson. Whether or not Tom recognised Allan's supremacy as a golfer, the rest of the golfing world had done so with little reservation. And if Tom did not feel that he was the natural successor to Allan's mantle, most of the golfing world did. Those who had their reservations were concerned with the much-discussed great Musselburgh pretender, the renowned Willie Park.

10 The 'Honest Toun' Park

Willie Park burst onto the golfing scene in October 1854 and for the next 30 years was Tom's greatest rival. He was from Musselburgh, locally known as the 'Honest Toun', that had spawned some great golfers and had long been an irritant to St Andrews' claim of golfing supremacy. Willie was undoubtedly the greatest of all the Musselburgh players, stamping his authority on the game by winning the first Open Championship in 1860. However, it was his audacious challenges for very high stakes that captured the public's imagination and brought thousands to the links to witness his confrontations with Tom Morris.

Born in 1833, he came from a background very different from that of Tom. He and his brothers, Archie and David, were born in the nearby village of Wallyford, while Mungo and Jack, the younger of the five Park boys, were born in the town of Musselburgh. Their father, James, was described as 'a sturdy Scottish ploughman', and was said by his grandson to have belonged to a breed of 'professionals' who played challenge matches for large stakes and to have been inspired by them.

The Park family moved into a cottage on the side of the highway that skirted Musselburgh links in the area called Linksfield. The Park boys simply had to cross the road to be on the links where they started to carry clubs at an early age for the gentlemen golfers who came down from Edinburgh. Willie and his brothers' start in golf would be much the same as Tom's, playing whenever they could with whatever clubs and balls that became available to them.

There were great Musselburgh players for the Parks to emulate. Tom Alexander was still about and making feathery balls when Willie was yet a boy. The Dunn twins were in their prime, although Willie Dunn's departure for Blackheath, London in 1851, followed by his brother Jamie two or three years later, would certainly have taken the competitive edge away from Musselburgh.[1] Willie Park was the doyen of the links, even as a teenager, and soon overcame Bob Cosgrove, Willie Dow and 'Grundy Geordie', the other leading Musselburgh men of the day.

While there is no record of Willie Park being apprenticed as a ball- or club-maker in Musselburgh or elsewhere, he does appear to have made both clubs and gutta balls in North Berwick and Musselburgh. He described himself as a 'Golf Ball Maker' in the challenges he issued in the newspapers from 1854, although he was listed in the Edinburgh trades' directories in the 1870s as a club and ball maker, as well as a professional golfer.[2] His second son, Willie Jnr, who joined his father around 1885, was an astute businessman as well as a great player and expanded the business to international status by 1890.

As a young man Willie Park's income was mainly derived from playing and, apart from what he made caddying or partnering gentlemen players, he was dependent upon the money matches that he could arrange. Needless to say, he quickly ran out of takers on Musselburgh links and very soon had to start looking beyond his home course for lucrative matches.

Tom Morris would most likely have come across the sixteen-year-old Park in Musselburgh during the course of the great foursomes match of 1849 when he and Allan took on the Dunn brothers. If he did not, he would certainly have heard about him soon after. The stories of Park playing for money, the odds he gave, as well as some of the wagers he made, were common fare in the golfing 'howfs' of the day. Tom or Allan being matched against him on the links would be a recurring topic of the sporting gentry in Edinburgh and Glasgow, as well as in the Big Room of The Royal and Ancient and in officers' messes throughout the country.

Two events probably conspired to fire Willie Park's ambitions and entice him into the golfing firmament. The first of these was the announcement made in the *Ayr Advertiser* in early October 1853 that Tom Morris and Willie Dunn would attend the Autumn Meeting in St Andrews '. . . next week, and will there play any two in the world a match of two rounds.' The second was the reproduction of this challenge in the *Fifeshire Journal* by Henry Farnie, the recently appointed editor. Farnie was a knowledgeable golf enthusiast and the first journalist to report professional matches in the same way that prize-fights were recorded, blow by blow. Farnie's reports were soon given copy space in the national press and he was not averse to stating the purses on offer or the bets made.

It is simply not known if Willie Park was among the 'crack' Musselburgh players referred to by Farnie as appearing in St Andrews for The Royal and Ancient Autumn Meeting in 1853. If he was not there he would have learned of the betting and the excitement that surrounded the match that saw Tom Morris and Willie Dunn pitted against Allan Robertson and Sir Robert Hay. Tom and Willie did not, at first, play well and were down in the match after the first round when the betting was heavily against them. In the afternoon, they combined better, made up the four-hole deficit and went on to win comfortably. Much money changed hands that day and there was speculation about how much of it had found its way into Tom and Willie's pockets. It was not surprising that when Willie Park appeared on the scene at St Andrews, he had his backers ready and waiting.

On his first visit to the Autumn Meeting of The Royal and Ancient in October 1854, Willie, with his backers, threw down the challenge to Allan and Tom.[3] They received no response and it was left to George Morris, Tom's elder brother, doubtless encouraged by the local wags in the newly re-named St Andrews Golf Club, to take up the gauntlet. George was thrashed, and the Rev. John Kerr reported that, after Willie had won the first eight holes of the second round, he pleaded, 'For the love o' Gode gi'e me a hauf', and Allan remarked that 'He frichtens us a' wi' his lang driving'.

Tom, doubtless under pressure from the local sporting gentry, agreed to a two-round match at £50 a side the day after his brother's resounding defeat at Park's hands. If Tom thought that he could wrest back the honour of St Andrews and that of his family, it was a vain hope. There was much excitement in St Andrews over the outcome of this match. Tom was a favourite son who had gone away to Prestwick to better himself and here he was, having to uphold the honour of his 'Auld Grey Toun'. The first round was halved, but Willie Park won the second by five holes with four to play and consequently the match. There was much money lost that day in St Andrews, and Tom was consigned to the category of 'outsider', and referred to as 'Prestwick Tom'.

For Willie Park this was the match that really ignited his career. He had beaten Tom Morris, the only one of the big three players of the day who had dared to accept his challenge, and he had done it at St Andrews. Even the parochial *Fifeshire Journal*, not known for its unbiased reporting, conceded that, 'Possessing all the requisites of a good golfer – neat style, a long driver, cool as a cucumber whether playing a losing or a winning game, and equally handy with all the tools used in golf – he fully justified the confidence reposed in him by his backers.'

Tom suffered this, his first defeat at Willie Park's hands, on 19 October 1854 but had the satisfaction of taking the honours the following morning in a one-round match for an undisclosed sum. Willie pleaded for a second round but Tom was forced to decline because of commitments to other matches with J.O. Fairlie in the afternoon.

With still no response to his challenge from Allan Robertson, and no doubt buoyed up by his resounding victory over Tom, the 21-year-old Park resorted to extravagance, offering to play against the better ball of Allan and Tom.

This was an audacious and impudent challenge that he must have known would not be accepted. It was no doubt intended to embarrass Allan into playing him head-to-head. Allan resolutely refused to play the brash young pretender from Musselburgh and never did give Willie Park the satisfaction of matching him, and with good reason, for he would have nothing to gain and everything to lose. Allan was already universally accepted as the *de facto* champion, a position he took care to preserve. A win over Park would not alter his status but a loss would shatter the aura of invincibility that he had enjoyed in the golfing world for two decades.

In the week that followed, Tom took on Willie at North Berwick where he was again beaten, and at Musselburgh where he had a narrow victory over Park on his home green. The *Fifeshire Journal* reported that there was no money involved in the North Berwick encounter and no sum was mentioned for the match at Musselburgh. Tom and Willie appear to have played purely for the fun of it, which makes what followed all the more surprising.

Although no contemporary account exists, the golfing world must have been astonished when, on Saturday 4 November 1854, the following notice appeared in the *Edinburgh News*:

GOLFING.

A GREAT MATCH at GOLF was Played at ST ANDREWS LINKS on the 19th of October by THOMAS MORRIS, servant of the Prestwick Golf Club (late of St Andrews), and WILLIAM PARK, Golf Ball Maker, Musselburgh. This was played at St Andrews, North Berwick, and Musselburgh – Three Rounds on each Green – WILLIAM PARK beating MORRIS Nine Holes at the conclusion of the game.

WILLIAM PARK Challenges Allan Robertson of St Andrews, or William Dunn, servant of the Blackheath Golf Club, London, or Thomas Morris, for Fifty Pounds, on the same Greens as formerly. Money Ready.

WILLIAM PARK, Golf Ball Maker, Millhill, Musselburgh.

There was no response to this from St Andrews, Blackheath or Prestwick. Tom and Willie met again in foursomes partnering gentlemen players and, on at least one occasion, in a head-to-head at Musselburgh which Tom won. Almost immediately after this, Willie raised the profile of his challenge, as well as the stakes.

On 11 October 1855, in the week before the Autumn Meeting at St Andrews, *Bell's Life* carried an advertisement, placed by Willie, offering to play anyone in a match over St Andrews, Musselburgh and North Berwick for £100 or £200 a side. This must reflect not only a considerable self-confidence, but also that money staked on match play was one of Willie's main sources of income – and that he had backers ready and willing to put up the cash.

Willie may not have received any formal response from either Tom or Allan, but he certainly whetted the appetite of the gambling men. The gathering for the Autumn Meeting in October 1855 was clearly in high expectation. The report in the *Scotsman* on 27 October that year begins,

> On Thursday, a match was played which created very great excitement amongst the golfers. The players consisted of the champion golfers of the day – viz, Allan Robertson of St Andrews (the king) and Tom Morris of Prestwick, against Dunnie of Blackheath and Park of Musselburgh. It is very difficult to state the total amount of bets made upon this round by numerous parties; but we believe we shall be rather under than above the mark when we say that from £300 to £400 depend on the issue. After a well contested match, the players came in with Allan and Tom having two holes and two strokes ahead of their opponents.

The *Scotsman* piece concluded with the news that the best was yet to come. Intimation was made that, at long last, 'Tom Morris has signified to Park his willingness to accept of the challenge for £100 . . . advertised by him some time ago to the "wide, wide" world.'

Tom's formal response to Willie's challenge came in *Bell's Life* on 25 October 1855.

It was not until 29 April 1856 that they met in this formally arranged contest, and the *Fifeshire Journal* reported on it from the outset, bringing the game of golf to the attention of the general public in places where it was almost unknown. It was a carefully arranged match played over the links at Musselburgh, North Berwick, Prestwick and St Andrews. The stake was £100 on the match, calculated by cumulative holes up over the 144 holes of golf. At each venue 36 holes were to be played, finishing at St Andrews on 10 May. We know, through the indiscretion of the editor of the *Fifeshire*

Journal, that the Earl of Wemyss was Tom's backer. It was an indiscretion that the editor would not repeat, for the Earl would not have taken kindly to the details of his betting at golf becoming public knowledge.

From the toss of a coin, Park won the right to choose the starting venue.

Betting was reported as '6 to 4 on Park and business brisk'. Play began at Musselburgh on Tuesday 29 April where Willie won by 8 holes. He added a further 5 holes to his lead at Prestwick on the Friday and Tom could only reduce his deficit by 2 holes after winning at North Berwick the following Tuesday. There must have been something of an anti-climax about the final leg at St Andrews on Saturday 10 May, although a huge crowd turned up to be addressed by Sir Hugh Playfair about the conduct expected, with Allan Robertson leading the marshalling. Tom played well, but although he reduced the 11 hole deficit by 5, Willie took the money with a 6 holes win.

Willie Park won this, their first formally arranged encounter, to the general amazement of the press in Glasgow and Ayr. In the *Fifeshire Journal* it was reported that the Earl of Wemyss, who was in London at the time, had instructed Tom to issue an immediate challenge for another match. This duly took place, starting at St Andrews on 26 October 1856 after the Autumn Meeting, and while the newspaper did not report on the progress of this match after it moved on to Prestwick with Tom trailing by 5 holes, the *Scotsman* did, and we learn that Willie Park again won the £100 stake. Willie Dunn had also risen to Park's challenge over the same four greens. Park was 12 holes up on Dunn at the conclusion of their match at St Andrews on Saturday 23 October and, after he trounced Tom by 5 holes three days later, the *Fifeshire Journal* appeared resigned to Willie's invincibility.

After the Grand National Tournament at St Andrews in 1858 something of a novelty match occurred that gained a great deal of attention. The brothers Tom and George Morris played and beat Willie and Mungo Park. Clearly buoyed by his victory with his brother, Tom and his backers immediately challenged Willie to a match for a £200 stake. This was an eagerly anticipated duel, and the excitement grew when it was announced that the challenge had been accepted and that the match would take place 'as soon as preliminaries are arranged'. Apprehension however ensued when the following reports appeared in the newspapers:

Grand Golf Match – William Park v. Tom Morris
– £100 A-Side.

We are enabled to state that a match at golf has now been arranged between the above named professionals, for £100 a-side, the best of 144 holes over the links, at St Andrews, Musselburgh, North

Berwick, and Prestwick, 36 holes to be played on each green. The stakes fall to be lodged with Stuart Grace, Esq., honorary secretary, Royal and Ancient Golf Club, on or before the 30th September. Morris's money is already posted. Park's is yet forthcoming. If it is not lodged tonight, however, the match is off.

Finally, there was widespread disappointment when it was announced:

PARK AGAINST MORRIS – MATCH OFF. – This match at golf which created no little stir amongst the gentlemen assembled at the meeting last week, is now declared off. Park's money, was, as intimated in our impression of last week, due on Thursday last. Not forthcoming then, he craved and obtained an extension of his time to Monday last, when again he craved a further delay to Tuesday night, which was granted – but when Tuesday came, no deposit of his portion of the stakes appeared. So no alternative was left but to declare the game off from that cause. We should like to hear an explanation of Park's conduct.

So the great challenger was humiliated and the betting gentlemen of the links were on this occasion denied their sport. It is not difficult to understand why Willie's backers were not forthcoming with the stake, for Tom's form had been good in matches after the meetings at North Berwick, Prestwick and St Andrews. The Musselburgh brigade may have been justifiably optimistic with their money in the past, but they were shrewd enough to know that the situation had changed and Park was not likely to beat Tom on his current form.

In the 25 years that followed, Tom and Willie would be responsible for more than a 'fair bit' of money changing hands at Musselburgh, St Andrews, Prestwick and North Berwick. The gambling men's demand for their matches never abated, and few golf reports were concluded without the rumour of some ongoing arrangements of an encounter between Morris and Park.

Arrangements were ultimately successful for another great four-greens match after the Autumn Meeting at St Andrews in 1862. Announced as 'The Great Golf Match' in the *Scotsman* between 'Tom Morris of Prestwick (a St Andrews bred player), and William Park of Musselburgh (bred on his own links), for the sum of £100 and the championship'.

The big event began in the third week of November at Musselburgh and was concluded on 2 December at St Andrews. Tom was the victor on all four greens. On Willie's home links at Musselburgh, Tom enjoyed a 2-hole win. On his own links at Prestwick he won by 5 holes, taking a 7 hole lead to North Berwick where he increased the margin by a further 4 holes. His 11-hole lead certainly reduced the betting temperature at St Andrews but it did little to dampen the public's enthusiasm for the match. The 2nd of December was a 'cloudy raw day, but not unfavourable for the game – an immense assemblage turned out to witness the two rounds.' Although the outcome of the 'big match' was all but determined, there was big betting on the outcome of the two rounds at St Andrews. If Willie's backers were hopeful of recouping some of their losses of the previous two weeks it was a hope misplaced, for Tom was 4 holes ahead after 9 holes and 15 holes up overall in the match. Tom won a further two holes before Willie withdrew on the 13th green. The *Fifeshire Journal* was euphoric, while the *Scotsman*, with restraint, wrote, 'Tom Morris' triumph has been somewhat unparalleled in the annals of golfing, he having won on all the four links, and by a heavier majority than almost ever fell to the lot of a golfer in such a match'.

These four green matches were extensively reported in the press and keenly followed by the nobility, gentry and ordinary citizens. There can be little doubt that these matches raised the profile of golf and, increasingly, thousands flocked to the links to be part of the excitement.

The tussles between Tom and Willie did, however, continue over the years and there is no doubt that they had great respect for each other as players. Some of their encounters were recorded in detail while others passed with a mere mention in the sporting press of the day. Tom and Andrew Strath took on and beat the Park brothers after the Autumn Meeting in 1863 and, one week later, Tom beat Willie for an 'undisclosed sum' at Dunbar. The events were, nevertheless, feasts to the golfing aficionados and eagerly anticipated by the caddies and local worthies as well as the sporting gentry. The matches were summed up by the late nineteenth-century golfing scribes as 'honours even'; this is a fair assessment, for Willie appears to have had the edge through much of the fifth decade while Tom enjoyed the honours through much of the sixth, although it is a summary that Willie would have disputed. After a report in the *Scotsman* of the events on the Links at St Andrews in May 1864, when Willie left the Town before a match was scheduled to take place between the Park brothers and Tom and Andrew Strath, Willie Dow took his place to partner David Park. The Musselburgh men were heavily defeated and, in the ensuing piece in the paper, Tom was referred to as 'the champion'. It was an error that Willie Park was not prepared to let pass and he duly wrote a letter to the editor, not only pointing this out, but also noting that he and David had earlier bettered the Morris and Strath score.

Willie Park clearly had a high sense of his own worth and, perhaps understandably, smarted at the ready and universal reference to Tom Morris as 'Tom' and 'the Champion Golfer', while he was constantly referred to as 'Park', and frequently as the Musselburgh contender, even when he was the holder of the Open Championship Belt.

Comparing their playing abilities, Willie was described as a long and accurate driver and a deadly putter – his 'grand lay-deads' being legendary. Overall, from contemporary reports, Willie was probably the more brilliant player while Tom was steadier.[4] With regard to their personal relationship there is evidence that the two had a great deal of mutual respect which extended to 'the warm and kindly terms in which they spoke of one another'. W. Dalrymple wrote, 'Auld Willie once said to me, with a half smile, half combative cock of his head: "I aye likit best to play against Old Tom", and that Tom had said in a speech at a celebratory dinner, "there was no disguising the fact that William Park was as good a golfer as ever lifted a club".' Although there was some animosity between the golfing townships of Musselburgh and St Andrews, this clearly did not extend to Tom and Willie themselves. In strokeplay competitions, they were more often than not paired together, but the organisers surely did this in response to the betting brigade. In head-to-head matches they famously played for large stakes put up by backers, but, on many occasions, did so for nominal amounts in clearly hastily arranged games, frequently with amateur playing-partners in foursomes.

Given the popularity of their contests and the attractive financial outcomes for themselves, they must have considered that they were in some kind of partnership, notwithstanding the fierce competitive spirit between the two of them.

As their matches progressed through Musselburgh, Prestwick and North Berwick to St Andrews, their following grew and the press reports gained the same prominence as was given to race meetings and prize-fights. The matches between Tom and Willie Park, throughout 1856 in particular, may have provided the appetite and stimulus to mounting some sort of national competition, for the interest in and reporting of their play was widespread. So much so that a movement led by Colonel Fairlie started to gather support which came to fruition with a Grand National Golf Tournament held at St Andrews in 1857.

11 Genesis of Tournament Golf

In 1856, Fairlie began his project for a National Tournament. Until then, organised amateur golf competitions were club events restricted to members. Of course there were matches between friends from different clubs and even challenge matches between clubs, but the proposal for a national tournament was altogether new and on a different scale.

A meeting of the Prestwick Committee in October of that year resolved to consult with other leading clubs on the possibility of a national inter-club event for gentlemen players. It was proposed that this should be a foursomes knockout competition, two players from each club, to take place either at St Andrews or Prestwick, and the winning club 'shall be considered the champion club till the next tournament, and be entitled to the prize'.

Some eight months after Prestwick had first proposed a National Tournament, their minutes record that the suggestion 'has been very well received by most of the Scotch Clubs and also that of Blackheath'. More consultations took place and a majority chose St Andrews as the venue. Thirteen Clubs responded positively and entered a foursomes pair.[1]

Named by the organising Committee the 'Grand National Golf Club Tournament', the very first of its kind, it was held on the last three days of July 1857. It was essentially an inter-club knock-out competition and, as can be expected of such a pioneering venture, it did not run entirely smoothly. Not only did the Honourable Company's team fail to turn up, only one member of the Panmure team appeared, and one member of the North Berwick team arrived too late on the opening day. North Berwick was granted a bye into the second round, but then both members of their team were also members of the organising committee!

The tournament in its foursomes matchplay format was won by George Glennie and Captain John Stewart of Fasnacloich, both renowned on the Scottish links and both full-blooded Scotsmen, but on this occasion representing Blackheath in London.[2]

The *Fifeshire Journal* reported:

> The interest manifested in the golf tournament continued unabated until the closing day. During the remaining days of the meeting the excitement at the Links was greater than even on an October or May gathering of members of the Royal and Ancient. The parties all along appeared to pay marked attention – crowding round the home hole on the return of the combatants.

The paper also effused:

> Over thirty-five ladies of the leading families of the county and beyond, led by Lady Catherine Whyte-Melville, Lady Charles Kerr and Lady Playfair, graced the occasion, as did most of the nobility and gentry of the district.

Clearly the event was a social success.

This tournament was of the utmost importance to the development and future of the game. It was the first attempt at running a national competition, open to all clubs, and it can therefore with justification be described as the forerunner of every tournament and championship played since. It was a defining moment in the game and set golf off on a different and more organized route which would lead directly to the Open Championship and all subsequent tournaments.

The part played by Tom Morris and Allan Robertson in the running of this event is acknowledged by their inclusion in what is a historically very significant photograph. It depicts the competitors, together with the Convener of the Committee, John Whyte-Melville and the umpire, Sir Hugh Lyon Playfair, formally assembled outside the newly erected clubhouse.[3] That Tom and Allan were included at all, and that they were placed in such a prominent position in the photograph, speaks volumes. Not only does it reflect their importance to the proceedings, but it also shows the status they enjoyed on the Links with the gentlemen of The Royal and Ancient Golf Club. Such recognition, in a formal setting, of two artisans, is probably unprecedented and without parallel in any comparable situation in the class-obsessed society of Victorian Britain. If evidence is required of the importance of Allan Robertson and Tom Morris in golf at all levels in the mid-nineteenth century, this photograph provides it.

Although there were clearly hiccups, this first tournament was judged a great success, attracting extensive press reporting with very favourable commentary. Certainly the organisers and participants seemed satisfied, for at its conclusion, a new committee was formed to draw up the conditions for the next year's event.

For 1858, the format of the Grand National Tournament was changed to singles matchplay. The entry was still restricted to 'gentlemen players' who were members of recognized clubs, playing 'even-handed', in other words without handicap allowance. It was reported that the play of the eventual winner, Robert Chambers Jnr, was so poor immediately before the Tournament that he had to be persuaded by Tom Morris to enter. The organizing committee, somewhat strangely, decided that both contestants of halved matches would go through into the next round. This ruling produced the bizarre situation whereby the winner of the tournament won only two of his seven matches, the first and then the final against David Wallace of Balgrummo. The *Fife Herald* must have echoed the sentiments of everyone when it observed, 'some improvement could yet be made on the system of play'.

Another tournament was held in 1859, this time divided into 'scratch' players and lesser golfers playing under handicap. The event was described as 'wanting a deal of the excitement observable last year on the same occasion', and this would appear to have been a view generally held. The Royal and Ancient also blamed the event for the poor attendance at the Club's Autumn Meeting held shortly after in September, and decided not to hold the Tournament again.

While these were the first attempts at organising national tournaments, they were perhaps pursued with less vigour and enthusiasm than Colonel Fairlie and his friends in the Prestwick Club would have wished. Furthermore, these tournaments were exclusive and held in order to determine only the best amateur gentleman player. The impetus for what followed with regard to tournament play came from Prestwick, with St Andrews no doubt being kept informed of planning and progress. Fairlie and the members at Prestwick were off on an altogether different tack. What they envisaged was a strokeplay national tournament for professional players only, with none of the byes and halved match problems of matchplay.

In May 1860, doubtless after consulting Tom and much discussion with the members at Prestwick, Fairlie and the Club committee set about structuring and organising what would effectively become the first Open Championship. The Club presented a handsome belt of red morocco leather decorated with silver embossed golfing scenes as the trophy. This belt, 'The Challenge Belt', was the same in every respect as prize-fighting belts of the time. The Belt cost £25, which was raised by subscription from the Prestwick members, a stipulation being, again consistent with belts awarded for prize-fighting championships, that if any competitor won the Belt for three successive years, it would become his.

The Challenge Belt was to be competed for eleven times between 1860 and 1870, when Tommy Morris took possession of it after his three consecutive victories. These contests are universally recognised and referred to today as the first Open Golf Championships.

From the outset, the competition for the Challenge Belt was designated as stroke play over three rounds of the twelve-hole Prestwick green. The winner could, on depositing with the Club a £25 bond, take the Belt away, returning it the following year, or it could be left in Prestwick. Each pair of competitors would be accompanied by a marker and a committee of four was formed to enforce the Rules of Golf of the Prestwick Club and the competition and to make any decisions not covered by them 'in the spirit of the game'.

Notice of the event appeared in the national press and letters sent to clubs made it absolutely clear that only professional players could compete. Fairlie was not at home at Coodham at the time and he asked Mr Campbell, the then Treasurer at Prestwick, to contact the principal clubs to inform them of the date, format and eligibility for the event, suggesting that he consult with Tom Morris regarding this. Only eleven clubs were written to directly, requesting them 'to name and send the best players on your Links, not exceeding three in number'.[4] In addition, the letter also stated, 'It is understood that they must be known and respectable Cadies'. A notice appeared in the newspapers on 2 October 1860 repeating these conditions and adding, 'Professional Players not being Keepers of Links are to produce a certificate of respectability from the Treasurer of the Golf Club to which they are attached.' The field was therefore somewhat restricted, even for the 'Professionals', as the Prestwick Club was apparently determined to exclude undesirables from their competition. Clearly the respectability of the Champion Golfer was as important as his talent.

This Challenge Belt competition would also appear to have been conceived as an extension of the local sporting entertainments. It was set to take place during the Autumn Meeting of the Prestwick Golf Club, which in turn, was timed to coincide with the Ayr horse race meeting, when the majority of the gentry would be in the vicinity.

Some three weeks before Abraham Lincoln became President of the United States of America, the first contest for the Challenge Belt took place on 17 October 1860 in Prestwick. The field was small, but this was not surprising when one considers that while the winner would be accredited

Champion Golfer and awarded the Challenge Belt for the ensuing year, there was no prize money. The competitors would doubtless be able to earn money from additional challenge matches amongst their ranks, set up by the Club members, as well as partnering the gentlemen golfers in private contests during the week. There would surely be something for everyone. Tom Morris and Willie Park, however, were recognised to be in a class of their own, possibly further deterring those who might otherwise have been prepared to travel to Prestwick. Only six competitors made the journey, thus, together with the locals Tom Morris and Charlie Hunter, the field was brought to eight.

Willie Park had played at Prestwick in 1856, 1857 and again in 1858, but it is doubtful if Bob Andrew, known as 'The Rook', from Perth, or Andrew Strath and George Daniel Brown had played on Tom's links. Brown entered from Blackheath in London and Alexander Smith and William Steel came across from Edinburgh with Willie Park. Neither Smith nor Steel distinguished themselves and never again entered the lists for the Challenge Belt.

The gentlemen and golfers at Prestwick were familiar with Willie Park and knew him as a threat; the others they would have watched during a practice round over the links and not rated. The betting was heavily on Tom but there were many among the gentlemen from Glasgow and Edinburgh who were prepared to back Park, especially if given good odds.

Before play began, the players were assembled in front of the Red Lion and the rules of the contest explained. Each had to sign his acceptance. Two rounds of the 12-hole course were played before lunch, which was taken at the Red Lion. The Club carried the luncheon costs for the eight players at one shilling each. There was no prize money on offer but at least there was a good lunch.

To the incredulity of the people of Prestwick and many of the gentlemen of the Club, Park took a three-stroke lead after the first round, a 55 to Tom's 58, then held the lead after the second when both took 59. Although Tom had a last round of 59 to Willie's 60, Park took the Belt by two strokes. Prestwick was stunned. The general shock and disbelief about the outcome can be deduced from George Glennie's letter from London to the Prestwick Treasurer, dated 19 October, only two days after the event, in which he bitterly regrets the result.

The *Ayrshire Advertiser* also bemoaned that:

> The most veteran frequenters of the Links will admit that in all their experience of Morris, they never saw him come to grief so

often, because it is well known that the battle of Bunker's Hill is an engagement which he has very seldom to fight.

Tom atoned for his supporters' sufferings in some measure by playing Willie Park the next day in a match of three rounds for a £20 stake. Tom won three holes up with two to play and, hopefully, all was forgiven.

Tom's defeat apart, this inaugural event may not have been all that the members at Prestwick had anticipated. The field was small and, apart from Park, Morris and Andrew Strath, the rest of the competitors did not come within 13 strokes of the winner. The minutes of the Spring Meeting of the Club of 1861 make it clear that a restructuring of the Challenge Belt Competition to include gentlemen players was intended: 'proposed by Mr Fairlie that the challenge belt be open to be played for by gentlemen players, members of the following clubs:– St Andrews, Honourable Company of Edinburgh Golfers, North Berwick, Prestwick, Blackheath, Carnoustie, Perth and Leven.'

The motion was seconded by Rev. Pollock, and carried unanimously.

One can certainly understand the Prestwick members' disappointment. Their attitude may also have been influenced by the fact that immediately before they sat down to their meeting, Willie Park had again defeated Tom by four strokes over one round of the course. They may well have been concerned that the Challenge Belt might find a permanent home in Musselburgh after only three years. Whatever the reason, the Spring Meeting minutes make clear that the members were resolved on a change in playing eligibility and, in retrospect, it is clear that Fairlie's proposal was an attempt to augment the field with able amateurs.

If Tom and his supporters had been disappointed by his defeat at the hands of Willie Park in the first contest for the Belt, their spirits were raised in the second year. The 1861 event, the first truly 'Open' with amateurs in the field, attracted the cream of the gentlemen players. All the leading professionals entered the lists, despite the fact that there was no prize money. The twin brothers Willie and Jamie Dunn of Blackheath made a special journey up from London: the leading players from St Andrews, Perth, Musselburgh and Edinburgh were all there. It was also really 'Open', in the sense that there were apparently no restrictions with regard to the 'respectability' of the professional players.

From the numbers following Morris and Park, there was little doubt that it was generally perceived as a two-horse race, the remainder of the field being 'thrown out of the chances of success'.

And so it proved, for after the first of the three 12-hole rounds, Tom and Willie were level and in the lead. There was cause for concern for Tom's supporters when Park took a two-stroke lead on completion of the second round. Even the local newspaper related that 'the opinion became very prevalent that [Park] would be able to retain his laurels'.

Shortly after the start of the third and last round, however, Willie was in trouble. At the 2nd hole, in making a very daring attempt to 'cross the Alps' in two, he finished in 'one of the worst hazards on the green'. This cost him three strokes, and the newspaper commented that it was 'by no means the first occasion on which he has been severely punished for similar avarice and temerity'. Tom had, by this point, made up his deficit and was soon two ahead, an advantage which he lost at the 5th and 6th holes. Willie played the three subsequent holes indifferently and found himself three strokes behind. The short 11th was the crucial hole; Tom holed-out in two after 'a fine iron shot and a finer putt', while Willie took three. Tom was then four ahead with only the last hole to play.

The *Ayr Advertiser* relates:

> Driving a magnificent ball from the teeing ground towards home, it landed in a bed of fog at the edge of a pool of water . . . To come to grief at such a time was most provoking, and the spectators thought Tom would pick out the ball and forfeit a stroke; but with self-reliance, rising to the emergency, he dexterously sent it bounding into the air, and ultimately halving the last hole, finished in a splendid round of 53, and secured the national guerdon of golfing skill.

The newspaper continued with a criticism:

> Considerable disappointment was expressed that there should not have been a formal investiture of the belt by some of the officials of the club on the spot, although the modesty with which Tom wears his honours, we presume it was more in consonance with his own feelings to have been relieved from participating in any such ceremony.

Tom had handsomely avenged his defeat by Willie Park of the previous year, improving on Willie's winning score by 11 strokes. The gentlemen amateurs, while bringing some additional *éclat* to the proceedings and doubtless augmenting the crowd, were nowhere. Colonel Fairlie finished best with a score of 184, 21 strokes behind the winner. It was fitting that

Tom's mentor and friend, who had been responsible for bringing him to Prestwick in 1851, and who was really the founder of the Open Championship, should be the first Leading Amateur.

The 1862 Challenge Belt was a sorry affair, with only four professionals and four amateurs entering, Willie Park alone making the journey from East Lothian. One reason for the low turnout of professionals could have been the perceived invincibility of Tom Morris and Willie Park, who had so completely dominated the two previous contests. Another, no doubt, was the total absence of any prize money. The cost of travelling to Prestwick, together with board and lodgings, may well have deterred an artisan player. In addition there was no recognition for the 'Leading Amateur'.

Tom won the 1862 Challenge Belt competition with 163 strokes, the same score as in the previous year, and by the huge margin of thirteen strokes ahead of Willie Park in second place.[5] It was in this year that the church was first represented in the field in the figure of Rev. Pollok, who unfortunately failed to distinguish the cloth by not returning a card.

If the Prestwick Golf Club was unaware of the difficulties many potential competitors had in meeting the costs of contesting the Challenge Belt, others were not. The earliest intimation of a prize money fund comes from a letter addressed to Tom Morris from the Edinburgh Burgess Golfing Society. The letter, dated 7 September 1863, a week before the event, simply states that the Society was prepared to underwrite a prize of £2 to the runner-up for the Belt. The writer asks Tom if 'he would let this be known and assures him that the money will be with him in good time'.

This offer must have prompted Prestwick to introduce prize money for the professional contestants at the 1863 event: £5 for the runner-up, £3 to the third placed and £2 to the fourth, but still nothing for the winner!

Fourteen competitors entered the 1863 event, the most to date. Willie Park won, with Tom two strokes behind. Tom was therefore denied winning the Belt outright by his great adversary and was later to remark that it was Prestwick's Cardinal Bunker and Willie Park that had prevented him from claiming the Belt as his own on that occasion. Willie got the Belt to show off for a year, but no money, while Tom, in second place, came out £5 richer. Doubtless Willie had something to say about that and clearly somebody listened because, in 1864, when Tom again won the Belt, he received £6, the second-placed Andrew Strath £5, the Rook in third place £3 and Willie in fourth place, £1. Willie Park must have thought that Prestwick was conspiring against him, for in all but one of these years, in the post-championship money matches set up between himself and Tom, he was beaten.

He did, however, have his fair share of the money in the matches he played at other venues throughout the 1850s and into the 1860s. But things were changing, with the number of players involved increasing and the game being played to a higher standard by amateurs and professionals alike.

Changes were also taking place in the reporting of golf in the national press. Before the founding of the Challenge Belt contest and the Open Championship, and apart from the big professional money matches, golf received little attention outside Scotland. The *Scotsman*, the *Edinburgh News* and the *Glasgow Herald*, all with nationwide circulation, were sporadic and inconsistent in covering golfing events. Such reporting that did regularly take place was concerned with the play of gentlemen and the results of club meetings. This situation changed as the Open Championship became established as a regular feature of the sporting calendar, because of the gambling interests in it. *Bell's Life in London and Sporting Chronicle*, as well as *Sporting Life*, for example, carried the results of early professional contests. These were the gambling men's papers, giving news not only of horse racing and boxing, but also of quoits, ratting, dog racing and other more parochial sports that attracted the gambling set, such as 'northern knur and spell' and hare coursing. With the Open Championship, golf entered the pages of the national gambling press, and within ten years, became featured in the detailed recording of matches and the odds on offer.[6]

While all this was happening, young Tommy Morris was approaching his teens, and about to raise the game of golf to a new level, a level that few at the time would have imagined possible.

12 'Cast in the Very Mould of a Golfer'

The Burgh School at Prestwick was only a few yards from Nancy Morris's front door on to the High Street. Tommy went to the school with James and Robert Hunter from across the road at the Red Lion and with Johnny Allan, the stonemason's son from just down the road. They were contained in one classroom ruled by Mr Williamson, with the minister of the Kirk looking in every so often to put the fear of God into them. How much of an impression the Burgh School made upon them we can only guess but what we can be sure of is that they started to play golf on the links at Prestwick just as soon as they could lay their hands on a club.

Elizabeth Morris, two years younger than brother Tommy, and William Hunter joined them in the Burgh School with Jamie and Matthew Allan, but it was only for a year, before Tommy and James Hunter were taken out of the school and sent to Ayr to the great Academy there. James would excel and win prizes: Tommy would not.

Tommy's education at Ayr Academy was not cheap. From a penny a week at the Burgh School to over a shilling in the Academy would have been a noticeable expense to the Morris household. Tom was paid by the quarter, just under £50 a year with £6 a year deducted for his house rent. This was more than a fair wage for a man in his position. A farm worker was lucky to take home £10 a year with milk and meal in his tied cottage. The Burgh schoolmaster was not earning £30 a year and in St Andrews, Willie Alexander and Sandy Herd were being paid £6 between them to keep the Links, albeit not on a full-time basis. Tom was well enough off to have to pay the poor tax, a privilege reserved for only the better off among the working classes.[1]

The fact that Tom and Nancy were prepared to pay Ayr Academy fees and send Tommy the three miles into town every day, testifies not only to their financial well-being, but also to their aspirations for his future. How much Tommy derived from his experience of what was one of the best schools in

Scotland at that time is difficult to say. He would certainly have been seated beside the sons of the merchant and landed classes. He would have learned the language, mannerisms and manners of the well-to-do and been familiar with their habits and hobbies. Later in life, Tommy Morris, through his Ayr Academy education, would have been at ease in a wide spectrum of society and very far from seeing himself as a servant to anybody.

Prestwick Golf Club had a juvenile section in the early 1860s and the competition results were published in the local newspaper. It is not surprising that Tommy did not figure in the lists because as the son of the Club servant he would be excluded from membership even though he attended the same school and in the summer evenings would doubtless play golf on the links with the young members.

His regular playing partners were almost certainly James Hunter and Johnny Allan. Both emerged as outstanding players, winning the Eglinton Medal of the Prestwick Mechanics, which in 1858 was re-named the Prestwick St Nicholas Golf Club. James would remain an outstanding amateur, while Johnny would finally become professional to the North Devon and West of England Golf Club at Westward Ho! and compete in professional tournaments. All three would come to contest the Open with different degrees of success.

Tommy had his first recorded outing at the Perth Open Tournament in April 1864 in an event organised by the Royal Perth and King James VI Clubs. He was twelve years old and arrived with his father intent upon playing in the big event. The committee, however, considered that 'his close connection with the game paternally', rendered him ineligible to play in the amateur part of the tournament; not being a professional either, he was debarred from taking part at all. It is hardly surprising that he was refused entry to the professional competition. Win or lose, the presence of a twelve-year-old in the field could be an embarrassment to the professionals and would hardly add stature to the event.

Tom Morris won the Perth tournament after a play-off with Willie Park, but in spite of being barred from the tournament, it was young Tommy who really stole the show. The organizers were sympathetic to Tommy's exclusion and, whether from knowing of young Tommy's play or from a reluctance to disappoint the boy, they set up a match between him and William Greig, who was considered at the time to be the best boy player, on the Inch at Perth.

Tommy at once gave notice of the skill and style that was shortly to outclass all other players of his day and propel him to the very summit of golf. A contemporary newspaper reported:

> But perhaps the most interesting match of the day was between Master Morris, son of the redoubtable 'Tom', and Master William Greig of, as it seems, Perth juvenile golfing celebrity. They are really wonderful players, for their years, both of them. We had no idea that very-young-Perth could produce so proficient a golfer as Master Greig. He played with astonishing neatness and precision, but the honours of the day were in store for his competitor. Master Morris seems to have been both born and bred to golf. He has been cast in the very mould of a golfer and plays with all the steadiness and certainty in embryo of his father.

Tommy gave an exhibition of his prowess against an overwhelmed Willie Greig. The local press devoted more space to Tommy's exploits than to the tournament proper, and much was subsequently written about his performance. A silver collection was raised from the crowd that followed the boys which, as the newspaper reported, 'exceeded the numbers following the principal players'.

Such was the importance of the event in Perth that Mr Henderson, photographer, took a studio-posed photograph of the leading professional contestants. While young Tommy was excluded from the professional tournament, he was nevertheless included in the photograph: the first time father and son were depicted together and probably the first time that Tommy had posed for the camera.

When Tom and his son appeared on the Inch at Perth, it is recalled that Willie Park asked, 'for why have ye brought yer laddie, Tom?', and Tom's reply, 'You'll see for why soon enough.' Soon enough came some two years later in a tournament at Carnoustie, when Tommy beat a field made up of all of the leading players of the day. Immediately after this he took on and beat Willie Park in matchplay for a £20 stake. If there was any question of the fifteen-year-old deserving his place in tournament fields it must have been answered that day.

In 1864 at Perth, Tommy was already conveying his infectious excitement to the game and his dash and vigour made his play a spectacle. It was something that he would learn to use to best advantage in the years to come for he, more than anyone, was responsible for capturing the imagination of the public and turning golf into a popular spectator sport.

Returning to Prestwick via St Andrews, after the excitement of Perth, must have been unsettling for Tommy. His friends, James Hunter and Johnny Allan, had already left school. James had begun work in Ayr, in a timber yard belonging to his father's cousin, where he made a precocious start in timber trading, learning a business that would ultimately found his and the Morris's family wealth. Johnny Allan had started work with his father in his stonemason's yard in Prestwick. Obviously unhappy there, he would soon make his escape, first to the Links of St Andrews and Aberdeen, then finally to Westward Ho!, North Devon.

Tom and Nancy would be becoming increasingly concerned that their youngest son John was growing up unable to walk. His hip deformity was probably due to a congenital defect that today would be corrected soon after birth. With no known treatment available at the time, John was destined to rely on a trolley for any mobility. With this, he would propel himself about his father's workplace, where he did what he could in binding and whipping club shafts and dressing and painting gutta balls.

Movement for John was difficult in Prestwick with the house front door opening on to the busy road through the village and his future must have been of great concern to Tom and Nancy. Of more concern was the fact that the Club was planning to build a clubhouse down the Wrack Road on the links with accommodation for the professional. If the family moved there, John would be isolated on his trolley, a prospect that neither Tom nor Nancy could contemplate. What life he had in the street would be taken from him down at the links.

Elizabeth would leave the Burgh School in her tenth year to find employment as a dressmaker, possibly with Charlie Hunter's sister Mary, only a few yards up the High Street.

There were changes taking place all around the Morris household in Prestwick. William and Elizabeth Hunter in the Red Lion were planning their retirement. Their daughter Mary had married John Raeside and it was Mary and John who were left to run the inn together when William and Elizabeth moved to the cottage on their land at Everton, just up the road. The Prestwick St Nicholas Club had started the series of moves that would separate it completely from the Prestwick Club's course and take it a mile up the Ayr Road to its own course and independence.

Tom and Nancy were held in the highest regard by the golfers and townspeople of Prestwick. After a special Testimonial Meeting held on 2 February 1861, with three special prizes on offer, the Prestwick St Nicholas Club entertained Tom at dinner in the hall of the Red Lion. Mr Prain, the Captain, presented Tom with 'an elegant gold watch' not, he said, 'as a requital for his services, but only as recognition of the obligations under which the Club had so long been laid'.

On New Years Day in 1863, after the traditional meeting on the links, the Prestwick St Nicholas Club held another dinner in the Red Lion to honour Tom. The local paper reported that the Captain of the club, Mr R. Howie Smith, who warmly complimented him on his victory over Willie Park in their £100-a-side marathon over four links, proposed the health of Tom Morris. Not only did they warmly drink to his health but they also presented him with a handsome timepiece as a New Year's gift from the Club. Nancy, although not present at this all-male affair, was presented, through her husband, with a brooch, in appreciation of her kindness and attention in promoting the comfort of the Club's members.

13 'The Apostles of Golf'

The recognition that Tom Morris was receiving was not merely confined to Prestwick. His marathon match with Willie Park in 1862 had caught the public attention and newspapers had covered their exploits in half-page reports. Willie and Tom between them had completely dominated the first five Open Championships and Tom's third victory in 1864 brought him national repute and an altogether new social recognition.

But there were also significant changes taking place in the game itself, way beyond the confines of St Andrews, Prestwick and East Lothian. Golf was on the move and about to blossom on links lands far to the south, in a place that Tom already knew and not simply as an address on parcels of golf clubs and balls.

While Tom was labouring on his course on the Prestwick links in 1853, Major General William Driscoll Gosset, then a lowly captain in the Royal Engineers engaged in the Trigonometrical Survey of Scotland, was stationed at Ayr. The Captain was introduced to golf at Prestwick when he drew up the first map of the course, which he presented to the Club and which can be seen hanging on the clubhouse wall today. At about the same time, his cousin, the Reverend Isaac Gosset of Northam Priory, near Westward Ho! in North Devon, was initiated into golf in St Andrews by his brother-in-law, General Moncrieff.

On a visit to Northam in 1854, Captain Gosset suggested to his cousin that the Northam Burrows, the great sprawl of links land around Bideford Bay, was eminently suitable for golf. In the words of the Rev. Gosset's son, George, 'from that date onward golf was played on the Burrows'.[1]

Tom supplied the Gossets of Northam with golf clubs and balls in 1858 and his bill for £5 9s 6d included wooden clubs at 3s 6d, irons at 4s 6d, and gutta balls at 1s each. He probably supplied others taking up golf on the Northam Burrows, because, by 1864, there were enough regular players to form a club.

The North Devon and West of England Golf Club was formed on 18 May 1864. It is particularly significant that the founding membership, while containing some recognisable Scots golfing names, was largely made up of new converts to the game. At least three-quarters of the members had never played before, yet it was through them that golf was introduced into English society.

In August 1864, Tom Morris arrived at Bideford station to spend ten days as the guest of the Reverend Isaac Gosset and his family at Northam Priory. In Isaac Gosset's words, 'on August 8th Tom Morris arrived to assist in laying out the links. He played in foursomes daily and attracted some of the county magnates as spectators. He found walking up Bone Hill at the end of a day's golf a bit trying. He put in eight days play.'

The Reverend Gosset kept a record of Tom's play every day and even worked out his average for each hole on the course that he had laid out on his first day there.

On 10 November 1864 the Club held its first dinner with 'thirty two or more members in attendance'. It would eventually become the 'Royal North Devon Golf Club', known as 'Westward Ho!' for short, and go from strength to strength. This Club, although not the oldest, was, more than any other, responsible for establishing golf in England.

Although golf had for long been played at Blackheath in London and on Kersal Moor near Manchester, it was by expatriate Scots in the main, with few English participants. At Westward Ho! the game was taken up by men (and women as early as 1868) who had no connection with Scotland and who had hitherto never even seen it played.

The Reverend Isaac Gosset, the self-styled, 'Apostle of Golf', is acclaimed as the 'Father of English Golf'; this is not hyperbole, but he was a mere acolyte of Tom Morris who preached the virtues of the game wherever and whenever he could. All who met him at Westward Ho! held Tom Morris in the greatest affection. He first visited Northam in 1860, some four years before the Club was founded, staying a month with the Reverend Gosset, when he 're-arranged the course'. By the time of his second visit in 1864, he was treated as a celebrity by the golfers of North Devon, who showered him with gifts and mementos. Isaac Gosset knew what he was doing when he brought Tom Morris to Devon to demonstrate how the game should be played and to teach his friends how to play it. Tom's quiet confidence, humility and reliability, the character traits in his work and play that had taken him to Prestwick, were what Isaac Gosset sought to put on show at Westward Ho! They were also the features that the gentlemen of The Royal and Ancient were then demanding at St Andrews.

One cannot determine when exactly in 1864 the word came to Tom from St Andrews that The Royal and Ancient wanted him to return there to take charge of the Links. He would have been aware that there had been a great deal of dissatisfaction expressed about the condition of the St Andrews course in the *Fifeshire Journal*, with letters of complaint extending as far back as the late 1850s. Tom would likely have been well sounded out at the Autumn Meeting in 1863 with discussions ongoing until final agreements were reached in the summer of 1864. The gentlemen players from St Andrews, who frequently enjoyed the links at Prestwick and extolled its virtues, may well have fuelled this dissatisfaction. Da' Anderson had been given charge of the Links in the early 1850s soon after Tom had left for Prestwick, but had given up the job because of criticism and interference – and the fact that he was underpaid. Watty Alexander and Sandy Herd had then tended the Links for a combined salary of £6 a year and, after 1860, Sandy had taken the responsibility upon himself. But clearly all was not well and he, too, tendered his resignation.

In 1864 The Royal and Ancient authorised its Green Committee to appoint a custodian of the Links, 'at a salary considerably larger than that hitherto given'. The sum of £50 was noted as being the 'considerably larger' amount, with a further £20 for any addition expenditure required. A minute of the Club, dated 4 May 1864, records: 'Major Boothby moved that Thos Morris of Prestwick, formerly St Andrews, be brought here as a professional golfer on the understanding that he shall have entire charge of the golf course and be responsible for it being kept in proper order, and that he shall be the servant of the Club under the direction and control of the committee in charge of the green.'

Major Boothby did not get his motion passed unopposed. No less a figure than Mr John Whyte-Melville was against Tom's appointment. Why he opposed Tom was not recorded. Whyte-Melville was a leading figure in the Club who would certainly have known Tom since his earliest emergence on the Links of St Andrews. He would also have known of his achievements at Prestwick and of his status as a professional player. Whyte Melville's opposition to Tom's appointment remains a delightful mystery.[2]

It is clear, however, that it had long been The Royal and Ancient's objective to appoint Tom Morris to oversee the Links. At the Autumn Meeting in October 1859, less than a month after Allan Robertson's funeral, the *Fifeshire Journal* reported that at a meeting of the Club, 'the subject of a successor to the much-lamented Allan Robertson was discussed' and that 'the feeling of the meeting lay almost entirely with Tom Morris, Prestwick'. The paper went on to speak of Tom's talents and impeccable qualifications and to express the hope that although 'some little difficulties interpose', the Club would be able to resolve these and that he would be persuaded to return to St Andrews. The 'little difficulties' could have been Tom's loyalty to Fairlie and the Prestwick Club, as well as to his friends in the Mechanics Club. It is also entirely possible that any offer made to him was not commensurate with his expectations. In any event he stayed in Prestwick for another five years.

Tom had doubtless discussed sometime in 1864 with Mr Bethune and Major Boothby the possibility of moving back to St Andrews and had agreed to their proposal. He was in the Town for The Royal and Ancient's Spring Meeting in May and was back again in July with Colonel Fairlie, when some members gathered for the summer season. Certainly, by that time, an agreement must have been reached and Fairlie would have known of it.

Tom tendered his letter of resignation to the Prestwick Club, dated August 1864, intimating his intention to leave in November. This letter is probably the only one in existence that we can be sure was written by him. The grammar, punctuation and spelling errors support his own contention that he was not altogether proficient with book or pen.

The Prestwick St Nicholas Golf Club gave Tom a grand farewell dinner in Prestwick Town Hall, which started at three in the afternoon and went on until midnight. It must have been a very emotional experience for him, because as well as being presented with a fine and suitably inscribed gold hunter watch, he was also much toasted, lauded and applauded. The Ayr newspaper reported the event and the *Fifeshire Journal* carried a copy. They gave an account of the toasts and the speeches but what they could not recount were the feelings of Tom and his fellow founding Members of the Mechanics Club at that time. The Club had been renamed the Prestwick St Nicholas Golf Club: they had seen it grow and develop into a club managing its own course, playing matches against Perth and St Andrews and recognised as the model for all local and artisan clubs throughout the country.

In the Red Lion, William and Elizabeth Hunter, together with their friends and neighbours, also had a special supper for Tom and Nancy to mark their leaving Prestwick. Doubtless all of the children that had grown up together were also there. Nancy was presented with a fine inscribed brooch 'from all her friends and neighbours in Prestwick'. It must have been a very moving occasion for them both, for the friends they had made in Prestwick would remain close and loyal for the rest of their lives.

14 Home to Roost

At the same time as General William T. Sherman was routing Confederate forces on his 'march to the sea' through Georgia in the American Civil War, Tom Morris and his family were moving back to St Andrews. 'Golf Notes' in the St Andrews news section of the *Fifeshire Journal* of 24 November 1864 reads:

> The Green is in excellent condition and many gentlemen are daily practicing their favourite game. The Saturday afternoons are a fruitful source for our tradesmen who then play as long as light will serve them. Tom Morris has arrived to enter upon his duties as Conservator of the Links and we doubt not that his return amongst us will add more item to the popularity of the national game.

These few words fail to reflect the significance of Tom's return to the place of his birth, for it was to catalyse the Town, the Links and golf into a new age. For the next forty years, Tom would be at the centre, as well as the helm of golf as it developed into the game we know today.

While Tom took up his appointment on 19 December 1864, it was not until the New Year that he was presented with his tools of office – a barrow, spade and shovel – and formally told by the Club's Green Committee of the duties expected of him. The minutes record:

> Tom Morris being called, it was explained that he was to have the charge of the links, that his duties were to keep the putting greens in good order, to repair such portions of the links as required it and to make the holes. The committee is willing, when heavy work (such as carting etc.) is required, to grant him assistance at the rate of one man's labour for two days in the week, he superintending and assisting in the work.

Tom had been to and fro between St Andrews and Prestwick at least twice a year during his thirteen years away, but the changes taking place in the Town must have astonished him and Nancy. Hope Street, Howard Place and Abbotsford Crescent were nearing completion and a fine row of houses, Gillespie Terrace, where Robert Chambers and James Balfour owned properties, ran into another row of Georgian-styled houses called Playfair Terrace. Mrs Broughton, the widow of Captain Broughton, lived there, as did the widowed Lady Playfair. The foundation stone of Hope Park Church was newly laid and, up at the Northgait where Tom was born and raised, the cottages were being knocked down so that new houses could be built in their place. The Royal and Ancient Golf Club, renamed as such in 1834 and previously simply known as 'The Old Club', was now popularly referred to as 'The Royal and Ancient'.

The railway spur from Leuchars to St Andrews, which was finally completed in 1852, had brought far-reaching changes. 'Residenters' had built many fine houses and a new type of wealthy city folk from Edinburgh and Glasgow was resorting to the proliferating hotels to 'weekend' in the Town. It was on the Links, however, that the real effect of the railway was to be seen. Play on the course was now such that it had to be regulated and players rushing from the train onto the Links had to be intercepted to stop them playing away to the 2nd hole.

Tom and Nancy moved their family into a property in Golf Place. The 1864 Valuation Roll for St Andrews refers to it as a house and shop and it could not have been very large, for it had a rental value of only £2 per annum.[1]

Clearly the little house in Golf Place was a temporary dwelling for Tom and Nancy and their three boys, with Lizzie staying on in Prestwick before moving to live with her Grandmother Bayne in the nearby village of Leuchars. If not clear then, it would soon become evident, that Lizzie had set her heart upon James Hunter in Prestwick. Jof, at six years old, was entered into the junior classes at the Madras College, while Tommy was set to making balls and helping out in Tom's shop. The four-year-old John, with his limited mobility, would still be in the house with his mother. In two rooms, with one forming the workplace, this must have been cramped and far from comfortable with no privacy whatsoever; in fact not much different from that which they had left in Prestwick.

For Tommy, St Andrews must have been an exciting place, and their move back eagerly anticipated from his visits through the years. The great sweep of the West Sands, with the long rolling waves breaking on it and the busy Links that saw constant play every day, must have inspired the fourteen-year-old boy. Here he had competition to test him from boys of his own age who were as seasoned as himself on the Links. Andrew Smith and James Kirk were both newly out of the Madras College and learning business behind the commercial counters of the Town. They would emerge as players competing at the highest levels in the amateur game. Davie Strath, then apprenticed as a clerk in an office in St Andrews, became an early friend and rival for Tommy on the Links. Their lives would become inextricably linked. There was also Young Bob Kirk, working with his father making balls next door in Golf Place, and Jamie Anderson, also making balls with his father, Old Da', just round the corner in Pilmour Place. It was the play of young Bob Kirk and Jamie Anderson that would sharpen Tommy and make him work for his money. They were Tommy's seniors in years, but no more than a good match for him at the golf. There would be plenty of golf with opponents who rarely played without wagering some money on the match.

If Tommy had reservations about leaving his friends in Prestwick's busy township, they would be quickly forgotten because, life on the Links aside, St Andrews was never a dull place. The Morris family had barely settled, for instance, when the brig *Napoleon* went onto the rocks to the east of the Town near Boarhills. Doubtless Tommy would have been there with his new friends, along with the hundreds of others who watched, as attempts to get a line on board failed and all hands perished in the sea before their eyes.

Tommy's first competitive play in St Andrews was on New Year's Day, 1865. It was the annual competition of the Operatives Golf Club, a club made up of the caddies and club- and ball-makers, who were the 'professional' players of the day. There had been snow and frost for a week, but the weather cleared, leaving only patches of white in the hollows on the Links. Jamie Anderson won, holing the course in ninety-eight strokes, with George Daniel Brown, young Bob Kirk and William Mason, who was being given strokes or 'odds', tying on ninety-nine in second place. Tommy came fifth with a score of 100, with 'odds', and old Bob Kirk was next with three strokes more. The young Tommy was blooded now, integrated into golf in the Town and launched into the coterie of caddies and crack players making up the local elite of the Links. But he would not be given 'odds' for long.

Meanwhile, back at Prestwick, the Club was having less than satisfactory success in finding a permanent replacement for Tom following his departure a few months earlier. Four applicants sought the position: Charlie Hunter of Prestwick, Andrew Strath of St Andrews, Jamie Dunn, then at Blackheath, and Tom's elder brother, George. In enlightened, true democratic style, the whole membership of the club was invited to vote on the various candidates, the result being Hunter 16 votes, Strath 10, Dunn 1 and Morris nil. Charlie Hunter, Tom's protégé and friend, was thus appointed to succeed his mentor, but it was to prove a temporary position. Eight months after notifying his acceptance of the job he wrote in May 1865 to the Club tendering his resignation, 'In consequence of having received a more lucrative appointment at Blackheath'. He was in fact replacing Willie Dunn who had just been sacked. Consequently, the Prestwick Club appointed Andrew Strath, a 27-year-old from a large St Andrews family of five sons and a daughter, and the eldest of the four brothers who would emerge from this family and leave their mark upon golf.[2]

Andrew Strath won the Challenge Belt, the Open Championship, in 1865, his first year at Prestwick. Clearly, knowledge of the links, with its blind holes and extensive areas of whin bushes, was an advantage. Tom could only manage fifth place behind Willie Park and Willie Dow from Musselburgh and Bob Kirk from St Andrews. Tom was certainly off his game, or perhaps his mind was on other things. Young Tommy was in the Open field for the first time, and with the inexperience of youth was not having a good day. He withdrew after the second round, even though a stroke better than his father.

After the Spring Meeting at Prestwick the following year, a purse was raised to match Tom and Andrew Strath over two rounds of the links. Betting was very heavy and, according to the *Ayr Advertiser*, the crowd was 'greater than ever seen before on the Green'. Tom won by the comfortable margin of seven up with six to play. He had defeated Willie Park in 1863 and again in 1864 by the same margin over Prestwick links and his defeat of Andrew Strath, the 'Champion Golfer of 1865', only added to his legendary status amongst the Prestwick locals.

Andrew Strath won the Belt just this once. He would play again in 1866 and 1867, but by the time of the Open Championship in 1868 he was dead. The tuberculosis that ravaged the Strath family took Andrew in his thirty-third year. Only one of the Strath brothers, George, enjoyed the fruits of old age. Andrew suffered for three months before his death in February 1868, leaving his wife Euphemia to die a year later in St Andrews. His three children, living with the extended Strath family in St Andrews, all died young. It is clear that the members at Prestwick much liked and appreciated Andrew, as witnessed by the subscription raised by the Club to support his widow and children.

After Andrew Strath died, Charlie Hunter was brought back from Blackheath to tend the Club at Prestwick where he remained in post for the rest of his life. Charlie's humour, manners and affability were learned at the knee of Tom Morris, who in his turn had learned them at the feet of Allan Robertson. The attitude and style of the Club Professional were set in place in Prestwick over these years and yardsticks laid down for generations to come.

Tom was certainly setting the standards in St Andrews. After the Spring Meeting of 1865, the local paper was so impressed by the way that Thomas Morris conducted and organised the gentlemen's games that it made special comment about it. Thereafter, in the paper, he was simply referred to as 'Tom'. That year he played some very successful foursomes matches against stiff opposition, partnering Thomas Hodge who ran a boarding school for young gentlemen in the Town. Hodge was a highly skilled amateur artist who left memorable watercolour paintings and sketches of the Links, as well as of the gentlemen players, professionals and caddies of the day. It is clear from these that his favourite subject was Tom Morris. Hodge, like Colonel Fairlie, was an all-round sportsman who came to golf late and played it well.

The standards Tom set himself were frequently too high. He had a tendency to be foolhardy with the 'odds' that he gave to gentlemen players, but when he took on Robert Clark and Gilbert Mitchell Innes's better ball, he was probably being silly. The *Fifeshire Journal* called this match the 'first three-ball match ever played', which merely reflected how little the editor knew, since a professional playing the better ball of two gentlemen players was commonplace. What made this match special was that not only had Tom taught Clark and Mitchell Innes at Prestwick, but he had also publicly called them the top gentlemen players of their generation. The pair beat him on the eighteenth green, but only just, for Tom's putt to halve the match came to rest on the lip of the hole.

Tom was also setting standards off the course by becoming a man of property. He was probably the first man making his living solely from golf to become a property owner.

Whether Tom had a vision of the future, or whether it was out of necessity to accommodate his disabled son John, while providing better domestic accommodation as well as a workplace, we will never know, but Tom took the plunge into property ownership in 1866. It was a bold step that could not have been taken without the support of friends. Thomas Milton was a friend and he was also the Provost of St Andrews. As a contemporary of Tom's, he came from a wealthy family in the Town and had attended the Grammar School and University. They had played on the Links together as boys and had remained friends. It is possible that Thomas Milton may have had some part, through his position as the Provost and a member of the

Club, in bringing Tom back from Prestwick and he may well have talked to Tom, providing an inducement about acquiring property and establishing a business in the Town. In any event, it was Milton who advanced Tom a £400 bond to buy No. 6 Pilmour Links, secured by a charge on the property and a life insurance policy taken out by Tom several years earlier for £100 payable on his death.[3]

Tom not only owned the Pilmour Links house but also the shop that went with it on the Links end of the feu. It had been the workplace that Hugh Philp, the premier club-maker of his day, had made out of Willie Fairful's cart shed in 1832 and which George Daniel Brown, 'club and ball-maker', had occupied since his arrival in the Town from London in 1861.

Richard Bartholomew Child purchased this property from Mrs Philp in 1861. Mr Child, then resident in Henley-on-Thames, was a 'retired ale merchant' of some considerable means, whose daughter had married George Daniel Brown in 1858. Brown was born in 1836 into a family of coopers in Waltham Green, Middlesex, and passed his early life in Putney, a London borough. He entered the inaugural 1860 Open Championship from the Blackheath Golf Club in London, the first non-Scot to compete in the Open, and moved to St Andrews soon after. He played in the 1861 Championship from St Andrews, again failing to distinguish himself, but finished a creditable fifth in the 1863 event, his last appearance. He took part in the 1864 Perth Tournament but other than reports of matches he played in St Andrews (on one occasion partnering Willie Park against Tom and Andrew Strath in 1861 when he and Willie were beaten) there is no record of any further tournament play. From his absence from any local records after 1866, it is safe to conclude that he left the Town. There is a delightful irony in the fact that it was an Englishman, indeed a Cockney, who established the first golf shop in St Andrews and by definition, the world. G. D. Brown described himself as a club- and ball-maker, and examples of both exist today stamped with his name. He not only advertised his shop and workplace on the Links, but also extolled the range of his wares.

Brown occupied the workshop premises for five years and in that time renovated the building by extending the shed roof that is seen in the earliest photographs. Later photographs show the new gable boldly bearing his name in large letters, perhaps something that was viewed with some distaste by the locals. He did not occupy the house at 6 Pilmour Links. Mr Child rented it to a seamstress, while the Browns lived above the shop in the newly constructed living accommodation.[4]

Tom clearly had a low opinion of George Daniel Brown, a view he shared with Andrew Lang, the popular writer and poet of the day. Lang relates:

One G D Brown with a cricket style, and any amount of conceit, had Philp's shop for a time after Forgan left, and took up business for himself. He would floor me if there was money on it. I had none; nor did I bet even when I might have made a good thing of it; but Tom gave me £10 to stake against him. I never heard any more of the challenge of G D Brown. This no one knows till now. But Tom took the brag out of the upstart by this cunning ruse.

By acquiring both Brown's premises and his 'extensive stock', as is shown in the notice from the local paper and *The Golfer's Year Book for 1866*, Tom had shrewdly set himself up in immediate business at the most advantageous site on the Links. The property was ideal for Tom in every respect. Situated at the top of the Links on Sandyhill, opposite the last green and the 1st tee, it was the likely place for a player to buy a ball or have a club refurbished. From Nancy's point of view, with the house and workshop separated by a garden, it must have seemed idyllic. It was the first time in her married life that she had not lived with clubs and balls, to say nothing of the smell of wood glue and the clutter of men standing around talking about their golf. But most importantly, the house and workshop were virtually on the same level and the seven-year-old John could propel his trolley back and forth without assistance and so develop some independence and lead a fuller life.

15 'Leddies Gowf' and Caddie Cantrips

The growth of the Town, and the improvements made in it, resulted in greater commercial activity and in no area more so than golf. St Andrews was fortunate in having expansive beaches for sea bathing as well as ancient monuments and extensive cliffs and stone quarries. Sea-bathing had become fashionable among the health-conscious Victorians. Exploring ancient ruins, as well as chipping at rocks to uncover fossil remains, was a pursuit for both gentlemen and ladies of a scientific frame of mind. St Andrews, with its resident community of intellectuals in the University and gentry in The Royal and Ancient Golf Club, became a choice summer resort for the increasingly socially aware middle classes from the heartlands of industry.

Golf, which had hitherto largely been a winter pursuit, quickly became an all-year-round game on St Andrews Links. Many, who had only known of the game through hearsay and newspaper reports, took it up after witnessing it in the course of a railway excursion to the Town, perhaps undertaken to visit the Castle and Cathedral ruins, or during a holiday taken for sea-bathing on the recommendations of their doctor.

It was the development of St Andrews as a premier seaside resort that resulted in the summer golf boom. A company provided bathing huts, which were wheeled cabins, moved by horses keeping pace with the tide so that ladies could descend straight into the sea. These had a magnetic attraction for the Town's young blades and the Town Council had to pass a by-law making it an offence for any male person over the age of ten to be within 100 yards of the ladies' huts.

Putting also became popular on the green that Playfair had set out on the bank just below Tom's shop. Few gentlemen, seduced into putting with the ladies, would be able to resist the temptation to try their hand at the real thing on the Links.

This putting green, or 'Short Course' as it came to be known, came about after the caddies made holes to idle away their time while awaiting their 'men' coming out to play. The Short Course was situated where the grand houses and Rusack's Hotel now stand on the Links Road, where a few of the more energetic caddies had cut the grass and generally improved the area as a putting surface. This was their undoing, for it was not long before some of the ladies, who had similar waiting problems and who may have had aspirations to golf, took to playing on this Short Course. Mrs James Wolfe Murray, the daughter of John Whyte-Melville of Mount Melville by St Andrews, raised not a few eyebrows and some whispers, when she took to the Links proper in 1855. Others soon followed her, but they were few in number, for the majority were either content to keep themselves to the caddies' Short Course, or were sensitive about intruding on their menfolks' terrain.

As the numbers of ladies increased, the caddies were more frequently deprived of their green and they were in no position to complain. Encouraging the wrath of the ladies was something that might irritate the gentlemen, whose play, after all, was their bread and butter. There must have been contretemps because, in 1866, the Town Council raised the possibility of a short course for ladies only. In 1867 the Green Committee of The Royal and Ancient applied itself to the problem and D.L. Burn proposed that the area to the west of the last loop of the Swilken Burn, before it meets the sea, be cleared of whins to make a putting course for the ladies. Mrs Boothby and her daughter would appear to have been the main driving force when Tom engaged extra labour to clear the land and make what came to be known, and is still known, as the Himalayas Putting Green. The ladies formed their own club, the St Andrews Ladies Golf Club, and for a small fee, were granted exclusive rights to this green by Mr Cheape, the Laird of Strathtyrum and owner of the Links.

The Club was an immediate success but it was not without controversy. The townspeople were very sensitive about what many perceived to be a creeping exclusivity about the Links from The Royal and Ancient. Setting aside one part of the Links for the exclusive use of one club, albeit a ladies club, was interpreted as the thin edge of the wedge and was stoutly resisted. This placed Tom in a difficult position. Notices were posted prohibiting anyone other than members of the Ladies Club from using the Putting Green and Tom, as Links Superintendent, had to police and enforce the ruling.

This edict was eventually put to the test by James Denham, a close friend and neighbour of the Morris family at Pilmour Links. Due to a railway accident, Denham was unable to play golf but he was an enthusiastic putter who had enjoyed many summer evenings putting with Tom and the others of the golfing fraternity. Most peculiarly, according to the press reports of what transpired, James Denham and young Bob Kirk called at Tom Morris's shop one evening to announce that they were about to putt on the Ladies Green. Clearly they were giving notice to Tom that he should eject them from the putting green and this he duly did. Denham brought an action but lost the subsequent court case. Tom's testimony was singularly impartial although he was a participant in what was clearly a test case. The outcome was to have repercussions for years to come and would also resurface with some significance some thirty years later when The Royal and Ancient purchased the Links from the Strathtyrum estate.

Tom's stance was unpopular and the public perception of him at the time was not good. There were letters to the editor of the local paper on the matter and threats of prosecutions. Tom made some attempt to improve the caddies' Short Course adjacent to the Links Road to assuage public feelings and he also built another close to the railway station. But the matter rumbled on for some time until the Ladies Course, as it came to be known, was eventually opened to all.

With the increase in play came an increase in the need for caddies. Tom found himself in an invidious position, for much had changed since his departure for Prestwick. Such was the demand that young boys could find easy and ready employment on the Links and some were unruly. The Royal and Ancient published in May 1863 the first notice regarding 'Rules and Discipline of Caddies', and appointed Robert Forgan and James Wilson, as well as the Club Steward, to 'fix upon the proper boys to select as caddies and to take supervision of them.' Forgan and Wilson had tried to control matters but their efforts met with little success. Upon Tom's return to St Andrews at the end of 1864, the Club published 'Proposed Rules regarding PAY AND DISCIPLINE OF CADDIES'. This notice also announced that Tom Morris had been appointed 'Keeper of the Green' and that Members should engage their caddies, as well as directing any complaints about them, through him.

With Tom in constant attendance on the Links, it is not surprising that he was given full control of the caddies and, although he could never have found it an easy job, some order began to prevail. The caddies respected him for his kindly attention to them. Tom certainly knew their ways and, more importantly, he knew them personally. He could refer to fathers and grandfathers of any unruly young lad and he could help and encourage the weak and meek and put down the belligerent. He was a great player, 'St Andrews' best', and was therefore an authoritative figure by rights on the Links and, if there were any unaware of this fact, there would be others determined to make a living in the game who would be quick to let them know. The 'caddy problem', as it was referred to in the local press, was one that lasted throughout his tenure on the Links and brought him joy and dismay in roughly equal measure.

Every cloud, however, has a silver lining. Increasing activity on the Links meant that demand for golf clubs was burgeoning and Tom was in the right place with the right premises to satisfy that demand. By 1870, in addition to his sons, he was employing three men making clubs and balls and the numbers would steadily increase to eight through the next three decades.

Tom Morris was now a man of property and a man of business, but he was still a golfer. No Spring or Autumn Meeting at Prestwick or St Andrews passed without him in attendance. His loyalty to Colonel Fairlie was continuous on both greens, for when Fairlie was playing, Tom was by his side with the Colonel's clubs under his arm. Fairlie's health was, however, failing fast. He did not make the journey from Coodham to St Andrews after 1865, and his last medal outing at Prestwick was in 1866 when he and Tom suffered a thrashing over 24 holes by the young blades, Mitchell Innes and Andrew Strath. They never played foursomes together again and, sadly, Fairlie did not live to see Tommy's ascent to the top of the game.

16 A Champion in the Making

Tommy had his first attempt at the Challenge Belt in 1865 when he was just 14 years old. The signs were already there of the temperament that would propel him to the very top, but the distractions and frustrations of youth were also present. His father Tom was the defending Champion that year and was playing badly. Tommy was a stroke better than his father when he gave up after 24 holes of the 36-hole Championship, but he was back in Prestwick and there were doubtless other things to do and people to see.

Tommy was entered as Tom Morris Jnr from Glasgow and it has been guardedly concluded that this was a mistake in registering his entry. It is not difficult to imagine an unknowing scribe asking the boy the question, 'And where have you come from laddie?' and the naive boy answering, 'Glasgow', since he had just got off the Glasgow train. There is, however, some evidence that Tommy did spend some time in Glasgow about this time.

In his book *Golf in Perth and Perthshire*, Peter Baxter relates how Bennet Lang came to have his start as a club maker in Tom Morris's shop in St Andrews. Ben Lang left school in Perth to take up an apprenticeship with a firm of engineers in Glasgow. 'Here he met young Tom Morris,' relates Baxter. Lang was 'strolling in the vicinity of Alexandra Park one evening when he heard a voice saying, "play eighteen more!" Investigating the quarter from whence the sound had emerged, he was amused to see a young man engaged laboriously trying to dislodge a ball which had got fixed in a fissure of one of the rocks in that "sporting" course. The intimacy with young Tom Morris led to Lang going to St Andrews and learning golf club making with Old Tom.'[1]

There is certainly no record of Tommy's play in St Andrews in 1865 after the New Years Day play of the Operatives Golf Club. It is probably also significant that Tommy did not play in the 1865 tournament at Montrose when the members of the Operatives were there together with every other player of significance in the game.[2]

Baxter's account of Lang's meeting with Tommy is cursory and frustratingly ambiguous. It is likely that, having provided an Ayr Academy education for their eldest son, Tom and Nancy would have nursed ambitions for him as an apprenticeship in Glasgow's engineering boom. Lang, a fifteen-year-old and a year Tommy's senior, may well have been present on the North Inch at Perth the year before when Tommy had matched Master Greig and may then have established a connection with Tommy. What is certain is that Tommy was in St Andrews by the spring of 1866, and that by 1867 Lang was living in the Town, working in Tom's shop and playing golf.[3]

But if Tommy himself gave any thought to an occupation outside golf it did not last long. His roots and his life were inextricably linked with golf and his flowering in the game was as inevitable as summer following spring. In 1866 Tommy really started to bloom. The gentlemen of The Royal and Ancient were noticing his play in St Andrews and, although they did not yet invite him to partner them in matches, it was thought that he brought a new style of play into the game.

The graceful swing or sweep of the club that the early writers so much admired was not something that Tommy pretended to. Willie Park's long sweep with a distinct loop at the top may have been effective and his father's 'hunkered' and somewhat laboured swing might have produced results. Yet Tommy, without the restraints of experience, swung the club with a flourish and a dash, the like of which had not been seen before. The Rev. W. Proudfoot wrote, 'Tommy was the embodiment of masterful energy. Every muscle of his well-knit frame seemed summoned into service. He stood well back from the ball, and with dashing, pressing, forceful style of driving, which seldom failed, sent it whizzing on its far and sure flight.'

His swing was quick and wristy. He hit the ball hard and when he needed it to go further he hit it harder, eschewing the maxim that pressing courts disaster. It was said that he could break a shaft with the force of his preliminary waggle on addressing the ball. He accepted no conventions and created a variety of shots hitherto unknown. The rut iron, a club with a very small, lofted head that most players carried to extricate the ball from ruts or rabbit scrapes, he used to great effect, floating the ball up to the flag in a wide variety of approach strokes. In essence Tommy followed Allan Robertson in developing the lofted shot to the flag.

He carried two putters and used them both differently. On a good surface he putted with a wooden-headed putter that had a longish shaft with which he was described as 'invincible', while on poorer greens he used an iron-headed driving club with a little loft on it and with a very short shaft. He had, in fact, invented the 'jigger', the pitch-and-run approach shot that would become popular on all links courses in years to come.

As well as a new range of shots, Tommy also brought a fresh attitude to the game and it was one that was not altogether appreciated by his elders and betters; an attitude that might be described as self-confidence bordering on arrogance. It was also hinted at the time that Tommy had a disrespectful attitude, with a touch of the mercenary about him, and that he could be altogether too familiar. Certainly Tommy must have found his position difficult on many occasions, because at Ayr Academy he could well have been seated next to a boy destined to become one of the gentlemen players who might now call upon his services as a foursomes partner.

The Chartists, the forerunners of the trades union movement, were gaining ground in society at large and the question of privilege as a birth-right was one of the intensely debated issues of the day. Tommy and his friends in Prestwick were ambitious. Witnessing the 'good life' at first hand every day in school and on the links must have made them even more so. His childhood friend and sister's beau, James Hunter, for instance, certainly coupled hard work and determination with ambition, making him a very wealthy man. Tommy was naturally flamboyant but he clearly had a similar drive and determination to better himself. It was most probably this, as much as his lifestyle, that brought him into conflict with his father and which was much commented upon at the time.

Unlike his father, Tommy not only welcomed challenges but also issued them. He was not prepared to leave the rewards for his play to the whims of benefactors and often played and partnered for an agreed sum. The pots and spin-offs from the bets were secondary. He simply revolutionized the game as it then was, and every professional golfer who followed after him benefited.

Tommy may have come into the golfing public's eye as a boy in Perth in 1864, but it was at Carnoustie in September 1867 that he showed his true mettle. Tommy Morris, at the age of sixteen, won his first tournament. Against a field made up of the best from St Andrews, Musselburgh, Perth and Prestwick, after three rounds of the 10-hole course, he was tied for the lead with Willie Park and Bob Andrews on a score of 140. The subsequent one-round play-off was reported by the *Dundee Advertiser* to have created much interest and 'a great number of spectators accompanied them round the Links'. The newspaper also noted that 'Morris headed his opponents from the first, and kept and improved his lead to the end, coming in the winner with a splendid score of 42', which was four strokes ahead of Bob Andrews, Willie Park having retired when he 'had the misfortune to send his ball into the Burn'. The newspaper also reported that Tommy's score 'was the theme of admiration of both professionals and amateurs, and three hearty cheers were given for the youthful champion when he "holed" his last shot'. The Earl of Dalhousie had put up the £20 cash professional prize money and Tommy had won half of it, and no doubt the approbation of his father who had thought little of his chances in the play-off, remarking, 'He's ower young'.

A post-tournament match took place between Willie Park and Tommy for £5. The young contender thrashed the champion over three rounds by 8 up and 7 to play. His play at Carnoustie that week was a portent of what was to come.

Tommy's fast-growing friendship with Davie Strath, Andrew's youngest brother, was put to the test on the Links at St Andrews after the 1866 Spring Meeting. The gentlemen collected together a sum of £20 (the local paper suggested) and the two boys played two rounds of the course for it. Tommy triumphed, but only just. Against Davie Strath in a post-tournament match watched by a large crowd, however, he lost on the last green when Davie holed a long putt. The two would be matched again and again throughout the years, sometimes head-to-head, sometimes in foursomes play with a gentleman partner when the odds had to be bargained.

Tommy's headgear marked the stages in his life. He went from being a boy wearing the traditional round cheesecutter cap with a shiny polished leather peak, to a youth with a felt cap, until he arrived at manhood with his defining blue glengarry bonnet.

There can be little doubt that Tommy was a flamboyant figure who played to the crowd. As his headgear changed so did his attire, imitating the dandy of the day with Beau Brummell lapels and waistcoat piping. His swing, always fast, took on a flourish that 'near spun him off his feet', and sent the glengarry flying from his head, to be returned to him from a scramble of admirers.

But if his game was flashy it was also effective. In 1866 Willie Park won the Champion's Belt, two strokes clear of his brother David. Tommy was a long way down the field, nine strokes behind his father and nearly twenty behind Willie Park. In 1867 Tom had his last victory for the Belt, with Tommy five strokes away, placed fourth behind Willie Park and Andrew Strath. The signs were already there; Tommy was learning and learning fast. If Tom Morris and Willie Park were not aware then, it would not be long before they realised that their period of supremacy was drawing to an end.

It is not difficult to explain Tommy's ascent. Maturity and increasing physical strength, the ability to know when, and when not, to take risks, how to make strokes and how to save them, turned Tommy into the complete golfer. But development of the competitive edge was also important. Johnny Allan had come through from Prestwick to work at the club maker's bench for a year in 1865. Johnny brought the strength he had developed in his father's stonemason's yard to the game and he, together with Davie Strath and young Bob Kirk, made the going in St Andrews far from easy. But two other already established players were coming to prominence. In St Andrews there was Jamie Anderson, and in Musselburgh, Bob Ferguson was making an impression on Willie Park.

The Morrises would have first encountered Bob Ferguson as a youth of eighteen at the Leith Tournament in 1867. He was the surprise winner of the £10 purse on offer then and, as a result of this famous victory, Sir Charles Tennant was prepared to back him against all-comers over the links at Musselburgh. It is clear that Bob regarded Tommy with great affection and held him in some esteem. The two played many money and exhibition matches in the Lothians and Fife and it is from Bob's reminiscences that we have the best overall account of Tommy's play, particularly his devastating putting. Bob insisted that Tommy was the greatest player in the world and the finest golfer that he ever played against. After suffering a heavy defeat at Luffness, Bob remarked that he had never seen golf played like it. 'Time and again,' he said, 'Tommy would make his putt and watch the ball progress towards the hole with the words to his caddy, "Pick it out the hole, laddie".'

Jamie Anderson was already a part of their every day lives in St Andrews and although nine years older, he was one of Tommy's regular playing partners. The Andersons, as neighbours and family friends, were particularly close to the Morris family. Tom had made feathery balls with Da', Jamie's father, in Allan Robertson's front room and Jof, when still a boy, carried Jamie's clubs and was his frequent playing partner as a man. Jamie Anderson partnered and opposed Tommy in foursomes matches but there is no record of them challenging for a large sum of money. Jamie left no record of his impressions either of Tommy or of golf in his time. Like his father, Jamie was a retiring person: unlike him, he enjoyed the drink a little too much, which eventually led to his downfall.

17 The Finest Rounds Ever Played

In 1868, Tommy won his first Champion's Belt with the phenomenal score of 154, eight strokes better than the previous best of Andrew Strath in 1865. His father took second place, three strokes adrift, with Bob Andrew from Perth in third place and Willie Park in fourth.[1]

The outcome of this championship is remarkable. For the first and, almost certainly, the last time, a son and his father took first and second places respectively in the Open. Tommy was only 17 and his father was 47 years old.

When the time came round again for the 1869 Autumn Meeting of the Prestwick Club and the Challenge Belt competition, Tommy was ready.

David Strath entered the field for the first time that year, having just left his secure job at a clerk's desk to make a life in golf. Tom was not playing particularly well and one can only surmise that the pressure of laying out courses and work on the Links of St Andrews were taking their toll. For whatever reason, his play was indifferent in the event, and for that matter, anywhere else, that year.

Tommy was at his best, however, and was to remain at his best. He won the Challenge Belt again in 1869 with the remarkable score of 157, eleven strokes ahead of Bob Kirk in second place, with Davie Strath third and Jamie Anderson fourth. Neither Willie Park nor Bob Andrew showed up at Prestwick that year and the field was small. This may well have been due to the acceptance of Tommy's invincibility, for the talk in every golfing howf in the land was about the play in St Andrews. Firstly Jamie Anderson and then, only weeks later, Tommy, on two successive occasions that summer, had equalled Allan Robertson's record 79 strokes over the St Andrews Links. Tommy had also swept all before him at Burntisland and North Berwick where he had won every prize on offer over the two-day meetings.

In that year's Open, the excitement at Prestwick was undoubtedly about Tommy's hole in one in the first round at the 8th, the 166-yard Station

Hole. It was the first recorded at Prestwick and the first in the Open Championship. Tommy was breaking new ground in every respect.

Jamie Anderson's first attempt at the Belt came in 1869, while Bob Ferguson of Musselburgh had already made an appearance the previous year, creditably finishing in 5th place. Both were Tommy's seniors by several years and both were established winners. The reason for their absence from the earlier championships could not have been penury because Jamie had been prepared to travel to Montrose, Perth and Leith to play. Bob Ferguson had made the same journeys as well as to St Andrews. Lack of self-belief seems to have been the problem. Both probably considered Willie Park and Tom Morris to have a stranglehold on the Championship. The emergence of young Tommy and the fact that both had beaten the Park and Morris old brigade, seems to have broken down psychological barriers. Bob Ferguson had clearly eclipsed Willie Park at Musselburgh and, at St Andrews, Jamie Anderson had created a stir on 19 August 1869 by setting a new course record with a round of 77. When Tommy recorded the same score in May 1870, the newspapers made much of it and Jamie Anderson had to take it upon himself to write to the editor of the *Fifeshire Journal* to remind him of his precedence.

It is worth reflecting on these two rounds of golf, for they were an achievement that is probably unsurpassed in the game. The heads of the wooden clubs were, by today's standards, not at all conducive to sending the ball a long way and the irons had no markings on the face, so backspin was virtually impossible. The performance of the hand-hammered gutta ball was substantially less than the revolutionary rubber-cored ball introduced at the beginning of the twentieth century, and a world away from the today's high-technology balls.

It is the consideration of the course that they played that confounds and amazes. Even with the availability of the horse-drawn mower, the fairways were little more than rough tracks of grass interspersed with whin bushes on both sides. Bunkers were natural sandy scrapes, or sometimes simply huge sand dunes, pitted with rabbit holes, completely unkempt and untended in any way. The greens were in general no better than today's fairways and would be derided by today's golfers. From a combination of maps and contemporary accounts, we can put together a picture of how the course appeared in 1870. What we cannot do, however, is describe the accuracy or the power and dexterity required to play the course at St Andrews in 77 strokes at that time.[2]

It was the 1870 competition for the Belt that was Tommy's greatest challenge because, if he became victorious, he would win the trophy outright. He certainly prepared well for the task. He travelled the length and breadth of the country playing competitive golf, and his progress was extensively covered in the press. He went down to Westward Ho! in Devon, playing against Johnny Allan and Bob Kirk, then to London at Blackheath where he was matched against Bob Kirk again. On his way north, he went next to the Liverpool Golf Club at Hoylake, the course that Tommy's uncle George had laid out the year before and that his cousin, Jack Morris, had been left to look after.[3]

It is clear from contemporary newspaper accounts that Tommy had achieved sporting celebrity status. His play filled many column inches and when, on 3 May 1870, he went round the St Andrews Links in 77 strokes, his supremacy was widely noted. After this time, every national newspaper carried the results of golfing events in the *Sporting Intelligence* columns.

There can be no doubting that Tommy's travels and the newspaper coverage he was attracting were responsible for the increase in the size of the 1870 field for the Champion's Belt. He may also have been responsible for James Hunter, his boyhood friend from the Red Lion at Prestwick, entering the fray. James had already established a reputation as a player at Prestwick, as well as at St Andrews, where he was a frequent visitor with Tom's daughter, Lizzie Morris, their childhood friendship having flowered into courtship and a promise of betrothal.

The *Ayr Advertiser* named the entries for the Belt that year but also devoted a full column to Tommy. It is clear that Prestwick considered him a favourite son and equally clear that Tommy relished his popularity there. The crowd that flocked to see the competition for the Belt was huge, the like of which would not be seen again for many years. Complaints about the spectators were many and vociferous. The newspapers opined that the majority were 'clearly completely new to the sport', and were 'decidedly unruly in most part'.

If the crowd was unruly, it did not affect Tommy in the slightest. Indeed, he must have been inspired by it. His first round of twelve holes in 47 strokes, taking into account the clubs, the gutta ball and the rudimentary greenkeeping of the day, is arguably the greatest ever played. It was certainly the lowest for Prestwick and therefore for the Championship; Tommy's score was never bettered for as long as the gutta ball was in use. If his play at many of the holes merits a eulogy, then his three at the opening hole, a mighty five hundred and ten yards generally held to be the equivalent of a par six with hickory clubs and gutta ball, deserves an anthem. That Tommy holed his third shot with a cleek was stupendous. Even walking the links as they are today, one is left awe-struck and doubting.

Tommy built on his first-round lead, producing the three lowest rounds played in the Championship, 47, 51 and 51, for a total of 149 to win by a margin of 12 strokes, leaving the press of the day, as well as the rest of the field, stunned. Davie Strath and Bob Kirk were joint runners up on 161, with Tom in fourth place on 162; Willie Park was a further eleven shots behind Tom. It was Tommy's finest hour and certainly a great day for all the Morris family and their friends in Prestwick, as well as their cohorts from St Andrews. Tommy had won the Challenge Belt for the last time; indeed it was the last time that anybody would win it. His third successive win made the Belt his personal property.

It was a great day in Prestwick, but it was a bittersweet one for Tom. Colonel James Ogilvy Fairlie had died only four weeks before the Autumn Meeting and Tom would have felt keenly his absence on this great day. His great benefactor, friend, sometime partner and mentor, had not lived to see his 'laddie' make the Belt his own.

The celebrations of Tommy's success in Prestwick were continued in St Andrews. By the evening of Saturday, 17 September 1870, everyone in St Andrews would have learned that Tommy Morris, and his father, Davie Strath and Bob Kirk, were all about to return from the Open Golf Championship at Prestwick. Some folk would walk down the Links and out on the Station Road behind the 17th green to meet the train as it puffed its way along the Eden estuary and across the Links into the station. Others, the womenfolk and the elderly and infirm, with perhaps a few of the gentlemen players maintaining their dignity, would simply linger about Tom Morris's shop doorway and wait to welcome the conquerors home.

There would certainly have been little play on the Links that day, and if any player had been so out of touch as to seek a caddy for his clubs he would have got short shrift. St Andrews Links, and indeed the whole Town, was in a high state of excitement, for the news had long since spread that Young Tommy Morris had made the Belt his own. But it was not simply that he had won it that swelled the public pride, for that was near enough a foregone conclusion; it was the fact that he had won it by 12 strokes from his two close friends and rivals, young Bob Kirk and Davie Strath. More than that, his father was only a further stroke adrift and Jamie Anderson, on his first outing, was not far behind. St Andrews had virtually made a clean sweep of the great Championship at Prestwick if Bob Kirk, then resident at Blackheath but a St Andrean nonetheless, was included. More important still was the fact that neither the renowned Willie Park nor any of his tribe from Musselburgh had come close to the St Andrews brigade. Yes indeed, it was a great day for the 'Auld Grey Toon', and it was a great night as well. Young Tommy's friends carried him shoulder high from the train, all the way up the Links and into Mr Leslie's Golf Inn, where an enthusiastic reception awaited them.

A flag had flown outside Tom Morris's shop since Thursday when the news had first come through from Prestwick. Hardly surprising then, that everyone who was anyone on the Links had gathered in the Golf Inn to celebrate Young Tommy's success, drink a toast to his and everyone else's health and maybe try on the Championship Belt. And if anybody was prepared to sing, recite a verse, or even feel inclined to say a few words, he would doubtless be given a receptive hearing.

James Denham took the floor to propose a toast to Tommy, saying that although no one doubted that he would do it, his achievement was nevertheless truly remarkable and one unlikely to be repeated. Tommy, in response, thanked his friends for their warm welcome home, the like of which he had never expected. He said that he had set out to make the Belt his own three years ago but, (doubtless with a nod to Davie Strath, Bobby Kirk and finally his father), his friends had not made his task easy. Then Henry Farnie of the *Fifeshire Journal*, who was there to record it all, made a toast to Old Tom. In reply, Tom said that he had very nearly won three in a row himself in 1863, but the Cardinal's Bunker at Prestwick had put paid to his hopes in the second round that year.

Tom must have reflected upon a remarkable year. Not only was his son established as the undisputable Champion Golfer of his time, but Tom himself, through his own achievements and with a little reflected glory, had become something of a celebrity. For any golfer coming to St Andrews to play, or even merely to watch, whether nobility, celebrity or ordinary person, a meeting and a word with Tom Morris was an integral part of that experience. Tom had met Dr Simpson, the first man to use chloroform in anaesthesia, when a party of medical men came over from Edinburgh to watch him and Tommy take on Davie Strath and Jamie Anderson. A whole host of men of letters came to stay with Mr Blackwood, the publisher, who rented Strathtyrum House from the Cheapes. Men like Dean Stanley, Thomas Hughes, James Froude, John Everett Millais, Charles Kingsley and Anthony Trollope, names that meant little enough to Tom, but neverthe-less merited a mention in the local paper and caused quite a stir in the Town and on the Links. Tom may not have been aware of it, but he and golf were emerging as topics of conversation in society. To the majority, entirely unfamiliar with the game, he and golf were synonymous.

But 1870 was also the year when Tom had given of his best against Willie Park and had nothing to show for it, despite weeks of training and preparation. He had even set aside his pipe to get himself into perfect fitness. In the spring, the gambling men had persuaded him to take on Willie in another marathon match over four links and one hundred and forty four holes of golf. They had raised £100 a side for it, just as they had done in 1856 and 1858 when Willie won, and again in 1868 when Tom took the honours. He had never expected it to happen again, indeed he had vowed that it would not, but on Thursday 14 April, he walked out of his shop at ten o'clock in the morning to greet Willie Park. The newspaper reported that the crowd was so large that a rope was needed to keep them back and Colonel Dougall, the referee, had to appeal for order before they even played away from the 1st tee. It was a close run thing at St Andrews, but it ended with Willie one up on the day with 108 holes left to play.

The crowd at Prestwick on the next Thursday was just as large but thankfully more orderly. Tom took a 5-hole lead in the first round, but Willie pulled it back through the other two rounds, leaving Tom only one up at the end of play. At North Berwick on the following Tuesday they left the course with Tom holding a 1-hole lead. There were only 36 holes left at Musselburgh on Friday, when Tom and Willie met to resolve the match, together with a crowd of some six to seven thousand people and young Mr Robert Chambers, the referee.

From the start the crowd was out of control and Mr Chambers threatened to abandon the match after only three holes if order was not restored. With Tom being jeered and jostled, they somehow got round the course twice, although the very partisan crowd made it near impossible to move, far less swing a club.

In an article appearing some twenty years later in the magazine *Golf*, A.H. Doleman related that,

> At Mrs Foreman's, Tom missed a short putt which gave Willie the hole and made him two up and six to play on the match. The excitement was intense, and Park's supporters cheered lustily. Tom went into Mrs Foreman's, as Willie thought, merely for a refreshment, but never returned to play. After waiting nearly half an hour, Willie played out the remaining six holes, and claimed the match. The conduct of the referee on this occasion was much blamed at the time . . .

Willie was up in the match when Mr Chambers called a halt and they apparently retired to, or, more accurately, sought refuge in, Mrs Foreman's pub. The referee felt that they should try again the next day, but Willie would have none of it and played on by himself, claiming the match and the purse. The *Golf* article drew responses from others who had witnessed the match and they proved as partisan then as they had twenty years earlier. Doleman, a Musselburgh man, considered the allegation of undue partisanship to be exaggerated. Others, particularly from St Andrews, took an entirely different view. The entire proceedings at Musselburgh were farcical and made even more so when the betting men brought in an arbitrator who took six months to settle the issue as 'game null and void'. Life was never dull at the golf with Willie Park.

18 Renovations in Making the Play

In the 1860s when Tom took up his tenure on the Links, The Royal and Ancient Golf Club had improvements in mind, as did the Town Council. The Council had introduced bathing coaches to the West Sands in 1864; tree planting was being extended in South Street and general improvements made to the Cathedral and Castle accesses. The Royal and Ancient Clubhouse was in the process of having a striking bay window added to the frontage which was completed in September 1866. A veranda with outdoor seating would be added to complement it.

The 1850s and 1860s were an age of improvement in society in general but in agriculture the rate of change was spectacular. Growing flax and lin-seed had given way in Fife to cereal production and, with the introduction of mechanisation such as McCormick's reaper from America and Shank's newly developed grass mower, there was an excess of local land labourers. In 1855 Allan Robertson made the six-hole course for the Cupar Golf Club, and although it is not known to what extent he re-shaped this agricultural land, it is hard to imagine that the fast-growing summer grasses were con-trolled without the use of the horse-drawn cutting blade or the mower for the greens. This course, on the meadowland at Tailabout on the banks of the river Eden, was probably the first proper inland course to be built on good agricultural land. Doubtless the Fife lairds in The Royal and Ancient made every piece of mechanical machinery available to Tom for what followed.

Almost immediately on his arrival in St Andrews, Tom was engaged in overseeing the construction of a road across the 1st and 18th fairways. Today it is whimsically called 'Granny Clark's Wynd', and was opened in May 1866 to facilitate the movement of holidaymakers to and from the West Sands. At the same time, he completed the 'redding-up' and reseeding of the rough ground to the west, between this road and the Burn, the area of land where Halket's Bunker was once situated. The *St Andrews Gazette* agreed that 'the area is no longer the mess that it was'.

The road across the Links was constructed after an event that must have distressed golfers at the time but greatly pleased the agricultural community. In October 1865, high surging seas deposited a huge amount of wrack (seaweed) on the West Sands. This material was the only source of fertiliser for fields, other than farmyard manure, and was a bonanza to the local farmers who immediately set about recovering it before it could be lost to the next tide. Expediently, the farmers carted the wrack only a few yards to security on to the 1st fairway. The prodigious amount of material was built into great middens that took up most of the right hand side between the Burn and The Royal and Ancient Clubhouse.

In the weeks that followed, the farmers transferred the wrack midden to the fields and in the process wrought terrible damage on the course, paying little heed to the established roadway across the fairway. The ruts made by the narrow-wheeled carts were widespread and as well as re- establishing the road to make sure that such damage could not be caused again, re-turfing of the whole area was also begun and lasted for the next three years. This was the first major improvement on the Links. It led to the complete banking and control of the Burn and made what is now the 1st green possible, and ultimately the right hand side of the Old Course as we know it today.

In retrospect it becomes clear that a general plan of improvement for the Course and its surrounds was under way. It is equally clear that it was not Tom's plan alone. The first significant change had been made in 1857 when Allan Robertson had supervised the extension of the greens on all but the 9th and 18th to accommodate two holes. The scale of the changes that Tom oversaw between 1866 and 1879, however, was such that it required not only the financial muscle of the Club and the support of the Town Council, but also the co-operation of the Strathtyrum estate and the Cheape family. It also required the compliance of the house builders in the Town.

When Tom first put up his sign over the shop door, the Sandyhill area at the top of the Links in front of the old Union Parlour was rough and undulating. The strip of the 1st and 18th fairways all the way down to the Burn was similar with scatterings of sparse grassy patches that had long suffered from the intrusions of the sea. The Home, or 18th green, was situated some 30–40 yards in front of where the green is today and was reported to be 'on broken ground in a hollow, with the ground sloping down both sides'.

Above this, a trough or gully ran across the Links from opposite Tom's shop door, passing in front of the Clubhouse to the beach. The sole remnant of this today is 'The Valley of Sin', at the approach to the 18th green. The area above this gully up to the bank in front of the Clubhouse was used as a small putting green; the teeing ground for the 1st hole was on the other side of the gully from the Clubhouse towards the road. All of this, the rough Sandyhill and the hollow across the course, would be banked, levelled and smoothed during the winters of 1867 and 1868, leaving it roughly what it is today.[1]

At the Spring Meeting of The Royal and Ancient in May 1869, the new Home green came into play to general acclaim but it would take another twenty years for the 18th green to expand to what it is today. In 1869 it was less than half its present size with the hole sited, as it is now for every major championship, above 'The Valley of Sin'. It would be interesting to know whose idea it was to leave that treacherous little hollow when the gully was filled in and the whole levelled. Was it ever a bunker? Was it intended to be a bunker? Perhaps we will never know, but ever since its fateful founding in 1869, it has been the most telling place for a ball to come to rest, on an otherwise benign hole.

Tom's attentions were not confined to the top of the Links. In 1866, at the same time as the *St Andrews Gazette* was reporting that the first teeing ground was being set by the road (Granny Clark's Wynd) across the Links and that 'a notice was posted within the first hole that the last was shut up for repairs', the paper was also announcing that there were now 'fewer feezers' or 'cupped lies' on the Links. Tom had started directing the filling of divots and some roughly pitted areas with sand in January 1866. A year later, the newspaper was remarking upon the 'heaps of sand everywhere on the Links'. Tom was coating the Links with sand, contract-carted from the beach and deposited at strategic points about the Course. It was to be a recurring winter treatment, initially regarded with derision but eventually with general acclaim.

The building up and levelling of the land on which the present day first hole green is sited was completed in 1870 when the Swilken Burn was enclosed and its course to the sea fixed with stone-sided banking. The ground on which the green is formed is the product of infilling the Burn's banking with spoil from the Town's construction sites, as is the level land on the approaches to the Burn.

The Burn, which snakes its way across the 1st and 18th fairways, had long been a problem on the Links. Flooding at high spring tides and during heavy rain was a recurring event that Provost Playfair had done much to alleviate with the construction of breakwaters in the 1830s. The Burn, however, remained a muddy morass in places and its course was not helped with the banking up of the upper reaches when the Station Road Bridge was built in 1850 to carry the road behind the 17th green to the railway station. With copious amounts of good soil available from the Town's building sites, banking the Burn and levelling the land along its length became possible. This was an extensive task and although there is little note of it in the Club's minutes it must have been ongoing for several years, for the bottom of the Burn is today some three to four feet vertically below the level of the 1st green.[2] Fixing of the Burn's course generated today's 1st green, but it did more than that, for what followed would eventually transform the golf course.

Although the work of raising the level of the land is clear to see in the stonework along the length of the Burn, it is hard to reconcile the siting and structure of the Swilken Bridge with this event. The bridge has become a landmark in golf and its great antiquity is undoubted. On early maps it is labelled the 'Golfers Bridge', and its purpose was surely as a passage for golfers over the morass of the Burn. It can be seen as a feature in a *circa* 1740 oil painting of the Links. It is also shown in many early photographs where, as in the painting, it can be seen as a more extensive structure than it is today. It is clear that when the Burn was banked much of the bridge was buried.

Today's 1st green came into play in the autumn of 1872, but the completion of it did not in itself make anti-clockwise play on the course possible. For that to happen much more extensive work on the golfing ground was needed.

In October 1870 the most telling, and in the long term, most significant event occurred. After the Autumn Meeting that year, the local press warned that extensive whin burning was about to be undertaken on the Links. The paper also gave due notice, under the headline 'Links Improvements', that big changes were about to take place. The piece reads:

> The extension of the golf course, which has been spoken of for some time past, seems about to be carried into effect. The course is already staked off [sic] and we learn that operations are to be carried out immediately to have it cleared of whins and bent. That it will eventually prove a boon to golfers is undoubted, but we fear that a considerable time must elapse before it becomes popular, as the roughness and spongy nature of the ground will make play more difficult. But while our golfers are to enjoy a greater liberty, we fear that those of our citizens who are in the habit of making a promenade of that portion of the links will be inclined to complain a little at the curtailment of their pleasure ground.

In the event, there were no complaints. Despite the awful sight of the burning and uprooting of the whins, no letters to the editor appeared. It comes as a surprise that in a council chamber divided bitterly over almost every issue and in a township with a vociferous conservative minority, no one appears to have voiced an objection to the changes.

The area that was burned and from which the whin roots and bent were removed, extended from today's 2nd tee to the intersection of the 7th and 11th fairways, almost the entire length of the northern side of the course. This clearance considerably increased the width of the course, laying bare land that would require very extensive work to make it fit for golf. It would lay the basis for the further extension of the greens and for the outgoing fairways on the modern-day anti-clockwise course. Much manpower and expense would however be needed. This is reflected in the minute books of The Royal and Ancient Club where the annual expenditure for upkeep of the Links, which had long averaged less than £50 a year, more than doubled abruptly in 1876-77 and persisted at this level throughout the next decade.

Links land fit for golf may have been readily won from the whins with effort and manpower, but protecting it from wind and waves at the High Hole, where the course runs into the Eden Estuary, was another matter. It was the area of the Course that caused Tom and his predecessors the greatest anguish and it took knowledge and guile to stabilise it.

It is clear, from a report of a conversation with his friend David Louden in 1907, that Tom's greatest difficulty with maintenance of the Course was caused by the green and its surrounds of the High Hole, the 7th and 11th. Tom is quoted as saying that the High Hole:

> has gi'en me mair bother than a' the rest o' them put together. The Hole was a great deal nearer the Eden in oor young day than it is noo; an' the neighbourhood o' the hole was aye changin' an' the hole itsel sometimes filled up efter a heavy storm at sea. The saund drifted up wi' the gale an' the puttin' green was often little better than a bunker. As ane o' my auld cronies ance said to me: "It's whiles ae thing, an' whiles anither an' whiles a' thing mixed thegither." There was naething to kep the saund. But, aboot the 'ear 1847 – the last year o' the "featheries" – Charlie Howie, the nurseyman at Law Park, took it in his head to saw [sow] what he ca'd Sea-Lyme Gress, which, he said, throve fine at Kinkell Cave an' the Dennis Wark. He sent to Holland for aboot half a stane o' seed, an' sawed it along the bank o' the Eden, an' it throve fine

there awa'. It keppit the saund round aboot its wiry roots, an' in time reclaimed a guide lump o' grund. At the present time it is aboot eighteen yairds ayont the auld edge which used to be proppit up 'wi' planks, ye mind. A new green has been made at a lower level on the grund reclaimed by the Lyme Grass. The High Hole was also the first on the Links that had a sheet-iron case put in to keep it in proper shape. I fell on that plan efter a gude deal o' study, an' it suited to a tee. Then, when ither holes got raggit roond their edges, I had them dune up i' the same wye, an' that was the beginnin' o' the modern style o' the hole tin.'

Although the major changes that Tom oversaw on the Links were carried out between 1865 and 1872, he continued to develop and improve the course throughout the 1870s and 1880s. With the completion of what is today the 1st green and with the extensive clearance of the whins all along the north or sea side, an altogether new course emerged. As the greens were extended it became possible to play both clockwise and anti-clockwise. We will never know if this was part of a grand plan because it is unrecorded. It is clear, however, that what may have been a novelty at the time quickly became an expedient solution to the problems of wear and tear for, by the late 1870s, Tom was switching the direction of play regularly. It was in 1876 that the modern-day layout had its first tournament play with the Open Championship of that year.

Tom's amiability, diplomacy and tact may have played some part in carrying out these extensive changes without objections. He was clearly clever in eliciting support and astute in keeping the public informed. The changes on the Links between 1866 and 1880 would probably have met with furious objection had they have been perceived to have come from The Royal and Ancient Club alone. Tom, through his network of caddies and townsmen golfers, almost certainly paved the way for a smooth passage, not only through the local golfing community, but also through the council chamber. Although he may have crucially won the townspeople's support, an altogether higher authority must have had a hand in dealing with Mr Cheape of Strathtyrum, the owner of the Links.

At the conclusion of club dinners it was a long-standing tradition to raise a glass to toast Mr Cheape – 'Laird of the Links'. Three generations of Cheapes had done their bit to preserve the Links for golf. When the family had first come into ownership of the Links in the early 1800s, the estate set 'march stones', to designate the limits of the golfing ground. The Cheape estate had also seen to it that the tenant of Balgove Farm respected these limits and was, furthermore, expected to police the ground to see that no harm came to it. The 'march stones', which can be seen to this day, were inscribed with a 'G' on one side and 'C' on the other, representing 'Golf' and 'Cheape'. About 26 stones were put in place to set the limits of the golfing ground. Some became redundant and disappeared on the western side with the building of the railway line and the station along the length of the present day 16th and 17th holes, and by the construction of the estate wall along much of the 14th fairway. Some of these stones have been removed altogether to accommodate modern greenkeeping machinery and some have been relocated, but enough remain to show the extent of the renovations on the Links that took place. Those that can be seen today in the middle of the 4th, 5th and 7th fairways designate what was then the eastern limits of the course before the whins were removed, and their locations reflect the extent of Tom's renovations.

Improvements to the course never ceased, as the Club accounts of the time show. Tom's work extended to every department of play. As well as the new 18th and 1st greens being built, the 7th green was formed by extension of the 11th, the High Hole. The remaining greens were extended and partially re-turfed; the double green of the 6th and 12th holes was totally reconstructed and turf laid over what had hitherto been a sandy surface. Bunkers were also constructed and some filled in. In the early 1880s Tom introduced revetting of bunker faces to keep them in good order and had instituted the routine of divot filling.

It is clear that Tom was in a position to draw upon labour to carry out the extensive renovations at this time, but it is equally clear that the achievement was Herculean. That he found time for competition play, particularly his marathon with Willie Park in 1870 at the peak of his activities, was extraordinary. That he also had time to visit and advise on the development of new golfing greens, as well as maintaining his expanding business, must mean that he enjoyed much support. It is a delightful irony to read in the Ayrshire press that Tom arrived at Prestwick for the 1868 Open Championship 'at the eleventh hour due, it is said, to pressure of work at home'.

19 An Unlikely Match

There was no Open Golf Championship in 1871. Without the Belt to play for and no Colonel Fairlie to stir things and keep events moving forward, nothing happened. It would take another year to pass for a further initiative which inevitably came from Prestwick. With Tom Morris firmly established in St Andrews, it is hardly surprising that The Royal and Ancient should have a hand in it.

Various proposals were made for a new trophy and the continuation of the Open and early discussions took place between Prestwick, The Royal and Ancient and the Honourable Company based in Musselburgh. In April, at the Spring Meeting of the Prestwick Club, Gilbert Mitchell Innes put forward the motion:

> In contemplation of St Andrews, Musselburgh and other Clubs joining in the purchase of a belt to be played for over four or more greens it is not expedient for the Club to provide a belt to be played for solely at Prestwick.

Harry Hart, the Prestwick Secretary, however, clearly had ambitions to keep the Championship at Prestwick, because he proposed an amendment to the effect that the Club should provide a new belt and continue to host the Championship. While this amendment was defeated and the original motion passed, other issues were still to be decided. Both North Berwick and Westward Ho! were put forward as possible additional venues to Prestwick, St Andrews and Musselburgh. Without doubt, the financing of any new trophy and prize money would have featured prominently in the discussions. In the event, matters were not settled early enough for the Championship to be held at the usual time after the Autumn Meeting in 1871. However, two professional tournaments were held in that year, one at St Andrews which Tommy won, with Davie Strath second, and the other at Carnoustie where the positions were reversed.

By 11 September 1872 agreement had finally been reached between Prestwick, The Royal and Ancient and the Honourable Company. These three clubs were to stage the Championship in rotation, starting with Prestwick, followed by St Andrews and then Musselburgh. The Claret Jug, the 'Golf Champion Trophy', was commissioned at a cost of £30, the three clubs contributing equally. The total prize money was fixed at £20 with £8 for the winner and five other prizes. The Champion was also to receive a medal with his name and score engraved on the reverse side, a tradition continued to this day.

The Open Championship was resumed in October 1872 at Prestwick and Tommy began his assault for the 'Golf Champion Trophy', where he had left off with the Champion's Belt in 1870. His dominance, however, was not as absolute. He beat Davie Strath by just three strokes, taking 166 for the 36 holes. The field was small because the Championship had been organized hurriedly and the new trophy was not yet ready. The Claret Jug was finally completed in 1873 and the engraving of the Champion's name backdated to 1872. Tom Morris Jnr is the first name on it. This was his fourth successive victory in the Open Championship, a feat not equalled today, but it would be the only time that he won the new trophy.

It has been said that Tommy never achieved such heights again, but perhaps this was not the case. Tommy had pulled the game, and his contemporaries, up to a higher level and he had to live with the consequences. It is possible, of course, that he had lost some of that determined competitive edge, but he continued to play in challenge matches with much the same ratio of success and failure. He probably had problems in 'coming down to earth', because after winning the Belt outright in 1870 in Prestwick, his play back in St Andrews following The Royal and Ancient's Autumn Meeting was poor. In the 'Put-ins', by then called the ' Professional Prizes', for a total purse of £25, Tommy picked up his ball after only four holes. This event was the first outing in the professional ranks for Tommy's younger brother, fifteen-year-old Jof, who did not fare well. Davie Strath took the first prize with Bob Ferguson second and Tom third.

Tommy was far from a spent force, however, for within a month he beat Bob Ferguson over the three greens of Luffness, Musselburgh and North Berwick. Tommy beat him again after the Autumn Meetings in both 1872 and 1873 at St Andrews, atoning for Ferguson's win over the same links in 1871 and he and Davie Strath played some great matches with the outstanding amateurs Robert Clark and Gilbert Mitchell Innes. Tommy was as active as ever, perhaps more so, and even took on James Wolfe Murray who used a bow and arrow instead of club and ball, and was only narrowly beaten.[1] Moreover, if he was not successful in the field for the Champion's Trophy at St Andrews in 1873 and Musselburgh in 1874 he was not far off. His play at St Andrews during 1874 was held to be better than ever. In the course of a series of three-day matches with Davie Strath, held throughout the summer largely to entertain visitors, he equalled the course record of 77. He may no longer have been the official 'Champion Golfer' but he was still the supreme player.

In 1873 at St Andrews, the Championship was reduced to a lottery. Foul weather turned many of the greens to a quagmire with standing water everywhere, from which there was no relief. Tom Kidd won, with Jamie Anderson second and Tommy third, a clean sweep for the St Andrews men. At Musselburgh the following year Tommy was runner-up to Mungo Park, only two strokes behind him. Scoring was high, compared with previous championships, but it was the condition of the Musselburgh links, rather than poor play, that accounted for that. Tommy was far from being a spent force, but he may well have been a distracted golfer, for he had other things on his mind. Tommy Morris was courting Margaret Drinnen.

Although we have some knowledge of Margaret, we know nothing about how, where or when she met Tommy.[2] We can only speculate about this, but the match that he entered into with her was the most unlikely one that Tommy ever made, for their backgrounds and upbringings could not have been more different.

Margaret Drinnen was born in Carluke, Lanarkshire in 1841, in the very heartland of industrial Scotland. Margaret's father, Walter (Watty) Drinnen was a pit sinker, one of a team of miners who dug the shafts to open up the coal and ironstone seams.[3] The Drinnens had to move where Watty's work took him. By 1846, after moves all over Lanarkshire, he, his wife Helen and their six children were settled in 5, Crofthead Road, Crofthead, near Whitburn, one of a row of 129 identical small two-roomed cottages owned by the Coltness Iron Company. With six children, it is astonishing that they could also board John Syme from Bathgate, who worked with their eldest son George, in the ironstone mine of the Coltness Company, some two hundred yards from Crofthead Road. A younger Drinnen son, John, by the age of eleven, was an ironstone drawer in the same company's smelting works.

Whitburn lies between Edinburgh and Glasgow in West Lothian. In the nineteenth century it was a township of coal and ironstone miners living in rows of hastily built company cottages above which loomed the spoil wastes – the 'bings' as they are called in Scotland – of the coal pits and the ironstone mines. The sulphur dioxide in the atmosphere from the iron furnaces polluted the streams and poisoned the plant life in what was once open, fertile countryside. The population of Whitburn and its surrounding mining hamlets was made up of Irish labourers, miners from Yorkshire and those who had migrated for the money from farms to the graft of the mine or the sweat of the furnace floor. The hellish filth and squalor of mid-nineteenth century Whitburn is entirely outwith the experience of present times.

At the time of the census in 1851, Margaret, aged nine and her sister Agnes, aged thirteen, were apprenticed as lace tambourers in the village.[4] Watty had become a pit bottomer controlling the cage that raised and lowered the miners to the coalface. He, too, had been employed by the Coltness Company, but at the age of fifty-nine, he was no longer able to work and had to leave his company cottage. The family moved into another cottage in an even longer row at Millstone Hag, Whitburn, allocated to them because their eldest son George continued to live at home.

Although Watty and Helen had produced ten children, babies continued to arrive. In September 1859, Agnes, aged twenty-one, came home to give birth to her illegitimate son, William Drinnen. Later in the same year she married James Pettigrew, a coal miner from Bathgate. In 1862, Helen, aged nineteen, returned to have her son, also illegitimate and christened Andrew Drinnen. In 1864 she married John Brown, a Whitburn ironstone miner.

As for Margaret, at the age of twenty-five she bore an illegitimate daughter, Helen Stark Drinnen, on 26 May 1866. The baby died eight weeks later and in 1874, she married Tommy Morris, the Champion Golfer from St Andrews.

20 A Tied Match in West Lothian

Tommy probably thought about matrimony when, on 21 June 1874, he took communion in St Andrews Holy Trinity Kirk. His younger siblings, Elizabeth and Jof, had taken their first communion in Holy Trinity two years earlier. The marriage of Tommy Morris and Margaret Drinnen was announced from the pulpit on three successive Sundays and their banns were entered into the Session Book on 22 November 1874.

Tommy's parents did not make the journey to Whitburn on 25 November 1874 for the wedding. Nancy was already severely restricted by rheumatism, frequently in great pain and often required help in movement. On the day of the wedding, Tom hosted a party at St Andrews for Tommy's friends and the men from the workshop, in Honeyman's Golf Hotel, while Tommy took his brother John along as his best man and his sister Elizabeth as best maid, to witness his nuptials.

The marriage register records that the ceremony took place at 'Crofthead', a hamlet within the parish of Whitburn. This means that it did not take place in church (it was common practice in Scotland at the time not to have a church wedding), but almost certainly in the home of the bride's parents, or perhaps in another building. The officiating minister, the Rev. Thomas Bell, would have gone to wherever it was being held.

Remarkably, it was John, and not the older brother Jof, who was Tommy's chief supporter and who witnessed the proceedings and signed the Marriage Register. The paraplegic John needed a trolley for mobility and required lifting up steps, carrying on and off the trains and help onto seats, so someone must have made the journey with Tommy, for he could not have managed to transport John unassisted. With no reported details of the wedding in Whitburn, we can only guess who attended from St Andrews.

Tommy would probably have seen Whitburn and the cottage row at Millstone Hag before, but for John from his trolley, it must all have seemed like a different world, a world well away from genteel St Andrews, with the sand, the sea, and its green and pleasant links land.

It is strange that Tom did not attend his son's wedding. Even if Nancy needed help and nursing at home, there were surely many friends who would have looked after her in her husband's absence. Tom was, after all, away playing golf both the weeks either side of the wedding day and Tommy was undoubtedly the 'apple of his father's eye'.

Did Tom and Nancy disapprove of Margaret? They would certainly have known her well enough, for she had arrived in the Town some time after the census of 1871. Although her name does not appear in the St Andrews census of that year, when the banns of her marriage were called three years later, she was resident in a grand house on the Scores where she was employed as a housemaid. Yet no mention of Margaret was made at the time, despite the fact that Tommy was an enormously popular figure in the Town.

Nor were there, seemingly, any wedding photographs, or indeed any other photograph of Margaret. This is curious, given that St Andrews was well furnished with photographers and Tommy was photographed several times alone and several times with his father and sister. This, and the fact that neither of his parents attended the wedding, remains a mystery.

The fine house that Tommy acquired for his bride in Playfair Place, some one hundred yards up the road from where Tom and Nancy lived at 6 Pilmour Links, certainly attests to the financial well-being of Tommy, for its valuation was almost the same as his father's extensive property.[1] Not for Tommy and his bride the struggle to attain the first rung on the property ladder. The rental on their home was equivalent to the annual income of a trades journeyman, and the fact that Tommy was prepared to show off his financial well-being by renting such a substantial house for himself and his wife bears testimony to his independent attitude. He clearly did not subscribe to the Scots Presbyterian ethos that someone from the working classes simply did not flaunt newly-found prosperity. It is plain that Tommy and his bride were not in penury and were not prepared to live frugally.

What remains unclear are the reasons for the paucity of contemporary recorded information about Margaret. She was ten years older than Tommy and possibly more worldly-wise. The age difference might not have been considered significant at that time, but eight years earlier Margaret had given birth to a daughter out of wedlock. To the pious church-going Morris household, imbued with Victorian respectability, this, if they had known, might well have been a significant obstacle to their approval of her.

Margaret Drinnen was clearly an exceptional woman and some insight into her character can be found in the records of Whitburn Parish Church. Like her sisters, Margaret had acknowledged fornication and her child's illegitimacy before the elders of the Kirk in Whitburn and been admonished before the congregation. This rebuke amounted to 'naming and shaming', with the fornicator being made to sit in front of the church facing the congregation, while the minister admonished her for her sins. In some parishes the sinners sat on a special 'cutty stool', while in others they were forced to stand throughout the service, sometimes for two or three Sundays in succession. Margaret, however, was in some way different from her sisters, as the Whitburn Church records suggest she was spared much of this humiliation.

From the Session Minute Book of the Parish of Whitburn South, three entries can be compared, two relating to Margaret's elder sister Helen and the other to Margaret herself. Firstly, of Helen, we read:

> March 8th 1863. Helen Drinnen compeared before the session acknowledging that she had been guilty of the sin of fornication and this day underwent the discipline of the church and was again restored to its rights and privileges.

> March 15th 1863. With reference to the above minute, Helen Drinnen having been examined on the subject of baptism and its responsibility with approbation was this day admitted to stand as sponsor for her child in the ordinance of baptism.

Then of Margaret:

> July 8th 1866. Margaret Drinnen residing at Crofthead compeared before the session acknowledging guilt of fornication and was very affectionately rebuked and exhorted to walk worthy of her spiritual vocation, her child was at the same time baptised (her having, of course, convened with the moderator).

Margaret's record reads very differently from any other. Why? The fact that she was 'residing' at Crofthead suggests that this was not her usual home, yet we know from the record of the child's birth that she was born there. Margaret had either undergone some heart-wrenching ordeal, or she had put on an incredible performance for the moderator to escape with a mere 'affectionate rebuke'. That her child was baptised at the same time without further exhortation is astonishing. One explanation, however, could be that her daughter Helen was already seriously ill, dying thirteen days later.

Margaret clearly captivated the minister of Holy Trinity and the presbytery of St Andrews as the Rev. A.K.H. Boyd, writing in 1892, effused, 'she was a remarkably handsome and healthy young woman: most lovable in every way.'

In St Andrews, Tommy's marriage was a newsworthy topic and the local papers recorded it in the marriage announcement columns. In West Lothian there was no mention of it. Tommy may have enjoyed celebrity status on the links lands of Scotland, but in the grime of its industrial heartland he was a nobody.

21 American Connections

We may not know how Tommy Morris met Margaret Drinnen, but there is no question about how his sister Elizabeth, known as Lizzie, met James Hunter. Lizzie was born and raised in the Golf House in the High Street at Prestwick, directly across the road from James's home in the Red Lion Inn. The two families were the closest of friends with James being her big brother Tommy's best friend and constant companion. Lizzie and James would be as familiar with each other's households as they were with their own and there could not have been a time in Lizzie's conscious life when James Hunter was not a part of it. If Margaret Drinnen was an unlikely match for Tommy, James Hunter and Lizzie were a pair, so to speak, from the start.

When her family moved from Prestwick to St Andrews in November 1864, Lizzie remained in Prestwick for four years before moving to Leuchars, near St Andrews, to live with her maternal grandmother. She was, however, far from being remote from her family while at Prestwick, for her father and brother Tommy were back there several times a year. Prestwick was all that Lizzie had known and James and his family were the centre of her life.

We also know that she and James were often in St Andrews during their years of courting. The Morris family was proud to keep a record of James's rounds on the St Andrews course where his average score was in the low eighties. James was a golfer, not quite in the top class, but nevertheless good. He was a leading light in the Prestwick St Nicholas Golf Club and a contestant for the Open Championship in 1870 when Tommy claimed the Belt as his own. James was well known in St Andrews and played home-and-home matches with Mr Petrie and Mr Stonehouse, St Andrews businessmen, at Prestwick and St Andrews. He was a successful entrepreneur and enough of a social figure to be present at the re-founding of the Glasgow Golf Club in 1870. Indeed, he and Walter Smith played the inaugural match against Tom and the Captain of the Club, the Lord Provost of Glasgow. The *Fifeshire Journal* reported the event, remarking that Tom had been invited 'to give éclat to the proceedings at South Park on the 10th of March.' That James was involved was at once an acknowledgement of his association with Tom and recognition of his business and social success.

James left Ayr Academy at the age of thirteen and entered the offices of his father's cousin in Ayr. The Hunter business was timber and James made an early and precocious start in it. At the age of fifteen he made the first of his travels to the New World. As a purchasing agent for Stewart of London, a company of timber importers, he went to Canada where he learned the timber shipping business, living in various port cities. In 1869 James left Greenock for Darien in Georgia, USA where he would buy standing timber, arranging its lumbering and shipping back to Britain for sale and distribution. By 1870, and only twenty years old, he had started his own business which was to flourish. In 1880 he was employing his younger brother, Robert, as clerk in his office on the Darien waterfront where he had already established his own wharf and sawmill.

The ships that James Hunter contracted in Greenock, Liverpool and the Baltic ports had their own triangular trade. From Glasgow or Liverpool they would sail to Lisbon with manufactured goods. From Lisbon, their cargo augmented with wine, they would catch the trade winds for the Azores and America and for the return voyage back to Europe they would be laden with James Hunter's timbers from the pine forests of Georgia. Perhaps as a result of this link, James became the Portuguese Vice-Consul in Darien and later in Mobile, Alabama.

Darien was a small rural township, the administrative seat of McIntosh County on the Darien River, a branch of the mighty Altamaha at its river delta. Today the town has a population of some ten thousand, and is not much changed in size or numbers from that where a twenty-year-old James Hunter landed in 1869.

Darien was first settled by Scottish Highlanders in 1736 and named after the ill-fated expedition and settlement of 1697 on the Isthmus of Darien in Panama which put paid to Scotland's attempt at colonization. The English had already built Fort George on the site in 1721, their first fort on Georgia soil, as a barrier against the Spanish in Florida.

The Scots settlers in Darien drew up a constitution, the first article of which stated that no man should own slaves. It was a dreadful irony that, near the conclusion of the American Civil War, 'Black Yankees in Blue Coats' should descend upon the township from the sea and raze it to the ground. The Fifty-Fourth Regiment of Massachusetts Negroes had sailed from Battery Wharf in Boston, led by Colonel Shaw. At the mouth of the Darien River, Shaw met Colonel Montgomery, a man with a bushwhacking background from Kansas. He gave the order for the looting and burning of the settlement in June 1863.

When James arrived in 1869, Darien was well on its way to recovery. A huge quantity of yellow timber was exported from Darien in 1870, bound for American and overseas ports. The timber, from the great sugar pine forests of heartland Georgia, was floated down the Altamaha River in rafts to the steam-driven sawmills of Darien. It was into this booming timber business that James brought his energy and expertise, to make the fortune that would provide for the Hunter and Morris families for generations to come.

Tom and Nancy may not have attended the nuptials of Tommy and Margaret in Whitburn, but they were certainly present at the wedding of their daughter Lizzie to James Hunter in Holy Trinity Church, St Andrews, on 4 March 1875. James's brother, William was his 'best man' and Mary Bruce attended Lizzie as her bridesmaid. Once again there was a celebratory supper for the workshop men in the Golf Inn and this time the marriage was reported in both the Fife and Ayrshire newspapers. Two days after their wedding, James and Lizzie left Scotland to set up home in Darien.

Their route to Darien was circuitous. James took his new wife to Canada where he maintained interests with the London-based company that had given him his first opportunities in the timber business. While at Quebec, he seems to have followed in the footsteps of his father-in-law in the promotion of golf. John Foote of Quebec's *Morning Chronicle* wrote of James Hunter in the *Field* in October 1875: 'In July last a smothering enthusiasm was rekindled by the appearance amongst us of an accomplished golfer, and we at once organised the Quebec Golf Club'. At the end of July, James and Lizzie moved south to Darien, Georgia. He was, however, back in Quebec in October for the first competition of the new club which he won by a large margin. He was never heard of in Quebec again.

James had built a fine house on Second Street in Darien that stands to this day and is still known locally as the Hunter House, a clapboard building only a few yards from the waterfront and the wharves where he plied his business. James and Lizzie engaged two African-American servants, a boy called July Tog and a middle-aged lady, Catherine Gignihat, both of whom would long remain in the household. The neighbours and business associates of James would have warmly welcomed Lizzie, and she was certainly well provided for with her fine house and servants. Darien, however, must have been a shock for her: it was a rough lumber township in the deep south of America and a world away from St Andrews.

In contrast to the mellow warmth of a Scottish summer, the July heat of Darien is oppressive. The Georgia tidewater summer heat is exacerbated by the high relative humidity and while there is enough shade below the tall pines, there is no respite from the relentless damp heat.

In the 1870s Darien was a busy, vigorous little township strung along the waterfront of wharfs and sawmills. Timber was its mainstay and indeed its only reason for existing. Trees cut and trimmed in the forests were brought down the Altamaha River in great log rafts. Some logs were trimmed and cut into planks in Darien's mills but the vast majority left the little port as logs in specialist bow-loading ships that transported the massive tree trunks in their entirety. These ships arrived at Darien with ballast of stones that were off-loaded in set places and in such volume that they came to form small islands. James Hunter built his wharfs from such ballast from Scotland, together with great log pilings with planked walkways that remain a feature of Darien's waterfront and all of the little townships of the Georgia tidewater.

Back in St Andrews, despite the absence of James and Lizzie, these were halcyon times for Tom and Nancy. Tom's business, although cramped for space, was going well. He was being widely complimented on his improvements to the Links and for the construction of the Ladies' Golfing Green. He was also in demand from all quarters to lay out new courses. His own play was good and his middle son, Jof, was increasingly taking Tommy's place as his foursomes partner in matches as far afield as Aberdeen and Luffness.

Tommy was also doing well, although at St Andrews in 1873 the combination of poor weather and Tom Kidd and then the following year at Musselburgh, Mungo Park and poor greens, had deprived him of his Champion status: he was still the man to beat. His dashing exhibition matches with Davie Strath and Bob Ferguson were in great demand everywhere.

More routinely, there were the usual matches after the Spring Meeting of 1870. Captain Stewart and Tom played a match against Mr Rae and Tommy that drew a large crowd. The captain and Tom played well in the first round before faltering in the second to a 5 and 4 defeat. Jof also kept his end up partnering Mr Bennett against the Honourable Charles Carnegie and Bob Dow from Montrose to win 3 up and 2 to play. Tom and Tommy kept to their winning ways, beating Davie Strath and Jamie Anderson by a 7 and 5 margin in a two-round foursomes match for a £10 purse. To wind up the meeting, Tom and Jof beat Davie Strath and Bob Dow 2 up at the 17th hole.

The father and son partnership drew crowds all summer. Tommy Morris was enough of a celebrity on the Links for the newspapers simply to refer to him as 'Tommy' and to record the details of his rounds while ignoring those of others. The Morrises took on Jamie Anderson and Davie Strath for a £20 purse in June, in front of a large crowd, and won handsomely. They repeated the match again in July, also for £20, before an even larger crowd. It was exhibition golf and an attraction for the summer holidaymakers. These events served to popularise the game and they also added greatly to Tommy's own stature and popularity. Tommy and Davie took their performance to the links at Aberdeen where Prince Leopold, the youngest son of Queen Victoria and himself Patron of the Aberdeen Club, followed their £20 match. Even the Edinburgh newspapers remarked on the crowds that Tommy attracted to North Berwick for his two round-match with Bob Ferguson.

These were the Morris family's happiest years. With his renovations on the Links supported and lauded in the Club and the Town, Tom Morris could also bask in the reflected glory of Tommy's acclaim. His shop was the busy nerve centre of golf in the Town and of the game at large. John's limited mobility was no impediment to his employment with the men in the shop as he could propel himself unaided through the garden from the house into the workplace. Nancy would have a stream of letters from Lizzie and James in America that she could read and re-read to Jof and John and her friends who stopped by for a cup of tea. There would be talk of the alligators in the creeks of the Georgia Tidewater, the comings and goings of the timber ships and of the Native American Indians and Lizzie's coloured servants in the house in Darien. These were happy times that Tom Morris must have reflected upon throughout the rest of his life.

22 Recognition and National Acclaim

Tommy Morris undoubtedly transformed golf in the course of his lifetime. He was ably assisted by his father and enjoyed a supporting cast of young players, who were all enthusiastic about the money to be made and eager to make a name for themselves. Davie Strath and Jamie Anderson were immediately at hand in St Andrews and Bob Ferguson of Musselburgh was willing and ready for any match. In England, Bob Kirk at Blackheath and Johnny Allan at Westward Ho! were keen to be involved and Jack Morris of Hoylake was always on for a foursome with tempting money attached to it.

All were young and eager. They were men of their time, a time of opportunity and self-improvement. Queen Victoria may have been in a retiring frame of mind following the early death in 1861 of her husband and consort, Prince Albert, but the country at large was not. Society was in transition, as the newly founded middle-class swelled and the artisans formed working mens' institutes and mechanics societies. Sport was becoming organised with the formation of football, rugby, cricket and athletic associations; rambling clubs were taking the urban working classes into the countryside and railway excursions were creating a craze for leisure time mobility.

There was, however, no sudden burst of golfing activity. The general public was almost certainly aware of the game played on the linkslands of Fife and the Lothians, but it was far from being a popular sport. From the press coverage both at local and national level, it is clear that golf's popularity was growing steadily. There were particular events that attracted the sporting swells and these were brought to the general public's attention in the national press. This propelled interest in the game into pubs, men's clubs and society rooms throughout the country.

Tommy Morris's outright win of the Champion's Belt at Prestwick in 1870 was one such event. It was as nothing, however, compared to the coverage of events surrounding the Park/Morris match in the same year. The preparation and planning for this event was widely reported for weeks in advance along with the details of betting and current form. It could be said to be the first hyped sporting contest, because the coverage far exceeded anything that had gone before in the prize-fighting ring or on the football field. The fact that their match ended in controversy added fuel to the fire of public interest and served to set the stage for the popularity of all future golfing contests.

After this, golf matches came thick and fast. We do not know whether the principal exponents of the game, the professionals of St Andrews and Musselburgh, were quick to exploit the opportunity, or whether the public appetite for the matchplay contest was such that challenges were driven by demand. Professional matches that had hitherto been restricted to events following the Spring and Autumn meetings of the principal golfing societies at St Andrews, Prestwick, Musselburgh and North Berwick, were soon taking place further afield and throughout the year, particularly during the summer season. Matches previously contested for 'prizes' or sums put up by gentlemen as a betting vehicle, became attractions sponsored by enterprising businessmen.

The advent of the mechanical grass mower undoubtedly helped to make more summer play possible. In less than a decade, golf evolved into an all-year-round pursuit of men from a broad spectrum of society. The demand for these contests was at least in part driven by the summer resorters and those who served them, the hotel proprietors, the boarding-house keepers and businessmen of the Town Council chambers, who saw revenue in the crowds that flocked to witness these spectacles. In Fife, at Leven, Elie and Burntisland, professional prizes were established and in the Lothians, both Dunbar and North Berwick were quick to promote similar attractions to those at St Andrews. Commerce was turning golf into a spectator sport. Sea bathing may have been the prime mover for the resorters, but the theatre of matchplay golf was the main amusement.

Such entertainment needs a stage, a director, a cast of characters and a star. St Andrews had them all. The dramatic sweep of the Links with its long expanse of beach and sea was the setting. Tom Morris was the director and a whole host of caddies and players who were prepared to take club to ball at a moment's notice were the cast. Tommy Morris, however, was the star. The summer visitors could witness his matches at first hand on the Links and read about what they had seen in the following day's press. A middle-class man with his family and even a working-class day-tripper travelling by train from Glasgow or Edinburgh could rub shoulders with a celebrity.

The starring role that Tommy played is easily seen in the increasingly lengthy press reports of his matches. No matter who his opponent or partner was, the press reported it. When Davie Strath took on Willie Park and subsequently Bob Ferguson over Musselburgh and Luffness in 1870, the *Scotman's* report took up little more than a paragraph. Tommy's matches in the same week in May against the same opponents over the same venues warranted a column; his presence always ensured extensive press coverage. Even the most trivial of his matches, such as those played against the better ball of two amateurs, each receiving strokes, was reported with the stake given and a full account of the holes played.

In the summer of 1870 the routine of what were really exhibition matches was established when Tom and Tommy returned from Westward Ho! and Hoylake in June. In Scotland, the *Scotsman* and the *Herald*, and in England, the *Field* and *The Times*, had reported on their activities, and within weeks the *St Andrews Citizen* was giving notice of matches being arranged on the Links that summer. In July, for instance, the Medical Faculty of Edinburgh University put up a £25 purse for a match between the Morrises and Davie Strath partnering Jamie Anderson. A similar match was staged in August for the entertainment of a trainload of excursionists from Peebles who, it was reported, followed the match in pouring rain.

Within a year, these matches were summer season fixtures and over successive summers they drew increasingly large crowds. Tom and the flamboyant Tommy, together with Davie Strath and Jamie Anderson, played foursomes golf in partnerships that switched regularly. The most popular events were, however, those in which father and son were partnered and it was through the reporting of these events that Tom began to be referred to as 'Old Tom'. It was a name that stuck, and it was soon sufficient for the press to simply refer to 'Old Tom' and 'Young Tommy' in their reports.

Tommy appears to have partnered whoever was at hand. He took James Hunter along as his foursomes partner in a four-round match against Bob Ferguson and David Park, Willie's younger brother, at Musselburgh in March 1871.[1] The Musselburgh men won by one hole, but in subsequent singles matches Tommy beat Bob by five holes, while James fell to David Park by sixteen holes.

Summer was being referred to as the golfing season by the end of 1871. In less than three years the number of professional events had more than doubled, exhibition matches had become public entertainment and the game a spectator sport. Press coverage of golfing events was a regular feature and prior notices of matches were posted in the sporting columns. The general public started to attend in the same way that it went to athletic contests and football matches. Golf suddenly became a topic of parlour conversation.

The game entered the Victorian home because of the social cachet associated with it. Golf was played by gentlemen of all ages. It was a game with decorum, played by men who wore jackets and ties; a caddy carried the clubs; there was little huffing and puffing and, although it required vigour, there was little or no sweat. The game was stylish, requiring skill and dexterity and it was played sociably with formality and rigid etiquette. Golf was the sort of sport that ladies could accompany their gentlemen to watch on a warm sunny summer afternoon and experience at first hand the excitement. Golf was tailor-made for the pretentiously genteel, emerging middle class of Victorian Britain.

In October 1874, under the headline, 'The Popularity of the Game of Golf in Scotland', a piece in *The Times*, Britain's leading newspaper, gave the game the stamp of absolute respectability. The *St Andrews Citizen*, parochial and with a small circulation, still in its infancy and pretentious beyond its years, took delight in reproducing and poking fun at the article. The *Times* piece reads:

> There are districts and burghs where every second inhabitant is a golfer. It is the game of the country gentry, of the busy professional man, of the bourgeoisie of flourishing centres of trade, of many of the artisans, and even of the roughs. People who have never taken a golf club in their hands have a high regard for it as a game which is eminently respectable. It is the one amusement which any 'douse' man may pursue, irrespective of his calling, and lose neither respect nor social consideration.

Sporting Scotland and much of England was preoccupied with the activities on the Links of St Andrews throughout the summer of 1873. The friendship and rivalry of Tommy Morris and Davie Strath first caught the public imagination with the outcome of the Open Championship at Prestwick in 1872 when Tommy won and Davie came second.

The first account of Tommy and Davie Strath on the Links was in May 1869. After Tommy and his father had suffered an ignominious defeat to David Park and Bob Ferguson in a £50-a-side match, Tommy and Davie took the Musselburgh pair on for the same sum and won handsomely. In the months that followed they beat every combination matched against them and were opposed in foursome with a variety of playing partners.

Tommy and Davie's first head-to-head match that caught public interest was in May 1869 after the Spring Meeting of The Royal and Ancient and there was a lot of betting attached to it. Tommy won with a four-hole margin. He would never find it so easy again.

Over the five years that followed, in head-to-head matches and in four-somes with amateur or professional partners, honours were pretty even. Although Tommy was continually referred to as 'The Champion Golfer', there were those prepared to back Davie Strath in a 'grand match' where consistency, endurance and determination were as important as finesse. The young men's close friendship, together with their competitiveness and superiority in the game, whetted the public appetite and raised the pulse of the betting men. Their matches gradually grew in importance to compare with the major prize fights of the day and were as widely reported.

'The Great Golf Match at St Andrews', as it was headlined in the *Field* of 2 August and reported in the national daily press, took place between Tommy and Davie Strath in the last week in July 1873. Played over three days and six rounds of the Course for a purse of £50 (or £100 depend-ing upon the report), the *Scotsman* considered it 'the most important golf match played since 1870 when Tom Morris encountered Willie Park over the best four greens in Scotland.' It must have been generally perceived as such, for the *Field* remarked that 'before the match commenced a large concourse of spectators had assembled on the green,' and concluded that 'all praise was due to Major Boothby (umpire) and others for the order they maintained.'

Davie Strath was the victor in this encounter by three holes, but such was the excitement generated that a return match for the same purse was played four weeks later. Again, Jamie Anderson carried Tommy's clubs and Tom Kidd caddied for Davie Strath. Captain Maitland Dougal discharged the duties of umpire in front of what *The Scotsman* called 'a large and fash-ionable assemblage.' *The Field* of 30 August reported every stroke played, 'as the match is exciting considerable interest in all parts of the kingdom, we make no apology for entering into details.' *The Sportsman*, one of the most widely circulated newspapers of the day amongst the gambling fra-ternity, went further with the details of this encounter. Tommy, it claimed, was putting up £50 to Davie's £40 and that more than £2,000 nationwide was being bet on the outcome, £600 allegedly in Liverpool alone.

Tommy won this match by 4 holes. It was concluded on Friday and on the following Monday and Tuesday, they were out again, Tommy part-nering his father in a four-round foursomes for £25 against Davie Strath and Mr Gilbert Mitchell Innes. Tommy and his father took the laurels by

13 holes in front of an 'excited and fashionable crowd', according to *The Scotsman*.

Even the *Ladies' Home Journal* felt obliged to bring the game to the attention of its readers, albeit through the patriarchal and condescending pen of Henry Kingsley. His headline assumed some knowledge of events in September 1873, for it reads:

> The Great St Andrews Golf Match.
>
> There is no doubt that the great and charming game of golf is winning its way slowly and steadily. The Scotch know a good game when they find one. They found golf or goff in England when they conquered us, and they have made a speciality of it ever since. Next to a nice ecclesiastical case (an intrusive case is generally the most amusing) a Scotchman loves a game of golf. At the present moment, the Established Church, Free Kirk, United Presbyterian, Episcopalian, and, for aught we know, some of the old Scotch Roman Catholics, have got something extraneous to argue about. Young Tom Morris is playing Strath at St Andrews. The madness is not confined to Scotland; that most sober of papers, the *Daily News*, which has no particular connection with Scotland, has every detail of the great game wired to London, regardless of expense. *The Times* itself does the same. The claimant's nose is quite pulled out of joint by these two young Scotchmen, at least in the opinion of every man who has ever seen the game of golf.

These were lucrative events for Tommy Morris and Davie Strath for, quite apart from the purse on offer, their cronies were always at hand to pass a cap among the crowd for a collection, 'silver if you please, sir.' Over the 1872 summer season Tommy earned in excess of £200 in prize money. It is impossible to assess what he received for foursomes matches and made in wagers, or 'presents', from grateful backers, but his prize money alone that year equates to over £20,000 in present day terms.

It is not surprising that neither Tommy nor Davie left St Andrews to take up professional appointments elsewhere. As early as 1869, *The Field* reported Tommy's receipt of Blackheath's offer of the position of resident professional. Tommy did not go to London but his friend Bob Kirk did; he was reported to have accepted an appointment at Stirling in 1870 but that also came to nothing. Similarly, despite the fact that the *St Andrews Citizen* reported in May 1871 'the imminent departure of Davie Strath for New York', detailing his farewell dinner and presentation with a new set of clubs,

Davie also remained in the Town. These young men may have hungered to see the big outside world, but they clearly had too much of a good thing going in St Andrews, and everywhere else that the game was played, to contemplate leaving.

Tommy was indubitably the central figure in the game. Described as 'a tall, handsome athlete, and unmatched at all parts of the game', he brought a new flavour to golf and introduced a new attitude to those playing it. Together with Davie Strath, he introduced a new dash to the game. Like Willie Park, he issued challenges that were posted in *Bell's Life in London* and *The Sportsman*, but unlike Park, Tommy did not direct his challenges at any particular player. Tommy and Davie were prepared to take on anybody, any time, any place, for any stake, in singles matchplay or foursomes golf. Unsurprisingly no one rose to the challenge.[2]

They were both very popular and, from their photographs, somewhat dashing figures in St Andrews. Together they were instrumental in founding the St Andrews Rose Golf Club in 1868. Made up in the main of former pupils of the Madras College, the Rose Club members were young men who were socially aware and ambitious. Certainly they appeared determined to make an impression in the Town when it held its inaugural ball in January 1872, as it was on a scale hitherto unseen in the working classes of the community, surpassing any local social event that had gone before. The St Andrews press was clearly impressed with the assembly, the music and the catering. The decor of the Town Hall appears to have been spectacular with pride of place given, centre stage, to Tommy's Championship Belt.

The word has come down through the generations that Tommy and Davie mixed with the 'fast set' and there is some suggestion of this in the wagers on foursomes matches with amateur partners. Then there was Tommy's relationship with one Mr Frederick Fair.

Fred Fair was certainly of the fast set. Tommy played regularly with him throughout the summer of 1874, partnering him in foursomes against Davie Strath and various other partners, possibly Fair's friends from London. Fair and his friends' names appear in *The Field's* reports of matches played at Blackheath and Clapham Common, usually involving one or other of the Molesworth brothers. Mr Fair, as *The Times* carefully worded it, 'now or lately residing in St Andrews,' was called as a co-respondent in a widely reported divorce case brought by Mr Thomas Gardyne of Forfar against his wife, 'currently residing somewhere in London'.

Tommy certainly had the money to mix with this set and it is clear that it caused some resentment. The professional players from Musselburgh neither made, nor had the opportunity to make, the income earned by the

St Andrews players. It was hinted in *The Scotsman* that the row after the September meeting at North Berwick, when Tommy was awarded the £20 first prize after the disqualification of Cosgrove, was the result of the Musselburgh players' generally held opinion that favouritism was shown to the players from St Andrews. The Musselburgh men may have had a case, for in the press and the public's perception, the Park brothers and Bob Ferguson played only supporting roles in the contests with the Morrises and Davie Strath, even when they won. To the general public, golf and St Andrews were synonymous, and this was anathema to the Musselburgh men.

St Andrews had long since eclipsed Musselburgh as the premier golfing venue and the Morris family was at the focal centre of golf in the Town. The Musselburgh men may have resented St Andrews and the Morrises pre-eminence in the game, but they had much to be thankful for as well. St Andrews and the Morrises had brought golf to the attention of the masses and created a public appetite for the game. The rewards may not have been evenly spread amongst those who made a living from the game, but everyone benefited from its rising popularity.

From this time on, every young man who played the game well in Musselburgh, St Andrews or anywhere else, reaped the rewards of Tommy's flair and his father's quiet charm; characteristics that they had somehow transferred to the game itself.

23 The Beginning of the End

The good times for Tom and Nancy were not to last. The summer bo-nanza of visitors to St Andrews for the golf and the sea-bathing had not even begun, when preparations were started for a match to take place over the North Berwick links in September 1875. From the outset there was widespread interest in the newspapers. Tom and Tommy Morris, father and son from St Andrews, against the brothers Willie and Mungo Park from Musselburgh, every one of them past Open Champions. It was a repeat of the previous year's match at North Berwick, when the Park broth-ers had won. It was just another contest for the Morris family, but after this match nothing would ever be the same again.

Arranged for Saturday 4 September, information about the encounter was soon being extensively reported in the newspapers throughout Scot-land. Even the Edinburgh, Aberdeen and Glasgow press were remarking upon the amount of betting and the current form of all four participants.

Professional golf tournaments were part of the summer entertainment of the Scottish East Coast seaside resorts. In North Berwick, the Town Council, led by Provost Brodie, together with a number of summer resi-dents, put together an annual purse for a professional tournament that drew huge numbers of spectators and made for lively commerce for the town. The presence of Tommy Morris was mandatory and a Morris versus Park match guaranteed a bonanza.

Tommy and Davie Strath had played a tight head to head at Leven's Dubbieside links and following the professional matches held at Burntisland the week after, the odds shifted heavily in favour of the Morrises. All four contestants in the forthcoming big North Berwick match were at Burntis-land, where Tommy won comfortably from Bob Ferguson who tied with Davie Strath in second place. Tom was fourth with both Mungo and Willie Park well down the field. Afterwards, Tommy and his brother Jof took on Bob Ferguson and Willie Paxton from Musselburgh for fifteen shillings to five shillings put up by Mr Robert Clark; the Morris brothers won by 4 and 3. Throughout that summer Tommy Morris appeared invincible.

When the North Berwick Professional Tournament was played on the Thursday before to the much-discussed Morris/Park match, the odds were thrown into confusion. Tommy played badly in the first round and his father worse. Both Willie and Mungo played well. In the last round, however, Tommy found his form and beat Willie by a single stroke to win the event. This was not without controversy; Cosgrove from Musselburgh had returned a card one stroke better than Tommy which the referee refused to accept because 'it was marked incorrectly'. Cosgrove complained bitterly and at length but his disqualification stood.

This controversy almost put paid to the eagerly awaited Parks versus Morrises match and it brought to a head the long-held animosity between Musselburgh and St Andrews. J. Campbell and R. Cosgrove from Musselburgh and W. Dunn, also from the 'Honest Toun', but at that time acting as professional at North Berwick, were all disqualified for incorrectly marked cards. When the referee Mr Hume, a respected solicitor, announced this, an ugly scene ensued during which Willie Park and the other Musselburgh players stated that unless Cosgrove was awarded the £7 first prize, 'they would play no more with any of the St Andrews men'. A foursome match between Willie Park and Bob Ferguson against Tommy and Davie Strath, which was about to begin when the announcement was made, was immediately called off. As reported in *The Scotsman*, the Musselburgh men left the course with Willie threatening to withdraw from the 'important' match the next day. 'In the event of it breaking down', the paper suggested, 'some other match will no doubt take its place'. The hullabaloo about the disqualification was soon put aside when Pringle and Paxton replaced Park and Ferguson on the tee and the foursome match began. But Willie Park was never likely to withdraw from a Morris match. He and Mungo had taken the money with a 3 and 2 win over the Morrises the previous year and were not likely to pass up the opportunity of a £25 pot.

On Saturday 4 September 1875 at 11 a.m., the match that had been talked about for months played off on the links at North Berwick. Tommy hit the first ball and, after the first three holes were halved, the Parks drew first blood at the 4th. With two rounds of the 9-hole course completed, however, the St Andrews pair was 4 up. After a break of an hour for lunch, the third round was played and halved. In the fourth and last round, the Parks rallied and won four holes back to stand all square with two holes to play. The St Andrews partnership of father and son took the penultimate hole and halved the last to win the match by one hole and take the £25 pot.

What followed has gone down in golfing history, as well as local folklore. It certainly must have been a most painful and sad experience for Tommy Morris and for everyone who knew him. In St Andrews that Saturday afternoon, Tommy's wife, Margaret, died while giving birth to a stillborn child.

The newspapers gave differing accounts as to how the news was received on the links at North Berwick and the events that followed. Drama has been added to the tragedy by a multitude of scribes since, but the fullest and probably the most accurate account was given in *The Scotsman* on Monday, 6 September. According to this report, the match was over and the Morrises declared the winners, when a telegram was handed to Tommy,

> announcing that his wife was dangerously ill and requesting that he should get back to St Andrews with all possible haste. With no train from North Berwick that would make the connection with the last Fife train from Edinburgh, the Morrises were about to set off by road when Mr Lewis, a summer resident in the town, offered to sail them across the Firth of Forth in his yacht moored in the harbour.

This offer was accepted and the craft had just cleared the harbour mouth and was hoisting sail when a messenger reached the pier with a second telegram 'stating that Mrs Morris had given birth to a son, but that both mother and child were dead.'

The Scotsman continued:

> The purport of this message being made known to a number of Tommy's friends who had been seeing him off, they agreed, although the yacht was within easy hailing distance, to allow it to sail without acquainting those on board with the distressing news, fearing that the shock to the unhappy husband would be too great. Meanwhile rumours of what had taken place found their way to the green where the match between Park and Strath was in progress, and spreading among the groups on the Links, cast a gloom over the remainder of the play, much sympathy being everywhere expressed for Morris who had been married for scarcely a year.

Tom Morris added this *Scotsman* report to his scrapbook of newspaper cuttings, and although he lived for another thirty-two years, it was the last entry that he would ever make in it.[1]

The press in St Andrews stated only that:

immediately on the conclusion of the match the mournful tidings were received by telegram from St Andrews of the death of young Tommy's wife which cast a sad gloom amongst his many friends in North Berwick. After the foursome, Park and Strath played a single of two rounds that Park won by one hole. Park and Strath again played on Monday a match of four rounds for £10. Strath won two up.

The casual way with which the St Andrews paper juxtaposes the news of Margaret's death with the golf results jars even today. But if the St Andrews' press of the day failed to provide space in its pages to record much of the melancholic event, a century later it would take 'JKR' half a page to make myth of it and certainly high drama. In 1975 we read that the yacht had, upon arrival at St Andrews:

nosed onto the little harbour and Tommy had leaped onto the pier in the gathering dusk. A solemn crowd had assembled and mutely it opened ranks to watch him, Glengarry in hand, stride unseeing up the cliff path of the Kirkhill and past the Cathedral's haunted tower. At the top, he broke into a run and stumbled past the Ladyhead fisher folk at their doors; on down cobbled North Street. Only when he was confronted in his little house in Playfair Place by the Auld Town Kirk minister, Dr A K H Boyd, did full realisation finally strike the young champion with agonising impact. His Maggie was dead.

Dr Boyd recorded in his 1892 *Reminiscences*:

She was a remarkably handsome and healthy young woman: most lovable in every way . . . that fine girl (she was no more) had her first child, and at once ran down and died . . . I was in the house whenever they arrived. What can one say in such an hour? I will never forget the poor young man's stony look; stricken was the word: and how, all of a sudden he started up and cried, 'It's not true!' I have seen many sorrowful things: but not many like that Saturday night.

Margaret Drinnen's death was a tragedy that still induces feelings of sorrow and grief. It is all the sadder that the details of her death expose writers of the accounts given as romantic and fanciful. There is no contemporary eye-witness account of Tommy's landing in St Andrews and we have no knowledge of who met the craft at the pier head or who broke the sad news to him. The 'little house' in which Tommy confronted the minister might have been 'little' by Dr Boyd's standards, but by any other yardstick, with a rateable value of £28, it was no mean dwelling, for it had housed a family of five with a domestic servant before Tommy and Margaret's tenancy. Then consider the description of Margaret Drinnen as 'little more than a girl'. She may well have been a beautiful and handsome woman, but she was certainly no young lass. Margaret was thirty-three years old and had given birth to a daughter eight years earlier.

The only details of Margaret's life in St Andrews of which we can be certain is that she died in the afternoon of 4 September 1875 and that she and her stillborn son were buried in the Morris family grave in the Cathedral graveyard on the following Tuesday. It is interesting that Margaret's name is misspelt on the Morris family tombstone in the Cathedral Cemetery in St Andrews. It is the only instance in any records where her name is spelled 'Drennan'. There remains confusion about the correct spelling of her name; her birth is registered as Drinnen, which we have to assume is correct, although her marriage certificate is spelled Drinnan. While the tombstone was engraved some years after her death, did no one in the Morris family know how to spell her name?

Three days later Willie Park won his fourth and last Open Championship at Prestwick. There was no Morris in the field.

24 The Ultimate Tragedy

The press of the Lothians and Fife failed to print an obituary of Margaret Drinnen. The absence of any notice in the St Andrews news columns is hard to understand. The enormity of the tragedy has been passed down through the generations in the Town, but no mention has ever been made of her background. Although female friends and relatives at that time did not attend funeral services or internments, they did attend the 'chesting', when the dead person was placed in the coffin and the minister held a short service in the family home. We do not know if any of her relatives from Whitburn participated in the mourning.

After her death there would appear to have been no further contact with the Drinnens of Whitburn and Margaret's family descendants today knew nothing of their connections with the famous Morris family of St Andrews. There is no evidence whatsoever that anyone in the Town, either at the time or since, had any knowledge of her background or that she had given birth out of wedlock – something certainly scandalous in Presbyterian Scotland at that time. The story of her marriage and death, however, has been told and retold many times. Was Margaret not altogether accepted by the Morrises, or was the tragedy of her short marriage too painful a subject to be dwelt upon? We may never know. What we do know is that Margaret Drinnen came and went in less than a year and left a myth that has resonated down through the years.

Tommy was undoubtedly distraught. Contemporary writers remarked on this and the local newspaper, not given much to emotion and even less to sensation, commented upon it. It would be surprising if Tommy had not suffered severe anguish; they were married for less than a year and, considering the differences in their backgrounds and ages, he must have been devoted to her.

It was said that he had to be persuaded to play golf again. But the sparkling form, which had brought him such success in the matches and tournaments he played earlier that year, had deserted him. At the close of The Royal and Ancient's Autumn Meeting, however, he was back on the Links. Jof Morris played first on Friday 30 September against Mungo Park and won by one hole. In the afternoon Tommy partnered Mr F. B. Elliot of The Royal and Ancient against Davie Strath and Captain Boyd; by all accounts, it was a desultory match with Strath and Boyd winning by five holes.

On Saturday 1 October, less than a month after Margaret's death, a large crowd gathered to watch Tommy and his father take on Davie Strath and Bob Martin for a purse put up by a group of gentlemen from The Royal and Ancient. The hole-by-hole account in the local press shows the standard of play was extremely high, with Tommy's putting being extensively remarked upon. The Morrises were 4-up with five holes to play but they lost the last five. Tommy was said to have broken down but the scoring hardly reflects this. Everyone who plays the game knows how fortunes can swing. The only hole that was played badly was the last where Davie Strath had a good drive while Tommy barely cleared the Burn. The hole and the match were lost to a four.

Tommy's alleged 'breakdown' in this match is not supported by facts. In the afternoon he was out again, this time for the professional prizes, the 'Put-ins'. There was £30 in the pot and the only outsiders in the field were Mungo Park and Cosgrove from Musselburgh. Jamie Anderson took the first prize of £12, Davie Strath was second with £8, and Tommy fifth with £2. Tom Morris, Tom Kidd, Jof, Mungo Park and Bob Martin, as well as twelve others, were in the field. Only six strokes separated first from fifth place. Tommy was not playing well that Saturday, but he was not playing badly either. After the emotional turmoil he had been through in the previous four weeks, it is astonishing that he was playing at all.

There was, however, some cause for celebration among the St Andrews golfing fraternity, for Davie Strath's banns of marriage had been cried in the Kirk and, on 21 November 1875, he married Agnes Ronald of Rosebank in Dundee. Tommy, still in mourning, would not have attended the wedding but he would have been there in spirit. Davie Strath, as so many contemporary writers attested, was a good and loyal friend to Tommy Morris. There was also the excitement in the news of a great golfing challenge issued from Westward Ho!, North Devon.

At the end of November, Captain Molesworth, a forceful character from the Westward Ho! links, came north for a golfing tour of Scotland with his three sons, Arthur, George and Reginald. They visited Prestwick and St Andrews, but even before they had arrived, the news of the challenge match had broken and spread to the national press.

The Captain himself was an indifferent, although enthusiastic player, but his sons had ability. Captain Molesworth put himself and his boys up against Sir William Houldsworth, who was the owner of the late Colonel Fairlie's estate at Coodham as well as being the proprietor of the Coltness Iron and Coal Company, and three of his friends, firstly at Prestwick and then at St Andrews.

Honours were even at Prestwick but at St Andrews the Devon men won by three matches to one with Arthur Molesworth winning both his matches against good opposition, as he had regularly done in the past at both Westward Ho! and Hoylake.

Arthur was clearly the golfer in the Molesworth family. He considered himself to be an able player and his self-confidence was such that he was prepared to match himself for any sum against any professional in Scotland with the receipt of a third, that is a stroke given every three holes. It has been said that Tommy had to be persuaded to take up this challenge. The local paper, however, did not remark upon any reluctance on Tommy's part and, if he was reluctant, it would be the first and only match at which he had ever balked.

The match was announced in the press on Thursday, 25 November 1875, and the stake given as £50. When the contest started on St Andrew's Day, Tuesday 30 November, the stake was stated to be £100. Before play began on that Tuesday morning, the stakes had been clarified and, of the £100 on offer, £50 was staked on the outcome of rounds and £50 on the match. This was to be a 'marathon' by any standards. Played over six days, with two 18-hole rounds a day, it totalled 216 holes of golf. The match was planned for the Tuesday and Wednesday, with Thursday a rest day. Play would continue on Friday and Saturday with, of course, no play on the Sunday. The final two days were scheduled for the following Monday and Tuesday.

Play began at 10.30 each morning with an interval of one hour between the morning and afternoon rounds. Mr T. T. Oliphant of The Royal and Ancient Club was acknowledged umpire and Mr J.G. Denham held the stakes. The matches followed the now recognised anti-clockwise route of the course known to the modern-day player. Mr Molesworth received strokes at the 2nd, 5th and 8th holes out and at the 11th, and 14th and 17th holes in.

Reports about the match differ: the Reverend Tulloch claimed that the account given in the *Badminton Golf Book* was incorrect and in this respect he is right. According to *The Scotsman*, the Reverend Tulloch's reporting is inaccurate too. The details are of no consequence. It is the outcome that is important and all agree on that.

On the Tuesday morning a bitterly cold wind from the northeast with flurries of snow greeted the players on the 1st tee. Tommy did not start well. Both players took 45 strokes for the first nine holes, with Tommy taking 51 for the back nine to Arthur Molesworth's 58. In the afternoon, Tommy had exactly the same score as his first round, while his opponent took 50 out and 51 back. With his six strokes handicap allowance, Molesworth was one hole down and one stroke behind Tommy in the morning round and down again by the same margin in the afternoon.

Wednesday was bitterly cold and crystal clear with no wind, but the hills to the north were blanketed with snow. Tommy was in better form that day and after two days of play was 12 holes up on the match and the winner of all four rounds.

As arranged there was no play on Thursday. After four rounds of golf over two days of bitterly cold wintry conditions both players had certainly earned a rest day. Newspaper coverage was already extensive and *The Scotsman* progressed from reporting it as 'Golf Match at St Andrews', in its Sporting Intelligence column, to 'The Great Match at St Andrews'. *The Times* also carried a cursory report on the progress of the match. This was a 'big' match in every way.

Play recommenced on Friday morning under a blue cloudless sky and, as the press reported, a fine 'bracing atmosphere'. Molesworth was in great form and, in the morning round won four holes and took four strokes off Tommy's lead. Tommy redressed the balance in the afternoon and levelled the day's play, maintaining the same differential in the overall match.

Saturday was again cold but also blustery; despite the weather, as the press reported, the crowd was, 'immense and by their anxiety at the hole side very often seriously incommoded the players'. *The Scotsman* reported that the 'conditions under which Saturday's round came off were unique in the chronicles of golf matches'. It had snowed overnight and men armed with brooms and shovels preceded the players to clear the greens. Ball spotters were necessary at every hole even though both players had resorted to playing with red-painted balls. Colouring may have made finding the balls possible but it did not prevent them gathering snow as they rolled.

Scoring reflected the conditions, with Tommy playing particularly badly in the morning, giving Molesworth a 2-stroke lead and a 1-hole win to deduct from his 12-hole deficit. In the afternoon, Tommy played better but not well enough to match Molesworth, who recorded a 3-stroke win and a further two holes to his credit. At the end of the first four days of play, Tommy held a substantial lead, being nine holes up and 11 strokes ahead.

He had won five of the eight rounds played. It was Saturday night and Tommy would be ready to meet his friends with a drink round a warm fire.

There was no play on Sunday. There never was play on Sunday. Tommy was back again living under his father's roof and he would be in the church every Sunday morning. It had snowed again on Saturday night – the church parade would have been through a light covering of snow.

More snow on Sunday night left the Links with three inches of a snowy mantle, with drifts one and two feet deep. On Monday morning at 10.30 when they assembled on the 1st tee, *The Scotsman* reported that 'Tommy appealed to his backers to have the match abandoned but Mr Molesworth would not consent to delay, and the game was gone on with'. Tommy's lead was such that one wonders about the Molesworth's motives in not accepting an abandonment. Certainly young Molesworth had rallied on the Saturday and, with his strokes, had reduced the deficit through both rounds that day, perhaps giving grounds for optimism. The press, however, lamented that the conditions reduced the game to a lottery and this might not have been far from Molesworth's mind. If it was, he gambled badly.

On Monday morning, with a crowd as large as that on Saturday and the greens again being swept as they were played, the lottery began. While Molesworth, with his handicap allowance, was three strokes better and one hole up in the morning round, the afternoon saw a reversal with Tommy ending the day with an enhanced lead on the overall match of thirteen holes and two rounds.

It snowed yet again on Monday night. On Tuesday morning, although it had stopped, the Links had retained its blanket with drifts again up to two feet deep. No writer of the day recorded the reflections on the 1st tee on Tuesday morning, the last day of play. Their reticence speaks volumes, but it would be astonishing if some rational person had not remarked on the insanity of the whole proceedings. Certainly the *Fifeshire Journal* with clear restraint said, 'Newly fallen snow lay on the ground. Scarcely a hole passed without one or the other's balls buried out of sight in the snow. On the greens it was all dash and haphazard. Nothing but the lofting iron was of service.'

Tommy extended his lead in the morning round to fourteen holes and seventeen strokes. Despite playing through a snowstorm in the afternoon, they played all the holes because every stroke counted in the betting which was complicated and the details never fully disclosed. Bets were placed on holes, rounds and strokes. Tommy prevailed on all counts. He won the match by eleven holes with ten to play and by three rounds.

For his efforts, Tommy made at least £100 for his friends and backers. What he made for himself is not known but he certainly contributed to his legend. Although his personal reflections on the whole proceedings are not recorded he must have pondered upon how he had become involved in such madness.

Talk through the years in St Andrews is that Tommy never recovered from this match and that, through a combination of ill health and unhappiness, he began drinking heavily. Although these rumours were never written down, it would be entirely understandable if he had chosen to escape from his isolation and unhappiness through the bottle. Extravagant statements since claim that he drank himself into an early grave, but there is no evidence that Tommy drank to excess or that drink played any part in what was to follow.

Robert Clark, in his renowned and much respected *Golf: a Royal & Ancient Game* of 1876, had had included an account of the events immediately prior to Tommy's death.[1] Written in January 1876 by James Denham, a close family friend, within a month of the young man's sad demise, this must be viewed as the most accurate record:

> The deceased had returned home on Thursday, after two days' absence, in his usual health. The following evening – Christmas Eve – he supped at a private party with a few friends, and was in his accustomed cheerful spirits. On returning home at eleven he sat and conversed for sometime with his mother, who is an invalid. After retiring to bed in an adjoining room, his father, according to custom, went and bade him good night. The following morning his parents heard his usual movements, and about an hour after, upon his being called to breakfast, and no answer being obtained, the sad fact then became apparent that he had passed away, and so quickly that he did not appear to have been awakened out of sleep. The cause of so sudden and peaceful an end appeared, from a minute medical examination, to have been the sudden bursting of an artery under the right lung.

Tommy was reported to have 'become seriously unwell' in October, though the nature of his illness is unknown. He died on Christmas Day 1875, the time of death being given as ten o'clock in the morning. The available evidence suggests that he died from some cardiovascular disaster, probably a ruptured aneuryism of one of the main arteries at the back of the chest. It is not known whether his condition was inherited or acquired.[2] He was 24 years old.

25 Heartache

When Allan Robertson died in 1859, his death was recorded in the Scottish newspapers of the day. The growth of the game and Tommy's popularity throughout the whole of the United Kingdom was such that when he died, even *The Times*, the country's leading newspaper, carried an obituary. Papers in all parts of the land reported the news of Tommy's early death, written in language that attested to the respect, affection and admiration he enjoyed.

Tommy was buried on 29 December 1875 beside Margaret and their stillborn baby son in the St Andrews Cathedral graveyard. There was no golf that day in the Town. Shops, businesses and workplaces were closed so that everyone could attend.

The cortege procession that left No. 6 Pilmour Links was made up of men from all walks of life, from all quarters and from all levels of society. The hearse was followed by hundreds of men walking in solemn procession up City Road and through the West Port in a column that stretched the whole length of South Street and into the Cathedral Yard. Behind the hearse walked Tom and the Minister, the Reverend A. K. H. Boyd. Behind them were Tommy's brother Jof, his Uncle George, as well as cousin Jack up from Hoylake, followed by Davie Strath and Charlie Hunter, over from Prestwick. The local newspaper carried few details but it would be surprising if Johnny Allan, Jamie Anderson and Bob Kirk between them did not find a way of getting Tommy's brother, John, to the graveside to take a cord to guide the coffin into the grave. Many knew of Tommy's devotion to John and every effort would have been made to ensure that the disabled young man could pay his last respects.

Every golfer in the Town, as well as players from Crail, Earlsferry, Leven, Burntisland, and from over the Forth, including Musselburgh, Leith, Luffness, North Berwick and every other place that Tommy had played, were there to pay homage to him. Men from Perth and Montrose, Carnoustie and Aberdeen, whom Tommy had impressed with his play and touched with his warmth and friendliness, attended the funeral. Mr Mitchell-Innes, Mr Robert Chambers, Mr Arthur Balfour, Major Bethune, Provost Milton, his baillies and the town councillors were there. Even men who had never picked up a club but who knew Tommy from the howfs in the Town, men who were proud to say that they knew well Tommy Morris, the Champion Golfer, were there. Men who would swear blind that he was the finest chap that you could meet and as much a gentleman as anybody. They were all there, and although the turnout would have meant much to Tom and his family, it would have given them little comfort and only served to quicken their grief.

Time is the great healer, time and the promise of things to come. Word came from America that Lizzie had given birth to a boy on 15 March 1876 in Darien, Georgia. James had him christened Thomas Morris Hunter, five days later in Darien's little clapboard Presbyterian Church. (The family called him 'Tommie' after the American fashion.)

The news of Tommie Hunter's birth must have brought great joy to the Morris family, especially to Nancy, confined to her sick bed. The menfolk could escape to the workshop with all its distractions, but Nancy had no respite from her thoughts, other than the visits of her friends. The birth of Lizzie's Tommie must have seemed like a shaft of sunlight piercing the family gloom and at last provided a happy topic of conversation for Nancy.

But if the birth of the 'American' Tommie had lifted the spirits, they were not to be lifted for long. In May the news from Darien was bad. Tommie Morris Hunter had died on the 15th of that month and was buried the same day.

The *Darien Timber Gazette* carried the news of James and Lizzie's bereavement. Little Tommie had succumbed to the fever that annually raged through the swampland at the mouth of the Darien River on the Georgia Tidewater. At the onset of the sickness, Lizzie and her son had moved from the house in Second Street into the home of Captain Joseph Hilton and his wife, 'on The Ridge'. The Hiltons, an English family who had come into the Darien lumber business some twenty years earlier, had sited their home on slightly higher ground that was considered a healthier place for the sick child. Lizzie spent a week in the Hiltons' home nursing Tommie before he eventually died. In the little township over thirty other children died of the epidemic that month.

The family was numbed with grief. No intimation of the baby's death in Darien was made in the paper in St Andrews. The Ayrshire press carried the notice, but in St Andrews where Lizzie and James had married and made so many friends, no notice of the bereavement was made public. The Morris family's grief was already over-spent.

Life and golf, however, continued. Although Tom could only look back on 1876 with heartache, there can be no doubt that it was a splendid year for the Town. The harbour developments had started and the beautiful new houses in Hope Street and Abbottsford Place were complemented with the completion of the Hope Park Unitarian Kirk. Twelve boats were at the herring fishing and St Andrews was said to be as popular as Bournemouth for sea bathing. Golf was generally held to be as much a part of a gentleman's life as was shooting and fishing. Certainly in St Andrews, between the activities of golf and the bathing, there was barely a house left to be rented in the summer.

The great event of 1876 for St Andrews was undoubtedly the visit of His Royal Highness Prince Leopold, the youngest son of Queen Victoria. The Prince was to 'play-in' as the Captain of The Royal and Ancient Golf Club at the gathering for the Autumn Meeting and Tom Morris was to be there taking his place in the proceedings. Not surprisingly, the gathering of the members of the Club was great, as was the general public's interest.

The Prince and his entourage arrived at Mount Melville, the home of Mr John Whyte Melville, on Monday 20 September, where he stayed for five days, shooting, riding to hounds and playing golf.[1]

Much interest and importance were attached to the Royal visit and the preparations for it were intense, with both the Town and The Royal and Ancient Clubhouse undergoing a face-lift. The Prince's first entry into the Town, to be welcomed by the Provost and the baillies at the Town Hall, was a grand affair through the bedecked South Port and along a garlanded South Street. His second entry was to the Links and the ceremony of 'playing himself in' as Captain of The Royal and Ancient Golf Club.

Prince Leopold arrived at the Club with Whyte-Melville and, after some preparation in the Clubhouse, made his way down the newly constructed steps on to the freshly grown 1st tee. There he was introduced to Tom Morris who teed up the ball on a pinnacle of sand and proffered the Prince 'a handsomely finished play club'.[2] He hit a fair shot which showed that he was no novice but which, one suspects, astonished himself and certainly the waiting caddies, for it flew over their heads and the retrieval became a wild race. At the very moment that the ball was struck by the club, a small cannon was fired and His Royal Highness, by hitting the drive, had ceremonially won the Silver Club, the Royal Adelaide Medal and the right to become Captain of The Royal and Ancient Golf Club for the coming year. On returning the ball to the Prince, the unrecorded caddy was rewarded with a gold sovereign. This ceremony of the 'playing-in' of the new captain persists in this form to the present day.

The normal private events of the Club followed; the play for the various club medals and the Annual Dinner at which the Prince was invested with the Royal Adelaide Medal as Captain. Proceedings were concluded with the ball, a glittering event where His Royal Highness partnered the Countess of Rothes and at which the dining and dancing were reported to having continued 'to an early hour in the morning with great spirit'.

Mr Leslie Balfour won the Royal Medal of the Club, as he had the previous year and as he would again the following year. This year, however, the Prince presented the winner with an additional silver medal suitably inscribed to commemorate his year of captaincy.

Thursday was Tom's big day, when he partnered the Prince in a short match with Mr Whyte-Melville and Major Lockhart. The party played off shortly after noon with quite a crowd following. Three holes were played out before they crossed to the 16th tee to play back in. Tom and the Prince were one up when they turned back and they won the 16th to stand dormie two. They took the 'Burn Hole' and the match three holes up with one to play before also winning the 'Home' hole.

The Royal party left St Andrews by train on Friday morning with the Artillery Company lining the platform. Tom personally presented His Royal Highness with a pair of clubs and, as the train pulled out, the crowd was reported to have 'cheered enthusiastically'. A momentous Royal visit to the Town was over.

Tom must have subsequently looked back with considerable satisfaction and pride at the part he himself had played in the Royal visit. It was, alas, to be one of his few happy memories of 1876. He and his dwindling family were to suffer another devastating blow in November.

26 An Unmarked Grave in Australia

St Andrews was the venue for the Open Championship in 1876 and, with twenty-six entrants, it attracted the biggest field in any tournament to that date. As usual, play began immediately at the close of the Autumn Meeting of The Royal and Ancient Club. Had the venue been elsewhere, one can be certain that Tom would not have been there, for his wife Nancy was by this time gravely ill. He played well enough but on the whole the organization of play was unsatisfactory and uncharacteristic of events in which Tom had a hand. It would appear that with all the excitement of Prince Leopold's visit, the Club had overlooked arranging for exclusive use of the Course for the Open, which was to be played on a Saturday for the first time. From the start it did not go well.

In the course of the first round in the morning, a large number of Royal and Ancient Club members teed off alternately with the competitors and the chaos that ensued reflected badly on the Club. For the second round in the afternoon, things were even worse, for the local artisan players, on their only afternoon of the week off, joined in the melee on the 1st tee. *The Scotsman* bemoaned that the couples played off in a haphazard way, 'with the result that gentlemen got between the players and a good deal of hanging on was caused'. The *St Andrews Citizen* was scathing: 'The members of the Royal and Ancient might have exercised that courtesy which is invariably accorded them on their Medal days.' Matters were exacerbated by unruly visitors who had come to gawp at the Prince, and stayed on to watch the professional golfers.

The weather had not been good for the Prince's visit. It had rained, the course was heavy and the scores ran high. Davie Strath and Bob Martin were tied on 86 after the first round, sharing a 4-stroke lead. Bob Martin, an earlier afternoon starter in the second round, ran up a 90 while Strath, with a huge following gallery, had played 71 strokes when he reached the 14th tee. It was here that things went awry for Davie.

James Hutton, a 45-year-old cabinetmaker and businessman in the Town, was in the process of playing his approach shot to the 5th green when Davie Strath's ball, driven from the 14th tee, hit him on the forehead and felled him. Although Hutton recovered quickly and was able to leave the course on his feet, the incident clearly upset Davie and resulted in him dropping a stroke on that hole and also the next. Recovering his composure at the 16th hole, he stood on the 17th tee needing only to take ten strokes to finish and win.

Davie looked set to take the title as he played his third stroke into the 17th green. Some reports said the shot he played was a little strong, while others said that he hit a beautiful iron into the heart of the green. All are agreed, however, that his ball made contact with a player on the green. Davie made his five at the 17th but missed a short putt at the last hole, thus tying with Bob Martin on 176 total for the two rounds. Willie Park took third place with 183 and Tom, Willie Thomson from Elie and Mungo Park were two shots more on 185.

A play-off between Martin and Strath should have ensued and, indeed, would have taken place had not a protest 'by some of Martin's supporters' not been lodged with the Championship Committee demanding Davie's disqualification, 'on the ground that he had played to the green before the couple in front were off the green'. No rule covering such an eventuality existed then and it does not exist today. The incident on the 17th green was, and remains, a 'rub of the green'. There were no grounds for calling a penalty against Davie and the protest should have been dismissed out of hand by The Royal and Ancient.

What followed was little short of chaos. As well as the incident on the 17th green, the misfortune of Mr Hutton was raised and there was some question about the marker's accuracy in keeping Strath's card. When the Open was held at Prestwick, an 'umpire' was routinely appointed, but no such arrangement had been made at St Andrews for the 1876 event. The Committee met, but adjourned until the following Monday without arriving at any decision, ordering that 'the tie for first place should be played off under protest', at that time, when Tom, Willie Thomson and Mungo Park would also play off to settle the fourth place.

Davie Strath must have responded to this ruling with incredulity, as it placed him in an almost impossible position and certainly at a great disadvantage. He logically pointed out that there was no point in a play-off until a decision had been made on the matter, for should it go against him, there would be no need for one. He did not turn up for the replay on the Monday, whereupon Bob Martin was declared Champion and awarded the £10 first prize, with Davie Strath winning £5 for second place.

Few can fail to sympathise with Davie Strath, whose only sin was a possible breach of etiquette. As the most popular figure, the best golfer in the field and the natural inheritor of Tommy's crown, he had to contend with not only an unruly crowd but gross mismanagement of the event as well. He had left the Town earlier that year to take up an appointment as professional to the North Berwick Golf Club, while Bob Martin remained a fixture at the workbench in Tom Morris's shop in St Andrews. Tom would certainly have been consulted by the organising Committee about the handling of the objection to Strath's score and one can only speculate about the advice he gave. We will never know whether or not the decision about the play-off was entirely unbiased, but Bob Martin would go on to win another Open at St Andrews in 1885, while Davie's great chance to emulate his older brother Andrew's achievement was gone. After the debacle of the 1876 Open Championship, Davie Strath never played in St Andrews again.

Davie contested the Open at Musselburgh in 1877 over a course that 'left much to be desired': he took fourth place in a small field. It was to be his last Open, for in October 1878, Davie Strath boarded ship in Liverpool bound for Australia.

It was not until some two months later that the *Fifeshire Journal* printed the news that Davie Strath had gone to Melbourne for 'health reasons'. It was later reported in *The Scotsman* in June 1879 that he 'was far from well last summer, a hereditary lung infection having so developed itself towards the end of spring as completely to shatter what was formerly one of the strongest of constitutions.'

Like his brother Andrew, who had died ten years earlier in Prestwick, Davie was suffering from tuberculosis. Andrew Strath's demise in Prestwick was abrupt and Davie would have seen this at first hand and recognised the symptoms in himself. From a fit and powerful man, winning the Open in 1865, Andrew had run down in a matter of three months, no doubt to the spluttering, bloody death usually associated with consumption.

In 1878 there were as many places claiming 'cures' for this endemic disease as there were medical opinions on the matter. In particular, Dr Bird, an English physician in Melbourne who had studied medicine at St Andrews University, published in that year *Australian Climates, on their influence and prevention and arrest of Pulmonary Consumption*, which extolled the virtues of the South Australian climate for the treatment of consumption. This had a large circulation in the United Kingdom and received very flattering reviews in the *Lancet* and other medical journals, prompting sufferers who could afford the long journey to seek a cure in Melbourne.

In North Berwick, Davie Strath could enjoy the best of medical advice. Some of the most eminent physicians of the time were practising and teaching in Edinburgh University's prestigious medical school. Many of them golfed at North Berwick, and from these men Davie would have had a full prognosis. If one of his golfing Edinburgh doctors did not acquaint him with Bird's work, one can be certain that Charles Connacher, one of a number of childhood friends at St Andrews who had emigrated to Melbourne, would have. Desperation may have influenced Davie's decision to leave North Berwick, his bride of three years and two infant children, to find respite from his affliction on the other side of the world. Optimism could, however, have also played a part as well. Golf was certainly being played in Melbourne by immigrants from Scotland, and North East Fife in particular. If the South Australian climate provided relief from his illness, perhaps he was also contemplating the possibility of making a new life out there for himself and his family. For whatever reason, Davie set sail for Australia on 14 October 1878, one week before the Open Championship at Prestwick. He had a return ticket and he sailed cabin class at no trivial expense on board the *Eurynome*, one of the fastest sailing ships on the Australian run at that time.

The *Eurynome* made her customary rapid passage, berthing in Melbourne on 8 January 1879. During the last 45 days of the voyage, Davie fell ill with acute laryngitis, and his condition was such that he was carried from the ship on a litter and placed into the hands of Sergeant McAdam at Sandridge Police Station, He was subsequently taken to Royal Terrace in Fitzroy near the town centre and, as the press report states, 'into the company of friends'.

Weakened from the journey and debilitated with tubercular laryngitis, Davie lived just 20 days more, until 28 January 1879. He had £13 in his pocket and, no doubt foreseeing his end, had previously entrusted the *Eurynome*'s captain with £20 cash, with instructions that the sum be returned to his wife in North Berwick in the event of his death. He was interred in an unmarked grave in the Presbyterian section of Melbourne General Cemetery the next day.[1]

Davie was one of the best players of his generation, and from tee to green there was none better. Tommy, it was said, putted Davie out of the money time and time again. Davie Strath never won the Open and he was said at the time to be the best player never to win the Championship, an accolade that his record deserves. Time has reduced his name to a footnote in the saga of Tommy Morris, but Davie played a pivotal part, in his matches with Tommy, in bringing the game to the notice of a public that carried golf upwards to new heights. Today, Davie's name endures at the treacherous Strath bunker set in front of the 11th green, the 'High Hole In' on the Old Course at St Andrews.

27 'Generous with His Time and Spirit'

Jof did not take part in the matches after the 1876 Autumn Meeting or the Open Championship, even though they were played at the Morris's shop door in St Andrews. Nancy was now terminally ill and, on 1 November 1876, she died. She was a local woman with many friends in the Town, and although never in robust health, she was popular and much admired. With the workplace of her menfolk separated from the house by the length of the garden, she had never played the central part in the family business that she had in Prestwick. After a long and debilitating rheumatic illness, her demise could not have come as a shock. But after Tom had buried, in less than a year, his eldest son Tommy and his wife and their stillborn baby as well as mourned the death of his first grandchild in far off America, his wife's passing must have been a crushing blow. Now he and his two remaining sons, Jof and John, were alone in the house that had, only a little over a year ago, rung with vitality. Then word came from Darien that Lizzie was coming home.

Elizabeth Hunter, Tom's only daughter, arrived in St Andrews in March 1877. She was six months pregnant and doubtless exhausted after her three-week long journey, travelling by the packet boat from Darien to New York before embarking ship for Glasgow.

In June, Lizzie gave birth to a daughter, named Agnes Bayne Hunter after Lizzie's late mother, at No. 6 Pilmour Links. Tom registered the child's birth on 21 June 1877. The house that had known only death for the past two years now rang with the cries of a newborn baby and the bustle of the life around her. Lizzie and her friends would bring a new spirit to the house and to the lives of Tom, Jof and John and her presence would restore order and relieve them of the domestic daily chores.

Lizzie's arrival also brought a further and more critical respite for Tom. With her she brought her husband James's 'Note-of-Hand', to release Tom from his bond to Provost Thomas Milton. We can never know if Provost

Milton was pressing for the money or if indebtedness to him so weighed upon Tom that he was eager to be free of it. There can be little doubt that with all of his troubles over the last two years, including the expenses incurred in three burials, Tom would have been financially stretched and certainly unable to repay Provost Milton from the workshop's revenues alone.

James Hunter purchased Thomas Morris's bond of £400 to Thomas Milton in March 1877, taking the property of No. 6 Pilmour Links and Tom's life insurance policy as security, exactly as Milton had done. If it was a weight off Tom's mind, his golfing reflected it. He played well and often that year, increasingly with Jof as his foursome partner. Jof acted as clerk and book-keeper in the workshop and as assistant when Tom was called upon to advise on the layout and construction of new golf courses that were starting to appear all over the country.

Increasingly, Bob Martin was left in charge of the workshop overseeing Bob Kirk and James Foulis, who was a cabinet-maker by training. John was also there, engaged in melting gutta percha and making balls. The business was successful but, unlike Forgan's next door, it was not driven into expansion to meet the steadily increasing demand for clubs and balls from all parts of the country and from across the Empire. Robert Forgan was no golfer but he was a businessman of ability. The Forgan business was to expand and develop steadily for the next hundred years. Forgan had a son, who was an equally indifferent player but who, if anything, was an even more astute man of commerce. The business incorporated modern machinery and manufacturing practices into the mass production of clubs and consequently flourished. But Forgan's did not only grow and develop manufacturing methods to meet demand; they were also innovative, bringing variety and novelty into the design of golf clubs to satisfy the whims of the rapidly expanding golfing public.

Tom's neighbours on the other side were the Andersons. Da' Anderson, with whom Tom had worked in Allan Robertson's front room making feather golf balls twenty-five years earlier, had built a more extensive property facing the Links on the north end of 5 Pilmour Links in 1870. His sons, Jamie and David, appear to have learned the club-making craft although we cannot be certain with whom. Jamie Anderson was an outstanding player and a close friend of the Morris family. His record attests to his ability, for he won the Open three years in succession from 1877 to 1879. Although two years senior, his time in competition on the Links with Tommy and Davie Strath was his formative period. With the demise of his two friends, Jamie, together with Bob Ferguson from Musselburgh, became the leading players for the next decade. Da's sons would come to establish a club and ball making business fronting the Links next door to Tom. David was the driving force in the Anderson brothers' businesses and was also a substantial player.

Despite having club-makers' shops on either side of him, it was nevertheless Tom's shop that became the focal centre for the life of the Links. Being in charge of the Course would have played some part in this, but more importantly, it was through the shop that gentlemen engaged their caddies and Tom's preparedness to have a word with anyone that stopped by was becoming legendary. 'Generous with his time and spirit' was how Leslie Balfour described him, and others would use similar expressions to attest to his popularity.

Prince Leopold returned to St Andrews in 1877 for the Autumn Meeting of The Royal and Ancient to play the Captain's role in the induction of his successor, John Inglis, the Lord Justice General of Scotland. Tom was again involved. Apart from performing his usual duty of teeing up the incoming Captain's ball at the 'driving-in' ceremony, he again partnered the Prince in a match against Whyte-Melville and the Prince's friend, William Skene. His association with royalty would doubtless further enhance the increasing respect he enjoyed.

There was a certain cachet in this gradually expanding world of golf of being associated with Tom Morris. Those determined to make a life in the game came to work with him in the shop for a year or two before moving on to make their names at some new golfing venue. Others came simply to play the game and, passing by the shop, stop for a while 'for a crack' or a 'blether' to hear golf gossip.

Donald Ross came to St Andrews from Dornoch as a result of Tom's visit to Easter Ross in order to lay out nine holes on the links there and, like so many others, stayed for a few months before moving on when the opportunity arose. We know nothing of how much Ross was involved with Tom in building courses in the United Kingdom, but his subsequent life and career in the United States is well documented and the courses he built there stand today as monuments to his genius. Young Bob Kirk returned to the Town from Blackheath and, despite the fact that his father was still running his own ball making business round the corner in Golf Place, he too chose to work in Tom's shop for four years.

Employing Bob Kirk and Bob Martin at the same time may not have made much business sense, but it made for some great golf. Tom played with them both as foursome partners, as well as with Jof, and they all travelled to tournaments throughout the season. One match that merits a mention because of the crowd and the attention it attracted was played between Tom and Bob Kirk against the brothers Jamie and David Anderson. It was for a purse of £40 put together from the gentlemen players and set to comprise four rounds of the St Andrews course over two days under the adjudication of Mr T.T. Oliphant of Rossie. The match took place on 17 and 18 March 1879. On the night of the 16th a heavy fall of snow left Scotland blanketed in white. Only St Andrews escaped the snow, and on the morning of the 17th the Links were clear and bathed in bright spring sunshine.

The local paper recorded that:

> Jamie Anderson was on his best form and young Bob Kirk, since his return to his native Green, got back much of his former rattling play. Tom Morris, on the other hand, did not give his partner the support he deserved; one of his favourite little mistakes in the putting having caused him a great deal of annoyance. David Anderson, too, who wants the steady style of his brother, was at times rather wayward.

Although Tom and Bob Kirk led from the first hole, the Anderson brothers recovered to level the first round. They led again in the second round to be three up at the turn. On the way in, snow began to fall and the Links were soon covered with a white mantle. Despite this and a piercing cold wind, play continued with Tom and Bob taking the day by one hole and four strokes. Typical of the weather vagaries in St Andrews, the next day, Saturday, was fresh and mild. Tom and Bob extended their lead to seven holes but the Andersons again pulled them back to only two holes by the end of the morning round. They held their lead, however, relinquishing only one hole to win on the home green. Tom and Bob stood four strokes better after four rounds.

Tom missed few tournaments. Now in his late fifties, he continued to play wherever the professionals assembled. Something of a professional circuit was emerging thanks to the efforts, it was said, of James Denham and members of The Royal and Ancient Club in putting together the monies and co-ordinating the Clubs. This circuit started after the Spring Meeting in St Andrews before moving to Musselburgh. Then, in the summer, it progressed to Burntisland and North Berwick, with Montrose and Carnoustie, Luffness and Leven, in turn sponsoring matches, before coming to an end after the Autumn Meetings at Prestwick and St Andrews. Tom played them all with Jof, Bob Martin and Bob Kirk from the shop, who together with

Jamie Anderson and Tom Kidd, made up the St Andrews contingent. Tom partnered one or other of them in challenge matches, mainly against Bob Ferguson and one of the Park brothers, throughout 1877 and 1878 at all of the venues. His head-to-head matches were becoming less frequent but he never missed a strokeplay tournament and was rarely out of the money. He and Willie Park were no longer regularly taking the laurels but they remained a strong presence and forces to be reckoned with.

James Hunter came home from Darien in May 1878 to see his daughter, Agnes, for the first time, and be reunited with Lizzie after nearly two years separation. James was by this time a wealthy man, and the owner of substantial land and property in Georgia. As well as the house that he had had built for Lizzie in Darien, he constructed wharves and warehouses on the waterfront and acquired vast tracts of sugar pine forests in the hinterland of the Georgia Tidewater.

James had been away in America when Tommy Morris had died and was buried in the Cathedral graveyard, but he was there for the unveiling of Tommy's memorial stone on the evening of Tuesday, 26 September 1878. Major Bethune and Mr J.G. Denham, acting as Honorary Treasurer and Secretary respectively, had raised a fund for the memorial with at least sixty golf clubs subscribing to the stone sculpted by John Rhind of Edinburgh. They had contacted all of the clubs where Tommy had played and left his indelible impression. It is significant and bears testimony to the admiration and affection that was generally felt for Tommy, that every club approached subscribed.

Miss Phelps performed the unveiling ceremony after a full-some oration by the Lord Justice General of Scotland, John Inglis, himself a golfer and the then current Captain of The Royal and Ancient.[1] Lizzie did not attend and we do not know why. It may be that she felt the absence of Tommy and Margaret too keenly on the return of James from America. She and James had called their son, born in Darien and christened and buried in the Presbyterian Church there, 'Tommie' Morris Hunter. It would certainly be understandable if all of the memories and associations were too much for her and she chose to stay at home with her brother John, for whom the Cathedral graveyard was inaccessible, and her year-old baby daughter, Agnes Bayne Hunter.

James stayed in St Andrews for over two years from July 1878 to September 1880, before returning to Darien, but he was far from idle; James Hunter was too active a man to fritter away his time. He travelled extensively throughout Scotland and England, making contracts with timber merchants for the pine that his woodsmen were felling and that his sawmills were cutting to stack in his warehouses on his wharves back in Darien. James also found time to golf in St Andrews and Prestwick and to make plans with Lizzie for the development of the house and garden at 6 Pilmour Links as well as Tom's workshop.

Although James was in the United Kingdom, he was not at home when his son, William Bruce Hunter, was born. Tom registered the birth on 13 June 1879. The boy was named after James's father, William, in Prestwick and Tom's mother's family, the Bruces, late of Crail but by then something of a name in Dundee and Leven.

Tom played a little less golf that year and through much of 1880. James Hunter advanced a second bond to him for £200 to extend the back of the shop to accommodate more bench space for a work force that had increased to eight. What golf he did play was successful enough. In June and July, he and Jof had wins at Aberdeen and Montrose and in August, with Tom Kidd as his partner, Tom beat Bob Ferguson and Willie Park at Burntisland and again at North Berwick.

At the end of August 1880 the three Allan brothers, Johnny, James and Matthew, arrived in St Andrews from Westward Ho! Doubtless they had made the journey to participate in the Open Championship of that year but they had also come to see James before he set sail on his return to the USA.

Tom must have welcomed the Allan boys with mixed emotions. This was the first time that they had all been together since Tommy's death. James Hunter, Johnny Allan and Tommy were particularly close in their Prestwick childhood and had played their early golf together. Tom must have felt his son's loss more keenly in the presence of James and Johnny than at any other time, although it would also have been a joyous occasion too, with Lizzie and James and their children. Lizzie was of an age with Jamie Allan, and Jof with Matthew. They had all attended school together in Prestwick and their reunion would bring happy memories, lapsing into sadness about Tommy's absence. Many of their reminiscences must have been painful for Tom; his and Nancy's living room at the Golf House in Prestwick and the Red Lion across the road were their collective second homes.

But there was much to celebrate: Lizzie's thriving young family and James's success in America, as well as the Allan brothers' new life at Bideford in Devon, where they were all in the process of marrying and settling down. Then there were Jof's successes on the links and John making a full life for himself in the shop. It must have been a particular joy for John to have all of his childhood heroes about him, to hear of their travels and experiences, because his own world extended little further than the shop front door.

And there was also the golf to be played. James Hunter partnered his father-in-law against Major Bethune, Thomas Hodge, Robert Stenhouse and others, while Jof took on and beat the Allan boys, one after another, and when Jof was done with them, Jamie Anderson beat them all over again. It was not surprising perhaps, that the Allans did not stay on in St Andrews for the Open Championship, which Jamie Anderson won for the third successive year.

After over a year at home with his wife and children, James left for Darien at the end of September 1880. He must have gone with a heavy heart, for he had made many new friends in the Town. If James had brought home his wealth and stories of the New World over the Atlantic, he was taking back with him equally rich stories of the Old World and of St Andrews in particular. When James dined out in Darien, he would have dined out well on the story of what he had witnessed on the Links, for he had been there at the onset of the 'Road War'.

28 The Road War

By 1880 the world was changing forever. Edison patented his incandescent electric light bulb, Bell transmitted the first wireless telephone message and the causes of typhoid and malaria were discovered. In St Andrews, some extraordinary events occurred that year that would change the face of the Town and its golf. These concerned what is now known as The Links, the road that runs down from Golf Place, past Forgan House and the Tom Morris shop to Gibson Place – therefore much of the length of the 18th hole of the Old Course. Today, the road is out of bounds of play, separated from the Course by a continuous line of white concrete posts and railings.

Before Saturday 31 January 1880, there was no road. A grassy bank, upon which the caddies had made a few holes for putting, ran from Tom's shop to the point where the road (today called Grannie Clark's Wynd) crossed the 18th and 1st holes. Tom had improved this putting area and the ladies enjoyed it for a time before he made their Himalayas putting green on the other side of the Swilken Burn. Provost Playfair had at one time directed that seats be placed on the bank for people to 'spectate the golf', and Thomas Hodge, the renowned amateur golfing artist, had often set his easel there and sketched the gentlemen and ladies at their leisure. This grassy bank was an integral part of the Course, bordered along its length by a continuous wall designating the backs of the Pilmour Links properties.

Ever since the Town Council had sold the Pilmour Links wedge of land from the Sandyhill down to the Swilken Burn in 1820, it had seen a slow and continuous development. Allan Robertson's house was the first to be built, soon to be followed by others to form what became Golf Place. Further construction work saw houses down the main turnpike road forming Pilmour Links and Gibson Place. The Links or north end of the plots remained gardens at the backs of the houses.

As the Town developed through the 1850s and 1860s with the building of the fine Georgian-style terraces of Hope Park, Howard Place and Playfair Terrace, there were those who saw the potential of the properties at Pilmour and particularly the land abutting the 18th hole. The plots were quickly bought up as they came on the market, and just as quickly subdivided and sold on with a handsome profit.[1]

The house owners of Pilmuir Links, who had sold the northern end of their gardens facing the Links for a pittance, were furious, and so too were many townspeople who viewed the new houses as privileged opportunism and blatant encroachment on the golf course.

The building work and the movement of carts and materials down past Tom's shop and along the edge of the Links soon reduced the land to a quagmire in the winter and a rutted dusty track in summer. The posts and chains that had been set up to prevent wheeled traffic encroaching upon Playfair's pretty bank, with its spectators' seats and short golf holes, had long since been dismantled to provide access for building materials in the first instance and to the properties themselves on completion. It was neither satisfactory nor practical to access the newly-built houses from the Links and from the beginning it was clear that a road would have to be constructed.

At the start of the construction work on the properties in 1874, the owners of the feus had petitioned the Town Council to remove the bank and lay down a road twenty-one feet wide on the edge of the Course from the corner of Golf Place down to Clark's Wynd. The road, they argued, would be a public amenity visually enhancing the Course with a line of posts and a chain to form a boundary between the golf course and the new road. In 1876, the Council concurred and established the Links Road Committee with the purpose of raising the cost of the road by public subscription as with The Scores road ten years earlier. The Committee was also charged to determine how the owners could be induced to carry out maintenance of the road while making no claims to ownership of it. The householders did not rise to this bait: together with The Royal and Ancient, they petitioned the Council, not only to build the road, but also to carry the costs of maintenance.

Presented with this petition, the Town Council was split evenly in two. One side, led by MacGregor and Carnegie, both owners of plots, put forward the view that the Links were not only for golfers but also for the community as a whole. The road, they argued, was necessary for the owners to reach their properties, while at the same time it would provide an additional facility for the townspeople passing to and from the railway station, situated on what is now the site of the Old Course Hotel. Because both men were interested parties, their views were expressed by Mr Thomas Truman Oliphant, a lawyer in practice in Anstruther, and a member of the Committee of Management of The Royal and Ancient, as well as an infrequently attending member of the Town Council.

Mr Paterson, of Kinburn House, led the Council faction against the new road. Paterson was a wealthy man, a lawyer, who had retired to the Town from business in the North of England. He was a member of The Royal and Ancient but was more interested in the Town's antiquities than he was in its golf. Initially he was in favour of the construction of the road but after familiarising himself with the ancient Links Charters, he pointed out that the Council was not entitled in law to sanction any change of use for any part of St Andrews' Links. He was a man devoted to conservation and defending the ancient rights of the townspeople, both with regard to the Links as a whole and the rights-of-way in and around the Town. Again and again, Paterson found himself in conflict with his fellow Councillors as rights-of-way were built over willy-nilly in the construction boom, to which the Council was turning a blind eye. Its other eye, however, remained open the while, alert to increasing Council income from rates revenue.

Paterson considered the proposed Links Road a road too far. He made it clear in a Council meeting that if the road were to be given the go-ahead, he would take out an interdict against the Council to prevent its construction. This he duly did after the Council had received a letter from Mr Whyte-Melville, as Chairman of the Committee of Management of The Royal and Ancient, giving the Club's blessing to the construction of the road and pledging to contribute to the expenses.

The Town Council passed a motion for the making of the road with a majority of one, despite Paterson claiming that at least six councillors had vested interests and should abstain. Exchanges within the council chamber between the two factions became fractious and personal and Provost Milton, chairing the proceedings, was so sorely tried that he regularly resigned his position at the Council's meetings. It took nearly a year for the Links Road Committee's motion to be adopted and the householders given the go-ahead for building their own road at their own expense on the Links land. Paterson took out his interdict in September 1878 and Tom Morris, together with Da' Anderson, their sons and many others, found themselves in court in front of the Lord Justice Ordinary, Lord Curriehill.

Like so many others, Tom and Da' were ambivalent about the construction of the Links Road. Despite having properties fronting the road, they took no stance on its building, although they had, as was brought out in

Court, initially, been in support of the project. This might have been before they realized that they would have to contribute to the estimated £61 for its construction or, as was also suggested in Court, it may have been before Mr Paterson, and his wealth, appealed to their sense of justice and civic well-being.

Both Tom and Da' were in a difficult situation in the courtroom. Da', who had already built his modest property next door to Tom's shop, had actually subscribed £3 to the Road Construction Fund. Tom had put his signature to a document in 1875 from The Royal and Ancient's Green Committee in support of the road construction.

What appears to have swung them behind Paterson and those opposed to the road, was the revelation of Paterson's hidden agenda which Tom let slip in cross-examination. Paterson was clearly determined upon a scheme to retrieve the Course and the Links for the Town, which had been sold by the Council almost a century earlier. For this cause, Tom was prepared, 'to give the roof off his own house'.[2]

Mr Paterson assembled twenty-one witnesses to pursue his case. As well as Tom, there was Da' and Jamie Anderson, Watty Alexander, Tom Kidd, Thomas Hodge the schoolmaster and artist, Jesse Hall the architect and Thomas Rodger the photographer. The defendants, MacGregor, Bain and others, deployed an even greater cast, with thirty-six witnesses consisting of leading members of The Royal and Ancient, with only Bob Kirk, the ball-maker, and Robert Stenhouse the grocer, representing the local golfers.[3] The Town Council defended its position by calling only Andrew Aikman, the respected local golfer, grocer and town councillor.

Despite the evidence against the road given by three Open Champions, Tom Morris, Jamie Anderson and Tom Kidd, in his summary Lord Gifford said: 'the evidence of skilled golfers is all one way. Indeed, many of them appear to regard the proposed road as an improvement to the ground, considered purely and solely as a golfing ground. This seems to be enough to dispose of the whole case.'

So the case and costs were found against Mr Paterson, but Lord Curriehill issued a solemn warning to the Council and any others with an eye to speculation: 'It is fixed that the Magistrates of a burgh are not entitled to alienate open ground of the description but that they must hold it for the use and enjoyment of the community of the burgh, as it has been used for times past, according to use and wont.'

This did not end the matter. The case was appealed to the Court of Session, unsuccessfully. Intimation was made that there would be an appeal lodged in the House of Lords, the highest court in the United Kingdom.

Clearly alarmed at the prospect, the Town Council gave the building of the Links Road top priority. Construction began on Saturday 31 January 1880 and all hell was let loose.

Road works began with the levelling of the ground between the Sandyhill corner of Golf Place and Clark's Wynd. Bottoming and road metal was laid with no opposition. On the Monday following, however, things changed dramatically. Mr Paterson and his supporters, Tom amongst them, had raised a large gang of labourers with four horses and carts and all the equipment necessary to remove what had been laid of the road. This they did quickly and very enthusiastically, only to find that the faster they removed it, the faster it was relaid. Again and again, the road was laid and relaid, each time being lifted, carted away and dumped, only to be carted back again. A huge crowd assembled and chaos ensued. The police, brought from Cupar and outlying districts, were powerless to intervene because there was no breach of the peace. All the work of laying and lifting the road was carried out in an orderly, organised and polite manner. To all intents and purposes, two gangs of men were at work, albeit with one gang immediately undoing what the other had just completed, but nevertheless in peaceful accord. Members of the Town Council who intervened literally had the ground taken from under their feet.

It says little for the councillors that they resorted to both subterfuge and stealth to have their way. They made it known to the opposition's road lifting labourers that they would receive more money for laying the road, so they immediately switched sides. Road laying now progressed quickly, with both sets of labourers engaged in construction. Mr Paterson tried the same ploy and succeeded by raising the stakes. Road lifting progressed even more quickly. The lifting had not gone far, however, before the councillors raised the stakes even higher, to £1 a day, more than a week's wages. Needless to say, the councillors won the day.

With no labour and no horses and carts available for hire in St Andrews, an agent for the protesters was dispatched to the nearby village of Strathkinness, some four miles from St Andrews, to recruit men and horsepower. But the agent was 'got at' en route by the opposition and arrived in Strathkinness well the worse for drink, and fit for nothing but bed and sleeping off his excesses. Worse still, a Council representative, passing himself off as an agent for Mr Paterson, managed to waylay, at Guardbridge, Irish labourers raised from Dundee. He deviously explained that they were too late, and doubtless after a drink and a small something for their troubles, they returned home.

With no help forthcoming, the townspeople against the road brought their own wheelbarrows and shovels and set about removing it. This time, however, the councillors had contracted their labour force not only to lay the road but also to see that it remained laid. There then followed a hullabaloo that raged well into the night, with wheelbarrows damaged and a pitched battle with spades and staves that thankfully produced no really serious casualties, but which required much alcohol both to stoke and to assuage the fires of valour. Mr Welch, a Council member who was opposed to the road, counted fifty-three men 'made mortal drunk by and at the expense of the Town Council'. He made no mention of those in a similar state on his own side. Mr Welch was, incidentally, a significant figure in the local Temperance Movement.

Tuesday morning dawned with a large force of men recruited from Strathkinness dedicated to road lifting. Again a huge crowd assembled and the Town was closed for commerce. The men from Strathkinness, with two horses and carts, were assembled in nearby City Road to march upon the new road. The Town Council applying for, and being granted, an interdict against the opposition, avoided pitched battle at the eleventh hour. With both the Chief Constable of Fife and the Procurator Fiscal present and prepared to read the Riot Act, the Strathkinness battalion retired with their horses and carts after due reward for their appearance was paid.

The road was laid and it remained laid, but matters and scores were far from settled. Both the local and national press covered the events and letters to the editors that followed were both vitriolic and revealing. Mr Denham, writing from his home in Edinburgh, let it be known that T.T. Oliphant, who had long protested his disinterest in the matter, was in the process of renting the Harris house when General Moncrieff's lease expired, for his brother-in-law, Mr J. Auldjo Jameson, an eminent Edinburgh lawyer. Jameson had acted for the householders in the Court of Session hearing of the case. Few also failed to notice that both Lord Moncrieff and Lord Justice Clerk were balloted for membership of The Royal and Ancient on 14 February, less than a month after the completion of the road. Both had sat on the Court of Session that had turned down Paterson's appeal.

The Morris family would have watched the ridiculous affray on the road from the shop door and read the acrimonious letters exchanged in the press. Even if Tom and Jof did not actually participate, there is no doubt where their sentiments lay.

The whole episode had caused 'more bad blood and bitterness than anything in the town in the memory of living man', as Oliphant is reported to have exclaimed in the council chamber. A few months later, it would lead to humiliation in the Morris household.

29 A Felon in the Family

In July 1880, some six months after the Links Road was laid, posts connected by chains were erected, designating the limits of the 'golfing green' and making the road out-of-bounds of play. To the local golfers this was rubbing salt into a seeping wound, because no prior notice had been given and no motion put before the Council. No one was surprised when the posts and chains became targets for vandalism. Letters to the editor in the St Andrews newspaper make clear that the local golfers perceived the posts as a symbol of their own impotence in the affairs of the Links.

The *St Andrews Citizen* reported that on the night of Saturday 7 August, Jof Morris together with Andrew Perrie, a stonemason, and two caddies, Walter Gourlay and William Honeyman, were found lying on the Links close to three of the posts that they were alleged to have pulled from the ground. It was not until the following morning that they were arrested and charged with malicious mischief and Breach of the Peace.

The four had spent the evening drinking in George Leslie's Golf Inn, but according to Leslie they had left at eleven o'clock quite sober. At about this time, Mr David Scott the joiner, who had been contracted to set the posts and chains, was out walking on the Links in the darkness with the Procurator Fiscal, Mr Woodcock, and two police officers, Inspector Stuart Maiden and Constable Robert Lang. Hearing a noise in the darkness close to Grannie Clark's Wynd, they had gone to investigate and found Jof and his friends lying on the grass, 'with their caps over their faces and whispering to one another'. In what followed, Jof declared that Procurator Fiscal Woodcock had assaulted him and demanded that the policemen arrest him immediately. Some attempt was apparently made to calm Jof who was incensed that the police would do not so and he continued to 'swear at the Procurator and the posts until his father came to take him away'. His anger unabated, he continued to complain about the Procurator, shouting that he would 'take £500 off him in damages in the Court of Session and tie him up there for two years'. It says something for Jof's tenacity that he did send a letter of complaint to the Lord Advocate.

In Cupar Sheriff Court in front of Sheriff Lamond, Mr McKechnie, an advocate from Edinburgh, represented Jof and his friends. Jof entered a plea of not guilty to a Breach of the Peace charge and of using foul and abusive language to both the Procurator Fiscal and police officers in the course of their duty. Charges of vandalism and malicious mischief were dropped. Under cross-examination, Woodcock conceded that Jof Morris 'is usually a quiet lad', but would not agree that he had 'pushed him about'. Both Inspector Maiden and Constable Lang said that they had never had any prior connection with Morris, Gourlay or Honeyman, but that Andrew Perrie had previous convictions.

David Scott, the joiner, was least evasive under cross-examination, and under pressure from the Sheriff, explained that he had not only been paid to put up the posts but also to check with the Procurator that they remained in place. He said that the posts were six feet long and eight inches square and that they were sunk three feet into the ground. One man alone could not, he said, remove them. He related that the contract for the posts was for £40 and reluctantly named T.T. Oliphant as the party who had contracted him to set the posts. He also acknowledged that both he and the Procurator were aware that there was a move afoot to pull them from the ground, but that his presence on the Links in the dark that evening and his meeting with the Procurator, had nothing to do with the posts whatsoever. He, together with Mr Woodcock, had been attracted to the spot by the noise and drunken behaviour of the four accused.

The defence called on George Leslie, the proprietor of the Golf Inn, and Mrs Nicoll the wife of Sergeant Nicoll, a town councillor whose property overlooked Grannie Clark's Wynd. Neither had seen nor heard any disturbance although both had been outdoors for at least part of the time. Jamie Anderson and his lodgers also attested to having heard nothing despite the fact that 'every sound from the road was heard in the house'. Tom Morris was also called, and he, too, had heard nothing during his late evening walk with his dog until the Inspector had called on him to collect his son.

Mr McKechnie, in summing up, said that the charge of Breach of the Peace was incidental to the grosser charge of malicious mischief and would never have been heard but for the posts and chains. He said that the right to erect the posts and chains was in dispute and further added that no one had proved that the lads had removed them. The Sheriff responded by saying that he had no doubt about who had pulled up the posts and chains, and that Morris certainly was in Breach of the Peace. The case was dismissed against Honeyman, Gourley and Pirie, but Jof was found guilty.

Jof was sentenced to ten days imprisonment and bound over to 'Keep the Peace' for six months under penalty of £10 or thirty days in prison. The Sheriff said that he would 'normally have imposed a fine but that the action of the posts was one of a greater scheme concerning the road and that any fine he imposed would be paid for him'. McKechnie was heard to say to Jof, in a voice loud enough for the whole court to hear, that he would be out in a day.

Immediately after the court proceedings closed, a petition to the Lord Justice General, the Lord Justice Clerk, and the Lord Commissioners of Judiciary, was drawn up to suspend and squash the sentence and was taken over to Edinburgh that same Monday afternoon by Mr Thomas Mitchell, Jof's solicitor. On Tuesday a warrant for liberation was obtained from Lord President Inglis, and Jof, under caution of £10 for his reappearance, was set free from Cupar prison.

When Tom received the telegram from Cupar and announced its contents at the shop door, a number of caddies set out for Cupar to convey Jof home. In a carriage and pair, Jof and his friends reached St Andrews in mid-afternoon and started a procession about the Town. A large crowd followed the carriage that stopped outside the houses of town councillors, jeering at those who were all for the Road's construction and cheering those who were against it. Eventually Jof was deposited outside his father's house in Pilmour Links from where he reappeared in response to ongoing cheers to thank everyone for their well-wishes. Jof appealed his conviction and sentence successfully in the Court of Judiciary and his name was cleared and struck from the record.

These events reflected the high feelings that were running in the Town, as Jof was the most law-abiding, abstemious and mild-mannered of men. Of course they also reflect the regard in which the Morris family was held, because other miscreants were treated less mercifully and few had their names struck from the record. Jof's misdemeanour was clearly treated as a special case.

For the Town, the Road Case was over. For Mr Paterson, there was still trouble to come. Mr Bennett, a fellow councillor, who was vehemently opposed to the Road, had in July pointed out the inconsistency in The Royal and Ancient's stance on the issue. His point was that the Club had opposed the sale of the fues of Pilmour in 1820; the Council had granted it the land at the top of the Links on which they had built their clubhouse in 1854 in exchange for the withdrawal of this opposition; the Club was now endorsing the encroachment of the golf course for a road that could be construed to be mainly for the convenience of a few of its members. John Paterson wrote to the Committee of Management to the effect that this issue was likely to be raised in the council chamber. This letter, which also appeared in the *St Andrews Citizen*, said that he had heard that there was 'a serious intention to test the validity of title of the club to the site of the clubhouse'. He also stated that other matters had been promoted at Council, 'rather to forward the private views – some of them of a patrimonial character of some of your members of committee'. It was an accusation that matters within the Club had been raised out of self-interest.

The newspapers caught the story and the *Telegraph* reported that Paterson was likely to be 'blackballed', an erroneous conclusion since the man was already a member of The Royal and Ancient. More informed sources in *The Scotsman* reported that he was likely to be brought before an Extraordinary General Meeting of the Club to explain himself under Rule 28 of the Constitution. As in most clubs, this rule allowed for the expulsion of a member if his conduct 'endangers the character or good order of the Club'. An expulsion would require a two-thirds majority, but in the event no vote was called although an Extraordinary General Meeting was held. At this gathering, John Whyte-Melville read a letter from Paterson claiming that he himself had never made any imputation on any member, but was merely reporting what he had heard from other members of the Town Council.

Tom's position in the Road Case was ambiguous. On the one hand, he was fiercely protective of the Links and the rights of the St Andrews citizenry to access them. On the other hand, he was an employee of The Royal and Ancient that had, as administrators of the Links, given its blessing to the construction of the road that he had at the outset supported. His ambivalence was not appreciated in the Town, and not for the first time. He had built the the Ladies Short Course (the Himalayas Putting Green) on what had been a part of the Links where townspeople had for long bleached their linen on the whins. When a notice was put up restricting access to all but the members of the Ladies Golf Club, Tom was required to carry out the restriction order.

George Bruce, a local 'lad o' pairts', a town councillor, a businessman as well as a poet and champion of locals' rights, wrote verse about the Ladies Course that pilloried Tom. On the Road Case, however, he protested himself on the side of progress, and being a feu holder on Pilmuir Links as well as a town councillor, his position was hardly surprising. He composed a ditty that was popular at the time in which he depicted Tom as a 'Tom cat' who was more concerned about his own self-interest than the common weal. This was surely a case of the pot calling the kettle black, but it was a very confusing time from which no one emerged with honour and few were unscathed.

So it was that the Links Road was completed and set out-of-bounds, to the discomfiture of every 'slicer' of the ball on the Links ever since. The width of the 1st and 18th fairway was reduced to 85 yards with out-of-bounds to the right on both holes. The Road War saw scenes more remarkable than those in the Rabbit Wars 75 years earlier. In both instances, the townspeople were divided over the use and abuse of the Links, as they have continued to be divided over every major issue about them ever since.

30 The Last Great Match

For years there had been speculation about the possibility of Tom and Willie Park being matched again over four greens: a contest of 144 holes. There had been talk of it ever since their great match twelve years earlier was abandoned because the Musselburgh crowd had made further play impossible. A rematch had almost come about on several occasions, but, for one reason or another, negotiations had always broken down. Then, in 1882, the last gasp of the old gambling guard finally brought matters to a conclusion.

The first intimation of the match was made in the *St Andrews Citizen* on 22 April and it was soon followed up in the Scottish national press. The report said that backers had been secured for a £100 a side match to be played over the four greens of Musselburgh, St Andrews, Prestwick and North Berwick, starting at Musselburgh on the 12th and ending at North Berwick on 22 May. A separate match was arranged to be played between the two former Champions over the Aberdeen links on 28 May. One week later, a report read that, 'new backers' were involved, and the Aberdeen match was cancelled; Tom would instead play Tom Kidd at Aberdeen. The Morris-Park match would begin at Musselburgh as agreed, but play would now commence on 9 May. Both sides agreed on the referee and the stake-holders: the stakes were lodged with an 'independent party'. 36 holes of match-play were to be played on each green: four rounds at Musselburgh and North Berwick, two at St Andrews and three at Prestwick. Early betting was said to be heavily on Park.

Estimates for the crowd that gathered on the links at Musselburgh on 9 May 1882 vary between two and three thousand, but by the close of play it was certainly the higher figure. There had been much concern about the crowd at Musselburgh because the events that disrupted the 1870 encounter were still in the minds of many, and resentment about that outcome had persisted. Ropes had been made available for control of the crowd, and the referee who was appointed, Mr Gillespie, was a well-known and formidable Edinburgh advocate.

In the event, the crowd was well behaved, and after four rounds of his home green, Willie Park was one stroke ahead and one hole up on the match. Musselburgh had been played through a strong wind from the west and the course was said to be in poor condition, with the grass about the holes 'bumpy and bad'. It was reported that Tom had the better of the long game but that his putting was poor.

The weather in St Andrews was mild with a light breeze off Lucklaw Hill on Friday the 12th when they assembled for the second match. Betting was very much favouring Park, and the odds for a Tom victory were lengthening. Play was not of the highest standard from the outset. They halved the first round, both taking 92 strokes, when again Tom's long game was steady but his putting poor. The afternoon round was much the same, but Willie stole a hole with a long putt, taking 90 to Tom's 91, so ending the day and the match one hole up.

The Ayrshire papers were not optimistic about Tom's chances at Prestwick. Their reports on the current state of the contest considered Willie's matchplay reputation and contrasted their finishes in recent Open Championships. Somebody had done their homework; the odds on Park shortened even more. What the Ayrshire press failed to mention was that a putting touch could come and go like a shower of rain. The touch with the putter that had carried Willie Park through Musselburgh and St Andrews deserted him at Prestwick.

Again there was a large turn out of spectators on the morning of Tuesday 16 May, a blustery and overcast day. Both men started as they had left off at St Andrews with little between them. Both took 59 strokes for the first 12 holes, Willie scrambling halved holes with deft putting. It was in the second round that Willie's putting touch deserted him. Tom again played a steady 59 while Willie scored 64. Tom went from a deficit of two holes to a 3-hole lead in just 12 holes. By the end of the day at Prestwick, he extended that to an 8-hole lead, taking another steady 60 to Willie's 65 in the last round. The turnaround in the match was abrupt, and the events of the day must have sent the gambling men into frantic hedging of bets.

All of the newspapers refer to the number of gentlemen present at North Berwick on the blustery cold morning of Friday 19 May. One can only guess at their expectations, because many would have taken the early odds on Willie. Others, perhaps with insight and aware of the difference in the stamina of the two men, would have made allowances for their age and taken the risk, with the opportunity of the long odds offered on Tom after the second round at St Andrews.

Willie fought back well and found himself three holes up on Tom after the first two rounds, but still two holes down on the match. Tom, however, held his ground and took three holes early in the afternoon round to win comfortably, five holes up and three to play. In 144 holes of golf, Tom won 48, Willie 41 and 55 were halved. Tom had fully justified the faith of his backers, had upheld the honour of St Andrews and, more importantly, had convincingly avenged his unexpected defeat at the hands of Park in 1854. St Andreans would never again refer to him as 'Prestwick Tom'.

Over all of the four greens, the golf had not been good, but it was an evenly matched contest. The reports suggest that if Tom had been at all able to putt at Musselburgh and St Andrews he would have won at all four venues. If the difference in their play was so discernible, it says much about Willie's state of health. It is clear that he was not the figure that he once was, and his play was not what it had been only two years previously. Tom was sixty years old and Willie, twelve years his junior, should have had the marked advantage.

Tom Morris was an extremely healthy and robust man. Whether or not there is any truth in the claim that he took a daily dip in the sea, a claim made by others but not by himself, there is no doubt that he was a swimmer and enjoyed sea bathing, which had become a fad with the health-conscious Victorians. By the mid-1870s, St Andrews was a booming resort, and in the 1880s was already the gentry's resort of choice for sea bathing. In his *Reminiscences of West Country Golf*, the well-known, if somewhat fanciful, sports writer at the time, 'Rockwood', relates how a gentleman staying in a cottage next to Bailey Wilson's house in Prestwick in the early 1860s, raised the alarm one cold frosty morning when he saw a man on the beach trying to drown himself. It turned out, he said, to be Tom Morris breaking the ice to enjoy his usual morning dip in the sea. It is from this passage in Rockwood's book that the claim of Tom's 'usual morning dip in the sea' comes. It would perhaps be more plausible if the author had not written about Tom 'breaking the ice'. The Gulf Stream laps the west coast of Scotland, and there is minimal chance of the bay of Ayr freezing over. Rockwood was in no doubt that 'Tom's wonderful state of preservation' was attributable to his daily sea-bathing habit which, had it been true, would have caused a sensation in St Andrews and brought out every Victorian tourist and delighted caddy to witness the event.

We also learn that it was his practice to sleep 'with his window down a foot at the top'. The Reverend Tulloch tops this by relating that when he saw Tom's northeast bedroom window it was 'quite halfway down'. Also, he reports that Tom had told him of waking up one morning to find a coverlet of snow over his bedspread. It had snowed during the night and the north-easterly wind had blown the flakes in and over his bed. Tom must either have been a very sound sleeper, or his bed was well-heaped with blankets. He could equally well have been a great maker of myths.

The fact remains that, in spite of his 60 years, Tom was a very fit man. This enabled him to enjoy his longevity in the game. Like other informed men of his time, he was conscious of his health and the factors that influenced it. He would also have known the importance of personal fitness in competitive sport. Newspapers of the day carried long articles on the training regimes of prize fighters and even on mental concentration in sport and the development of speed and stamina. Tom did train long and hard for his four greens marathon match with Willie Park in 1870, as he had done previously in 1864. Doubtless he recalled what he had learned from Colonel Fairlie, himself an outstanding athlete in his day and knowledgeable in the way that Victorian gentlemen were about sporting matters. Tom's training for the Park match in 1882 bore dividends, for he beat his younger opponent and it is clear that his physical fitness played a part in this victory. Although at Musselburgh and St Andrews Park took the laurels, stamina prevailed and the margins by which Tom won at Prestwick and North Berwick undid all Willie Park's earlier good work.

Reporting on that match, contemporary writers remarked upon Willie Park's frailty. But for a frail man, Willie played a powerful game of golf and, at a time when life expectancy was not much over fifty years, he played for a remarkably long time. His tall and lean frame, with its slow and deliberate movements, contrasted with Tom's stocky robust vigour.

It is intriguing that Willie never caught the popular Victorian imagination in the manner that Tom did. Willie was arguably the greater player but never capitalised on his greatness. Willie's son, like Tom's, was an Open Champion, although Willie Jnr was never the dominant force in the game that Tommy was. The ascendancy of the Morris name over that of Park is not due to chance; it has more to do with character and romance. Tommy Morris's colourful personality, his successes, the affection felt for him, his early death, all of these moved the Morris name from the links into the parlours. The wavering fortunes of the Musselburgh course contrasted with the ever-increasing popularity of the Links at St Andrews. In the game, the Park name may have been pre-eminent in East Lothian, but in the wider world it gradually became a footnote. Tom Morris not only controlled the Links, but his name, accessibility and the location of

This studio photograph of Tom Morris by Thomas Rodger was probably taken after Morris and Robertson's win over the Dunn twins in 1849 and before Tom left St Andrews for Prestwick in 1851 (by courtesy of Rhod McEwan).

This studio photograph of Allan Robertson by Thomas Rodger was probably taken at the same time as the one of Tom Morris on the previous page, shortly after the win over the Dunn twins in 1849 (from a private collection)

Willie and Jamie, the identical Dunn twins from Musselburgh, were Morris and Robertson's early adversaries (by courtesy of Bob Gowland).

James Ogilvie Fairlie is seen completing his swing in this posed photograph by Thomas Rodger from the 1850s. On the right, Tom Morris stands behind him with clubs characteristically under his arm.

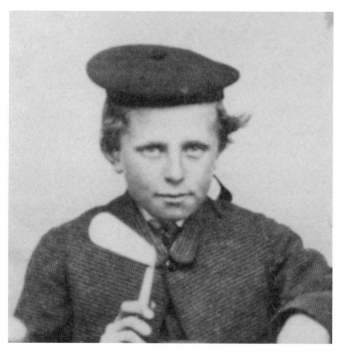

Young Tom Morris at the age of 12. This, the earliest photograph of Tommy Morris, was taken by Henderson in Perth, when he posed with the participating professionals who objected to his participation in the 1864 tournament (from a private collection).

This St Andrews studio photograph of young Tom Morris was probably posed after his first significant win at the Carnoustie Tournament in 1867, aged 16 (from a private collection).

The Challenge Belt. This was presented to the Open Champion from the inauguration of the Open Championship in 1860 until Tommy won it outright after his third successive victory in 1870. Thereafter, the 'Claret Jug', today's Open Championship Trophy, was instituted and Tommy was its first winner (by courtesy of The Royal and Ancient Golf Club of St Andrews).

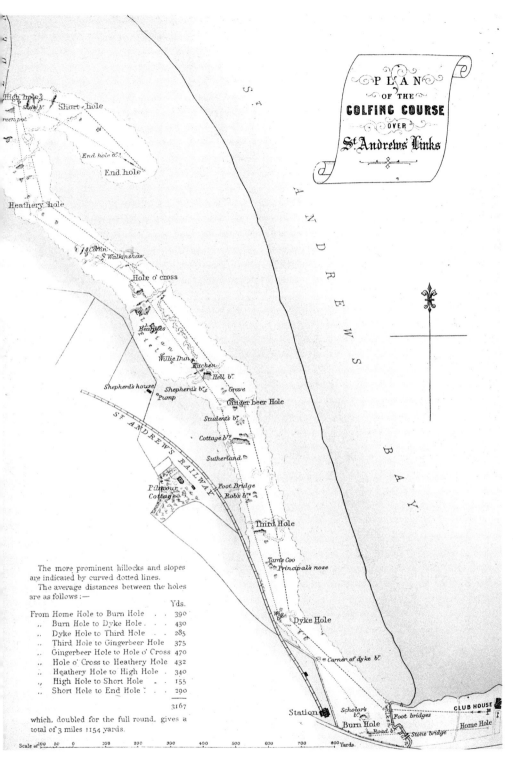

This plan of the Old Course at St Andrews in 1875 was the first map of the Old Course after the completion of Tom Morris's work, that made for circular play both clockwise and counter-clockwise (by courtesy of Mrs Ann Langton).

Davie Strath aged 28 years.

PRESTWICK GOLF CLUB.

THE CHAMPION BELT. *1870*

Mr. *T. Morris Junr.*

1st Round. Strokes.	Holes.	2nd Round. Strokes.
3	1	5
5	2	5
3	3	3
5	4	5
6	5	6
3	6	3
3	7	3
4	8	4
4	9	5
3	10	3
4	11	4
4	12	4
47		51
	1st Round,	47
	Total,	

Morris

3RD ROUND.

Holes.	Strokes.
1	5
2	5
3	
4	7
5	4
6	5
7	3
8	3
9	5
10	4
11	3
12	4
	51
1st Round,	47
2nd Round,	51
Total,	149

Tommy Morris's 1870 Open Championship scorecard. His score of 149 was 12 strokes ahead of the joint runners-up, Bob Kirk and David Strath (by courtesy of Prestwick Golf Club).

Tommy Morris wearing the Challenge Belt. This studio portrait by Archie Downie was taken after Tommy had gained the Belt as his own. He and Davie Strath (opposite), two young men, friends and adversaries, were, through their flamboyance, style and play, largely responsible for popularising golf (from a private collection).

MEMORIAL TO THE LATE TOM MORRIS, JUNR.

A very general wish having been expressed that a Memorial should be erected to the Memory of the late Tom Morris, Junr., by placing a suitable monument over his last resting place ; and, as he was so widely known, and universally admired for his honest and manly exertions by which he rose to the first place in the golfing world, and for his frank and courteous conduct towards all classes, which made him respected wherever golf was played, it has been thought desirable that an opportunity should be afforded to all who knew him, and have witnessed his extraordinary golfing powers, of joining in this tribute to his memory.

Major Bethune has kindly consented to act as Treasurer for a fund for this purpose ; and as it is desirable that it should include subscriptions from golfers throughout the different greens, the following gentlemen have agreed to receive any sums sent to them at the under-named places ; and the Hon. Secretaries of the various Golf Clubs :—

St Andrews, ...Major R. BETHUNE, Union Club ; Mr G. Murray, Post-Office.
Musselburgh, ...Captain KINLOCH, Honourable Company of Golfers ; JAMES MILLER, Esq.,
                                                Musselburgh Golf Club.
North-Berwick, ...Provost BRODIE.
Prestwick, ...HARRY HART, Esq , Prestwi
Glasgow, ...Mr A. W. SMITH, Glasgow Golf Club.
Leven, ...CHARLES ANDERSON, Esq., Leven Golf Club.
Carnoustie, ...Jas. G. ORCHAR, Esq., Dalhousie Golf Club.
Perth, ...Hon. Secretary, King James Golf Club.
Montrose, ...Hon. Secretary, Royal Albert Golf Club.
Aberdeen, ...Hon. Secretary, Aberdeen Golf Club.
Blackheath, ...GEORGE GLENNIE, Esq., Blackheath Golf Club.
Westward-Ho, ...Captain MOLESWORTH, Royal North Devon and West of England Golf Club.
Wimbledon, ...DAVID I. LAMB, Esq., Wimbledon Golf Club.
Liverpool, ...JAMES TWEEDIE, Esq., Royal Liverpool Golf Club, Hoylake.

Any communication may be addressed to JAMES G. DENHAM, Hon. Secy., 3 Pilmour Place, ST ANDREWS.

The memorial to young Tom Morris that can be seen today in the Cathedral graveyard in St Andrews was raised by subscription from this circular sent to all the Golf Clubs of the day in 1876 (from a private collection).

Jof, Tom Morris's second son, was a significant professional player who took third place in the Open Championship in 1876, behind his close friends Jamie Anderson and Bob Kirk (from a private collection).

The Links Road along the length of the 18th fairway, shown here in the 1880s, was laid in 1880 despite strong opposition from many townspeople, who felt strongly enough to dig it up and mount a vigorous opposition to it being re-laid (by courtesy of Mrs Ann Langton).

This painting by W. A. Dick, a local shopkeeper, was displayed in his shop window. In the fore-ground the road labourers are seen laying the road while being stoned by the opposing townspeople. Behind, the lumbering elephant (the Town Council), is being led by a donkey (the solicitor, Mr Oliphant). On the elephant sits a lark (Mr Lavarock) a member of the Council and supporter of the road as an 'improvement' (by courtesy of the St Andrews Preservation Trust Museum).

The Autumn Meeting of The Royal and Ancient Golf Club in 1862, by Thomas Hodge. After The R&A Clubhouse was completed at the top of the links in 1854, the Autumn Meeting became a significant social event, and ladies of fashion became a part of the links' scenery (by courtesy of The Royal and Ancient Golf Club of St Andrews).

Tom Morris's only daughter, Elizabeth, married her childhood sweetheart, James Hunter of Prestwick, in St Andrews in 1875. Their first home was in Darien, a small township on the Georgia Tidewater, where James had established a successful timber merchant's business (from a private collection).

Timber ships moored at the Hunter Wharfs, Darien, in 1878 (by courtesy of the Darien Chamber of Commerce).

The Hunter House in Darien today

The elderly Willie Park by John A. T. Bonner of Musselburgh (by courtesy of The Royal and Ancient Golf Club of St Andrews).

The elderly Tom Morris by Thomas Hodge of St Andrews. The two adversaries, Willie Park (opposite) and Tom Morris, brought about the golfing rivalry between Musselburgh and St Andrews. Matched over three decades, they played their last great match over four greens in 1882, when Tom was 60 years of age. The fitter and stronger Tom won this last contest, despite being some twelve years Willie's senior (by courtesy of Mrs Ann Langton).

Tom Morris, with Jof standing close beside him, stand central in the group of professionals and officials at the Troon Tournament in 1886 (by courtesy of Royal Troon Golf Club).

Tom with his workforce outside the shop on the Links Road in 1888 (by courtesy of Jim Healey, St Louis, MO, USA)

Tom with his grandchildren and their dog 'Silver', c. 1905 (from a private collection).

Tom with the gentlemen of The Royal and Ancient when acting as starter for the Autumn Meeting in 1902.

Tom Morris with ladies from the Tait family behind the 17th green in 1902 (from a private collection).

Tom Morris's funeral procession in South Street, St Andrews, on 27 May 1908 (from a private collection).

his shop, put him at the centre of the Victorian game, the focal point of which was St Andrews.

Tom had one further advantage over his fellow professionals for, in absolute terms, he was not poor and had no concerns about his financial well-being. He enjoyed continuous employment with a steady and substantial income. In both Prestwick and St Andrews he earned a considerable income from his play through competition and partnering gentlemen players in wager matches, which was in addition to his salaries for tending the Links and the Clubs. Furthermore, through the marriage of his daughter to James Hunter, his family was financially secure. Tom could play 'The Grand Old Man of Golf', because it was a part that he could afford to play.

By his sixtieth year in 1881, Tom's presence was venerated and anticipated at the Open Championships, even though he was no longer a serious competitor. Clearly Tom enjoyed the atmosphere and camaraderie of these events, relishing the play, enjoying the emerging talent, amateur and professional alike. He encouraged and cajoled St Andrews men into entering tournaments and any club maker in his shop who showed the slightest proficiency was automatically granted time off for tournament play. But Tom also enjoyed his own popularity; he loved nothing better than to hold court on the Ladies Putting Green, giving advice while modestly insisting that he was 'no a putter' himself.

In the years that followed his marathon match with Willie Park in 1882, Tom played a series of matches against Robert Dow of Montrose. Bob Dow, or Bob 'Doo', as he was affectionately known to the members of the Royal Albert Club, was no Willie Park, but he had his supporters in Montrose and, for small pots of £10 but more often £5, they played matches over their home greens throughout the 1880s. Although then in his late sixties, Tom invariably won, because he continued to be long off the tee and his touch around the greens was consistently good. He remained suspect with the putter in his hands, but his shot-saving was always remarkable, prompting Dow to shake his head in despair, declaring him 'a very canny player'. Tom and Dow also partnered gentlemen in matches, but these were small beer compared to the big money matches of old. Jof also played against George Low and one or other of the Simpsons of Carnoustie and Aberdeen, with mixed results. Campbell from Musselburgh was another always keen to match Jof in St Andrews during this period, again with varying outcomes.

Neither Tom nor Willie played in the Open in 1882. Willie Park did not make the journey to St Andrews for the Championship after their marathon match in 1882 due, *The Scotsman* reported, 'to lameness'. But if Willie was lame after their marathon match, Tom was positively indisposed. *The Scotsman* noted Tom's absence from the championship field:

> Tom Morris had, as usual, charge of the arrangements for despatching the couples and attending to the score cards and other incidental matters. He was unable to take part in the competition owing to a severe ailment in the leg, which has prevented his playing since the recent big match with Willie Park.

Willie did play at Musselburgh in 1883 but came well down the list; it was to be his last Open. Tom played on and, although he was never a serious contender in the Championship again, he did win a tournament at Hoylake in October 1884. This was his last big win, and it was against a field as good as any that could be assembled. He was in his sixty-third year and the press made much of it. What they failed to note was that his money-winning ways in competition stretched over almost fifty years and in that year alone he had competed in ten professional open golf competitions.

It is clear that Tom had charisma which Willie did not. It is also clear that Willie did not share Tom's innate optimism or his enjoyment of participation. Perhaps more important is that Willie did not have Tom's financial security and sense of well-being. These differences go some way to explain why Tom went on to become a revered national figure, while Willie sank into relative obscurity, as younger and more able men came to replace them at the forefront of the game.

31 Characterising the Game

Tom Morris stamped his character on golf throughout the course of the 1880s. He was the most popular figure in the game and his name was virtually synonymous with it. Tommy, with his flair and flamboyance, possibly contributed more in bringing the game to a broader public but it was Tom who was respected and, indeed, revered at all levels in Victorian society. The national press had made much of the manner and margin of his win in the 1882 marathon match with Willie Park but the changes wrought on the Links of St Andrews were also widely reported. Tom became the oracle and beginners emulated his calm acceptance of good or bad fortune in play. His innate characteristics of conviviality and congeniality, coupled with his pawky good humour, irrevocably came to be associated with golf at all levels.

In 1880 there were about sixty golf clubs in the British Isles, fourteen of which were already well established in England. By the end of the decade, the total numbers had increased to nearly three hundred with around a hundred clubs in England and Ireland, as the popularity of the game spread outside Scotland. Wherever a golf course was contemplated in Scotland, Tom Morris was consulted and his travels were extensive and frequent. Since his first English journey to Westward Ho! in 1860, he had returned to England to build, extend or renovate courses at Alnmouth, Manchester, Newcastle, Northampton, Watford and many other places; some associated with spas such as Harrogate or smart seaside hotels like Great Yarmouth and Scarborough. The impression that Tom made on his travels was important, but of equal import was the fact that wherever Tom went, a St Andrews professional golfer was likely to follow.

When he had laid out a new course, or perhaps revised or advised on an existing local attempt at creating a few holes, he would often be asked if he knew of a good man who might take charge of it. Winning a club championship in St Andrews became a passport to professional status at a golf club for which Tom Morris was looking for a man. Some would leave to become great names in the game, while others would merely settle into their new home to make their living, tending the golf course and attending, as Tom had well instructed them, to the members' needs. Peter Fernie, for instance, served with success at Wimbledon and Oxford without aspiring to more than two attempts at the Open, while his brother Willie, would make his name and put the newly founded course at Dumfries on the golfing map by winning the Open Championship at Musselburgh in 1883.

In England, golf began and developed in an altogether different way from Scotland. Wealthy converts to the game often built courses on their private estates or gave permission for others to do so. To such men, money was of little consequence; they demanded and got the best and the best in golf was clearly Tom Morris of St Andrews. He was much sought after, not just for designing and laying out courses, but also for altering existing ones as the game attained ever-higher standards. His fee was always the same, £1 per day plus expenses. He was not financially exploiting his position but rather carrying out the work because of his love of the game and making life easier for fledgling clubs to become established. His efforts as a golf course architect spanned 54 years, starting with Prestwick in 1851 and ending in Kirkcaldy and the Glasgow Club at Killermont in 1904. In that time he had worked on over a hundred courses.

Tom's work as a golf course architect, or more properly designer, was crude and rudimentary by comparison with today's sophisticated high technology. His job was to produce as interesting and reasonable a test of golf as possible with the resources at his disposal. That he was in such demand throughout the length and breadth of the land stands testament to him being the best exponent of this craft in his day. In many cases Tom would simply walk over a piece of ground and recommend, there and then, where tees and greens might be placed and, according to taste and budget, where bunkers might be dug and natural hazards brought into play. On other occasions he would spend days designing the course and would often return months later to see how it was developing. He had a great eye for where greens should be placed to best use the natural attributes of the land and he appears to have particularly favoured sloping plateau greens and those placed in hollows. To make the best use of the ground available, fairways often crossed each other and greens shared two holes. If he recommended a treatment for the land, it was based upon his own experiences from tending and developing the links at Prestwick and St Andrews and would no doubt have involved the liberal application of sand. He must have been good at what he did, otherwise he would not have been recalled, as at Aberlady on the Hope Estate, for the construction and reconstruction of Luffness, or invited to places as distant as Lahinch on the west coast of Ireland that required three days travel. Possibly his most significant recognition other than Prestwick and St Andrews, however, was his work in planning and staking out the holes for the Honourable Company of Edinburgh Golfers' new course at Muirfield in East Lothian in 1891.

The Honourable Company originally played over the Leith Links before moving to Musselburgh in 1836, where it remained for over fifty years. When it finally moved to Muirfield, it is recorded in the Rev. John Kerr's *The Golf Book of East Lothian* that David Plenderleith put into effect the design staked out by Tom Morris for sixteen holes. These holes were opened for play on 3 May 1891, when Tom enjoyed the honour of teeing the ball of Sir Alexander Kinloch who played the first stroke. Within a few months an additional two holes were brought into play in time for the 1892 Open Championship, and although it received complimentary reports in the newspapers of the day, Andra' Kirkaldy dismissed it as little more than 'an old water meadow'. The course was extensively altered before the 1901 Open, but it was not until 1919 that the present day Muirfield started to take its final form. Like most of the courses in which Tom had had a hand, the Muirfield of today bears no resemblance to that which he had originally laid out in 1892.

During the boom period of golf from the 1880s one can only guess at Tom's total contribution. Individual clubs' records are not very informative, but they certainly make clear the reverence in which he was held by all classes of society and by the landed gentry in particular. 'The Colonel', writing in Kerr's book, observed about the making of the Muirfield course, 'Old Tom is a veritable makkar – his is "the vision and the faculty divine" for making golf-greens; how I felt that as I walked beside him, he glancing "from heaven to earth, from earth to heaven", taking in the situation at every point!' Plenderleith, who had the responsibility of putting Tom's design into effect, is quoted as saying, 'It has been cunningly laid oot – ay, cunningly laid oot'.

There are numerous examples of his input in the construction of private courses, but his most unlikely creation must be that on South Uist in the Outer Hebrides. There he built a course for Sir Reginald and Lady Cathcart on the wonderful ten-mile strip of 'machair' or links land facing the Atlantic Ocean.

While Tom Dunn, and particularly young Willie Park, were also busy altering and laying out courses, there was clearly a certain cachet in having Tom associated with a newly established course. As the newspapers of the day reveal, his presence at an opening not only attracted public attention but also added a certain dignity. Having an outstanding Scottish professional in charge of the green was also a prerequisite for the leading clubs in England.

A glance through the Open records shows how widespread the game became in the course of the 1880s. From the Championship's narrow base of mainly St Andrews and East Lothian players, the spread and popularity of golf meant that not only was the number of contestants starting to increase, but unknowns were emerging from places where the game was still a novelty. In the 1882 Championship at St Andrews, players were drawn from Dumfries, Glasgow, Edinburgh and Leven in Scotland and from Wimbledon and Hoylake in England. Also, the formidable Simpson brothers and Douglas Rolland had emerged from Earlsferry, a fishing village on the south coast of Fife, to stamp their name and their birthplace on the game. By 1891, the numbers of professional contestants had doubled, with players from all over England, many of whom, like Tom Vardon, a Channel Islander, had no Scottish connections whatsoever.

Tom Morris, nevertheless, remained at the core of the Open Championship and it was through him that entries to the event were made. With increasing numbers, however, this informal system of entry clearly could not continue, and in 1891 The Royal and Ancient stipulated that entries would close three days before the event. With notice of the Championship posted only in the Scottish press and *The Field* in England, not everyone was made aware of the change, and some ten contestants found themselves only permitted to play 'under protest' of late entry. They had merely informed Tom that they would be playing and the matter had slipped his mind.

Tom had long been the conduit for professional contestants wishing to enter the Championship, as well as finding employment in the game, but golf was rapidly outgrowing him. Young men for whom he had found employment a decade earlier were themselves designing and constructing golf courses and their own protégés were emerging as great players. He knew them all from his travels or being introduced at his shop door and each, in their writings, were quick to express their regard and in many cases, their indebtedness to him.

Tom clearly found a special pleasure in the young and able on the links. Spirited young people appealed to him and he, with his wit, wisdom and vigour, had a special attraction for them. Horace Hutchinson, John Ball, Freddie Tait and James Robb, all had the ultimate compliment paid to them by Tom that he saw 'something of Tommy' in them. But it was

Douglas Rolland from Elie who was Tom's special favourite, and he took a keen interest in Dougie's movements and activities on and off the links: he was always ready to relate the latest 'Dougie Rolland story'. James Braid was Douglas Rolland's nephew, and Braid was subjected to Tom's gleeful reminiscences and fulsome praise of Dougie on every occasion they met.

Douglas Rolland was notorious for his exploits both on and off the links, epitomising the Scots word 'gallus' to perfection. He was a loveable rogue who recognised neither limit nor restraint. Doubtless Tom would have seen in Dougie Rolland much of the vitality, charm and flair on the links that had been absent from his life since the passing of Tommy.

Rolland first contested the Open Championship in 1882 at St Andrews while working as a stonemason in the Town. He was in the field at Musselburgh in 1883 and was runner-up to his Elie compatriot, Jack Simpson, then of Carnoustie, in 1884. After a widely reported home-and-home challenge match with John Ball at Hoylake, Rolland failed to appear at Cupar Sheriff Court to face a paternity suit. Sadly, with a charge of contempt of court hanging over him, the golfing press reported that he was not then able to return to Scotland and was therefore unable to contest the Open until it was played in England in 1894.[1] He had taken second place in 1884 and ten years later, at his fourth time of entry, he was again runner-up, this time to J.H. Taylor at Sandwich in Kent. At the Open Championship prize-giving ceremony in 1885, when the Kirkaldy brothers, Park Jnr, the Fernies, the Simpsons and all the leading players of the day were assembled, Tom is reported to have remarked wistfully, 'they should all thank the Lord that Dougie Rolland is holed-out in England'.

Douglas Rolland held down appointments at several clubs in England, among them Rye, Malvern, Limpsfield and Bexhill and from time to time he would return to his trade as a stonemason. Tom Morris was always ready to endorse him in his appointments, despite his wayward ways, and Douglas Rolland left every club he served with mutual expressions of regret and a legacy of enduring stories.

In complete contrast to the statuesque figure of Rolland, the diminutive Ben Sayers was Tom's other great favourite. Ben did not compare with Douglas as a player but his enthusiasm and interest in every aspect of the game was what Tom clearly enjoyed. Ben's manners, moderation and modesty, were said in St Andrews to be 'uncommon in a Musselburgh man'. He had been a circus acrobat, became a club-maker and was a much-loved figure in North Berwick, where he established the enduring club-making business that still bears his name. He was a frequent visitor to the shop in St Andrews and he and Tom were regular playing partners in exhibition events that were held to inaugurate a golf course or celebrate the opening of a new hotel. They were present at the opening of the Dunblane Hydropathic Hotel, at Highland Hotels in Crieff, Strathpeffer and Pitlochry and Marine Hotels at North Berwick and Elie.

Tom's travels, however, were not confined to consulting on course design and construction or to exhibition play. Through his sixties and seventies he continued playing competitive golf with the enthusiasm of his youth, albeit with diminished vigour and waning success. Times were changing, and with the emergence of Vardon, Taylor and Braid, Tom was becoming less the oracle than the oddity. He must have felt increasingly isolated, because all of his contemporaries and friends had either retired or were dead.

In January 1884, Tom Kidd died at his home in Rose Lane, St Andrews. He was from an old Town family of weavers that, like the Morrises, had turned to caddying when it was no longer possible to make a living with the handloom. Although Kidd had never been a principal player, he had participated in professional matches and was the surprise winner of the first Open played at St Andrews in 1873, when the weather reduced the event to a lottery. He defended his title unsuccessfully at Musselburgh, but after that he never ventured further afield than Elie and Leven, where he competed successfully, and in St Andrews, where he played in his last Open in 1882. He and Tom enjoyed many successes in foursome matches in St Andrews and, most famously, in Burntisland when, in August 1879, they beat Bob Ferguson and Willie Park by two holes. Earlier that year he beat Bob Ferguson over his home links at Musselburgh. Tom Kidd died of heart disease after suffering ill health for over a year.

In 1886, young Bob Kirk, after months of debilitation, died in his sleep at 4 Pilmour Links. Although Bob's death could not have come as a shock, his absence from Tom's shop and life on the Links must have left a void. He was a neighbour and friend of the Morris family as well as a sometime employee. He had taken up the appointment of professional at Blackheath, which had initially been offered to Tommy Morris and, because of his travels, he was familiar with all of the great players in the game. During his Blackheath stay, he played frequently in competition with Jamie Allan and Jack Morris at Westward Ho! and Hoylake. Undoubtedly, Bob and Jamie Allan's greatest hour came in August 1879 when they played for a £200 stake over the four greens of Westward Ho!, Hoylake, Prestwick and St Andrews. Jamie won at all four venues. Although Bob was only 41 years old when he died, he was one of Tom's old guard, always ready for the challenge and prepared to travel anywhere to compete. He never won an Open, although he threatened often enough.

In October 1888, George Morris, Tom's elder brother, died in Edinburgh after a prolonged illness. Suddenly Tom was aware of his own age and mortality.

32 Death in Alabama

In Darien, Georgia, James Hunter's business had prospered. He made further acquisitions of timberland after his return to America in 1879 and added extensions to his wharves and mills in 1880 and 1881. In 1880 James brought his younger brother Robert to Darien to act as his clerk and book-keeper; two years later, two other brothers from Prestwick were to follow. Robert was already highly experienced, having run the Scottish end of the Hunter business and the full measure of his skill would emerge in the years to come when Tom and his family would reap the benefits of his business experience.

Robert Hunter married Marian Shannon of Newry, Ireland in 1875. When they moved to Darien with their family, they lived in James's house on Second Street when he moved to Mobile, Alabama, in 1882. Robert and Marian retained the services of July Tog and Catherine Gignihat, the African-American servants who had attended to James since the house was built.

Shortly afterwards, James and Robert enlisted the help of two nephews in Prestwick, James and Andrew Manson, to work in the business in Darien. Their father, Thomas, was a founding member of the Prestwick St Nicholas Golf Club and both the Manson brothers were stalwarts of it. Other members of the Manson family would ultimately make their home in Darien and later Mobile. They, together with James and Robert Hunter and their families, became prominent citizens within their communities and would become the driving force in establishing golf in the southern states of America. Robert is remembered as the 'Father of Mobile golf'.

James came back home to St Andrews from Mobile at the end of June 1883 and, perhaps not surprisingly, Lizzie became pregnant again. In July 1884, she gave birth to Elizabeth Gray Hunter, named after James's recently deceased mother from Prestwick, after whom Lizzie herself had been called. James was not at home in St Andrews when Gray, as she became known, was born and again Tom registered this, his fourth grandchild's birth.

Preparation for James Hunter's return to St Andrews had been made well in advance. He had made a further £200 bond available to Tom in 1882 to finance the renovation of the workshop, and more importantly, to convert the attic floor above the workshop into good living accommodation. Tom's total indebtedness to James, as registered in the Fife Sasines, now exceeded £800.

Before 1882, Tom's shop had changed very little since he acquired it in March 1866. Indeed, little had changed since Hugh Philp had died and his nephew Robert Forgan had taken over the premises in 1856. George Daniel Brown, who had occupied the building since Forgan moved his business next door, had made living accommodation above the shop, renovating the roof and adding his name in large white letters on the gable end. Prior to these alterations, the cart shed that Thomas Fairful had originally built on the site would still have been recognisable to anyone of Tom's age. The changes that were made in 1882 were, however, substantial, and apart from various additions to the shop and house, the property has remained much the same to the present day.

The conversion of the upper storey was completed in April 1882 and consisted of five rooms, including a large living room, with two rooms adjoining it overlooking the Links. Access was by an outside stair from the garden at the back, where there was a lavatory that the workshop men also used. The front of the shop was remodelled in stone from Nydie's quarry and the extended gable to the east was formed in concrete, a then novel material, in its first application in the Town.[1]

The property above the shop is today called 'Tom Morris House', a name going back to at least 1935 and possibly to about 1900. It was built with the express purpose of providing independent accommodation for Tom's sons, Jof and John. Up to this time they had lived at 6 Pilmour Links with Lizzie and her children in increasingly cramped conditions, as Agnes, now five, and Bruce, aged three, grew up. Accommodating John's difficulties in moving about and Jof's increasingly troublesome rheumatism in a house with two children and a baby, as well as Tom, could never have been easy. If James Hunter was to have any place for his work, and space to enjoy family life with his children, Jof and John would have to be relocated. They moved into their new accommodation and Tom, when he realised that he could keep a virtually round-the-clock vigil on the Home Green from the window, soon moved in as well.

James Hunter came back home every year to spend time with his wife Lizzie and the children. From St Andrews he could enjoy his golf and the social life, as well as expand his business contacts in the United Kingdom.

James was a golfer of no mean ability and, despite his long absences, was a popular figure in St Andrews. He played regularly and competitively in a broad spectrum of company, twice entering the Open Championship lists. In 1883 he was the inaugural winner of the Hall Blyth medal at Hoylake where he was a member. He had much golf during his stay in St Andrews where he and Major Bethune enjoyed many matches against Tom and Colonel Boothby. James also captained a Thistle Golf Club side against a University team and was a regular competitor in both the Thistle and Rose Clubs' medals. Entering fully into the golfing scene, he donated prizes of club shafts to the St Andrews Club.[2]

James had registered his will in Cupar, Fife, in September 1877. In the event of his death, Tom, together with Charlie Hunter of Prestwick and James Glover Denham, his neighbour at Pilmour Links, were nominated as his trustees. Mr Denham resided in St Andrews for many years after a business career in London; he was a golfing enthusiast who did much to further the professional game and improve the lot of the caddies. He and Major Bethune had formed the nucleus of the committee that organised the Cathedral graveyard memorial to Tommy, to whom they were particularly close. The other trustee, Charlie Hunter, was James's cousin and four years his senior. Charlie Hunter had inherited Tom's mantle at Prestwick Golf Club and had carried Tom's clubs throughout his encounters on the Prestwick links against Willie Park.

At the end of October 1885, only three months after Gray's first birthday and with Lizzie again pregnant, James Hunter returned to America, where he announced his intention of becoming a citizen of the United States.

By the time of James's departure for the United States, the pregnant Lizzie and her family were living in some style at 6 Pilmour Links. The house had been developed both internally and externally. The attic room in which Tommy had died was gone. A second storey had been added with the classical Georgian proportions popular at the time. A fine doorway was built and the old cottage windows re-designed to match the new larger ones on the first floor. An extension had been added at the rear to accommodate an inside-flushing water closet. The whole house was topped off with a fine balustrade giving it the appearance of a small country house, unique in the Town. It was the finest house on Pilmour Links and much admired. At the rear, unseen from either the Links end or Pilmour Links, the garden was similarly treated. Although the path was retained for John to propel his trolley between the house and the workshop, the garden was redesigned with flower beds and box hedges. A little summerhouse was placed to catch as much of the sun as the enclosed garden would allow. Finally, a fine wicker fence was set behind the workshop to demarcate and limit the spread of workshop debris. Lizzie had a very fine house and garden, a fine young family and a successful, widely admired and much respected husband. With her father and brothers about her and a broad spectrum of friends in the Town, she must have been contented enough. She took regular holidays in America with her husband and would appear to have been blissfully happy. Her happiness, however, was not to last.

On 31 January 1886 James Hunter died in Mobile, Alabama. His pregnant wife Lizzie received the news by telegram two days later. His death was reported in the Ayrshire and Fifeshire newspapers as well as the national press in Britain. The state newspapers of Georgia and Alabama recorded his passing as 'a major loss of a central business figure, an entrepreneur and a man of great foresight and vision.' James had died, the *St Andrews Citizen* reported, 'as the result of an accident in the course of conducting his business as a timber merchant'. His body was dispatched from Mobile to St Andrews and it was accompanied by his youngest brother, Andrew. It reached home on Friday, 18 February 1886.

The burial of James Hunter took place the next day. He was interred beside Tommy Morris, who had been his lifelong friend as well as his brother-in-law, his sister-in-law Margaret Morris, and his mother-in-law Agnes Morris, who had known him since his childhood in Prestwick.

A large number of his business associates and friends from Prestwick attended the funeral. His son, William Bruce Hunter, aged seven, with his grandfather Tom Morris, led the cortege, followed by Jof and James's brother, Andrew. There followed relatives and friends from Prestwick, led by his cousin and trustee, Charlie Hunter, and business associates from Glasgow and Liverpool. Many townspeople attended, including his other trustee, James Denham, Major Bethune, Mr Keiller-Bruce, Colonel Boothby and Mr Everard, together with Mr Stonehouse, Mr Aikman and other businessmen of the Town with whom he had played golf.

After leaving St Andrews some three months earlier for what was to be the last time, James Hunter had travelled to Mobile, stopping only briefly at Darien, Georgia on the way. But for his perspicacity and business acumen, he might never have been in Mobile. James had foreseen the decline of Darien as the eastern seaboard's premier timber port. Georgia was running out of its pines. Continuous felling meant that less accessible land had to be purchased, and hauling the logs to the rafts on the Altamaha River to be floated down to Darien was becoming uneconomical. James saw the sugar pines of Alabama as the next area of opportunity.

James Hunter had already purchased land in the Alabama counties of Washington, Monroe, Mobile and Choctaw and also off the coast on Farmers Island, Blakely Island and Pitts Island. James owned more than 100,000 acres of land in Alabama alone, where he contracted 20 sawmills and employed over 500 men. The location of one of these mills in Washington County he named 'Prestwick', a township and name that survives today. James moved to Alabama, leaving Robert to manage the business in Darien. He also left Robert and his family in the house that he had built for Lizzie, a house that stands to this day and is referred to locally as the Hunter House. When Robert subsequently moved to Mobile, the Manson family would come to live in it until recent times.

The life that James Hunter led in Alabama was altogether different from that of the family man in St Andrews. James owned a fine house on Government Street in Mobile which Robert and his family would come to occupy but, throughout his years in Mobile, James rented a suite of rooms in the Battle House, the premier hotel and watering hole in the heart of the rapidly developing township.

James Hunter was not only the largest timber shipper in Mobile, he was also, at the age of 37, considered to be one of the leading businessmen in the State. Profiles of him appeared in the American press as he acquired land and built sawmills and wharves up the Alabama River and along the creeks of Mobile Bay. He was reported to have over 200 ships in service at any one time plying the timber trade from his wharves in Mobile, Pascagoola, Darien and St Simon's Island.

But James's life in Mobile was far from all work and no play. If he was a leading player at the heart of business in the town, he was also a leading light at the core of its social scene. The ground floor of the Battle House Hotel was, as the saying goes, 'where the action was', in Mobile. The parlour was the businessmen's bar and its gaming rooms attracted 'high rollers' from all along the Mexican Gulf Coast and beyond. It was proudly held to maintain and convey the energy and spirit of the South and, in Mobile, to be the spiritual home of Southern charm and hospitality.

The Battle House was also the meeting place of the Athelstane, the Manassus and the Infant Mystics Societies and James was a member of them all. These secret societies derived from the time soon after the Civil War and were made up of those who 'reluctantly accepted the Union' and were considered part of the white South's recovery – their way of saying that they still had power. Whether this was the case or not, they outwardly appeared to have been concerned mainly with organising charitable and social events; the Infant Mystics in particular played the leading role in organising Mardi Gras and running masked balls. 'Rich bachelors at play', would sum up some of the activities, and in Mobile, James Hunter would appear to have worked as hard and played as hard as any of them. He certainly enjoyed an entirely different lifestyle to that with his wife and children thousands of miles away in St Andrews.

The manner and circumstances of his death very much reflected the way he lived in Mobile. At 5 o'clock on Sunday afternoon, 31 January 1886, James persuaded two of his Battle House friends, Dr Rhett Goode and Mr John Motley, to accompany him on a social visit to the Norwegian barque *Martin Luther*. The ship was being loaded with James's timber two miles up the Alabama River at his wharf towards Three Mile Creek. The skipper, Captain Arensen, was a friend of long standing and a man whose company James clearly enjoyed. Despite the fact that James had promised John Motley that he would have him back in Mobile by six o'clock, they were still enjoying Norwegian hospitality at nine o'clock. Rhett Goode actually asked Captain Arensen if he could have them put ashore, but James would have none of it and kept them there until long after darkness had fallen, so that they required lanterns to see their way into James's rowing boat.

Dr Goode related how he had entered the small boat first and taken his seat in the stem. Mr Motley had followed to take his seat in the stern. The newspaper reported that James 'came down the rope and started to take a seat in the middle of the boat, but fell into the water'. Dr Goode related, 'I thought at first it was a practical joke and that we would all have a good laugh at Hunter because of his ducking,' adding, 'He was an expert swimmer I knew.'

But James did not surface and an oar thrown into the water where he fell simply drifted away. Captain Arensen and two of his sailors rowed downstream and within six minutes saw his foot and hand above the water. They had him on the wharf quickly and applied artificial resuscitation until Dr Goode arrived to declare him dead.

James's body was wrapped in the ship's flag and by half-past ten it was in the mortuary of Alba and Carmelich, the undertakers. Dr Goode was present throughout the embalming and took the opportunity to carry out something of an autopsy when he recorded fatty degeneration of the heart with an enlarged ventricle. He concluded that James had died of 'heart disease', although neither he as his doctor, nor Robert Hunter his brother, had any inkling of such a condition. Dr Goode was reported to have found 'his condition such that he was liable to die at any moment. The situation at the time had nothing to do with his death. He would have died just the same if he had been in the Battle House parlour or anywhere else at the time.'

James Hunter's body was laid out in his Battle House suite where a funeral service was held at four o'clock on Monday afternoon. There was a large attendance, with many making the journey from Pascagoola in Mississippi, as well as a profusion of floral tributes. Those from the Athelstane, Manassus and Infant Mystics Societies were spectacular and would be preserved to accompany Andrew Hunter and James's body to St Andrews. There were also wreaths from all of the leading business lights in Mobile, as well as a large floral anchor from Rhett Goode, a pillow with the initial 'J.H.' worked in 'immertalles' from Mrs St John; Mrs Quigley sent a basket of flowers and Mrs Gaylord and Mrs Waller sent bouquets.

Dr Burgett conducted the service, which closed with words of sympathy 'for the sorrowing widow and children on the other side of the Atlantic,' and a prayer. At half-past six, after all had paid their last respects, ten pall-bearers, all business associates and residents of the Battle House apart from one African-American stevedore from the wharves of Pascagoola, bore the body to the undertakers. At a quarter past eight, Andrew accompanied the body and a selection of floral tributes to the depot of the Louisville and Nashville Railroad, where they were placed on the midnight train to New York and thence onward by ship to St Andrews.

The story has been passed down in St Andrews that James's body arrived in a cask of brandy, giving rise to the enduring black humour in the question of what happened to the brandy. There is some evidence for this, disguised in the Mobile Probate Court records of the settlement of his estate. Among the first items on the list of expenditures immediately following his death is ten dollars for 'duty on ginger ale'; a sum that would have purchased enough ginger ale to float a timber ship at the time. However, the fact that the body was embalmed makes this story doubtful. Interestingly, in the sale of his Battle House effects, his collection of wines sold for $56 and his spirits for $50, while his clothing and the rest of his personal effects raised only $45. Either James maintained a very fine cellar or he was not sartorially inclined.

James' body was interred in the Cathedral Graveyard the day after its arrival in St Andrews and the spectacular floral tribute from the Infant Mystics Society in Mobile was placed upon his grave. Sadly, only those who attended the interment ceremony saw the flowers, for they were stolen from the grave that night. Some months later, a small chinaware wreath inside a glass vase bearing the words 'In Loving Memory' was also stolen, prompting Jof Morris to write to the local newspaper complaining about desecration in the burial ground. The consequences of James Hunter's death would reverberate in the family for many years to come.

22 Family Affairs

Resolving the estate of his son-in-law was not a simple undertaking for Tom Morris and he needed all the friends he had. Doubtless he, James Denham and Charlie Hunter, put their heads together after the funeral in St Andrews and came to the conclusion that they could not handle this alone. As trustees they had the right to appoint whomsoever they thought might best serve the interests of the estate.

On 7 March 1886, less than a month after the funeral, Tom and Mr Denham met in Edinburgh. Then on 29 March, armed with the legal documents required in order to appoint two new trustees who had the business experience that the Trust needed, Tom met Charlie Hunter in Prestwick. The men they chose had been friends of James Hunter in St Andrews: Robert Bethune of Nydie was a Major on the retired list of the British Army and was Laird of the lands of Nydie and the owner of Nydie Quarry, the quarry from which had come the grey sandstone to form the fabric for much of the Town developments. Bethune was a golfer with whom James had played in St Andrews and a member of The Royal and Ancient Golf Club. Alexander Keiller-Bruce was the second appointment.[1] He was from Dundee where his mother was of the Keiller family, the eminent jam makers of that city, who produced the world's first commercial marmalade in 1797. His father had died early and his mother remarried Mr Govan of Smith & Govan, Chemists in St Andrews. Keiller-Bruce inherited the business and became a leading figure in the Town as Dean of Guild on the Town Council. He had been well known to James, his wife and daughter being Lizzie's friends. Keiller-Bruce, however, would pose a problem for Tom in years to come.

On 11 June 1887 in Mobile, Robert Hunter petitioned Judge Price Williams Jnr of the Probate Court of Mobile County, to take out Letters of Administration for his brother's estate in America. His petition was granted and the Mobile County Court formally informed the trustees in St Andrews of the arrangement.

And everything was indeed satisfactory. Robert sent cheques to the Trust between September 1890 and May 1892 totalling £12,752, equivalent today of more than £1 million.[2] This was a fabulous sum of money, which can be placed in perspective only when one considers that the wage of a manual worker at the time was no more than £25 per year.

Robert Hunter himself had prospered in the meantime. Based in Mobile, he changed the name of the company to Robert Hunter and Company, Timber Merchants. Shortly afterwards, in 1887, he joined Arthur Shirley Benn, James's English friend from his days in both Canada and Georgia and together they formed Hunter, Benn and Company, after buying out Lizzie Morris, James's widow in St Andrews. Robert Hunter brought Robert and John Manson of Prestwick over to the United States in 1886. They were made directors of Hunter, Benn & Company and were responsible for running the Darien end of the business. They were enthusiastic golfers and by the 1890s had established the Darien Golf Club on the swampy land on the Altamaha Delta of the Georgia Tidewater: no mean achievement at that time. William and Andrew Hunter, who were siblings of James and Robert, had also emigrated, taking up positions in the Hunter business. All of the Hunter brothers were golfers and all played leading roles in establishing golf in Mobile.

Tom Morris could never have expected to be involved in the handling of such vast sums of money as those which resulted from James's estate. His situation would have been widely talked about in the Town for nothing can remain secret in any small township, least of all St Andrews, where one caddy might overhear a confidential exchange on the Links which would become common knowledge throughout the Town before the round was completed.

Tom continued to golf, to travel and, increasingly, to hold court outside the front door of the shop where he would sit with his grandchildren in the sunshine and talk to passers-by. Accompanied by them and their dog, Silver, he enjoyed walks on the Links while watching the play of the emerging talent in the club-makers' competitions. The pride and pleasure he took in his grandchildren, who called him 'Bosie', was obvious to all. He enjoyed nothing more than parading them on the putting green on summer evenings and, dressed in their best, leading them to St Mary's Church on Sunday mornings, bearing the youngest, Jamesina, born five months after her father's death, high on his shoulders.

Tom's elder grandchildren, Agnes and Bruce, were pupils at the Madras College where their younger sisters, Gray and Jamesina would also come to join them. They were active and popular in the Town, as was their mother,

Lizzie, who although in prolonged mourning for her husband, was involved in the society of the Church and in the Sunday School at St Mary's at the east end of Market Street: from their earliest years, all were participants on the Links. Agnes would experience golfing success in St Andrews as well as in Germany after her marriage to Willie Rusack. Her brother, Bruce, as he was known in the family, enjoyed extensive amateur golfing honours throughout Scotland and England. Like her brother, Gray would come to contest National Amateur Championships.

Lizzie's family was a source of pride to Tom. His family competitions on the Himalayas Putting Green were commented upon in the local press, as was his attendance at a Madras College prize-giving ceremony to see Agnes receive her reading award. Photographs taken by the St Andrews photographer Fairweather show Agnes putting, with Tom and Silver in the background. If his grandchildren were a source of pride they also clearly brought him much joy.

The years throughout the 1880s and early 1890s must have been golden ones for Tom as they brought both comfort and social acclaim. He was made an Elder of Holy Trinity Kirk with duties at its second charge at St Mary's. He was a member and stalwart of the Curling Club, as well as the Burns Club, enjoying the cronyism of the land-owning men of the Town and the University. Tom and his family had become stout and resolute middle-class Victorians.

Although he had his daughter's family and those of his first cousins living in the Town as well as in nearby Tayport and Dundee, it was to his mother's family, the Bruces, late of Crail and Anstruther that his own family remained closest. In local parlance, Jean Bruce's two brothers had done well for themselves. Her elder brother had married into the jam-making Keiller family in Dundee and adopted the hyphenated Keiller-Bruce name. Her younger brother, who had trained as a tailor in Anstruther, was the proprietor of a tailors and haberdashers emporium in Leven, employing five men and three women. The Bruces of Leven had a fine house at Scoonie where Mr Bruce, a widower, resided with his three daughters and his son. Both father and son were leading figures in the Leven Thistle Golf Club. The Bruce family were as stolidly middle class as was Lizzie Hunter in St Andrews. Kate Bruce had been bridesmaid when Lizzie married James so it is not surprising that it was to the Bruces that she turned for help and support during her travels.

Lizzie travelled to visit James in America twice, returning with him to St Andrews, and on each occasion leaving Agnes Bruce from Leven in charge of her children and household. Agnes was the same age as Lizzie; she was a spinster whose role in life seems to have been running her father's home in Scoonie with her two sisters, serving her father and brother. She appears to have helped out in St Andrews not only during Lizzie's visits to America, but also at times when Lizzie took her family to Florence Cottage, the house that James had had built in Prestwick, next door to his parent's retirement home, Hunter House, in the High Street.

In 1891, Lizzie took her younger brother John and her family to Florence Cottage with their 17-year-old housemaid from St Andrews. This could not have been an easy undertaking for the paraplegic John, nor for those that accompanied him, and it says much about Lizzie, as it also does about John's closeness to his nieces and nephew. It also reflects the close connections that the Morris family retained in Prestwick.

Both the 1881 and 1891 census show that Tom was resident in the Pilmour Links house while John and Jof were listed as living in the flat above the shop on the Links Road. In the Pilmour Links house, as well as a living-in maid, Lizzie's family also employed a daily help, doubtless to serve both properties for cleaning and laundry work. In the workshop, Tom was employing eight men by 1891, although he himself could have played little part in their management and productivity for, as well as supervising work on the Links, he appears to have played golf on a daily basis.

Tom played regularly with the members and guests of The Royal and Ancient, most frequently with Mr Everard, who would become the Club's historian, and with Thomas Hodge, amateur artist who was the owner and head of a private boys school in the Town. Increasingly Tom's games, no matter how casual, attracted small crowds of spectators with whom he would walk and chat casually. The Ladies Short Course, by then called the Himalayas Putting Green, was another of his favourite venues. Tom slipped easily and readily into the role of resident celebrity.

Tom clearly relished his renown. Parody poems and references to him in *Punch* and other magazines were collected and pinned to the wall in the shop, where caddies and visitors alike would gather to read them. His mail increased and the stream of visitors became a flood. Newspaper accounts of meetings, tournaments and matches began with a paragraph about his presence or absence at the event. He clearly worked tirelessly at the promotion of the game but he was also enjoying himself.

Few Town Hall *soirées* or visiting troupe of entertainers' performances passed without his attendance, often with his grandchildren in the front row and few without some 'ditty' addressed to him. He attended club and social event dinners and, when pressed, was ready with a 'vote of thanks'. Few charitable committees sat without him, for his name was enough to guarantee support and he appears to have gladly lent it to any worthwhile cause. Any fledgling golf club that called upon him for advice in laying out its course, or even to simply appear at its opening day ceremony, could count on his help.

Tom Morris had emerged from the great age of Victorian patronage to become a great Victorian patron himself.

34 The Gathering Storm

Considering the extent of Tom's out-of-town activities, it is hard to see how and when he performed his duties as Links Superintendent. In his early years after his return to St Andrews, between 1865 and 1879, Tom must have been very active, as that was the time when the most extensive changes were made on the Course. Whins and heather were cleared and fairways widened. Some greens had accommodated two holes from as early as 1830, but it was Allan Robertson whom the Green Committee of The Royal and Ancient had charged with properly establishing them in 1856. Tom not only extended the double greens but also created entirely new ones. The 18th green was formed in 1869, and what is today the 1st green at the side of the Swilken Burn was established for play in 1872.

Hitherto play on the Course had been clockwise. Today's 17th green was also the 1st green, the 16th was the 2nd and so on. With the construction of the 1st green it ultimately became possible to play the Course anti-clockwise. By the late 1870s Tom was regularly changing the direction of play and both the novelty and the general improvement of the Course in consequence was much appreciated. Laudatory notices of the quality of the Course appeared regularly in the press virtually from the time of his taking up stewardship and, singing his praises, became a regular feature in the *St Andrews Citizen* after every Autumn Meeting.

From 1876 David Honeyman ably assisted Tom full-time on the Links. David was a scratch golfer, fiercely loyal to Tom and assiduous in his attendance, if not perhaps his efforts on the Links. There was much humour about Tom and Honeyman's activities throughout their years together. They were the topic of several cartoons and attributed with conversations of the 'Pat and Mick' kind, but if Honeyman was loyal to Tom, it was a loyalty that was reciprocated, because in 1889 Tom advanced David Honeyman a bond from the estate of James Hunter to purchase a house on North Street.

David Honeyman's son, also called David, was also engaged on the Links. He too, was an able player and was a popular singer in the Town and a member of the church choir. Young David married in 1895 before leaving to take up an appointment as a professional in Mexico where he lived for five years before moving to the USA.

The extent of the Honeyman and Tom's achievements on the Links is hard to gauge. They could draw upon Town Council workmen and redundant caddies in the winter months to augment the labour force but we know little of their conceptual contributions. Tom has been attributed with bunker placing and re-turfing of greens which, even if of his conception, required the official ratification of the Green Committee. This committee was made up of three or more members of the Committee of Management of The Royal and Ancient and would appear to have been a passive body, keeping no minutes of meetings until circumstances compelled it to do so in 1890.

Although we know little of the origins of most Old Course bunkers, the Green Committee's records reveal a little of how those on the right hand side of today's 2nd, 3rd, 4th and 5th holes came to be. In 1899 the Committee invited several leading amateur players to help position bunkers on the 2nd through to the 5th as well as the 9th holes. From The Royal and Ancient, Argyll Robertson, Fairlie, Everard, Balfour Melville, Macfie, Low and Freddie Tait were amongst them, as well as William Greig, a local artisan golfer. Clearly Tom must have supervised the construction of these bunkers but would appear to have played only an accompanying role in their numbers and siting. Before 1890, however, it seems that Tom had an entirely free hand in all that transpired on the Links and much of the decision making was left to him.

Tom certainly made extensive renovations but without detailed records from the Green Committee or reference in the press, we cannot conclude what renovations were of his own volition and what the Committee directed. The construction of the 1st and 18th greens were certainly supervised by him as was the reconstruction of what is now the 6th/12th green and the extension of the double green of the 7th and 11th holes.

There is some suggestion that the introduction and construction of fixed separate teeing grounds was his idea. This is not surprising for the practice of teeing-up, initially in 1754 within one club-length from the previous hole, must have made putting through duffers' divots hazardous and frustrating. Being responsible for the quality of the greens, this damage must have perplexed Tom. The teeing distance from the hole was gradually lengthened to not less than six and not more than eight club-lengths. It is not surprising that when separate teeing grounds for all the holes were introduced in 1875, they merited a mention in the press and their adoption was instantaneous and widespread. One wonders why it took so long for Tom and the Green Committee to come to such an obvious solution to what must have long been a nagging problem.

Tom had other problems, too. Although honoured and revered in St Andrews and the locker rooms of The Royal and Ancient and the Honourable Company, his frequent absences from the St Andrews Links during his course construction, 'consultancies', were causing some disquiet. When compared to the standards of the new and blossoming courses in England in particular, the Course was increasingly found wanting.

From the onset of his tenure as Superintendent of St Andrews Links, Tom Morris performed a social juggling act that required considerable diplomatic skill. Serving the interests of The Royal and Ancient Golf Club, his paymasters, while at the same time attending to the townspeople's rights of access, their play and that of visitors, was no easy matter. Tom had no formal designated right to his power on the Links, yet he governed every aspect of it with benevolent tyranny and the fact that he maintained concord between all interested parties is amazing.

Horace Hutchinson made the perspicacious observation that 'his unfailing courtesy, kindliness, tact and perfect temper have kept all the various interests, that are a little apt to run counter to each other at St Andrews, jogging along without friction.' There can be no doubt that Tom was a despot on the Links and Hutchinson provides a brilliant insight into the nature of this:

> Town clubs, students' clubs and the Royal and Ancient, have all done, like good little boys, what 'Old Tom' has told them to do all these years – has told them with such a way of telling that they had not the least idea that they were being ordered about – Tom also not precisely understanding what sort of tyrant he was; and so they have all gone along together in friendly wise, as if shamed into mutual friendliness by the perfect gentleness of the old man, their common mentor.

Things were, however, changing, and it was becoming clear that a seventy-year-old, no matter what esteem, respect or vigour he enjoyed, could not continue to satisfy all interests. With the increasing popularity of the game, more and more people resorted to the Town primarily to play golf. Hotels were proliferating and the letting of rooms to summer visitors made a major contribution to the income of many family households. If the increasing numbers of golfing visitors brought problems of access to the Course, they also brought problems of wear and tear and it was Tom Morris's responsibility to see that this was put to rights.

Tom had set greenkeeping standards from the outset at Prestwick. His nephew, Jack Morris at Hoylake and Charlie Hunter at Prestwick, had enhanced these standards with the encouragement of green committees that were both active and knowledgeable. He himself had raised standards further with his improvements at St Andrews but these required increased maintenance and made greater demands upon labour. His travels as a course consultant placed additional burdens on his time and, coupled with his advancing years, were taking their toll on his efforts. Time caught up with Tom Morris at the start of the 1890s when he first experienced its ravages with the Green Committee of The Royal and Ancient Golf Club.

David Lamb was appointed Chairman of this Committee in 1891 and his first action was to establish a minute book. It is clear that problems were developing with the upkeep of the Course. Not only was there press criticism of its condition during the 1891 Open Championship, but also the fact that the Green Committee felt that it had now become necessary to keep a minute book, suggests that all was not well. It becomes clear in the 1891 minutes that the Committee was set to be more attentive to the decision making in the day-to-day running of the Course and to establish standards of maintenance. It would henceforth instruct Tom and keep a closer eye on his activities on the Links:

> It was agreed to instruct the greenkeeper to have all the bunkers properly dug up and in the future to see that no grass was allowed to grow where it should not be in them. The greenkeeper having been called up was then and there instructed to see that in future the grass was properly rolled after rain; this only having been done up to this date in the most casual way once or twice a year at most.

Although one can only speculate about the feelings of the Green Committee, this was clearly not the comfortable assembly that had gone before and it must have been a confrontational meeting for Tom. He was told to employ two other men to dig the bunkers and further informed that shortage of labour was not to be used as an excuse for the greens not being properly rolled.

This was not simply a new committee flexing its muscles, for it is clear from the September minutes of the Management Committee of The Royal and Ancient, that there was general dissatisfaction with Tom's endeavours on the Links:

> There was read a complaint signed by several members regarding the management of the links and the frequent absences of Tom Morris, the custodian. After careful consideration the meeting resolved that David Honeyman, who has been employed on the links for some time, should be appointed foreman and be responsible for the work done.

It is noteworthy that it was the 'frequent absences' that were referred to as the root of the problems. Tom had never felt the need to seek permission to go away to advise on the building of golf courses, or to participate in competition or exhibition matches, and there is no record of the Green Committee hitherto complaining. He saw himself not only as the green-keeper but also as the custodian of the Links of St Andrews; indeed he was frequently referred to as such. He was an icon in the rapidly expanding world of golf and knew himself to be an important figure in every department and at all levels in it. His word had always been law on the Links: his judgement had never been questioned and he knew that the public perceived him as an ambassador for the Town, The Royal and Ancient and the game itself. The face of golf was, however, changing and the authority of St Andrews was being questioned as the Course was increasingly contrasted and compared with the great new courses emerging in England. The Royal and Ancient was undisputedly regarded as the premier golf club but a new breed of men was coming to the fore in the game at large, and they were not reticent in criticism of it. *Golf* magazine, the first publication dedicated exclusively to the game and published weekly, was founded in 1890 and from the outset it was sometimes critical of the old order. Leading amateur players were emerging from England where little consideration was afforded to tradition or heritage, and these men were finding a foothold in committees of The Royal and Ancient Club. For them it was efficiency, quality and productivity that mattered. They were not, in general, the gentry of old, but men of business who were less tolerant of sentiment in running the affairs of their Club.

Subsequent minutes of the Green Committee make clear that instructions for the maintenance of the Course went directly to David Honeyman, bypassing Tom completely, and that the new arrangement was made absolutely clear to him and that he agreed with it. The Committee instructed Honeyman, for instance, to re-turf the whole of the 6th green. He was also charged with making new holes on the greens on Monday mornings, as well as being issued with detailed instructions for rolling, fertilising and top dressing with a soil and sand mixture.

Tom may have agreed to the new arrangements in committee, but actual execution on the Links was another matter. The fact that he continued to do things his own way and that the committee was not altogether sure how to handle the matter, becomes clear in the minutes of September 1893. We learn that Mr Everard, a long-time friend and confidant of the Morris family, had resigned from the committee and that Allan Macfie had replaced him. In November, however, Macfie also tendered his resignation to the Secretary in a letter that summarised the dissatisfaction he felt:

> Dear Grace,
>
> I have thought the matter over, and I am afraid I must decline to serve on the green committee. As long as the green committee is a mere collective puppet in Tom Morris's hands, I think that it is a perfect farce having one at all; until a green committee would be supported by the general feeling of the club in any dispute with Morris, which is far from the case at present, there is no earthly use in trying to improve the course in any way.

Macfie was obviously neither a man who would pull his punches nor hesitate to speak his mind. He was also not alone in his criticism of Tom's laxity and in the frustration felt at his highhandedness. But The Royal and Ancient membership was clearly divided in its support of the Green Committee. Macfie's resignation reflected the fact that the majority in the Club, although probably supportive of the committee's efforts, would rather that Tom Morris be left undisturbed.

While the members of the Green Committee were having their problems with Tom Morris, he in turn was also having his own difficulties with them. Mr H. W. Hope, the founder of the Luffness Club in East Lothian, related to Rev. John Kerr in 1895 that:

> Tom Morris has often told me of the immense difficulty he has always had, and still has, at St Andrews, to get the green committee to consent to the necessary work and regulations for keeping the course in order. I refer especially to the sanding, and the shifting of the play from one part of the ground to another . . . No green has . . . a good chance of being kept in good order . . . unless they have a man like Tom Morris to organize, superintend, and direct

the work, and is ready to insist upon the necessary work being carried out, however much the best of golfers may grumble at what is being done.

Tom also enjoyed the support of many local people in his efforts, as letters to the editor of the *St Andrews Citizen* show at the time. His routine sanding of the Course, which initially met with derision, was widely recognised as the panacea to all ills by the locals and, when he refused a committee directive to roll the greens, its insistence prompted outrage.

It is not difficult to rationalise the dissatisfaction with Tom's maintenance of the Course and his indifference to committee directives. The Royal and Ancient's membership was burgeoning and the new wave of men, able golfers in the main, played their golf on swards much richer than a Scottish links could naturally sustain and at places without the burden of the past that cluttered decision-making in St Andrews. Courses like Prestwick, Troon, Hoylake, Lytham and Sandwich could initiate changes and improvements as they wished. These clubs owned, or had complete control of, their courses and were free to bring about change as the membership saw fit. In St Andrews, The Royal and Ancient may have carried the expense of upkeep and improvement, but radical change was another matter and any restriction in play would almost certainly bring about conflict with the townspeople.

Radical change was, however, a feature of the times. The death of Queen Victoria in 1901 ended an era that had seen Britain become the most powerful country in the world, while at the same time changing the face of society with manufacturing industry. The free and easy relationship between master and servant that was all Tom Morris had known, was eroded in the founding of the factory system of the Industrial Revolution, and was lost altogether with the emergence of the new middle class with its managerial attitudes. The working class responded with the founding of the Labour Party and strikes organized by coalminers, steelworkers and jute factory workers, tested the hegemony of inheritance and capital. The graduation of women from Scotland's universities, the abolition of elementary school fees and the election of representatives on county councils reflected reform in society and the completion of the Forth and Tay Railway Bridges reflected its mobility.

The old order was changing fast. Alterations to the physical landscape of St Andrews may not have been marked and the social changes not immediately evident, but they were there nonetheless. Tom Morris was left to juggle the demands of the clients of the newly founded hotels and their proprietors, with the increasingly belligerent townspeople vociferously demanding their rights on the Links. Maintaining the status quo could not have been easy and, if it was not clear to Tom, it was apparent to the members of the Green Committee that it was becoming impossible.

Having a word with Tom Morris was an essential part of a sojourn to St Andrews; hiring a caddy and gaining access to the Course was part of that 'having a word' by men unaccustomed to casual response or 'waiting their turn'. Access to the Course often required waiting in line and the 'irreverent caddy' to a gentleman of past times was perceived as a 'disrespectful rogue' by men accustomed to the forelock touching folk of the factory floor. Queuing up for the 1st tee behind a fisherman, a farm labourer or a plumber, was incomprehensible to many accustomed to the privilege of precedence. Congestion was a problem that Tom could handle with effort and quiet tact but the social conflict must have completely bewildered him. To Tom, all men were equal on the golf course, despite their different stations in life. Each section of society had the right to organize their own clubs and affairs and to play their golf where, when and with whom they chose. This was a laudable philosophy perhaps, but absolutely impractical in a situation where one club was bearing all the costs of maintenance and upkeep, while everyone else was enjoying the facilities at no cost whatsoever. As servant of the Green Committee of The Royal and Ancient Golf Club, it was Tom's responsibility to see that his masters had a course to play, maintained to the best of his capabilities and with organized access to it. But he was also a townsman whose life, like that of his employees and many of his friends, was dependent upon the Links through those resorting to the Town to play. In the changing society of the time, his position was impossible to maintain and was, indeed, archaic.

Change had to be brought about, even if only to maintain the existing state of affairs on the Links. The ever-increasing visitor numbers resulted in a very congested course, particularly in the period June to September, with townspeople, as well as Royal and Ancient members, finding it more and more difficult to play when they wished. In addition, the heavy amount of traffic brought about a crisis in course maintenance. It was against this background that The Royal and Ancient determined to resolve the situation by seeking ways of building a new golf course, a relief course effectively, on other available land on the Links of St Andrews.

35 Links in Conflict

It comes as no surprise to learn that, by the end of the 1880s, The Royal and Ancient was considering the possibility of constructing a second golf course on St Andrews Links. Despite the fact that this Club was carrying the cost of upkeep, a member had no guarantee of access to the Course at a time he wished. Apart from Tom Morris organising a caddy and being on hand to make sure that members found a place on the 1st tee amongst the throng of Town players and visitors, they had no more benefits than any other player. This situation must have been an increasingly frequent topic of discussion in the Big Room of the Club and members who had travelled some distance from their home courses, which may have been strictly private, must have felt agitated, if not aggrieved, by having to wait in line. Alexander Cheape of Strathtyrum, proprietor of the Links and a member, would have been aware of the situation and supportive of the Club's ambition to build a second course.

In 1890 Mr Cheape let The Royal and Ancient know that he might be prepared to sell the Links. The Club jumped at the chance of outright ownership and made an offer thought to be £3,000. Mr Cheape eventually turned this down on the grounds that it would materially diminish the letting value of some of his adjacent farmland at Balgove but, crucially, promised to give the Club first refusal if he changed his mind.

There are no secrets in a small township. The Town Council must have known that The Royal and Ancient were well along the way to relieving Mr Cheape of land that, in agricultural terms, was of little use other than for intermittently grazing sheep. Improvement or development of the Links as a whole was impossible because of the nature of the land and obligation, by ancient charter, to preserve the golfing ground. Proprietorship of St Andrews Links may have brought kudos but little in terms of revenue.

Clearly aware of The Royal and Ancient's interest in buying the Links and under pressure from all quarters, the Town Council formed a committee in April 1893, 'to consider the propriety and practicality of increasing the golfing facilities on the Links'. This was in response to talk in the Town of The Royal and Ancient's approaches to the Cheape estate with a view to constructing a second course exclusively for the use of its members. In retrospect, it is difficult to understand why the Council had not acted earlier, because the Course was the principal asset of the Town and the fact was that the Town did not own the very thing that was sustaining it. It is not surprising that this committee recommended that the Council should approach The Royal and Ancient to discuss the future disposition and entitlement of the Links.

Throughout the spring and early summer of 1893, the Club and the Town Council met in an effort to see if there was sufficient common ground to make any arrangement for joint purchase of the Links. Discussions foundered, however, on two points. Firstly, the Council had rightly concluded that the driving incentive for The Royal and Ancient was to acquire the Links in order to construct a private course for its members. This was unacceptable to the Council who wanted any new course to be open to the other St Andrews golf clubs as well as to the public. Secondly, the right of the public to walk over the Links was being challenged by the Club on the grounds that, in law, this was a privilege granted by the owner of the Links and not a right.

Throughout the course of their meetings, the Royal and Ancient gave the Town Council solemn assurance that, were the Club to obtain lease or ownership of the Links nothing would change. The Club would continue to manage and pay for the upkeep of the Course as before and the public would continue to have the right to play golf over it. However, the Council minutes of 3 May 1893 record that the members had concluded that the Club was '. . . apparently determined to acquire the links on their own behalf and to make a private golf course for the use of members of their own club'. In addition, the minute makes clear that the Club was questioning the right of the public to walk over the entire Links and that '. . . although strongly pressed on this point they declined to give any written obligation that they would not interfere with the public walking over the links'. The meetings had resulted in impasse: after a stormy meeting of the Council, a resolution was passed to approach Mr Cheape with an appeal for time and the opportunity to consider the purchase of the Links. In the council chamber, 18 of the 21 members moved to proceed with a plan to negotiate this purchase. Only two councillors, both members of The Royal and Ancient, voted against the motion, with the redoubtable George Bruce abstaining on the grounds that the rights of the townspeople to the Links were already established in ancient charter.

The Council made an approach to James Cheape, Alexander's successor, for his blessing, should the Town be able to put together a purchasing proposal. This led to an offer of £4,500 but Mr Cheape's agent replied that as negotiations were already in hand with another party, Mr Cheape was not in a position to deal with this offer.

This rebuff prompted the Council to write to The Royal and Ancient, as the 'other party', accusing it of 'intervening' in the matter. The Club was understandably indignant in its reply, pointing out that since it had been in serious negotiations with the Cheapes since 1890, it was the Council that had 'intervened'. Clearly relations between The Royal and Ancient and the Council, which had previously been described as 'convivial', had seriously deteriorated. Relations worsened even further when there was talk of the Council applying for a compulsory purchase order through Parliament.

Almost certainly the Town Council's approaches stimulated The Royal and Ancient, as well as Mr Cheape, because in April the Cheape Estate agreed to sell the Links to the Club under terms to be agreed. The price was £5,000 and the transaction was completed in the autumn of 1893. In response to the threat of compulsory acquisition of the Links by the Council, the Club's incumbent Captain, Andrew Graham Murray, one of the best legal brains in the country, advised the Club that any such attempt would not succeed if the Club, as the owners of the Links, objected to it.

Tom Morris maintained a very low profile during the course of this often bitter debate that went on both within and outside the council chamber and the Club. He had made it known that he strongly favoured public ownership of the Links during his cross-examination in the Road Case of 1878. He found himself in a difficult situation, however, when the Town Council called a public meeting to discuss the consequence of compulsory purchase by Act of Parliament, for, although fervent about the burgh's ownership of the Links, he was also a servant of The Royal and Ancient. Judiciously, he declined the invitation to attend a public meeting in the Volunteer Hall on 25 September 1893 which had been organised to gauge public opinion. His absence at the meeting was noted and commented upon when the townspeople expressed their overwhelming support for the Council's plan. The local press reported that it was 'a stormy meeting'. Captain Burn, the leader of an opposing ratepayers group, made frequent interruptions and when he was given the platform was howled down. At another meeting held by the dissident ratepayers and chaired by Captain Burn, Mr Hay Fleming, the popular local historian, was denied an opportunity to speak. Feelings were running high.

Both as an outcome of strength of opinion expressed in the public meetings as well as in the council chamber, the Town Council proceeded quickly in its efforts to acquire the Links for the Town. Dr Thomas Thornton of Dundee, an expert on Parliamentary procedures, was commissioned to advise the Council and, within a month, he recommended that the best course of action was to purchase the Links under a special Act of Parliament. The Town Council's decision to promote a private bill in Parliament for the compulsory acquisition of the Links from The Royal and Ancient Golf Club precipitated two years of sometimes acrimonious conflict between Club and Council over the ownership of the Links of St Andrews.

It also attracted widespread press commentary and much of it was written in vitriol. One commented that 'feelings were running high amongst some members of the Club about the desirability of having their own private golf course'. This possibility of The Royal and Ancient abandoning St Andrews altogether in favour of acquiring a private course elsewhere was being discussed within the press and by some members, but there is no record of it being officially discussed by the Club itself. The *St Andrews Citizen* commented, 'The Royal and Ancient might have been excused if . . . in these circumstances, they had severed their connection with the famous links, and sought a home for themselves, after the fashion of other clubs, elsewhere, and on ground which they could call their own'. The Honourable Company of Edinburgh Golfers had, only two years before, forsaken the public Musselburgh links for reasons similar to those now confronting the Club and had very successfully moved to Muirfield. This fact would not have been lost on any of the parties concerned in St Andrews. It is difficult to assess how real or large this threat to leave St Andrews was, but it is certain that Tom Morris would have vehemently opposed it.

Matters improved in late September 1893 when the Club informed the Council that, if within two years the necessary sanction was obtained from Parliament, the Club would hand over the Links to the Town, subject to mutually agreed conditions regarding the management of the courses. In addition, the Council was to repay the Club the £5,000 purchase price and any costs incurred in building a new course. While the Club and the Town were now co-operating in a common cause there was, however, to be a last minute serious disagreement. The stumbling blocks centred around who should control the courses and be the recipient of the green fees collected from visitors for play over the new course and how such fees would be applied. The position of The Royal and Ancient was clear. The Club had for long carried the running costs of the Course and, understandably, felt that it was its best custodian in the interests of all concerned. Additionally, it felt that any payments from visitors should go to the Club to help defray these costs. The Council, however, wanted to control the management of the courses, as well as receive any income generated. The parties could not agree to the final wording on these two points and The Royal and Ancient took the dramatic eleventh-hour step of presenting a petition against the Bill.

In opposing the Bill, The Royal and Ancient was now joining Mr Cheape and the ratepayers faction, who had previously lodged their objections. Captain Burn, of Ladies Golf Club fame, led the dissidents' group which included Dr Paterson, who ran a preparatory boarding school on the Scores and was a town councillor as well as being a Club member; Mr T.T. Oliphant, a principal figure in the Road War who was also a councillor and Club member; Mr C. Grace, the Town Clerk and Secretary of the Club, who was a vociferous supporter; Mr D. Mason, proprietor of the Golf Hotel; Mr Turpie, a plumber; Mr J. Macdougal, a gardener in the Town, and Major Bethune.

The ratepayers against the bill alleged that acquisition of the Links would throw a serious additional burden upon them, and the proposed one and a halfpenny in the pound rates increase was simply the start of things to come and ownership of the Links would be a financial burden and prove costly to the Town. They also claimed that they had never been consulted on the matter but this was unfounded, since there had been at least one specially convened public meeting in the Volunteer Hall and a Council election had taken place when every candidate returned had pledged support for the Bill. Captain Burn had done little for his cause with his disruptive behaviour at this meeting and, at a meeting called by him and his supporters, he lost credibility altogether when he refused to recognise Mr Hay-Fleming. The Royal and Ancient was at pains to distance itself from Captain Burn's group during the time it was opposing the Bill, as did Mr Cheape. This faction also called Tom Morris as an expert witness and he, together with the principals in the dispute, went to London to testify in front of a Select Committee. The hearing started on 1 May 1894 and was chaired by Sir James Kitson.

Three days into the hearing, counsel for the Council reported that agreement had been reached with The Royal and Ancient Club. The other objectors did not withdraw their opposition, however, and the proceedings therefore continued. In retrospect it is clear that the ratepayers faction was an impediment to the whole process and caused delay and expense to all concerned. What is less clear and difficult to understand is why Tom appeared in London as a witness for those against public ownership.

For someone who was 'prepared to give the roof off his own house' to see the Links owned by the Town, as he had declared himself in the Links Road case some fifteen years earlier, his appearance against the Act is a mystery. It is possible that he took the same position as that of George Bruce in accepting that the townspeople's access to all parts of the Links was safeguarded through ancient statutes. It is also possible that he was there as a servant of The Royal and Ancient Club, although this is surely unlikely since he was representing the ratepayers faction and it is doubtful if the Club would have placed him in a situation that would have compromised him with the townspeople.

It is more likely that he was alarmed when he heard of Provost Macgregor's proposal to turn the 1st and 18th fairways into a public amenities area and to have the Course start at the 2nd hole. Macgregor was not a golfer so he may perhaps be excused, but Tom could well have taken the view that his Course was safer in the hands of The Royal and Ancient than it was in the shifting sands of the council chamber. What is most probably the case is that the 73-year-old simply wanted things to remain as they were and for everyone to live in harmony. His position did, however, raise not a few eyebrows in the Town and it was not helped by Mr Everard's rather silly column in *The Pelican*, a London-based journal, reporting that Tom had 'chuckled' throughout the entire parliamentary proceedings at which he was present.

The legal minds were, however, clearly focused. The counsel for the Town, in pleading for compromise, substantially conceded the Club's position on the two points of disagreement. Effectively the agreement gave control of the management of the Links to The Royal and Ancient. The Club would continue to pay for the upkeep of the courses and pay the cost of building a new one. The St Andrews townspeople would have free access to the Course, as before, as well as any new course built, with green fees paid by visitors to be used to defray the cost of maintaining the courses. Little wonder that the chairman of the Council's Links Extension Committee, Tom's close friend George Murray, spoke glowingly of The Royal and Ancient's actions: 'The Club has done quite right . . . in giving the opportunity to the town of purchasing the links, it is acting very handsomely by the town'.

The Links Act of 1894 was given Royal Assent on 20 July 1894. The Links of St Andrews came into public ownership again and Tom Morris would not be required to 'give the roof off his house' after all.

36 New Facilities on the Links

St Andrews was beset with buoyant optimism in the early 1890s and understandably so. The list of visitors appearing in the local press throughout the summer months was lengthening. Property prices were booming as the Town's status as a resort grew, and the University was enjoying something of a new lease of life with more men of means and leisure finding St Andrews a desirable place to live.

Plans of improvement abounded in the Town and in the council chamber: many of them focused on the Links and the West Sands, with the object of providing resort facilities similar to those enjoyed in the celebrated seaside resorts in England. Tom Morris was regularly reported as a supporter of every plan and proposal put forward, possibly content in the knowledge that he had heard it all before and that nothing had come of any of them. St Andrews had neither an esplanade nor promenade and there was realistically little chance of the Town acquiring either without major capital investment and structural reorganisation of the 1st hole of the Course. Access to the West Sands was across the Course – a hazardous progress for sea-bathers who created a frustrating impediment for golfers striking off the 1st tee or for those playing to the Home Hole.

Early attempts were made to create a paved walkway round The Royal and Ancient Clubhouse in an attempt to divert walkers and carriages from the Links. One early project planned and to be financed by a Mr Steele, involved sinking railway sleepers into the beach by the Clubhouse and making a walkway by in-filling behind them. The tidal surge that ran east to west along the cliffs and across the flat expanse of beach behind the Clubhouse towards the mouth of the Swilken Burn, made short work of Steele's Folly (as it was popularly known), by washing away this half-hearted attempt at constructing an esplanade.

Tom was particularly in favour of Provost Paterson's plan for reclaiming land running from the Clubhouse to the point where the Swilken Burn meets the sea. It was Paterson's intention to build a promenade, the cost of which he was prepared to carry from his own pocket and, in 1888, the Town Council set up a committee to study a plan that he had had prepared by a firm of consulting civil engineers. Although the committee managed to agree the project in principle, they failed to agree on the exact line that the esplanade should take and, after much wrangling and adverse publicity, the Provost withdrew his generous bequest.

Councillor George Bruce, a prominent and highly respected figure in Victorian St Andrews, was a member of this committee and by far the most vociferous and vitriolic opponent of the Provost's plan.[1] Bruce had bigger things in mind for the approaches to the West Sands and was neither hesitant in airing his views nor for taking steps to put them into effect. He was knowledgeable about the tides and the likely outcomes of erosion caused by the sea. The only workable solution, he argued, was to build a barrier between the reef, known as Doo Craig, and the base of the cliffs to the east of the Clubhouse. This, he reasoned, would disrupt the tidal surge, thus preventing further erosion, while at the same time reclaiming more than an acre of land extending to the mouth of the Burn. His plan would enable a new road to be built and improve access to the West Sands and, more crucially for Tom Morris and the golfers, divert traffic from crossing the Links. Bruce also intended that the sea-bathing conditions would be made more pleasant by extending one of the Town's sewers further out to sea.

In 1893, George Bruce and his son Henry, who was trained as an architect and civil engineer, devised a plan to place four fishing boat hulks on the beach running outwards from opposite the Clubhouse. The high water mark on the beach was then within thirty feet of the building itself. When the plan became known, scorn was poured upon the Bruces in both the council chamber and in the streets of the Town, but nevertheless they went ahead, carrying through the initial construction stages at their own expense.

Four hulks were purchased, two from St Andrews and one each from Cellardyke and Anstruther. They were 63-foot herring boats of a construction peculiar to the Scots herring fleet that had already brought considerable wealth to the East Coast fishing burghs and would continue to do so for another fifty years.

Pulled up on to the beach, the hulks were set in place chained one to the other and filled with stones, rubble and concrete. The stones were moved from all along the beach by hand with the two Bruces working as hard as their men at the task, as did other independent supporters of the plan. Eventually, by driving in stakes, a barricade was built that held against the tide on the eastern side of the hulks. It did not take long for the whole scheme to catch the popular imagination, even within the council chamber, and the beach to the west of the line of hulks quickly became a dumping ground for the Town's refuse and waste from building sites, greatly helping the project. There were problems that had to be overcome, not least with the sewer that ran into the sea, perilously close to The Royal and Ancient's Clubhouse, which not only had to be moved but also extended.[2] Moving and extending this sewer was the cause of much disruption and made for an unpleasant time in the club; the rats that had followed the Town's refuse to the beach did not take long to appreciate the facilities of The Royal and Ancient Clubhouse.

Time is a great achiever and, together with effort and support from within the council chamber, a concrete wall was constructed along the north face of the newly formed embankment. Topsoil was spread over the enclosed area and soon a broad expanse of grass was available for the townspeople's leisure activities. George Bruce's scheme had worked remarkably well and a substantial area of land was reclaimed from the sea. The embankment was completed in May 1897.

In 1904, the Town Council came to recognise George Bruce's achievement and despite other proposals, resolved to name the new area 'The Bruce Embankment' in his honour. The Council further resolved that 'golf should not be played thereon'. Despite this resolution, a public putting green was laid out on the Bruce Embankment in 1914. It has been in continuous play ever since, interrupted only by the ephemeral tented village that springs up on it with every major golf tournament and which completely engulfs it during an Open Championship.

Construction of the relief, or New Course as it was already talked of, was already well under way as George Bruce's embankment came into being.

The Royal and Ancient had begun work on this New Course before the details of the Act of Parliament were agreed upon and Royal Assent was granted. A sub-committee of the Club had been formed, charged with the responsibility of creating this New Course and it wasted no time in setting about its objective. In November 1893, some nine months before the Act was passed, the *St Andrews Citizen* reported that the new course had been 'marked out by flags', and in February of the following year, *Golf* noted that construction work had started.

This was a major undertaking by the standards of the day. The cost to The Royal and Ancient was £2,000, with 45 men being initially employed in clearing whins, re-turfing where uprooting had taken place, and in preparing ground for the greens. Work continued throughout 1894, with all golfers eagerly awaiting the opening.

What passed for an opening ceremony took place on 10 April 1895 with Tom and Dr Duncan playing a match against Sheriff Henderson and his son, the result of which is unknown. What was recorded, however, was that Tom Morris had the honour of striking the first ball to open the Course. As Henderson was the chairman of The Royal and Ancient sub-committee set up to plan and prepare the course, this was yet another accolade for Tom, reflecting his status and the reverence in which he was held.

Lying between the Old Course and the sea, the general opinion was that 'The New' was a splendid course, in many respects similar to its ancient neighbour but several strokes more difficult. Full use had been made of the lie of the land, with many natural bunkers, as well as a few new ones. The greens and fairways were typically undulating, with the Home Green drawing particular praise from the *St Andrews Citizen* in 1895: 'The putting green . . . is a beautiful broad expanse of turf, not dead level . . . but with ridges and "saucers" and dips, which make putting what it really ought to be.' Everard wrote in *Golf*, 'The new links is no course for the slovenly player; driving must be straight and long . . . It is safe to prophesy that in a few years' time St Andrews will be able to boast of two courses unrivalled by any in the world.'

Not everybody, however, was happy with the New Course. Mr R. Cathcart, a respected member of The Royal and Ancient and the first Chairman of the joint Green Committee, wrote to the Secretary of the Club in 1898. He stated that the course would require to be greatly improved and much more money should be spent on it. As a result, the Green Committee were authorised to borrow money to effect the required improvements.

It is not clear what part Tom Morris had played in its design. There is no information about his input in the planning, either in the records of the Club or in the minutes of the Town Council and there are only vague references in the press. While he was in much demand throughout the British Isles for laying-out courses, being described by *Golf* magazine as '. . . the wily layer-out of courses from St Andrews', he would appear to have been marginalised in the design and construction of the New Course.

There was no shortage of knowledgeable golfers within the membership of The Royal and Ancient, and the design would have been the subject of much consultation and discussion. Benjamin Hall Blyth, for instance, was a member of the sub-committee and would have held and voiced strong views, as he had done over the construction of Muirfield two years previously. As a partner in the family civil engineering firm in Edinburgh that had built the grand Waverley Railway Station and the North Bridge over it, he was certainly experienced. It is not surprising that his man, Mr Duff, was put in charge of supervising the work and managing the forty-five men engaged in the construction. Hall Blyth almost certainly played a central part in also formulating the layout of the New Course and some would have it that he should be credited with its design.

At the time, Tom was in his mid seventies and being criticised both within the Club and the Town for the lack of time and attention he devoted to the upkeep of the Old Course. It is certainly possible that the sub-committee deliberately sidelined Tom regarding the design of the New Course.

There is conflicting evidence about the role he played. While letters appeared in the local newspapers complaining that Tom was not being allowed to play as great a part in the design as might be expected, *Golf* magazine commented in April 1895, 'Old Tom Morris has, of course, been supervisor-in-chief of the laying out of the course, but Mr Duff and Mr D. Honeyman, who have carried out his ideas, deserve high praise for their work.' Other local press reports commented that The Royal and Ancient sub-committee worked closely with Tom throughout and received much assistance from him. It is possible that Tom produced the initial outline layout of the course with the details being decided by Hall Blyth and the sub-committee.

He clearly did play some part in the design and it could well have been a very significant one, as both his knowledge and experience would have been important to the project. There is insufficient evidence, however, of his involvement to credit him with being the designer of the New Course, or that it should be designated a 'Tom Morris course' today. It is more than likely that the layout was arrived at by a consensus of knowledgeable members of The Royal and Ancient, including one or two first rate local golfers as well as, of course, Tom Morris.

In May 1896, The Royal and Ancient and the Town Council fulfilled the stipulation contained in the Links Act that the Links would be held in a joint feu. The Courses would be managed by a joint committee consisting of five members from the Club and two from the Council. Tom sat on, or was invited to, all of the Town Council's consultative or special committee meetings regarding the Links. As the Links Superintendent, he also attended meetings of both The Royal and Ancient and St Andrews Links Green Committees.

The meetings that caused him most consternation, however, must have been those at which the caddying question was raised, a topic recurring with increasing frequency.

37 A Time of Strife

In Allan Robertson's day the caddies were drawn from the ranks of the Town's weavers and the club- and ball-makers who were able players. In times of high demand fishermen and out-of-work tradesmen augmented their numbers. Robert Forgan and James Wilson had done what they could to muster and control the caddies after Allan's death in 1859, but it is clear that neither won the required respect nor conveyed the necessary authority to control the free spirits associated with the caddying lifestyle.

In 1864, The Royal and Ancient Club issued its members with *Proposed Rules Regarding the Pay and Discipline of Caddies*. These rules designated the categories of first- and second-class caddies, essentially separating proper caddies (then nearly all professional golfers) from mere club carriers, as well as fixing the rate of pay per round. When Tom returned to St Andrews that year, his remit on the Links was formalised, but it was also altogether different from Allan's. Although Tom's role in the government of caddies was not stipulated, what was expected of him from both the Club members, as well as the caddies, was a return to the old ways. Tom became able to control play on the Course with the same ease that Allan Robertson had done before him. Caddies had to pass muster before him and he could match the caddy to the man and his play. With the increase in play throughout the 1880s, however, the demand for caddies was such that everyone and anyone who could carry clubs found ready employment on the Links in the summer months and inevitably there was strife. Tom not only had to adjudicate in disputes between the regular and casual caddies but also between a player and the frequently outrageous demands of his caddy.

News of squabbling and outright fighting for carrying a man's clubs, even before he had alighted from the train at the railway station, made the national press and was parodied in cartoons in the periodicals of the day. Many youngsters, often playing truant from school, spent the day in the Swilken Burn in the hope of making some money retrieving golf balls from the water. Some were also not above muddying the water or standing on a ball in the mud to make sure that it was not found. It was a ploy that had been passed down through generations. There was a good market in second-hand gutta balls and caddies were able salesmen, airing their apparently knowledgeable views on the merits of particular balls. Retrieving balls from the Burn neither necessitated a long walk to look for them in the whins nor the uncertainty of finding them. As early as September 1866, the *St Andrews Gazette* reported that lynch law had broken out on the Links when 'a gallant Major' caught a boy who was muddying the Burn water to collect golf balls and had 'pitched him into the burn'. The boys also went to the extent of damming the mouth of the Burn to raise the water level to facilitate their work that year. Tom found a solution in paying a boy to stand guard at the Burn. Although there is no report on the success of this solution, it must have been difficult to find a youngster prepared to take on this job, as it would also have meant taking on the wrath of his friends.

Caddying had become the work of fishermen disinclined or unable to go to sea, as well as every other man who found strenuous effort unappealing, or was attracted to the lottery of a caddy's income so that he himself could play his golf. Instead of waiting at the 1st tee, the caddies took to waiting outside hotels, and it became difficult to hire a caddy on the tee. The national press reported on the squabble at St Andrews station and outside the hotels in the summer months and caddy jokes that became and, indeed, remain part of magazine fare, were born out of the melee on the Links at this time.

Tom Morris was formally appointed as Superintendent of the caddies in 1869. Any complaints had to be addressed, through him, to the Green Committee, who had the power to suspend or otherwise discipline any offenders. Lt. General George Moncrieff, while Provost of the Town, established evening classes for them in the Fishers School with prizes awarded for reading, writing and arithmetic, as well as for attendance and deportment. The Royal and Ancient also did its part to improve the lot of the caddy by setting up a welfare fund for clothing and other support through times of illness or hardship.

By 1890, the contracting of caddies that had hitherto taken place outside Tom Morris's shop under his supervision and adjudication, was out of control. It was clear that a more formal system would have to be established. In August 1890, The Royal and Ancient formed a caddies sub-committee to address the problem and the report it produced began the erosion of Tom's absolute power on the Links.

This report recommended the appointment of an officer through whom members were requested to engage their caddies and it also set recommended rates of pay. This proposal was generally adopted and the first Caddy Master appointed was Nicholas Robb, who had served twenty-three years in the Royal Navy before taking charge of the coastguard at Crail. He firstly established a register of recognised caddies and enforced the fixed rates of pay which varied between winter and summer and the Spring and Autumn Meetings. Rates were also designated for a professional playing with a gentleman, who, in addition, was obliged to pay the same amount for the professional's caddy.

Mr Robb's tenure of Caddy Master lasted a few years; conflict and elevation to Club Officer of The Royal and Ancient eventually took him indoors and in 1898, John Macgregor, a Black Watch soldier on the Reserve List, replaced him. Macgregor's term was brief, however, for after only a year, he was called to duty in the Boer War, where he was killed in action in the same campaign that took the life of Freddie Tait, the Amateur Champion of 1896 and 1898. Alexander Taylor took over from John Macgregor and he became a fixture on the 1st tee of the Old Course for many years.

Although the caddies were henceforth formally regulated, golf on the Course was not. Play from the 1st tee remained on a first-come, first-served basis, with caddies queuing on behalf of their men and Club members demanding priority. Needless to say, some ugly scenes ensued and Tom was summoned with increasing frequency. With the establishment of the Links Act in 1894, the Joint Committee's first decision was to appoint Andrew Greig as Starter on the Old Course.

This was a judicious appointment. He was a well-known and able man and a popular figure in the Town; his brother, Willie, was one of the best amateur players in Scotland. Tom attended the committee meeting when Andrew was appointed, most probably on his recommendation.

Tom Morris's word may have remained law on the Links, even though the new Green Committee had shown its teeth restructuring the labour force, but with the appointment of a Caddy Master and a Starter, his power base was significantly eroded. His hand was nevertheless still firmly at the helm. He was at Baillie John Milne's side when, representing the Town magistrates, the Baillie told the caddies that he insisted upon every caddy washing his hands and face and brushing his boots and clothes before going to the Links each morning. Whether Tom managed to keep a straight face or not is unrecorded.

With the implementation of the Links Act, the Town Council assumed responsibility for the caddies. This meant that the caddies came under the jurisdiction of the Burgh Court and Town's special by-laws. The Council produced its first set of rules for caddies in 1896, which was an almost exact copy of those in force at Musselburgh. Licensed caddies had come into being. They were required to wear a brass plate number badge at all times and they were not allowed to refuse an engagement, canvas for employment or argue about their rotation. They had to be decently clothed, strictly sober and prepared to conduct themselves in a 'civil, respectful and proper manner'. A caddy's license would be suspended or revoked if convicted of a crime and, contravention of the rules meant conviction before the magistrates with a penalty of £1, with 14 days imprisonment for non-payment.

Inevitably, in an occupation that attracted the free-and-easy maverick, there were many transgressions, and in a township where pride and prejudice were not unknown, the caddy's cumbersome brass plate was a stigma. But there were other unforeseen problems.

A professional golfer teaching a client would carry his man's clubs during a lesson and at least one conviction ensued from this practice. Andrew Kirkaldy was taken to court for carrying the Earl of Dudley's clubs. Andra' (as he was known) had told the Caddy Master that he would be carrying the clubs and had been warned against doing so. When Andra' returned to the 18th green carrying His Lordship's clubs he was charged and ordered to appear before the magistrates court. Tom was called as a witness to help determine the definition of a professional and contributed the unhelpful response to the magistrate, 'Ye ken as weel as me what the difference is between a professional golfer and a caddy.' Andra', however, needed no help from anybody. He conducted his own defence and, cross-examining Alexander Taylor, the Caddy Master, the following exchange ended the matter:

> 'Did you see Lord Dudley pay me?' Andra' asked the Caddy Master.
>
> 'I did not,' Mr Taylor replied.
>
> 'Tut, tut,' the Baillie Magistrate interjected. 'This is no case at all. Go away, Andrew.'

Andra' related that on his way home he met an old friend who said, 'Man, Andra', you missed your callin'. You ocht to have been a lawyer. But, Andra', just between you an' me, did you caddy for a fee or no?'

'Did you never try caddying for the good of your health?' Andra' replied.

He recounted the story in his autobiography *My Fifty Years at St Andrews* and tells how 'Tom Morris liked to get me on telling the story of my Police Court adventure.'

History tells us that Tom was more bemused than despairing about the changes taking place on the Links. The 'Venerable Grand Old Man of

Golf', as he was referred to in the press, was party to the general optimism abroad in the Town in his eternally youthful and enthusiastic way about every aspect of golf's progress. His grandchildren growing up about him kept him young in outlook and spirit, his shop door kept him abreast of gossip and the succession of golfing pilgrims kept his finger on the pulse of the game, wherever it was played.

Every notable figure in golf, and in much of society as well, was introduced to Tom and, even if they did not enjoy a round on the Course with him, would certainly be exposed to the full beam of his charm. H.H. Asquith, the then Liberal MP for East Fife and destined to be Prime Minister in 1908, had an annual summer holiday in St Andrews when he 'placed himself in Tom Morris's hands'. Asquith was Home Secretary in 1895 when he appeared in St Andrews for his annual holiday. Only weeks before, Tom had played a round with Arthur Balfour, the then First Lord of the Treasury, who would also come to be Prime Minister in 1902. The newspapers made much of both men's visits to the Town, as did *Punch*. In St Andrews there was much humour at the time about the 'Grand Company' that Tom was keeping and the popularity he was enjoying nationwide. He was said to have described Asquith, one of the great orators of the House of Commons, as 'a very well spoken man'. Balfour, an outstanding golfer who had published *Defence of Philosophic Doubt* some years earlier, Tom described as 'a thoughtful player, very sparing with his shots'. Whether or not these remarks are true we will never know, but they were frequently repeated at the time, as was the *Pelican* account of Asquith's appallingly bad golf that came from Everard's pen.

Tom may have had his problems with recalcitrant caddies and small boys on the Links. He may also have suffered the rants of George Bruce and those like him who resented the apparent hegemony of The Royal and Ancient, but there is no doubt that he was respected, no matter how grudgingly, at every level of society in St Andrews. Few local events were held without his presence. He opened flower shows and fêtes, presented prizes and proposed votes of thanks.

It is clear that Tom still enjoyed widespread respect within the Club. Mr MacFie may have taken exception to his high-handedness on the Links, but the general membership, and certainly the Green Committee, seem to have been prepared to endorse his decisions even in the face of complaints from the general public. After the Open Championship in 1895, Tom felt that it was time that the Course had a rest and, without referring to the Committee, promptly removed the flags from the greens and filled up the holes. In response to a barrage of complaints, the Committee was forced to publish a public apology that was posted in the local press, as well as in the Post Office and the Town Hall. It read:

> This Committee, learning that the golf holes on the Old Course have been filled up by the Custodian of the Links without authority, regret if any inconvenience should have been caused to the public and that such action should have been taken without notice and general agreement among golfers, but recognising that the Old Course is much in need of a rest, resolve to allow the holes to remain closed until 30th June.

What the caddies felt about the loss of their livelihood for a summer month was not recorded, but they doubtless made their feelings known to Tom at the shop door.

38 The High Priest of Golf

Golf burgeoned in the last decade of the nineteenth century. In retrospect, the Open Championship at Prestwick in 1890 was a groundbreaking event in the development of the game. Not only did an amateur golfer win the event for the first time, but he was an Englishman to boot! The *Glasgow Herald* considered John Ball from Hoylake to be the 'surprise winner' when he was declared the 'Champion Golfer of the Year' and, although it remained unsaid, the pride of the Scottish professionals must have been badly hurt. While Ball may not have been a household name in Scottish golf, he was already well known to Tom Morris and certainly familiar to the members at Prestwick and St Andrews, for he had already won the Amateur Championship.

The Amateur was the brainchild in 1885 of the Hoylake club, when Allan Macfie, a leading Scottish golfer, triumphed in the inaugural event. Entry was restricted to members of 'recognised' golf clubs in a move designed to keep out 'undesirables', so Macfie's claim to fame is questionable. For the 1886 event at St Andrews, which was open to all amateur golfers, 24 clubs subscribed to a magnificent silver vase. It speaks volumes about the reverence and respect with which Tom Morris was generally held that it is his unmistakable effigy that stands atop the Amateur Championship Trophy.

John Ball was not only the first amateur to win the Open Championship but he was also the first to hold both Open and Amateur titles in the same year. His achievement drew huge press coverage in England, and much of it was focused on the relative importance of the two titles. Some 44 players had contested the Amateur Championship at Hoylake in 1890 and Ball had to battle through four rounds of matchplay golf in two days to take the honours; by contrast, he was required only to play two rounds against a field of 30 to win the Open Championship. This commentary must have stung the Scots professionals and Tom in particular, because the event was very much identified with him and it was still through him that players intimated their intention to compete in it.

The format for the Open Championship had not changed since its inception in 1860. It was still contested over one day of play and for a prize fund that had altered little in 30 years. It was not generally perceived as the greatest test in the game and it certainly did not acknowledge the 'Champion Golfer of the Year' with a reward commensurate with the title. Change was long overdue and reorganisation was needed to invest the Open Championship with an added importance and raise its profile within the rapidly expanding game.

With the growth of the game in England and increasing press coverage of events, The Royal and Ancient was coming under some scrutiny as the perceived leading authority in golf, particularly from *Golf* magazine. Although invariably laudatory of 'Old Tom' and his efforts, the editor severely criticised The Royal and Ancient's arrangements for the Open Championship at St Andrews in 1891. Notice of less than a month had been given of the date and the English clubs appeared to have learned of it only through the usual notice posted in *The Field*. This date clashed with the Autumn Meeting of the Hoylake Club where John Ball, the previous year's winner, together with Horace Hutchinson and their younger compatriot, Harold Hilton, were members.

The short notice of the date was as it had always been. *Golf* was quick to point out that it was no longer adequate in the changing face of the game and used it as a wider criticism of the event and its organisation. Referring to the members of The Royal and Ancient, the editor bemoaned 'The administration of these (golfing interests) is frequently entrusted to gentlemen ludicrously out of touch with the wider golfing world, who . . . are not practical golfers, or acquainted in the slightest degree with the larger golfing community'. Even if, as *Golf* commented, 'The Royal and Ancient was out of touch with the wider world of golf beyond the limits of Fife', others in the game were not.

Tom Morris himself did not escape censure. It was through him that all professionals entered for the Championship and *Golf* commented, 'The memory of Tom Morris appears to have been relied upon as all-sufficient for the occasion; but, in at least one case, that veteran admittedly forgot all about a would-be competitor, while in others there was much conflict of testimony as to whether he had received names or not.'

Immediately after the conclusion of the Championship at St Andrews in 1891 the professionals held a meeting: Tom Morris was in the chair. It was unanimously agreed that 'an agitation should be commenced to bring about change in the organisation of the Open, to make it a more decisive test of golf and to invest it with an added importance more in accordance with the vast expansion of the game within the last few years.' The proposals which were put forward at this meeting were radical and far reaching: that play should be over 72 holes and two days, that the prize money should be substantially increased, particularly for the winner, and that an entrance fee of 5 shillings for competitors should be charged. Significantly, the inclusion of Open Championship venues south of the Border was also discussed.

This meeting was momentous in several respects, not least because it was the first time that the professional players had been bold enough to take the initiative in having a say in the game, but also in the far-reaching scope of the proposals. It was without doubt the progenitor of all the Professional Golfer Associations in the world today and Tom Morris was the driving force behind it. It is not surprising that Horace Hutchinson, in 1890, described Tom as 'The High Priest of this hierarchy of professional golf'.

Tom, of course, knew all of the professionals who attended the meeting, as well as Mr James McBain of Ayr, who acted as secretary. McBain was a member of the Prestwick St Nicholas and had enjoyed many matches with Tom, James Hunter and Jof at St Andrews and Prestwick. He was a journalist contributing to the Ayrshire press as well as the *Glasgow Herald* and, of course, *Golf* magazine.

The document drafted from this meeting was printed and widely circulated to all the leading clubs and players. The Committee of The Royal and Ancient merely minuted receipt of it, but the Honourable Company of Edinburgh Golfers, who were to host the next Championship in 1892, paid immediate heed. They not only announced the date of play in the Scottish and English press, including *Golf*, but also that the event was to be played over two days and 72 holes. Three days practice were to be made available and a 10 shillings entry fee for competitors charged, 'all of which, with £20 added by the Honourable Company, will be divided in money prizes among the Professional Golfers competing'.

The Honourable Company had done the honourable thing and implemented the professionals' proposals virtually in full. It also took one further revolutionary step in announcing that the event would be held at their new home, Muirfield, over the course that Tom Morris had laid out only a year earlier.

These arrangements went a long way to appeasing the critics of the Open Championship's organisation, but the shift of venue came as a body-blow to the Burgh of Musselburgh. It was a change that was also not welcomed by some of the traditionalists in the game. Although only a nine-hole course and, by the standards of the day, short and poorly main-tained, Musselburgh had staged six Open Championships, produced some great Champions and attracted a large viewing public. The town was never likely to take this slight lying down and a consortium promptly announced a tournament with a £100 prize fund, more than that of the Open, with the date deliberately set to clash with the Championship at Muirfield.

Tom's committee, through the pen of McBain and the columns of *Golf*, played some part in resolving the impasse that ensued between the Honourable Company and Musselburgh Town Council in East Lothian. The professionals made it clear that, although delighted with the proposed tournament at Musselburgh, they would contest the Open Championship, no matter where it was played. The Musselburgh movement saw sense and moved their event forward to the week before the Open. Tom did not participate in the Musselburgh event but every leading Scots and English professional did and the contest was close, with Willie Park Jnr triumph-ing over Tom Vardon and Andrew Kirkaldy. *Golf* deemed this event an 'unqualified success' and although enthusiastic about the 'arrangements' for the Championship proper at Muirfield a week later, some of the press condemned the course as a test unworthy of deciding an Open Champion.

Tom contested this inaugural Open Championship at Muirfield when Harold Hilton won and John Ball tied with Hugh Kirkaldy and Sandy Herd for second place. *Golf* applauded the arrangements, describing the spectators as 'select rather than numerous', the lack of numbers no doubt being due to the rather poor communications to the course with the near-est railway station being some three miles away at Drem.

The two outstanding amateurs from the Royal Liverpool Club had stamped their names indelibly on the history of the game. Ball had earlier won the Amateur at Sandwich that year when he had beaten Hilton in the final. Both would go on to further Amateur Championship successes and Hilton would take a second Open title when the event was held at Hoylake in 1897.

Tom and his fellow professionals, together with Hoylake's outstanding amateurs, were all in the field again at Prestwick in 1893 when Harry Hart, the Prestwick Club's long serving secretary, induced the final implementa-tion of the proposals made by the professionals in 1891. The Honourable Company had renovated the structure and organisation of the Open Cham-pionship in 1892 but the initial proposal to extend the playing venues to England came from Prestwick.

The proposal to place 'the Open Championship on a new and wider basis' also came from the Prestwick Club. Both Tom and James McBain had ready access to Harry Hart and the progressive membership at Prestwick, who would have been well disposed to see their Open brainchild flourish still further.

At a meeting of representatives of the Prestwick, Royal and Ancient and Honourable Company Clubs in Edinburgh in June 1893, agreement was reached to include as venues for the Open Championship, Royal Liverpool Golf Club at Hoylake and St George's Golf Club at Sandwich in Kent. Dates for the Championship were fixed and the conditions of entry and the prize fund determined, all very much along the lines that Tom's committee had proposed in its published paper in June 1892.

Tom played in his last Prestwick Open in 1893 through continuous rain in the worst weather he had experienced in the event. He fared badly but had the satisfaction of witnessing the young St Andrews brigade come to the fore, with Willie Auchterlonie winning, Sandy Herd taking third place and the Kirkaldy brothers tied for fourth.

He made the journey to the St George's Club at Sandwich in 1894 to see the Open Championship played for the first time outside Scotland. Although he did not enter for the event he did, however, play in it, for after four contestants withdrew, the Sandwich committee invited him to join the ranks. He played with a local member, Captain Tattersall and, after taking 100 in the third round, withdrew from the fourth. Tom was already familiar with the St Georges links and Dr William Laidlaw Purves, the man who had been the driving force behind establishing the Club. Tom had played in the professional matchplay tournament at Sandwich in 1888 when Peter Fernie put paid to the 67-year-old's pretentions in the first round.

There were 94 entrants for the first Championship played on an English links, even surpassing the huge field of 83 at St Andrews in 1891. If it was not apparent then, it would soon become clear that some sort of qualifying rules of entry would have to be introduced. With the new English professionals and the greatly increased number of amateurs entering the ranks, the field was approaching the unmanageable.

Play at Sandwich proved Tom and his committee to be correct in recommending venues for the Open Championship south of the border. J.H. Taylor from Westward Ho!, contesting his first Open, took the title, with Douglas Rolland, competing in the event for the first time in 10 years, in second place.

Tom Morris played in his last Open Championship in 1895 at St Andrews in the 35th playing of the event. He was 74 years old, over three times older than J.H. Taylor who retained the title. Although Tom did not play, he was present at the renovated Muirfield course in 1896 when Harry

Vardon made his first impression on the Claret Jug. Only family tragedies had prevented him playing in every Open Championship, but if he was not present at them all in person, he was certainly there in spirit, as he would be when the event was first played at Hoylake in 1897. Tom's departure from the playing ranks was co-incidental with the emergence of the great triumvirate of Vardon, Taylor and Braid, great champions all, who would come to dominate golf for the next two decades. These were men of the new age in the game, with a fresh and completely commercial attitude, with no sentimental attachment to the Open Championship. They would take up where Tom and his friends in St Andrews had left off in 1891 and come to introduce a new era to the game with the founding of the Professional Golfers Association.

Although no longer a participant, Tom continued to play a central part in influencing the progress of the Open and the development of professional golf. In August 1898, *Golf* reported that proposals for doubling the prize fund for the Open Championship had been 'put forward . . . in the name of a very strong Professional Committee, with Tom Morris at its head, and that fact alone entitles them to the respectful consideration of golfers'.

In February 1902, the 80-year-old Tom Morris was elected Honorary Vice-Captain of the newly founded Professional Golfers Association. Lord Derby and Prime Minister Balfour would come to be honoured as Honorary Presidents. Honorary Vice-Captaincy was a fitting recognition for the old man, not only for the part he had played in raising the status, respectability and kudos of the professional player, but also for the achievements of his lifetime in bringing the game to the forefront of public attention.

39 The Old Order Changes

Although Tom was the titular head of the Morris business that made clubs and balls and ran a golf shop, the time that he spent in it must have been greatly reduced as he attended to the sweeping changes taking place on the Links throughout the last quarter of the nineteenth century. Jof was effectively left in charge, keeping the books and controlling the paperwork. He, however, was afflicted with ill-health, and the role of workshop foreman was left to Bob Martin and increasingly to James Foulis, a cabinetmaker to trade who found a place as a club-maker with Tom in the early 1870s. In 1882, his 14-year-old son, also James, was apprenticed as a club-maker in the Morris workshop. This James Foulis would come to make a name for himself on the Links and in the expanding world of golf.

Throughout the late 1880s, young James Foulis is a frequently recurring name in the reports of medal competitions of the local clubs, yet he never ventured far from his home Links until, in 1895, he emigrated to America. Charles Blair Macdonald instigated his emigration and appointment as a professional golfer in Chicago. No one in St Andrews was surprised when, only a year later, they learned that James Foulis had won the US Open Golf Championship at Shinnecock Hills on Long Island.

William Lawrence gradually took over the onerous book-keeping task as Jof's ill health progressed. Lawrence was related to the Forgan family but unlike any other Forgan, he was a player of some repute, a champion of the St Andrews Rose Club and a force in the Thistle Club as well. Although he started work in his father's clothier and haberdashers business in St Andrews, he attended the University and became the dominie, the schoolmaster, in Crail. He was the driving force in the resurrection of golf at Kingsbarns in 1922 and remained loyally close to Tom's family for many years.

While the Morris business was thriving, it was not in the same league as Forgan's in terms of volume of output. From the outset, when Tom purchased his property and the contents of G.D. Brown's shop, he bought the necessary raw materials for club- and ball-making from Robert Forgan. By the late 1880s, Tom's workshop was engaged in little more than the assembly and finishing of clubs stamped with his name, the raw wood heads and shafts being made on the machines in the Forgan workshops next door.

The firm did have the best possible brand name, 'Tom Morris', and clubs and balls bearing this magic name were certainly in demand and were dispatched to all parts of the country and overseas to wherever golf was played. It would be wrong, however, to conclude that Tom and Jof were not commercially minded. They applied for at least two patents, one being in 1893 for 'an improved iron niblick', when Tom described himself on the application as 'Golf Club and Ball Manufacturer of St Andrews, in the County of Fife, North Britain.' Tom's 'improved niblick' could not have been a commercial success, for today examples of this patent are rarely seen, suggesting that very few were produced.

Robert Forgan embraced the new manufacturing technology and he invested heavily in it. In 1882, Forgan installed a gas engine that initially powered the lathes to turn and taper club shafts. Soon afterwards, he obtained his first copying lathe and the manufacture of wooden-headed golf clubs was transformed from a handcraft to an automated operation. This lathe revolutionised club-making, not only in terms of the time that it took to make a club, but also in the volume of production. In consequence, the price of woods fell dramatically as the assembly of the component parts of a club could be undertaken anywhere and by men with little or no expertise or training. From one master clubhead, the copying lathe could produce five in as many minutes, each a perfect replica of the master. These would be finished by sandpaper hand-dressing, the lead being run in the back of the head and stamped 'T. Morris' before varnishing. The club would be completed by attaching a shaft and fitting the grip. Tom Morris, like other club-makers in the country, bought Forgan's club heads and shafts by the score and assembled them to his own specifications.

From the introduction of the copying lathe Tom had his own 'master heads'. While his men finished the wooden-headed clubs to his own rigorous specification, it was Forgan's foresight and technical expertise that made Tom's workshop commercially viable.

The Tom Morris workshop also produced iron clubs. These heads were made and stamped with the Morris insignia by Robert White, Robert Wilson and later by Tom Stewart, all blacksmiths in the Town, as well as James Anderson of Anstruther. Tom's men would attach shafts to these iron heads and stamp the all-important words, 'Tom Morris, St Andrews', just below the grip.

Tom appears to have been sufficiently astute as to promote his own business wares when he opened a new golf course or played in an exhibition match, wherever and whenever the opportunity arose, as magazine articles and advertisements from the time show. He did not covet Royal Warranty, as Robert Forgan did next door; his own name was enough on his advertisements and listings in trade directories to attract sales. He claimed high quality and, with his name, charged more than other makers for his products. Demand was such that there was a continuous backlog of work in the shop.

Despite his sound business judgement, however, Tom Morris was never really a man of commerce. Unlike Robert Forgan, it was not the implements, but the game, that was important to him. He preached golf with almost missionary zeal, taking great delight in his shop's team wins in the club-makers' matches on the Links and equal delight when one or other of his men won a local club medal. For very little reward, he seems to have been prepared to travel the length and breadth of the United Kingdom to advise, plan and assist in the construction of golf courses and attend the most trivial of golfing gatherings. He also went to many amateur matches and meetings to add his support. Indeed, if one were to be cynical about it, one might suggest that he coveted the limelight, the adulation and, from the contemporary writings, the flattery associated with it. Certainly, he seems to have had an in-built awareness of public relations. In his later years, he went to the expense of having cards made of his portrait photographs, another of himself and Tommy together and yet another that showed him between Tommy and Jof. The latter card commemorated his two sons each holing the Links at 77 strokes, the 'Lowest Scores on St Andrews Links' (The fact that Jamie Anderson had established the first 77 score would appear to have been forgotten). He signed and presented these cards to the streams of visitors who went into his shop and stopped to shake his hand at the shop door. Self-aggrandisement perhaps, but also a promotion for his shop's wares for, to quote a late St Andrean, 'they got the postcard when they came out of the shop carrying their parcels'.

One nevertheless suspects that the world of business took second place to a game of golf, as few tournaments were held without Tom's presence. Jof was as assiduous as his father but by 1880 any thought that he could have succeeded at an Open Championship was past. Jof's greatest hour came in his maiden Open at Prestwick in 1878 when he was a central figure in one of the most exciting finishes the event has ever known. Jamie Anderson had four holes left to play when he learned that Jof, his close friend, had completed the three rounds with a score of 161. Jamie calculated that he had to finish in 16 strokes to win. In the event he produced what is probably the greatest finish ever seen in an Open Championship, holing the last four holes in what would be regarded today as four under par. He set out with a three, having holed a full iron shot, which was followed by a steady four at the next and then at the short hole he scored a hole-in-one, the second time such a feat had been accomplished in the Championship. After this, his five at the last was a formality. Jamie won by two strokes from Bob Kirk and by four from Jof in third place. Jof took eighth place at St Andrews the following year.

In 1880, like his father, Jof did not compete in the Open Championship at Musselburgh. The event was not well attended and the condition of the Musselburgh links came in for criticism in the press. Bob Ferguson had his first Open victory, with Musselburgh players occupying the first six places. Only Andrew Kirkaldy and Davie Corstorphine made the journey from St Andrews to Musselburgh, both having been smitten by championship golf the previous year. The local newspaper reported that the absence of the Morrises was due to the short notice of the event although Tom would have known of the timing from the earliest date. A more likely explanation is that the Morris household was still smarting at Jof's incarceration at Cupar Sheriff Court in the aftermath of the Road War. It was also the case that the Championship coincided with James Hunter's departure for America and both Jof and Tom were in Prestwick throughout the week following the event at Musselburgh.

At the 1881 Open Championship, the weather at Prestwick was atrocious and Jof did not return a card when Bob Ferguson had his second consecutive success. The conditions were such that the *Glasgow Herald* reported that the 'start was delayed by an hour and a half in an attempt to persuade markers to brave the storm'. Of the 22 starters, only eight cards were returned.

Neither Jof nor Tom entered the lists of the 1882 Open in St Andrews. Tom was, as usual, in charge of the proceedings, and it is most probably the case that he gave his full attention to the event. There had been some criticism of the organisation at St Andrews in 1879 and, after the debacle of 1876, Tom may have felt that his full attention was required to regulate play. New rules had been established earlier that year and the diameter of the hole had been fixed at four inches. The local paper reported that Tom 'gave a word of encouragement to each, in his usual happy kind of way, as they struck off from the tee'.

Jof played in five of the next six Open Champioships without distinction. His chance had come and gone in 1878. The rheumatoid arthritic affliction that had so plagued his mother's life had fallen to him and although not crippled with arthritis, his golf may have been affected by it. There is, however, some suggestion that Jof suffered from a form of depression. When he took to the Links after a long lay-off, the local paper suggested that his appearance was long overdue and that there was no earthly reason why, with his talent, he should not be a regular competitor.

Jof enjoyed only about a decade of serious professional golf when he competed with, and often beat, the best in the game. He could never have emerged from the shadow of his elder brother Tommy and perhaps too much was expected of him as Tom's son. His close friend and neighbour, Jamie Anderson, whose clubs he carried as a boy, was similarly afflicted with ill health and his playing days were over early.[1] Jamie's demise as a player was swift between 1882 and 1884, for he had compounded his illness with a taste and appetite for alcohol over which he had little control.

Jamie Anderson left St Andrews to take up an appointment at Ardeer in Ayrshire at the end of October in 1882. He did not make the journey to Musselburgh for the Open Championship in 1883, but did play at nearby Prestwick in 1884 when he finished well down the field. His last Open appearance was, fittingly, at St Andrews in 1888

Jamie remained at Ardeer for four years before moving to Perth where little is recorded of his time there. A hopeless alcoholic, he returned to St Andrews in 1898 when he became involved in a half-hearted attempt in business with the Kilrymont Golf Company that soon foundered. Jamie was declared bankrupt, and being destitute, a public order was made against him and he was taken into the County poorhouse in Thornton in August 1899. Jof, who had lent him money from time to time, held his possessions and, as his note-of-hand shows, it was to him that Jamie gave what little he had left in settlement of his debt.

Jamie Anderson died a pauper in the poorhouse at Thornton on 6 August 1905, a sad end for a three-times Open Champion. His body was returned to St Andrews where he was buried beside his son, David, who had died in the measles epidemic of 1863 when only eight months old. Jamie had erected a tombstone over the grave of his son, whose name lives on, carved upon it. Jamie's name was never added, but it too lives on, thrice engraved for posterity on the Claret Jug, the Open Championship Trophy.

In 1890 Tom played in the Open Championship at Prestwick. Things had changed dramatically in the thirty years since it was first played on the course that he had formed with his own hands. Prestwick had now an

18-hole course as good as any, as well as a fine clubhouse sitting at the head of the links, comparable in many respects to that of The Royal and Ancient Clubhouse at St Andrews. The great swath of links land all the way to Ayr had, however, been built upon. Troon, in the other direction, by then had become a sizeable township with a fine golf course that stretched as far as the Prestwick links.

Changes had also taken place in the game itself. Mr John Ball, the outstanding amateur from Hoylake, took the laurels in the 1890 Open Championship from a field ten times the size it had been thirty years earlier when Willie Park had snatched the inaugural Challenge Belt from Tom by two strokes. It is hardly surprising that Tom was the only contestant in the 1890 field who had played in that first Open Championship thirty years earlier.

Tom did not return a card at Prestwick but he did the following year in St Andrews in 1891 when the field had more than doubled. Hugh Kirkaldy won through wind at gale force with continuous rain: but the local news-paper had more to say about Tom in his 70th year returning a card than it did about Hugh's win. The novelty of his brother, Andrew, taking second place, two strokes behind, also detracted somewhat from Hugh Kirkaldy's success.

A whole new generation of players was coming to the fore in St Andrews. As well as Hugh, Andrew and John Kirkaldy, there was Willie and Laurie Auchterlonie, a whole raft of Herds, Alex, David, James and Fred as well as David Ayton, David Anderson, Jack and Andrew Burns. There were others of lesser importance. The majority were club-makers or tradesmen who would come to make their living from the game. But there were also those, like Bob Kinsman, who had no trade and who made their living in the caddy ranks and, in the best tradition of their craft, were drinking men of repute. Kinsman was finally imprisoned in Cupar in July 1883 for recurring belligerence. As well as beating his wife and two neighbours, the two constables who tried to restrain him also needed medical attention.

When boys, Tom had chased these men off the Links and he did not command from them the respect with which the young men emerging from other parts of the country regarded him. The young St Andrews blades were resentful of Tom's absolute unquestioned control. It was quite a widely held resentment. George Bruce in his *Destiny and Other Poems* refers to Tom as 'The Pope' and implies that, in every situation, Tom put the interests of The Royal and Ancient before those of the townspeople.

It is clear from Bruce's verse that Tom was becoming marginalised from his own kind, both in the Town and on the Links, and it is equally clear that although he enjoyed centre stage wherever golf was played, he was no longer 'one of the lads'. The photograph of the professional players assembled at the inauguration of Troon Golf Club speaks volumes. Tom and Jof are seen to be isolated in the very centre of the picture while all others appear to keep a respectful (or resentful) distance. This is hardly surprising, for Tom was on handshaking terms with the majority of the gentlemen players gathered for the event. Robert Hunter, Tom's son-in-law's brother, was an invited gentleman player and both he and Jof were residing in some style at Florence Cottage, Tom's daughter's house in Prestwick, for the duration of the event. These were not circumstances enjoyed by any other professional player of the day. His position and lifestyle in St Andrews was also not enjoyed by many and was resented by not a few.

With the benefit of over a hundred years' hindsight it is not difficult to understand Tom's attitude to the position that he found himself in. He appears to have been blissfully unaware of the social changes that had taken place about him. There was clearly status in pre-urbanisation Victorian society, but the relationship between master and servant, particularly in St Andrews, was an easygoing one largely based upon mutual respect. With the development of the cities and the factory system, a 'them-and-us' attitude grew and the expectation of privileges developed with the emergence of the managerial and professional middle classes. Tom treated everyone, irrespective of class, the same as he had always done. His easy familiarity with the upper classes was something that he had always enjoyed on the Links and it would appear to have been appreciated, at least by the older members of the Club. The younger men of the Links may have found this difficult to comprehend and may have interpreted his attitude to the gentlemen players as ingratiating and his equally casual relationship with them as condescending when he was, in fact, simply being himself.

Tom Morris was the patriarch of a successful family that had found itself middle class as the times had made it so. He was a celebrity, not through choice but through his longevity at the heart of golf, although his winning personality and open forthright friendliness also contributed. His position in the new class-conscious society was made all the more complicated by Andrew Lang's references to him as 'Professor Tom Morris' and 'Nestor of Golf' and having eulogised him in ballad form with the preposterously pretentious Latin subtitling 'Ecce, Senex Andreanus'. He may have been amused and delighted with the references to him in *Punch* and society magazines, but it alienated him from many in a township that relished its parochialism.

40 A Constant Benefactor

The sparks from George Bruce's verse may have kindled the young blades' resentment of Tom's absolute authority in St Andrews and beyond, but many were nevertheless indebted to him and it was something that they never forgot. Sandy Herd in his autobiography wrote about Tom finding him his first job as a club professional. Tom, he said, would keep them all informed of tournaments and provide support and encouragement for those wishing to make a life for themselves in the game. Newly founded clubs, even in America, would contact him to find a professional for them and his recommendation was always good enough to ensure an appointment.

Sandy Herd, whose grandfather was a weaver and virtually retained as a caddy by the Whyte-Melvilles, was familiar to Tom from childhood and was a particular favourite. His father and uncles were among Tom's closest and oldest friends and his grandfather was Tom's first recorded foursomes partner when they played against Allan Robertson and Sandy's brother Willie in 1842. It was Old Sandy who most frequently carried Tom's clubs and who had seen him through his early battles on the Links before he left for Prestwick. He had travelled to all of the courses with Tom and in his later years found a place beside John Morris at the back of the workshop making golf balls. The young Sandy would be of more than mere interest to Tom and his ultimate success in winning the Open in 1902 must have given everyone in Tom's shop much satisfaction.

Andrew Kirkaldy, or Andra', was altogether different. His family was from the West of Fife where his father was a miner who eventually moved to St Andrews, the three young Kirkaldy brothers soon becoming involved in the golf and caddying on the Links. Tom was clearly very supportive of them. Hugh was the best player of the three and came to win the Open at St Andrews in 1891, with Andra' runner-up and John a long way down the field.[1] Hugh died at the early age of 34 after closely challenging three further Open Championships.

Andra', however, was the character in the family and it is his name that endures. In 1879 he and Jamie Allan from Westward Ho! tied for second place behind Jamie Anderson in the Open Championship at St Andrews. In 1880, however, soon after the Open at Musselburgh, he was in Dundee carousing with some friends when they met a recruiting sergeant from the Highland Brigade and they all 'took the Queen's shilling' and enlisted in the Army. Andra' was a soldier for six years, serving mostly in India and in 1882, he saw action at the infamous battle of Tel-al-Kabir in the Egyptian campaign. He was wounded in the arm and leg, wounds that he was wont to curse in later years.

When Andra's six years soldiering ended in 1887, he took the sixpence a day on offer as a Reserve and came home to St Andrews. Showing that he had lost nothing of his ability during his time away, he took sixth place in the Open Championship of 1888. In the following year at Musselburgh, he met Willie Park Jnr in a play-off and, for the next few years, was rarely out of the running. Andra' had missed his chance while off soldiering, for he was soon overtaken by Vardon, Taylor and Braid, the triumvirate who came to dominate the game and the Open Championship for the next twenty years.

Tom found a place for Andra' as the Professional at Winchester where he first met the young J. H. Taylor, but his rough and ready outspoken ways were not exactly suited to the club servant role, especially in England. Within six months he was back home in St Andrews living as best he could from his income as a tournament professional and exhibition player, particularly with Ben Sayers and Sandy Herd. After Taylor's success in the 1895 Open at St Andrews, when Sandy was second and Andra' third, Taylor put out a challenge of £50 for two rounds of the Old Course. Andra' took him on and, much to the delight of the whole Town and Tom in particular, Andra' won on the last green. According to Andra's memoirs, Tom was overjoyed and said that 'the result had taken years off him'.

Andra' was, however, somewhat selective in his memoirs. Perhaps understandably, he failed to recall his other appearances, those in front of the magistrates. In the late 1880s and early 1890s he was fined ten shillings for fighting with a club-maker friend in South Street and again when the two got off the Dundee train, drunk and prematurely at Guardbridge, assaulted the Station Master on realising their error.

What Andra' also failed to recount in his memoirs was the anguish he caused Tom with regard to an appointment made for him in 1895 at the Shinnecock Hills Golf Club at Southampton, Long Island in the United States. A letter from Tom retained in the Club's archives shows that Tom had brokered Andra's appointment as professional there, that he had accepted the position and that the club had sent the money for his passage to America. Andra', however, had meantime got caught up in a series of exhibition matches with J. H. Taylor, and reneged on the arrangement, leaving Tom somewhat embarrassed.

Andra' spoke in glowing terms of his debt to Tom in his autobiography, and more importantly, the gruff, insensitive Andra' took it upon himself to express gratitude on behalf of the caddies. He related how Tom would often give a caddy with a family money in the winter when there was little work, always admonishing him that he spend it on meat and not on drink.

In 1910, Andrew Kirkaldy was appointed the first Honorary Professional of The Royal and Ancient Golf Club, a position he held with distinction until his death in 1934. His portrait in oils by Sir William Hutchison hangs in the Clubhouse as a permanent memorial to an exceptional, if slightly flawed but certainly popular, St Andrews man.

Donald Blue and Archie Stump were two caddies with whom Tom was much concerned. Both were characters living in the Model Lodging House in Logies Lane and were clearly 'a few pennies short o' the fu' shillin'. An old soldier, Donal', as he was known, was always kilted and very popular with the summer visitors who would match him against Stumpy for £5, simply to laugh at their game. Tom felt very strongly about these 'matches' and was behind some admonishing letters in the local paper written under the pen name *Dum Spiro Spero* by his friend David Louden. Both Donal' and Stumpy spent the winter months by the fire in Tom's shop with the workmen.

Andra', as well as Sandy Herd and others, related an enduring story of Tom's authority on the Links, although the time and actual match vary according to the writer, but it could well have been a recurring event. When a gentleman referee in a match appealed to the crowd for order on the 1st tee and when, despite this, the crowd made a rush to the bridges to cross the Swilken Burn, he made a further despairing appeal, again to no effect, Tom shouted out 'Stop! Did you not hear what the gentleman said?' The crowd came to an immediate halt and order was maintained from that moment on.

Sandy Herd was one of three Open Champions who came out of Andrew Scott's plasterer's yard. Jack Burns was another, and he too left the Town to take an appointment as a professional in England. Jack, however, returned after a year to take up a steady job as a plate-layer on the railway line. Forever after, when asked how he was playing, he would always reply that he had never been off 'the line' for years. Willie Fernie was also out of the plasterer's yard but was very different from his close friend Jack. Willie took a job at Dumfries before moving to Troon, where he became a renowned figure and participated with huge success in many tournaments and challenge matches, including winning the Open in 1883. Willie also designed golf courses in the West of Scotland as well as on the Isle of Skye and Isle of Arran.

Many more left St Andrews to travel as far afield as America and Canada at Tom's suggestion of a professional position. All five of the Herd boys found permanent and good jobs as professionals, with James winning the US Open the first time that the event was held over 72 holes.[2]

James Foulis left Tom's shop for Chicago after the members of the Rose Club and his work mates in the shop gave him a bumper dinner in the Cross Keys Hotel. Young David Honeyman left for Mexico, leaving his place on the Links with Tom and his father. Young David was a scratch player and a leading figure in the Liberal Club whose members also gave him a farewell dinner. James Ventor and James Tabor, both employed in Tom's workshop, took up appointments in Paris and Zurich respectively. Ventor and Tabor are not local names and one has to assume that they came to the Town to learn club- and ball-making. Both were skilled players, for Ventor won the Clubmakers' Medal in 1895 and Tabor, shortly before his departure for Zurich in 1902, was champion of the Liberal Club.

There was one born and bred St Andrean whom Tom insisted was the best and for whom a short employment in America was regretted. Fred MacKenzie was a great golfing talent. He won the 'Telegraph Cup', the precursor of the Scottish Amateur Championship, when he was only seventeen years old, and went on to win it three years in succession, as well as most other amateur tournaments. Fred represented Scotland against England at Hoylake when he played and beat Bernard Darwin with whom, in the process, he formed a lifelong friendship. Then, in 1902, Fred spent the summer in America for health reasons. While there, he unknowingly jeopardised his amateur status by taking sums of money for playing matches and teaching golf. Fred was unlucky because at that time The Royal and Ancient had been confronted with a problem from Hoylake that Horace Hutchinson had brought to general attention.

The redoubtable Douglas Rolland had entered for the first Amateur Championship. What was to be done about it? It had happened before when Dougie had entered a tournament at Dubbieside, Leven, after he had taken £6 as runner-up in the Open. The Innerleven Club had refused his entry even though Dougie pleaded that he was making his living as a stonemason and not as a professional golfer. He made the same point at Hoylake, and it was then that The Royal and Ancient made the enduring rule that if cash was accepted for playing golf, then the recipient was deemed henceforth to be a professional. It is interesting that when the Hoylake club declined his application, Hutchinson reported that Rolland had taken the refusal well.

Fred MacKenzie had no intention of becoming a professional. He had tasted life at the highest level of amateur golf when he represented Scotland against England and he was running a very successful family ironmonger's business in St Andrews. Tom remonstrated on Fred's behalf with The Royal and Ancient authorities but to no avail. The argument went that if one exception was made, hundreds would follow. Fred continued to play for another thirty years but never in competition. He was 23 years old when his golfing career came to an end but, for another thirty years, Fred Mackenzie was the player that every significant figure in the game sought out in St Andrews.

It was not only able players that benefited from Tom's attentions. He was renowned for his encouragement of the young and aspiring, as well as to those who came to the game later in life and 'caught the golfing bug'. Dons of the University, like Andrew Lang and Professor Tait's visiting science colleagues, were exposed to the glare of his charm and wrote devotedly about him. Then there were also the caddies and in particular their wives and families who were the recipients of his kindness. The feckless of the caddy ranks were always guided to a generous golf bag, and Tom would take particular care that the rewards for their labours reached their homes before it was exchanged for a tipple in the pub.

Tom Morris was not only the father figure of the game, but also a constant benefactor to all those golfers who needed his help.

41 In Social Limbo

With the increasing popularity of golf and the burgeoning numbers of professional and outstanding amateur players coming through, Tom found it increasingly difficult to keep a foot in every camp. Although he championed the caddies and encouraged every emerging young player, it was particularly difficult for him in a township where not a few were of the opinion that he behaved above his station and that he and his family had been too quick in forgetting their origins. Tom, they said, 'was little more than a caddy, though he would like you to forget it'.

The townspeople's perception of Tom is perhaps understandable when one reflects on the extent to which he was 'adopted' as a friend by the families of The Royal and Ancient members. He was also the darling of the well-to-do who came to reside in the Town, as well as the holidaymakers who clearly enjoyed his celebrity. He could be seen being driven about the Town in carriages and subsequently motorcars. He would greet gentry with familiarity and ladies solicitously, before perhaps, being taken out to tea or sharing pride of place at social functions. No presentation of prizes at the Ladies Golf Club could take place without his attendance and no charity bring-and-buy was held without his presence. He was a frequent guest of Professor and Mrs Tait in Edinburgh and the Blackwood publishing family at Strathtyrum House. When he was asked to lay out a course, or perhaps merely assess the suitability of a piece of land, he was invited as a guest and afforded the hospitality befitting a dignitary.

In the Town, however, there was some resentment about the way that he would throw up the sash window of his sitting room overlooking the 18th green and bellow, 'get aff that green'. No one was spared his command, young and old alike, as they walked across it or ventured on to it to try out a new putter; they were simply ordered off. There was even more resentment about the favouritism he showed to certain caddies and his brusque treatment of others. The verse of Andrew Lang and George Bruce leaves no doubt that he was generally perceived as the 'Lord of the Links' and that he behaved as such. To Lang, this was delightfully charming, but to Bruce, who felt that he was eschewing his roots, it was disgraceful.

Tom was certainly living like a lord in the fine family home that Lizzie and James Hunter had built and in the style that they aspired to. His closest friends and confidants were successfully middle-class and of some importance in the Town. Although he had two sisters living at the Cathedral end of North Street with his nieces and nephews, his closest family friends appear to have been the Bruce's of Leven, his cousin's family and as middle-class as his own. The workmen in his shop and his men on the Links may have regarded him as they always had, but to the townspeople he was certainly a man apart.

One example of his difficult situation concerned William Strath. Tom had known the Strath family all his life; the Strath brothers were born and brought up only yards from the Morris family home in North Street. Andrew was six years Tom's junior and had succeeded him as professional at Prestwick, while John, a year younger than Andrew, had become a plumber in St Andrews. William was born in 1842, followed by George in 1844 and David (Davie) in 1849. George was the first professional at Troon from 1884 to 1887 before he emigrated to America, his appointment being made at Tom's recommendation. Davie, Tommy's close friend and golfing adversary, was the professional at North Berwick from 1876 to 1878 when he left for Australia and an early death. Tom was a family friend and a central figure in the Strath brothers' lives.

But then William broke into Tom's shop and stole two golf clubs and a number of balls, not his first crime. A labourer and gardener, but more frequently a caddy and a player of sufficient stature to be matched against Bob Dow from Montrose for a small purse on at least two occasions, Willie had a whole string of convictions from 1860 until only months before his death in 1880. His first offence was assault with a golf club. He was accused of repeatedly striking William Mason over the legs outside James Wilson's shop in Golf Place. In 1877, Tom, Jof and John appeared before the magistrates to give evidence against Willie, whom they had seen breaking and entering into Mr Denham's house in Pilmour Links. Willie had strenuously denied the charge, claiming mistaken identity. When charged with breaking and entering Tom's shop, however, Willie freely admitted the crime. He had sold the clubs and balls for 2s 6d and felt entirely justified in doing so for, as he explained in the court, he felt that Tom Morris owed him the money.

Willie's reputation and the mounting number of charges of theft and drunken and disorderly behaviour brought against him, did not deter Tom engaging him as a caddy. On this occasion, Tom had engaged Willie for four days to caddy for a gentleman visitor who, because of bad weather, did not turn up to play one day. Willie felt that he should nevertheless have been paid, because although the gentleman was not prepared to play, he was prepared to caddy and was therefore due a day's pay. When this payment was not forthcoming, he broke into Tom's shop to seek recompense. Willie was convicted and sentenced but, as a loveable rogue, he carried the sympathy of many townspeople who felt that Tom had been somewhat severe in bringing the charge.

Certainly Tom had come a long way socially in thirty years. In 1888, the Thistle Golf Club of St Andrews honoured him with a dinner in Mason's Golf Hotel, at which he was presented with 'a very handsome and chastely-executed silver snuff-box . . . in recognition of his many achievements on his native and other greens, as well as of his 25 years' connection with the subscribing Club'. The newspaper report stated that it was 'Very neatly engraved on the lid . . . Presented to Tom Morris by the Thistle Golf Club. St Andrews, 1888', which wording was not quite correct.

In 1893 he was Vice-President of the Curling Club that had built a fine new pond across the road at the bottom of Gibson Place, opposite the Swilken Bridge, now the local golf club's car park. Major Bethune was the President and the membership comprised gentlemen of The Royal and Ancient and local businessmen; Tom was Vice-President. In the President versus the Vice-President match on New Years Day 1893, Tom 'skipped' a team made up of Major Carnegie, Colonel Marshall and Mr J. C. Constable. His team beat Major Bethune's comfortably. Tom was a curler of some ability, winning his first medal for curling in 1870, and was 'skip' for many years.

Only a fortnight after this event, Tom was invited to a dinner given by the St Andrews Guild Golf Club at which he shared the guest of honour position at the top table with the literary lion, Andrew Lang, as well as Findlay Douglas. St Andrews born and bred, Findlay Douglas of the National Golf Links of America was instrumental in founding the United States Golf Association, and as its President was the first person to embrace Bobby Jones when he stepped ashore in New York after completing the first two hurdles (the Amateur and Open Championships) of the Grand Slam of Golf in 1930.

A week after the Guild Club dinner, Tom was at the Town's Burns Club Dinner to celebrate the Bard's birthday, again with the gentlemen and business people of the Town. In his social rise, Tom had left a few caddies and friends behind and, not surprisingly, there were a few who nursed an unreasonable resentment.

On his 70th birthday, after he had enjoyed a round of golf with H.S.C. Everard and returned a creditable score of 83, Tom remarked that he had enjoyed more years of golf than most people had lived in a lifetime. Few of the friends with whom he had shared his formative years were left. Among those remaining in St Andrews was George Murray, the Provost and Postmaster. The two had been friends for many years and appear to have held every view in common. George, who was also a widower, bought a house nearby on the Links Road and Tom rented the ground floor for two years, using it as a showroom for his workshop's wares. The two were church elders and recognised as the venerable old men of the Town, attending church and taking their constitutional walks together.

David Louden, whom Tom had known since childhood, was another friend, a St Andrean by birth who had spent much of his life as a schoolmaster in the Borders. In 1874, he wrote a *Biographical Sketch of the Late . . . Sir Hugh Lyon Playfair* and was a frequent contributor to newspapers and magazines. The three made up a formidable trio of local dignitaries who were not the sort that you would meet in the pub and put the world to rights with; they were solidly and respectably middle-class citizens.

In his 80th year, Tom's day, according to a contemporary newspaper account, consisted of rising early to take a morning walk on the Links and decide with David Honeyman on the work at hand. He would be in the workshop when the men arrived at 7 a.m. in the winter, 6 a.m. in the summer months, and, after breakfasting, would collect his clubs and make himself available to play with any gentleman of the Club who required him. After lunch, his main meal of the day, he would be in the shop or on the Links, according to the time of the year and depending upon what was most demanding of his attention. After his tea, a light meal at 5 o'clock, he would read the newspaper before 'taking a turn' outdoors. Religiously, it is reported, that before turning in for the night, he would read from his Bible, 'the one with the big print'.

The account does not paint the picture of a demanding life and it does not include any reference to the sons about whom he must have been deeply concerned. Jof was now all but disabled with arthritis. The crippled John must always have found the back stairs up to the house above the shop difficult, and, confined to his trolley, the increasingly busy shop inhospitable.

John's life was curtailed abruptly on 22 February 1893. Despite his infirmity, John was a hale and hearty man only 34 years old. Always active and in robust good health, he worked daily in the workshop where he helped in making gutta-percha balls. He was also said to be a perfectionist at binding and whipping grips.

John was at work the day before his death and his behaviour was normal, finishing at his usual time. He died of a heart attack during the night, a 'heart spasm' as reported in the *St Andrews Citizen* on 24 February. John, or Jack as he was known in the shop, was well-liked by everyone, the caddies and his workmates in particular. Because of his infirmity, John could never play golf, but he was said to be very knowledgeable about the game and knew everyone who played it well. Significantly, the Simpson brothers from Carnoustie and Aberdeen, and Ben Sayers from North Berwick, attended his burial in the Cathedral Yard where he was interred beside his mother, Tommy and Margaret, and his brother-in-law James Hunter, all of whom had brought so much into his life.

John's death left a void in the Hunter household in Pilmour Links, as well as in the workshop and in Tom's life. He had been an integral part of the Hunter children's lives, a constant unchanging part, as he propelled himself about on his trolley, restricted to the confines of the house, the garden and the workshop. Lizzie and her children were clearly devoted to him as on at least two occasions they transported him to holiday with them in Prestwick, which could not have been an easy undertaking. His passing must have made a deep impact upon the young children's lives.

Quite apart from the loss of a friend and a much-loved and respected workmate, his death must also have had a dramatic effect in the workshop, where his trolley had to be accommodated and allowances made for what he could reach and where he could work. John was an able workman who accepted his disability and did what he could to earn his way in the family business. He knew and was familiar with everyone who entered the shop for he, more than anyone, was a constant feature in it.

To Tom, John's death must have been more painful than those of his family who had gone before, because he had witnessed his sufferings with the limitations of his life and, more importantly, had seen the fortitude with which he confronted his disability. Tom had seen greatness at first hand, had indeed felt the accolade accorded to greatness, but from within a family of remarkable men, Tom may have felt that John was the greatest of them all.

42 In Testimony

In his mid-70s, at an age when most would be seeking a comfortable armchair with peace and quiet to reminisce and take stock of their lives, Tom Morris was as active as ever. Indeed, from accounts of his travels and golfing engagements, it is safe to deduce that he was savouring his celebrity and relishing his social success.

Late Victorian society enjoyed its heroes and, in particular, those from the lower classes who, by dint of their ability, hard work, morality and loyalty, had raised themselves to respectability. Tom had all of the characteristics of the Victorian heroic figure and an abundance of masters ready to recognise his loyalty.

In July 1895, The Royal and Ancient appointed a committee to establish a Tom Morris Testimonial Fund. This was in response to articles and letters in the press following the successful completion of such a fund for W. G. Grace, the celebrated English cricketer who was to cricket what Tom was to golf. A. J. Balfour, the First Lord of the Treasury, together with other parliamentary figures in both the Commons and the Lords, had voiced their support for a similar fund and, from the number of letters in the press, the public was enthusiastic. Such was the response from within The Royal and Ancient that an Extraordinary General Meeting was called when it was agreed 'That the sum of £100 be voted from the funds of the Club towards the Tom Morris Testimonial Fund'. The public interest was such that the appeal raised over £1,240. With this sum, the committee decided to purchase a £500 annuity paying £80 a year, with the balance invested in the names of the trustees of the Club, the interest of which was to be paid to Tom in his lifetime. In the event of his death, it was proposed that the interest be paid to Tom's daughter, Mrs Hunter and her children, at the trustees' discretion. It is interesting that at the May Meeting of the Club the following year, Mrs Hunter and her children were deleted from the provision. Presumably, somebody must have discovered that she and her children were already very well provided for. The disbursement of the fund was not, however, to everyone's liking. From letters to the *St Andrews Citizen,* it is clear that some felt that, like W. G. Grace, Tom should have been given the capital sum in its entirety to use as he pleased. One report even suggested that he was not altogether happy with the arrangements made.

In addition to the income from his business, Tom was now in receipt of over £100 a year from the fund as well as his £50 salary as greenkeeper. The knowledge of his wealth would have raised a few eyebrows in the committee rooms and perhaps some unrepeatable expletives in the Town.

Tom is recorded in the local press as saying that the 'Club had done him proud': but it was the recognition of his services to the church that would bring him the greater satisfaction. The St Andrews Presbytery selected Tom as their representative at the General Assembly of the Church of Scotland in Edinburgh in May 1896. This was momentous social recognition for Tom. Previous representatives from the St Andrews, or indeed any other presbytery for that matter, were drawn from the local landowning and professional classes. As someone born into a weaver's household, raised to revere the Kirk and its ministers, Tom must have felt that this honour was the ultimate social accolade. He was clearly excited about attending the General Assembly. The letter to the Very Reverend James Rennie of Glasgow, which Jof penned and Tom signed, more than expresses the pride that he felt about it. Tom undoubtedly felt elated in May 1896 when he boarded the train for Edinburgh with Charles Grace and the Reverend Boyd. He stayed at the Tait family home for the week and was driven to and from the Grand Assembly rooms where he was treated like a lord.

Any euphoria, however, that Tom Morris was enjoying as the nineteenth century drew to its close was dashed in the summer of 1898. On 8 June, Lizzie died. She was his only daughter, who had forfeited her life with her husband to look after him and her brothers, and who had brought so much joy into his life with her marriage to James Hunter and the births of his only surviving grandchildren.

In the Town, the news was lost in the aftermath of the funeral of Lyon Playfair, 1st Baron Playfair of St Andrews. Playfair had died on 29 May, and Tom and Robert Forgan were listed in the local press at the end of two columns of dignitaries' names that attended his funeral in the Cathedral graveyard. For weeks afterwards, both the *St Andrews Citizen* and *Fifeshire Journal* devoted pages of print to his distinguished career.[1]

Intimation of Lizzie's death appeared in the Fife and Ayrshire newspapers: 'At 6 Pilmour Links, St Andrews, Mrs Elizabeth Hunter, widow of

James Hunter and daughter of Tom Morris, on the 8th of June. Funeral on Saturday 11th of June at 2 p.m.'

The only mention of Lizzie's death in the columns of the local paper read: 'Owing to the death of Mrs Hunter, daughter of Tom Morris, the veteran missed his first Championship meeting for thirty-five years. Old Tom reached his seventy-seventh birthday last Wednesday but did not celebrate it as usual by playing a round on the Links.' This terse commentary is incorrect. The Open Championship had been played 38 times and Tom had not attended in recent years on at least three occasions.

Lizzie died of pneumonia, and while of slight build and never robust, she was nevertheless a vigorous woman for most of her life. Although shy and socially retiring, privately she was joyous and witty. Like Tom and her late husband James, she was a devout churchgoer and a tireless worker for charitable causes, taking stalls and engaging in events at the charity bazaars run by the Townswomen's Guild and the Women's Guild of the Church. She was not a lady golfer, although her children and many of her close friends were. She had few friends in St Andrews and, given that she was born and raised in Prestwick, it is not surprising that she and her husband purchased a cottage and land there. She was a frequent visitor to Florence Cottage in Prestwick to where, even after James's death, she would transport her children with a maid and, on at least two occasions, John on his trolley. In St Andrews, her closest friends appear to have been her female second cousins, the daughters of Robert Bruce from Leven.

Robert Bruce was Tom's cousin; their respective fathers and mothers were siblings born in the Bruces' weaver's cottage in Kilrenny near Anstruther. Like Tom, Robert Bruce had come some way in society. He was a master tailor employing five men and three apprentice boys as well as his son, George, who was a good golfer and member of the Innerleven Club. His shop premises occupied a prominent place in Leven High Street and his residence at The Pleasance in Scoonie, Leven, was one of the grander houses of the township. Catherine Bruce had been Lizzie's bridesmaid and both she and her sisters, Helen and Agnes, acted as housekeepers in the Morris household when Lizzie visited Mobile or sojourned in Prestwick. After Lizzie's death, Agnes continued to help in the Morris household, nursing Tom through periods of illness and assisting Agnes, the eldest of Lizzie's daughters, who was left with the responsibility of running it.

Lizzie's life appears to have been one of total devotion to her husband, children, her father and her brothers. She died leaving Tom and Jof living above the shop and her children still residing at 6 Pilmour Links. Agnes Hunter was 21, Bruce 19, Gray 14 and Jamesina 12. Tom was their next-of-kin and he was 77 years old. The depth of his grief for his only daughter must have been heavily compounded by how keenly he felt the suffering of Gray and Jamesina.

Lizzie's will was much as James's had been. Tom and Mr Keiller-Bruce were nominated as trustees with full discretion over her estate. Tom immediately paid off his bond of £800 to James Hunter's estate, which was then wound up and amalgamated with Lizzie's into one trust.

Both James Denham and Major Bethune, both Hunter family trustees, were dead. Only Tom and Keiller-Bruce were left to administer affairs and immediately there was a problem. Keiller-Bruce, the grand man of local politics, a town councillor and managing director of Smith & Govan, the chemists in St Andrews, had vanished. We know this only from a study of the documents of Lizzie's will. The local newspapers did not report his departure from St Andrews; no court records pertain to his having committed any crime. His name ceased to appear in records of the church or the Town Council minutes. Provost Murray, Tom's closest friend, did not refer to Keiller-Bruce in any Council address and his name simply disappeared as an elder from the church records.

Mr Stuart Grace, the long time Secretary of The Royal and Ancient and Tom's mentor and friend, who had served as solicitor to both Tom and James Hunter, had died in 1895. Tom had been a pallbearer at his funeral that was of a scale befitting one of the Town's and the Club's main dignitaries. Tom had carried the insignia of The Royal and Ancient, leading the funeral procession through the Town and stood in silent tribute beside the Reverend A.K.H. Boyd at the graveside. Stuart Grace had guided Tom and Lizzie through the legal complexities following James's death in Mobile and his passing left a vacuum that was quickly and ably filled by his son, Charles Stuart Grace. It was he, acting on Tom's behalf, who had traced Keiller-Bruce to a house in Putney in London. Accompanied by Dr Paton, Lizzie's family doctor who had also become a close family friend, Mr Grace went to Putney and had Keiller-Bruce sign papers tendering his resignation as a trustee.

Keiller-Bruce's sudden departure from the Town is fascinating. He left behind a wife, son and a daughter. His son was already employed in the Smith and Govan business as manager and he continued as such. The family continued to live in their very grand house in Hepburn Gardens and maintained a chauffeur-driven motorcar. For whatever reason Keiller-Bruce abruptly left, a veil of secrecy was drawn over his departure and ranks were closed very firmly to see that no breath of scandal broke about it – no mean achievement in a town with the introspection and appetite for gossip of St Andrews.

If the pressure of responsibility for the well-being of his grandchildren, his shop and the Links, weighed heavily upon Tom Morris, he did not show it. Although, as the *Citizen* so bluntly put it, he was forced to miss the 1898 Open at Prestwick through the untimely demise of his daughter, it was not long before he was back in play on the Links.

Agnes, the eldest of the Hunter children, was left in charge of her younger sisters, Gray and Jamesina, who were both pupils at Madras College in the Town; William Bruce Hunter had already begun his apprenticeship as a marine engineer in Glasgow. Agnes was also being courted by Willie Rusack, a younger son of the family that had built the neighbouring Rusack Marine Hotel, with access both from Pilmour Links and from the Links Road itself.

On the Links, Tom continued to supervise the workforce of four men and attend to the overall management. *The Dundee Advertiser*, which had become the leading golf-reporting newspaper of the day and not given to flattery, reported on 11 January 1901, 'Notwithstanding the fact that Tom Morris, the veteran golfer is in his eightieth year, he still moves about freshly. Daily he is seen enjoying a walk on the classic Links and at the same time supervising with his keen eye the work of the green-keepers, while on other occasions, he can be observed wielding his club with youthful vigour. As showing his wonderful vitality it might be mentioned that on the closing day of the year and on the first day of the New Year, he engaged in a couple of rounds each day. He played a remarkable game for his age.'

In the same year, Tom's diplomacy was sorely tried by the stationmaster whose garden was coming to the fore in the golfing press as the 'world famous hazard on the Old Course'.[2] A high wall surrounding the garden caught any sliced second shots at the 17th hole. What was worse, the garden was not kept in the best state of tidiness, so not only did the wall have to be scaled after an errant ball, but also finding it was unlikely in the chaos of the garden. With a good sideline going in second-hand balls, it is not surprising that the stationmaster remained obstinate in his stance that balls entering his garden became his property. Both The Royal and Ancient and the Town Council had appealed to him in vain. It speaks volumes for Tom's diplomacy and tact that he not only negotiated a gate into the garden but also gained access for his greenkeepers to 'redd it up'!

Even in his eightieth year, Tom continued to travel widely and, although his tournament playing days were over, no important event took place on the Links of St Andrews without his attendance and few elsewhere where he was not present on the 1st tee. It is not surprising that his fellow professionals honoured him with honorary vice-captaincy of their newly founded Professional Golfers Association.

43 Honours as Willie Park Dies

In September 1901, some 50 professionals in England formed the London and Counties Golf Professional Association. J.H. Taylor chaired the first meeting and James Braid was elected captain. Mr A.J. Balfour, the distinguished golfer and politician destined to become Prime Minister, accepted the Presidency of the Association. The first sponsored tournament was held at the Tooting Bec Golf Club, South London, on 15 October 1901 and was won by the Chairman. As a strokeplay competition, it was a great success, with a silver collection from the spectators forming the basis of the Association's Benevolent Fund.

In February 1902, Sandy Herd spent two weeks back in St Andrews when he doubtless explained the purpose and objectives of the Association to Tom. Sandy must surely have been despatched to sound out the game's elder statesman on the matter, for later that month the announcement of Tom's appointment as Honorary Vice-Captain was made. On the 25th, *The Scotsman* reported that the Association had resolved to represent golfers from all parts of the kingdom, including club-makers and greenkeepers and that in honouring Tom 'the executive have also complimented Scotland and themselves at the same time, by the election of Tom Morris as honourary vice-captain of the Association'. Henceforth, they were to be known as the Professional Golfers Association (PGA).

It would be interesting to know Tom's thoughts on this momentous step. He himself had made his own way in golf from a time when a man made what living he could from carrying a gentleman's clubs and partnering him in foursomes play. He had seen Tommy and Davie Strath raise the profile of the professional player, while he himself had done much to make his profession respectable. Now those set on a life in the game had the security of collective representation and proper recognition.

Tom did not take lightly the honour that the new generation of young professionals bestowed upon him. He was always ready to be interviewed on any golfing topic and was prepared, when his foundering health permitted, to travel in support of Association-sponsored tournaments. In 1904, despite 'naggingly recurrent lumbago', he made the journey to the Irvine Bogside course in Ayrshire where Vardon, Taylor, Braid and all the other leading lights of the PGA were gathered for a purse put up by the Club at the solicitations of the Association. Significantly, he had not attended the gathering of the greats of the day at the Machrie course on Islay a year earlier. While he had no part in the making of this course, he had laid out the Uisguintuie course on the island in 1896, after crossing from Gourock round the Mull of Kintyre in a storm that forced the ferry to stand off Port Ellen for a day. The professionals fared little better on their journey to the Western Isles when, as *Golf Illustrated* put it, 'nearly all suffered from *mal de mer*, Sayers, Herd and White being the only three who were reported to have withstood the malady'. Their suffering was, however, well rewarded, for they played for a £100 first prize with a total prize fund in excess of £180, the biggest to date.

Tom's interest and enthusiasm for supporting golf throughout the country never waned and his activity in promoting the game's progress in St Andrews is best seen in the founding of the New Golf Club in 1902. At that time the local golfers had no clubhouse. St Andrews had many local clubs with about a dozen having their matches and medals reported in the press, but there was no clubhouse for the local players to store their clubs or relax after a round on the Links.

Tom had been a founder member of the Prestwick St Nicholas Golf Club and had proudly witnessed its development. He referred to it incessantly and chastised local businessmen for not having 'gumption' enough to do the same thing in St Andrews. Some local men did eventually call a meeting of all the clubs and a representative from each attended. A house was acquired on Gibson Place with its garden backing on to the Links and an architect and builder engaged to construct a 'big room' with lockers, built on the garden area, with a fine Georgian frontage onto the Links. Tom was made the first Honorary Member, strongly resisting a motion at the inaugural meeting to having the Club named the 'Tom Morris Golf Club.' Instead it was named the 'New Club' and the New Golf Club it would be. From inception the Club has had only one living Honorary Member. After Tom's death, Sandy Herd succeeded him and after his demise the honour fell to Bobby Jones. After Bobby's death, Arnold Palmer became the Honorary Member and he continues as such today.

Tom had witnessed golf on the Links from the 1830s when local men formed themselves into the Thistle Golf club and followed the example of

The Royal and Ancient with its medals and meetings. But the Town's golfers had never had a clubhouse. Now, with Tom firmly established in a chair by the window overlooking the Links, the local men had their own fine New Club with the decor and comforts of the 'Old Club', The Royal and Ancient. He had also witnessed even greater changes on the Links. He had cut the greens with a scythe and scooped out the holes with his bare hands in earlier times. Now, he oversaw David Honeyman and five other men employed with horse-pulled mowers on the fairways and push mowers on the ever-expanding greens. Now, the holes were being moved on a weekly basis using a patent hole-cutter to leave a metal sleeve that fixed the hole and its dimensions like concrete. Tom claimed to have invented the metal cup and there is no reason to doubt his word.

David Honeyman died suddenly on 7 June 1903. He was 67 years old. David came back from the Links in the late afternoon, had a heart attack and died in his home at 86 North Street, the house that Tom had made it possible for him to purchase. The news of David Honeyman's death was telegraphed to Tom in Prestwick where he was attending the Open Championship. If David Honeyman's demise signalled the end of an era on the Links for Tom, he must have reflected that an era had also come to an end in the greater world of golf when, on 25 July that same year, Willie Park died.

On the day that Willie Park lay dying in Musselburgh, Tom was having his portrait painted in Edinburgh. He was staying in Georgian splendour only a few miles away in Edinburgh's New Town, spending the weekend in the home of Professor and Mrs Tait. Professor of Natural Philosophy at Edinburgh University, Tait was the father of the recently deceased Freddie, the celebrated Amateur Champion and Black Watch officer who had died fighting the Boers at Koodosberg Drift three years earlier. Tom stayed with the Taits often, particularly during the period when Sir George Reid, the celebrated Scots artist, was painting the portrait of him commissioned by The Royal and Ancient. He was welcome at the Tait household for more than twenty years where much was made of him. The Tait family also maintained a house in Howard Place in St Andrews where Tom enjoyed their hospitality and in particular their motor car, in which he greatly delighted riding about the Town and the surrounding countryside.

That Monday morning in 1903 in Edinburgh, Tom must have read of Willie's death in *The Scotsman* where it was intimated, 'PARK – at Laurel Bank, Levenhall, Musselburgh on 28th inst., Wm Park sen. aged 70 yrs; deeply regretted. Funeral tomorrow (Tuesday) at 3 p.m. to Inveresk Churchyard. Friends omitted. Please accept this intimation, not invitation.'

What one would give for Tom's thoughts when he read this last line and further, after he had searched the paper for an obituary of his greatest adversary. Willie's obituary was to be found tucked away at the bottom of page four, a mere few inches of column space following after the results of Hansel Monday's play at Kilspindie for the Earl of Wemyss Cup, now the East Lothian County Cup.

With no heading, no preamble, it reads:

> On Saturday afternoon at his residence in Musselburgh Willie Park Sen. died. The deceased, who was 70 years of age, had up till nine years ago, followed the craft of clubmaker, first at Musselburgh, then at North Berwick and after 1875 at Musselburgh. He came to the front in the golfing world as a noted match player. When 21 years old he played against Old Tom Morris for £50 a-side which the Musselburgh man won. In 1882 the pair again met when Old Tom Morris was the victor. Park won the Open Golf Championship in 1860, 1863, 1866 and 1867. The deceased is survived by four sons and three daughters, all of whom have taken up golf.

In the *St Andrews Citizen*, the 'Golf Gossip' column noted, 'We regret to record the death on Saturday of Old Tom's most famous rival, Willie Park, known affectionately far and wide, as Auld Willie, at the age of 70'.

Tom must have reflected long and hard that week on Willie Park. No one could ever have known, or will ever know, what passed between these two men in the matches they played. The burden of responsibility for the many wagers they carried, other people's money, must have weighed heavily upon them. What bond they had, would have been unknown to anyone but themselves. For thirty years they had greeted one another on many greens. They were most frequently put out in the same group in stroke play competitions, but when they were not, there can be no doubt that their first enquiry on returning a card would have been news of the other's play.

Surely Willie Park deserved more of an accolade and one feels a sense of outrage across the years at the press rooms of the golfing scribes of the time. Doubtless Tom experienced the same sense of anger as he reflected upon the thousands who had clamoured after his matches with Willie Park on the greens of Musselburgh, Prestwick, North Berwick and St Andrews, and the gentlemen who opened their wallets and waved their money as they shouted the odds.

But as he sat over his breakfast in the Georgian elegance of Edinburgh, Tom's mind must have drifted back through the years that they had shared on the links and the different fortunes that life had dealt them. While Tom had played with royalty at St Andrews, Willie had remained playing for what he could on the unsung and then all but abandoned links at Musselburgh. To newcomers to the game that they had together brought into general public awareness, Tom was celebrated as the father figure while Willie was all but forgotten. The Park name was known, but it was known in the world of business where there is little romance. Young Willie Park, his son, was a leading business figure in golf. He was credited as a great builder of golf courses in Britain and North America. He was a great golfer as well, not in the same class as Tommy Morris and neither as famed nor fabled, but a great golfer nonetheless. Young Willie had won the Open Championship twice and had made more than a name for himself with his brothers in the golf courses that they created, as well as the international manufacturing and retail golf businesses they had built up.

Tom must have reflected on his own life that morning when he learned of Willie's death. Things might have been different if Tommy had lived. But that was not to be, and all that he had to show for Tommy was the Championship Belt and a monument to his memory in the Cathedral cemetery. Tom had lived a remarkably full life that was filled with great and joyful memories, but it was filled with hellish sadness as well. Now, here was the news of the passing of the great Willie Park, twelve years his junior, a man who had played a central part in his life, and he could not even pay his last respects. He must have asked himself, why? Surely Willie deserved better, if not a great funeral, then at least an accolade in the press. Surely Musselburgh would honour him in the same way that St Andrews had commemorated Tommy Morris. Tom must have taken some comfort in the thought that the people of the 'Honest Toun' would not allow the passing of their greatest son to go unheralded. Surely they would put up a monument to Willie Park as well? They never did.

44 The Evangelist and a Place of Pilgrimage

St Andrews seemed determined to see out the nineteenth century with a flourish. The new Cottage Hospital was nearing completion and the Council had stirred itself to build the Step Rock swimming pool. The Home of Golf, as St Andrews became popularly known at this time, again became a place of pilgrimage, but for reasons other than religion. Golf brought people to the Town from all over the world, as the great golfing boom that had raged through the United Kingdom, spread to the watering places of continental Europe and Ireland and finally the USA. In the early 1890s the presence in St Andrews of continental and American visitors, some of them expatriate Scots, merited more than a passing mention in the local press. By 1900, these visitors were almost commonplace and even the emigration of local golfers to take up posts in the US had become unremarkable.

One of the principal figures in spreading the gospel of the game was Charles Blair Macdonald. He can rightly be described as the evangelist of golf, for it was he who was responsible, more than anyone else, for bringing about the great golfing migration to the USA. C.B., as he became known, was born in Niagara Falls in the State of New York in 1855, but in every respect other than his birth, he epitomised the expatriate Scot and, indeed, the expatriate St Andrean.

His father had emigrated from Scotland to North America in 1848 and had amassed a fortune as a financier in Toronto, Canada and Chicago. It was from Chicago that he dispatched his 16-year-old son to St Andrews into the care of his grandfather, a dedicated golfer and member of The Royal and Ancient.

The impressions that St Andrews made on young C.B. when he first arrived were only sketchily recorded, but the quiet little seaside township must have contrasted sharply with the drab bustle of Chicago, still sagging from the Civil War and suffering in the aftermath of a devastating fire. He does not mention the University or his matriculation, but what he does record is his introduction to Tom Morris.

The American was too young to gain admission to The Royal and Ancient Club; that would come later, but the morning after his arrival his grandfather took him down to Tom's shop to be fitted out with clubs and a locker. As a St Andrean by heritage, a student in its University and a Macdonald to boot, young C.B. would be expected not only to play the game and play it well, but also to respect its rules and traditions. This he did with a fervour that would bring him notoriety in America and make him the bane of golf club locker rooms for the rest of his life.

One can only guess at Tom's reaction to the tall, well-built young American when he walked into the shop with his grandfather in September 1873, but it would be safe to conclude that if Tom did not find him interesting then Tommy and his golfing gang certainly would.

C.B. acknowledged that the game did not inspire him immediately but that it was not long before it did. Certainly he had arrived in the Town at a time when there was something of a golfing fever about. In the early 1870s, the regular matches that young Tommy engaged in on the Links attracted huge crowds and he, together with Davie Strath, Bob Kirk and Jamie Anderson, were popular figures whose matches and golfing adventures were the talk of the Town. Not surprising then, that the powerful American would come to find a place among them and make Tom Morris's shop his second home. Young Macdonald's exploits on the Links with Tommy and the other young golfing blades merited mention in *The Field* and the newly founded *Sporting Intelligence*, and these he proudly recalled in his biographical reminiscences some fifty years later.

In 1876, C.B. Macdonald returned to Chicago with a classmate from the University and immediately set out to attempt to play golf on a clearing that had been the site of Camp Douglas during the Civil War. But neither the time nor the place was favourable because, in American parlance, these were 'root, hog or die' days in Chicago and little if any outdoor sport was played at all. His golf was restricted to his frequent visits to St Andrews, and it was not until 1892 that he created his first seven holes on the estate of Senator John Farwell at Lake Forest, Illinois. A year later, in the spring of 1893, he built the first 18-hole course in America on a stock farm at Belmont, 24 miles west of Chicago.

Doubtless Tom was impressed when C.B. related his exploits during his visit in 1895. He must have been astounded in the summer of 1900 when he reported that there were now 26 clubs in the Chicago area alone and that he himself was the first official Amateur Golf Champion of the United

States of America. Tom would learn with possibly even more pleasure that Henry James Whigham had succeeded C.B. as Champion in 1896 and retained his title in 1897, for Tom had known Jim Whigham since his boyhood in Prestwick.

Whigham's father, David Dundas Whigham, had become one of Tom's most fervent supporters when he joined the Prestwick Club in 1860. D.D. Whigham was a lawyer who became the owner of a large and successful vintners business in Ayr. He had four sons, each becoming distinguished in different walks of life and all excellent golfers. After studying at Oxford, Henry 'Jim' Whigham became a journalist of repute in the US. He was wounded during his reporting of the War of Independence in Cuba and eventually became the editor of *Metropolitan* magazine. Tom would have been delighted but not at all surprised by Jim's successes in America. He had long been acclaimed at Prestwick the best golfer of the Whigham brothers and had distinguished himself at St Andrews, Westward Ho! and Liverpool as well. Had Tom lived to learn, years later, that Jim Whigham married C.B. Macdonald's daughter, he would doubtless have been amused.

Tom would also have been elated to hear from C.B. and Jim Whigham their first-hand account of Findlay Douglas's winning of the US Amateur in 1898, for Findlay was also a St Andrean of whom much was expected. Findlay had distinguished himself on the Links of St Andrews from a very early age. From his home in Market Street, he was educated at the Madras College where he was an acclaimed scholar and athlete as well as a golfer, before going on to excel at the University as well. C. B. Macdonald had been instrumental in securing employment for Findlay in New York and introduced him to the golfing set of Long Island. The long-hitting 22-year-old quickly established a name for himself in US golf and fulfilled expectations by winning and subsequently repeatedly challenging the final for the US Amateur title. To Tom, Findlay Douglas was the model St Andrean and he was forever extolling his virtues.

There is no doubt that in 1893 C.B. Macdonald was responsible for Jim Foulis' departure from Tom's shop to make a new life for himself and his brother in Chicago. Appointed by C.B. as professional at his newly founded Chicago Golf Club, he won the US Open Championship in 1896 at Shinnecock Hills. In St Andrews, Tom flew a flag from outside the shop to celebrate the event and had a printed announcement of Foulis's success in the window. His brothers followed him to Chicago and the Foulis boys and their friends played a pivotal part in founding the United States Professional Golfers Association. They were prolific in the construction of golf courses throughout the Mid-West of America and instrumental in establishing their friends from St Andrews in lucrative appointments at the golf courses they constructed. James Foulis learned the club-maker's craft in Tom's shop, and his father, who was Tom's first employee, was still working there when son James made his first visit home.[1]

Tom did more than anyone else to help and encourage local young men to make a name for themselves in the outside world and his pleasure in their success was boundless. But the young men needed little encouragement from him after both Findlay Douglas and James Foulis returned home in 1902 to tell of their successes. Although the dapper young Findlay cut a dash in the Town in his 'city-slicker' attire, it was Foulis who made the greater impression with the players on the Links and the men in the club-makers' workshops. Foulis had laid out twenty-seven of the thirty-five courses in and around Chicago, and on his home course he enjoyed the assistance of eight greenkeeping staff. His new-found wealth was obvious, but when he related the respect and the total lack of any social discrimination that he enjoyed in America, his former workmates were astonished. What had been a trickle of club-makers from St Andrews to the US became a veritable flood: others would soon follow from Elie, Carnoustie, Montrose and every other Scottish and English golfing place as well.

There was probably a little hyperbole in Findlay Douglas's remark that by 1900 a quarter of a million Americans had seen the light and were spending over $20 million on golf annually, but it was clear that golf was booming in the United States. There was at least one golf course in every state. Robert Hunter and the Manson brothers had long since played off in Georgia and were having regular matches with clubs in Florida. Robert and his son, James, had also firmly established golf in Mobile, Alabama. There were 165 courses in New York and 157 in Massachusetts, Texas already had five and California 17. The demand for golfing equipment was escalating and St Andrews was the principal beneficiary.

Tom Morris's workshop did not expand to meet the demand for golf clubs from America, but Robert Forgan's shop next door did. By 1895 Forgan was employing 50 trained men and had three clerks in his office. Ever with an eye to expanding his business, Robert Forgan readily advanced a sum of money to anyone securing employment in America. The sum was enough to cover the costs of travel and settling in the US and he also made extended credit available for his workshop's wares. This was not an entirely magnanimous gesture, for he was also establishing a conduit for the sale of his clubs and balls, as well as raising the profile of his name, in a burgeoning marketplace.

Forgan not only had the contacts on the ground for the sale of his wares but he also had an inside track in the US financial world. His eldest son, James, emigrated to the United States and became an established figure in Mid-West banking. He progressed to co-found the National Bank of Chicago with David, his younger brother, who claimed to be the first man to hit a golf ball in Minnesota. Through hundreds of city store outlets and dozens of professionals' shops in the US, to say nothing of the rapidly expanding home market, it is not surprising that Forgan's factory was turning out hundreds of thousands of clubs and shafts each year.

Robert Forgan, the head of the club making firm, died on 15 December 1900. His obituary notice in the local, as well as national press, was that of a successful businessman and Free Church bastion who had produced a family that had achieved at the highest level in the church and in the financial world of the US.[2]

On the courses of the New World, the players were more likely to be playing with a club bearing the insignia of the Prince of Wales Feathers and the Forgan name, than they were with one carrying the 'T. Morris' stamp. But in the bars and restaurants of the newly-founded country clubs, it was the Morris name that was the most revered, and C.B. Macdonald saw to it that few locker rooms were without Tom's image on the wall. Tom Morris had already attained iconic status in golf before it spread like a virus through America. The rich literature of golf had established his place in the history of the game: he was deemed to be the model golfer.

The early books on golf were written by men of Scots origin in the main, and the earliest of golf journalists were, if not of St Andrews origin, then certainly of St Andrews residence. These early scribes had ready access to Tom and he, always ready for a 'blether' or a 'crack', was only too delighted to tell them anything that they wanted to know – and often he would tell them anything that they wanted to hear. Few golf writers of late nineteenth century golf failed to quote him or at least refer to him as a source. And if Tom's memory was not what it had been, he was at least always able to come up with something.

Tom's homespun philosophy, which was particularly popular in gentlemen's magazines and the early golfing journals, was punctuated with quotations in his Fife vernacular and embellished with anecdotal humour. The general public's perception of the game, with the English gentleman player, the ragamuffin irreverent caddy and the dour subservient Scottish professional, was established through these journals. When their American counterparts appeared, they adopted this perception and tailored it to their own situation.

An account of a visit to St Andrews is a recurring feature in early American golf magazines, and a meeting with Tom Morris was an imperative to the piece, although much of what appeared was reproduced from what had gone before in the English journals, with further embellishment. Tom Morris went from icon to legend and eventually to myth.

It was not solely in golf journalism that a friendship with Tom Morris was a passport to an opportunity. Richard Tuft, who came to sponsor Donald Ross, would use his and Ross's early connections with Tom Morris as a by-line in their promotion of Pinehurst. Alfred Tillinghast, who would come to rival Ross as the supreme American builder of golf courses, was another visitor who, in 1896, had Tom pose with him for a photograph outside the shop and would thereafter refer to him with first name familiarity.

To the new converts to golf in America, a visit to St Andrews signalled their graduation in the game. A word with Tom Morris was something to relate to their friends, and if they could give his regards to the Scots professional at their country club and put on show the putter with which Young Tommy had won the Champion's Belt, they were on cloud nine.

The social and sporting status of having played at St Andrews and met the 'great ol' man' was established by the turn of the century and, after a lapse of 500 years, St Andrews had again become a place of pilgrimage.

45 Relinquishing the Barrow and the Spade

Tom's tenure as Custodian of St Andrews Links came to an end in June 1903 when he wrote his letter of resignation to Charles Stuart Grace, Secretary of The Royal and Ancient Golf Club. He was 82 years old. He had held the post for nearly 40 years and served at least six different Green Committee Chairmen. He was still being paid £50 a year by the Club for his services, the same sum that he had received at the onset of his employment in 1864.

It is clear that Tom did not want to retire and it took three attempts by the Royal and Ancient Committee to persuade him to do so. What is also clear is that the Committee was also mindful of the old man's feelings and of the importance to him of being publicly regarded as the central figure on the Links. It could not have been an easy situation for the Committee and one feels as much sympathy for its members as one does for Tom in his reluctance to face reality.

The condition of the St Andrews greens had caused concern for some time. Criticism had become commonplace and increasingly vociferous. Indeed, the greens had become a regular source of humour and it is from this date that the words 'mair saund, Honeyman' attributed to Tom by Thomas Hodge some twenty years earlier, became well known.

The Committee first confronted the situation in August 1900, when criticism of the condition of the Old Course was widespread. Constant comparison was made with other, by then well-established courses, some of which Tom had played a part in constructing and advising on their maintenance. Many of these courses were inland and laid out on land far more fertile than the barren links land of St Andrews. It became increasingly clear that the Green Committee had to act to raise standards on the Links

Doubtless after discussion with Tom, they resolved to advertise for 'a competent man to take charge of the St Andrews Links under the supervision of the Green Committee with Tom Morris'. Tom would continue to play his part, although the part that he would play was not entirely clear.

Mr C.B. Henderson of the New Luffness Golf Club was the successful candidate and was appointed at a weekly salary of 35 shillings and to start his duties on Monday, 1 October 1900. Mr Henderson's tenure as 'overseer' on the Links was neither a long nor a happy one. In April 1901 he was brought before the Committee and reprimanded for fighting with one of his staff. He was also reminded that he could be dismissed with a week's notice and, further, that he was to understand that his position was under that of Tom Morris, from whom he was to take orders. This reminder speaks volumes. Clearly, Mr Henderson and Tom did not always agree on green-keeping issues, and it also seems that the greenkeeping staff had divided loyalties. On 2 January 1902, the Committee decided to dispense with Mr Henderson's services and he was asked to leave in March.

Henderson had been appointed to St Andrews Links with glowing references and was a popular enough choice at the time. As a churchgoer and teetotaller, his fight with one of his staff seems oddly out of character and one cannot but suspect that the habits of Honeyman and the rest of the greenkeeping staff, developed under Tom, may have been more than the man could endure.

The Committee's solution to his departure would certainly support this conclusion. They decided at a meeting which Tom attended in January after Henderson's dismissal, that the responsibility for the holes and putting greens should be the responsibility of a new appointee, while the remainder of the Links should be in the charge of Honeyman under Tom Morris.

This restructuring of the Links management was a judiciously diplomatic solution to the problem of Tom's position, but it did not satisfy everyone on the Committee. Further meetings were held in January to discuss proposals regarding the structure of the greenkeeping staff. The minute of the meeting held on 19 January 1903 is telling:

> The Committee having for some time past had under considera-
> tion a proposal to alter the position of Tom Morris by making him
> a consulting Green Keeper with the same salary as at present, and
> to appoint as Green Keeper, another man who would have charge
> of the Links and undertake the superintendence of the workmen,
> and having now ascertained that Tom was not in favour of the
> suggested rearrangements but was desirous of remaining in his
> present position, resolved to take no further steps in the matter.

This statement beggars belief. Tom was 82-years-old, and after a mild stroke in the autumn of 1902, he was left restricted in his movements and slurred in his speech. It is clear that the Committee was in awe of him and simply unable to confront him with the reality of his situation.

But complaints about the condition of the greens continued and the Committee was soon forced again to tackle the problem of Tom's position. It appears that the members of it took the view that they had to persuade Tom to retire rather than simply tell him that he was being retired, in his own interests, due to his age and infirmity. At the 1903 May meeting of the Green Committee, the question of 'rearranging' the Links staff was again discussed. The upshot of this meeting was that the Rev. R.A. Hull 'kindly consented to see Tom Morris on the subject and to report thereon to a meeting of the Committee to be held on Saturday, 13th June'. In other words, the good Reverend was left with the job of making Tom an offer that he could not refuse: he proved to be the right man for this delicate job. He was an outstanding golfer, well respected in the Town and Tom's much-esteemed friend. Such was the pressure at the time that the Committee was very much dependent upon him finding a solution.

The reaction of the Committee when the Reverend reported back to them on 13 June is not recorded, but it was undoubtedly a collective sigh of relief. He was able to tell them that Tom would go quietly and that they were free to reorganise the management of the Links as they saw fit. Needless to say, the Committee was prepared to accept Tom's resignation, but, rather brilliantly, asked him to continue in office until they found a suitable replacement. They also undertook to continue to pay his salary for the rest of his life, appointing him 'Consulting Green Keeper'. Doubtless of more importance to the old man was the fact that he was also asked to 'continue to afford assistance as heretofore on Medal Days.' This request for him to continue in his role of Starter for The Royal and Ancient's medals was an enlightened one. It reveals more about Tom and the Committee's insight into his character than anything else. To Tom it was a statement of his worth and a measure of the esteem in which the gentlemen of The Royal and Ancient Golf Club held him. To Tom, recognition was everything. It was an affirmation of his importance and, more significantly, with his high-profile position of Starter, he was seen to be important.

Tom's letter of resignation dated the 19th was read to the Committee on 22 June 1903. He must have required some prompting to put his resignation in writing, for his letter reads:

I beg to acknowledge receipt of yours of seventeenth inst. with reference to my retiring from the charge of St Andrews Links. In reply I beg that you will kindly convey to the Committee of the Royal and Ancient Golf Club my sincere thanks for the way in which they have provided for me and for the kind acknowledgement of my past services. I am very pleased indeed that I am not entirely severed from duties connected with the Club and these I will do my utmost to execute to the best of my ability. Thanking you for your kind letter.

What the minute of the Green Committee fails to mention, however, is that David Honeyman had died on 6 June that year. This event, more than any other, must have signalled the end of the line for Tom. With the passing of Honeyman, his last connection with nearly forty years of service on the Links was broken. The end had indeed come.

It is a delightful irony that as the members of the Green Committee were gently and sensitively guiding, if not pushing, Tom into retirement, the self-same members of The Royal and Ancient Golf Club were honouring him by having his portrait painted in oils by Sir George Reid. It is noteworthy that one of the prime movers for commissioning the portrait was James Ogilvy Fairlie, the eldest son of Tom's late, great patron and friend, who had initiated his move to Prestwick and so changed his life and the face of golf almost sixty years earlier. Tom had taught James and his brothers to play golf on the links at Prestwick and in the parks of Coodham and all maintained close relationships with their old mentor.

There can be no doubting that The Royal and Ancient had treated Tom generously and with respect, while he in turn had served the Club and the Members loyally. With an annual income of over £100 per year from the 1895 Tom Morris Testimonial Fund, together with his £50 lifetime annual salary from the Club as 'Consulting Greenkeeper', Tom must have been one of the few people to have retired with a pension of more than three times his salary.

Perhaps Tom should have given up his place on the Links much earlier than he did and have resigned his post in 1890 when criticism of the condition of the Course was most vociferous. And perhaps he should have been persuaded to retire in the years immediately following, when early attempts were made to ease his responsibilities and modernise the Course management. Again and again, particularly before the Open in 1900, the condition of the Course was criticised in the press and in the new sporting journals. One wonders if Tom was aware of this criticism. His friends may well have kept it from him for his beloved Links were, as far as he was concerned, the yardstick against which all others were rated. The science of greenkeeping was in its infancy but there were members on the Green Committee who were not only widely read and travelled but who were also knowledgeable about botany and land management. Tom was no Luddite but he was particularly intransigent on several issues with regard to the machinery and fertilisers that had improved other courses and raised expectations in St Andrews. Robert Cathcart, the long-suffering Chairman of The Royal and Ancient Club's Green Committee, did his diplomatic best with Tom, treading the fine line between direction and confrontation.

Both he and Tom had survived MacFie's confrontation but no lesson seems to have been learned. MacFie was a knowledgeable, well-respected man and the first Amateur Champion, but he was deaf and was dependent upon lip-reading in communication, and this may have contributed to his impatience and intolerance. In any event, he failed to impose retirement upon Tom and it took others with greater tact, diplomacy and sensitivity to make sense prevail over sentimentality and obtain Tom's resignation.

It was an inspired move to maintain a position for Tom as Consulting Green Keeper, but more empathy and insight was reflected in maintaining his 'privilege' of superintending in the starter's box on Medal Days. Although Tom was employed by the Club, he was never officially appointed its golf professional, and as Custodian of the Links, he was not as such a Club servant. After the 1894 Links Act and the establishment of the St Andrews Green Committee, his salary continued, like all other Links expenses, to be paid by the Club.

His portrait was completed in 1903 and hung in the Big Room. Robert Cathcart's motion at the Annual General Meeting of that year clearly reflected the sentiments of the membership, who saw Tom as their own. Cathcart moved that it be unanimously resolved to record in the minutes:

> . . . the club's appreciation of Tom's long and faithful services as greenkeeper, the regret of the members that it should have become necessary for him to retire and their hope that he might be long spared to go about among them and take an interest in the links.

Hugh Hamilton from North Berwick, but at that time greenkeeper at Portmarnock, was appointed to the same position at St Andrews by The Royal and Ancient at a salary of £3 per week and, significantly, on condition that he did not keep a shop, carry on the business of club-maker or undertake work for other courses.

The Jubilee Course, constructed in 1897 as a beginners' 12-hole course, was extended by Hamilton, doubtless under Tom's watchful eye, to 18 holes in 1906, in an attempt to reduce pressure of play on the Old and New. Hamilton was also responsible for new bunkers to the right on the 2nd, 3rd, 4th and 5th holes of the Old Course and for the extensive application of artificial fertiliser on the fairways and greens. His efforts met with success but also with some criticism, most notably from the pen of Everard in *Golf Illustrated*:

> Some are beginning to grumble at – what do you think? – the bad lies through the course? The ill-kept putting greens? Not a bit of it; the grievance is that the lies are too good, the putting too easy, that the character of the putting greens has changed, and become too slow by reason of the grass on them; anybody can putt on a dull green, but it requires an artist to excel on it when it is hard, fiery and keen. This is the statement and it may give Hamilton food for thought.

H.S.C. Everard, it should be recalled, resigned from The Royal and Ancient Green Committee in 1890, when criticisms of Tom's efforts were first voiced. He was also a friend, and in his article one senses Tom's observations behind the somewhat backhanded acknowledgement of Hamilton's improvements. Although officially retired, Tom still had a voice, and acolytes hanging on his every word.

46 Playing Through

In retirement, Tom's life changed little, if at all; he continued to have his morning walk over the Links with Silver, his grandchildren's dog, but long since adopted as his constant companion. As a daily routine, Tom, George Murray and David Louden, would make their way down to the New Club where they would have a 'Black Strap'. If the 'crack' was good, they might sit for an hour or two or make the short walk further down the Links Road to the Swilken Burn and over the bridge to the back of the Road Hole green. When the weather was good, they perhaps made their way over to watch the ladies putting or simply sat at the shop door where their cronies and a few of the work-shy gathered to pass the time of day. This gathering was referred to as 'the parliament' in the Town, and after A.J. Balfour, Prime Minister, 1902–5, had stopped for a word after playing a round on the Course, the wags in the New Club insisted that Tom had put the country to rights.

However, lest it be concluded that Tom sank into a period of inactivity, a glance at the lists of courses in which he had some input quickly proves the contrary. It was business as usual; one week Aberdeenshire and the next the Isle of Man. He was in Islay in the Western Isles to look at one course site and in Cleveland in England to look at the completion of another. Astonishingly, he considered, although not surprisingly declined, an invitation to build a course and play some exhibition matches in Australia!

Although the last Open Championship in which he competed in 1895 at St Andrews was behind him, he continued to attend not only the event but every other significant tournament as well. He was no passive spectator, however, for no St Andrean was allowed to play off without a word from him. Mr James Robb, a native of St Andrews who worked as a clerk in a bank in the Town before being promoted to a position in Ayr where he had become a member and Champion of Prestwick St Nicholas, was especially targeted. Robb delighted in telling the story of how Tom approached him

on the 1st tee at the Amateur Championship at Muirfield in 1897 with
the words, 'Mind now Robb, ye'r playin' for the honour of the Auld Toun!'
James won The Amateur at Hoylake in 1906, but, sadly, Tom was not there
to see him gain the trophy.

In the autumn of 1902 Tom experienced what was described in the
local press as 'a very sharp illness'; but after two months he was back on
his feet again. He moved assisted by a chair on which he would rest and
with which he was able to reach the New Club before the New Year for his
Black Strap. By the late spring of 1903 he was moving freely enough to
dispense with the chair and have a few holes on the Links. But this illness
had shaken him and, although he made an apparently full recovery, his
activities were greatly curtailed. It has been suggested, and the word has
come down through the years in the Town, that Tom had suffered a mild
stroke at this time. It is understood that stiffness in his left leg affected his
gait and that the left side of his face was affected and resulted in a slight
slurring of his speech.

But if his activities were curtailed, his popularity remained undimin-
ished. In 1905, the millionaire and great Scottish civil benefactor, Andrew
Carnegie of Pittsburgh visited him. Carnegie ordered clubs for his Skibo
Castle course near Dornoch which Tom had laid out some years earlier.
When General Tom Thumb and his troupe of performing midgets came to
put on their show in the Town Hall, Tom met the General at the shop door.
Major Mite drove General Tom Thumb in his miniature landau pulled by
three goats in splendid livery. Tom shook little Tom Thumb's hand and
he went on his way, doubtless leaving Gray and Jamesina, Tom's younger
granddaughters, delighted.

Tom's public performance was also extended to the stage. In an 'Evening's
Entertainment' that the Oliphant family staged in the Town Hall with the
proceeds going to charity, Tom and Mr Everard performed an epic three
'tableaux vivants' performance. In the first scene, entitled 'The Stymie',
which was a kind of golfing snooker, the curtains spread to find, against a
backdrop of the Links, a frustrated Everard stymied by Tom who was looking on smugly. The curtains closed and opened again on the second scene,
entitled the 'Short Putt'. Everard had apparently holed his ball and Tom was
in the position of putting his. The audience was assumed to be sufficiently
knowledgeable about Tom's inability to hole short putts to appreciate his
situation. Now Everard was looking on smugly! The third tableau opened
to a triumphant Everard with Tom in a posture of 'characteristic annoyance
and astonishment' as the *Citizen* worded it. No mean acting feat for a man
in his eighties, for each tableau lasted some three minutes and a stationary

expression of annoyance and astonishment would test the most talented of thespians.

Tom was blessed with a strong constitution, but he became more and more frequently reminded of his mortality. In September 1905 he was confined to bed with a chest infection which left him seriously ill and from which he required two months to recover. But he was up and about in the Town at the beginning of 1906, albeit complaining about his increasing decrepitude.

If Tom was still active around the Town, Jof was not. After suffering long and hard with only infrequent respite from his rheumatoid arthritic condition, he died on 8 April 1906. Throughout his last five years, his only connection with the shop had been attending to business letters when he was able. His only involvement with the game had been through the St Andrews Golf Club where he assisted in the administration. Jof's death was not unexpected. He had been bedridden for some two months, just as his mother Nancy had been prior to her death thirty years earlier. Like his mother, Jof was 52 years old.

The funeral took place on Wednesday, 9 April, at noon. He was buried in the family grave below the effigy of his brother Tommy, in whose shadow he had spent his life. The golf clubs flew their flags at half- mast and the Town businesses closed for an extra hour to permit employees to pay their final respects, as Tom laid the last of his children to his final resting place. Tom was suffering from lumbago when Jof died and followed the hearse in a carriage, accompanied by his friends George Murray and David Louden.

Jof was well liked and respected by everyone who knew him. He was a good golfer who competed with and, in his day, beat the best. His brother Tommy and his father, however, eclipsed his life in every respect. A greater man might have left to find his own place in the sun, a lesser one might simply have hidden from the glare. Jof made his own place in the firmament of his father and brother, not a trivial achievement, and he merits respect for it.

Jof's death meant that Tom had outlived all of his children as well as his wife, daughter-in-law (Margaret Morris) and son-in-law (James Hunter). Three of his nephews and nieces and all of his school contemporaries in the Town had predeceased him .The family with which he was left, in his 85th year, was his daughter Lizzie's four children, his grandchildren, none of whom were then married. It was his longevity that left him surrounded by youth, and it was the youth about him that kept him young in outlook and vigorous in mind and body.

Tom had long since returned to live with his granddaughters, Agnes and Jamesina, at 6 Pilmour Links. His grandson, Bruce, had qualified as a marine engineer in Glasgow and was employed as an engineer's agent in Manchester. Gray, his other granddaughter, was living in Crieff. Other than his immediate family, he also had nephews and nieces in the Town. His sisters, Janet and Margaret, were his only siblings to remain in St Andrews, the others, with the exception of George, had emigrated. Janet was widowed after only four years of marriage to William Wallace, a butcher in the Town. She had made a living as a milliner and upholsterer before, at the age of 52, marrying Peter Marshall, a drainer from Kinglassie. He was a widower with two children, both of whom returned to Kinlassie after his death in 1879. Janet and Peter lived at 2 Pilmour Links before Peter's death when Janet moved her upholsterer's workshop to 44 North Street where she lived through ten years of second widowhood before her death, at the age of 82, in 1889. Margaret married Thomas Black, a St Andrews fisherman, and lived in North Castle Street, just round the corner from her sister. Margaret had six children, the youngest of whom, James Black was brought up by his Aunt Janet in North Street. Thomas Black was one of the most successful of the St Andrews fishermen, owning a boat crewed by five men as well as his son, David, with which he followed the herring round the coast of Britain. He was also an able golfer and was champion of the short-lived Fisherman's Golf Club in 1882. Margaret died in 1898.

Tom was to see the first of his grandchildren marry. Young Willie Rusack was courting Agnes, whose birth Tom had registered and who had been a constant in her grandfather's life from her birth. Willie was a master mariner, something of a poet and a close family friend. He was a year younger than Agnes when their banns were cried in St Mary's Church throughout February 1907 and their wedding on 8 March was something of a social event in the Town. Agnes and Willie stayed in the 6 Pilmour Links house continuing to look after Tom until the very end. Willie became Captain of the New Club and a town councillor. He was an able golfer and was considered an authority on golf course design and maintenance, building courses in America and Germany before he and Agnes settled into quiet retirement in Strathkinness, a village on the outskirts of St Andrews, where they both ended their days in the 1960s.

The back stair up to the accommodation above the shop became increasingly problematical for the elderly and partially infirm old man and he required constant supervision and assistance on the stair. After his illness in 1906, these rooms were not accessible to him, and after Jof's death in the old family house at 6 Pilmour Links, they were no longer used.

But Tom was failing fast. The burden of his years was telling upon him. In the two years after Jof's death, he spent much of his time sitting at the shop door watching play on the 18th green or making his slow way down to the New Club. There can be no doubt that the 'short sharp shock' he suffered in 1902 had taken its toll. In May 1906 he suffered recurring lumbago that restricted him to his bed or to a chair by the upstairs window of the flat above the shop. That year was the first time that he failed to appear on the tee for the Spring Meeting of The Royal and Ancient. His recovery from lumbago was slow and must have been frustrating for so active a man. From this date his movements were especially restricted.

On the afternoon of Sunday 24 May 1908 Tom 'took a daunder' down to the New Club with George Murray. They had both attended the morning service at St Mary's Church at the West End of Market Street. Both were elders of long standing in the Kirk, but their duties were not onerous. They would greet the parishioners at the church door, hand out the hymnals and when the time came after the sermon, they would pass among the congregation to collect the offering.

It being a Sunday, there would be no Black Strap at the New Club, as the licensing laws of the time forbade the consumption of alcohol on the Sabbath to all but *bona fide* travellers. They would take a cup of tea and watch the usual 'Sunday-best' parade of the citizenry on the Old Course. At about 4 o'clock Tom rose to make his way to the lavatory, then sited off the passageway to the Gibson Place entrance of the Club. Only two doors led off that passage; that to the right opened in to the lavatory while that on his left opened in to the cellar stairs, as it does to this day. Tom must have made the short walk hundreds of times, yet that day he turned left, opening the cellar door. It was a mistake that any absent-minded old man could have made, a momentary lapse of concentration or befuddlement, after rising from a soft seat in the warm afternoon sunshine.

Tom was found at the foot of the stair and he never regained consciousness. He was moved to the dining room of the New Club where Dr Paton examined him to find that the base of his skull had been severely fractured. Dr Paton held out little hope of recovery but Tom was, nevertheless, rushed by the horse-drawn ambulance van to the Cottage Hospital. There he was pronounced dead.

47 Now the Labourer's Task Is O'er

Every national newspaper carried the news of the death of Tom Morris. *The Times* of London printed a long obituary the day after and additionally highlighted his death in its 'Home Affairs' column. Other newspapers and magazines eulogised him in whole-page spreads that left few stones in his life unturned and drew plaudits from all the 'airts,' as he himself would have said with a chuckle. Dignitaries, such as former Prime Minister, Arthur Balfour, and a future one, Henry Asquith, as well as Andrew Lang, the literary lion, had more than a few words to say of the wonders of his ways. Legions emerged claiming closeness and insight and Rev. W. W. Tulloch took advantage of Tom's obituary notice in the *Glasgow Herald* to have an advertisement for his recently published book, *The Life of Tom Morris*, juxtaposed to it.

The townspeople of St Andrews said very little about him and merely mourned his passing. Tom was one of them, despite what the world had tried to make of him. Andrew Kirkaldy's words were quoted again and again for their parochial sentimentality: 'Tam Morris was a guid man. It'll be a while afore we see anither like him, and a damned sicht longer afore we'll see anither ane better.'

Tom had a funeral that would have graced a head of state. His body was taken from the Cottage Hospital to 6 Pilmour Links and laid out in his granddaughter Agnes's front room parlour. David Scott the undertaker made the arrangements, dressed him and placed his body into a grand oak coffin. On the morning of the funeral, this was moved to St Mary's Church at the West End of Market Street. Holy Trinity, the old Town Church was at that time undergoing renovation into the fine building that we know today.

The coffin was placed on a bier below the pulpit and family wreaths, and those from The Royal and Ancient, the Honourable Company, Prestwick Golf Club and the Kirk Session were set about it. Many other wreaths decorated the vestibule and were arranged up the steps to the church.

The Reverend Patrick Playfair, grand nephew of Sir Hugh Lyon Playfair, conducted the funeral service assisted by Reverend W. H. Letham, Tom's parish minister. The service began with the words 'I am the resurrection and the life'. The mourners, those who could get into the church and those outside who could not, then sang the second paraphrase 'Oh God of Bethel', and when they had done, the Reverend Letham read from verse 20 of First Corinthians, Chapter 15, 'I declare unto you the gospel which I preached unto you, which also ye have received, and wherein ye stand.'

There then followed the hymn 'When Our Heads are Bowed with Woe' before Reverend Playfair said in prayer:

> And in particular we now offer unto Thee our humble and hearty thanks for Thy great goodness in giving to us through very many years the good fellowship and work of him besides whose mortal remains we now bow our heads with resignation, although in deep sorrow. For his humble spirit, for his tender heart, for his constant courage, for his faithfulness to duty, for his chivalry, his courtesy and his kindness to all men, we give Thee praise and thanks. We remember before Thee with sincere gratitude his generous nature, his influence for good, his regard for Thy day, his love for Thine house, his zeal in Thy service, the honour, the esteem, the warm affection which he won through his simple nobility from multitudes in many lands. We bless Thee that his life has entered into ours; and we ask Thy grace, that we too may learn to glorify and serve Thee and to benefit others in whatsoever position Thou hast assigned to us.

The service was closed with the hymn 'Now the Labourer's Task is O'er', and everyone remained standing while the coffin was carried from the church as the organ played 'The Dead March'.

A long procession formed behind the glass walled hearse pulled by two black-plumed black horses, with two top-hatted attendants walking by their heads. Mr Robb, The Royal and Ancient Club Officer, headed the cortege, with Mr Hamilton, Links Superintendent, carrying the Club's Silver Clubs and Balls draped in black crepe. Behind them walked the male members of the Morris family, his grandson, the sons of his brothers and sisters, followed by the Captain and gentlemen of The Royal and Ancient Golf Club, with representatives from the Honourable Company of Edinburgh Golfers and Prestwick Golf Club. Members of the Parish Kirk Session followed them with the Provost and Baillies of the Town Council, then the professional golfers and the caddies, and finally the long procession of the general public. They moved off along St Mary's Place, turned right into Bell Street, then left along South Street to the Cathedral. The procession appeared endless, stretching out the whole length of South Street. Virtually every man in the small township of St Andrews was in the procession paying his last respects to a man they all knew, even if it only had been to nod and smile when passing Tom's shop door or entering the Kirk.

Andra' Kirkaldy was extremely proud of the fact that he was one of the six professional golfers who carried Tom's coffin from the road and down the steps and on through the long nave of the Cathedral's ruins to its final resting place by the Morris family grave. Doubtless so were Sandy Herd, Jack Burns, Willie and David Auchterlonie and Willie Crawford from North Berwick. Ben Sayers walked behind, not tall enough to play a supporting role.

There were too many mourners to get into the service at St Mary's Church and there were too many to get within earshot of the grave. They were spread about through the gravestones, round the ancient tower of St Rule and through the Cathedral ruins. Among them was Douglas Rolland, just another face in the crowd.

Tom's grandson, (William) Bruce Hunter, took the head cord and Mr Charles Grace took the foot. On either side of Bruce Hunter stood Tom's nephews, his brother George's sons, Jack from Hoylake and George from Edinburgh. James Black, another nephew, the son of his deceased sister Janet, and Charlie Hunter from Prestwick were next and Willie Rusack and the Earl of Stair completed the cords.

When Tom was finally lowered into the earth below Tommy's effigy on the cathedral wall and the minister had made the commendation and prayer, the mourners walked past the open grave in silent tribute.

The scores of wreaths were left around the graveside for a week and hundreds of townspeople came to read the messages of condolence. There were wreaths from the gentry of all parts of the country. From Mr Balfour, the former Prime Minister, from the Asquiths, and from the Grimmond and Boothby families.

There were wreaths from golf clubs throughout the country, some that no one had heard of, but all from places that Tom had looked over and set out where the holes should lie before declaring it 'as fine a place for golf as St Andrews itself'. Some places such as Hoylake and Westward Ho! sent wreaths from the inside and outside staff, as well as from the club members. The wreaths were still arriving days after the funeral, with simple messages from ordinary folk whose lives he had touched on a golf course somewhere;

from people that he had met on a train or simply as they had passed by the shop and he had talked to in that pawky, kindly way of his, and they had left with the feeling that they had met royalty. Many tributes were mere bunches of flowers gathered and placed there by the likes of a caddy's wife, as her token of gratitude to a man that had done what he could to keep her and her bairns in 'milk and meal' through the times when there was little work, or when her man was just unable to pass the pub door.

Tom Morris was laid to rest on Wednesday, 27 May 1908 at 3 p.m., but everything that he stood for lived on. In Prestwick and Hoylake, the loyalty of Charlie Hunter and Jack Morris was matched only by the appreciation of them by their Clubs' membership. Sandy Herd had reaped the rewards of diligence and perseverance in winning the Open Championship against the odds in a field that has rarely been bettered. Andra' Kirkaldy continued to convey the excitement and satisfaction of foursomes matchplay golf to men and women from all walks of life and to a new generation. Dozens of great players from Scotland had spread the gospel of fair play, honesty and consideration for others, the central tenets of golf, throughout the world. All of the features of the game that are held sacred by golfers were embodied in Tom Morris, the man, and today are synonymous with his name.

From an age of great Victorians, Tom Morris emerged, if not the greatest, certainly the most widely-known of sporting figures. From his humble origins in a weaver's cottage in North Street, St Andrews, in which golf was as integral a part as the loom, he nursed the game from little more than a parochial Scottish pastime to a worldwide phenomenon. Tom's testament is to be found not just in the 'Auld Grey Toon' of St Andrews, but also throughout the world, wherever golf is played. He is, indisputably, 'The Grand Old Man of Golf'.

Tom Morris was dead, but everything that he stood for in The Great Game lived on.

Epilogue

Tom died leaving grandchildren in St Andrews and nephews and nieces in Hoylake, Edinburgh, St Andrews and Canada. Agnes, his eldest granddaughter, married Willie Rusack who had early eschewed the family hotel business for the sea. After his marriage, Willie was active with his brother-in-law, William Bruce Hunter, in running the Tom Morris Golf shop. They opened a shop in Manchester, sited over Ye Olde Fishing Shop, which it is thought Bruce Hunter managed for a few years. Willie Rusack was an able golfer and member of the New Club, St Andrews where his brother David was Captain. In the early 1920s Willie and Agnes went to live in America where he represented the National Cash Register Company. In the 1930s they were involved in the Rusack family hotel business in the Harz Mountains region of Germany, where Agnes golfed competitively with some success. With the outbreak of the Second World War they returned to St Andrews, settling first in Bogward and finally in Strathkinness. The couple became a popular sight in the Town with the pony and trap that served all their travel needs through the war years and into the 1960s. Willie and Agnes left no children.

William Bruce Hunter trained as an engineer in Glasgow where he met and married Ellen Matheson. After their marriage, they lived in Manchester for a time before moving to Helensburgh, St Andrews, and then Wimbledon. Bruce Hunter, as he was known, was a good golfer who won club and regional events in Lancashire and the West of Scotland. He was a member of the New Club in St Andrews, representing it on numerous occasions and contesting the Open and Amateur Championships. Bruce suffered from tuberculosis and, in pursuit of a cure, left London for Davos in Switzerland where he died in a sanatorium in 1931. Bruce and Ellen had a son, who sadly predeceased them, and also a daughter, Doreen Gray, who was 19 years old at the time of her mother's death in 1935.

Elizabeth Gray Hunter, the third of the grandchildren, was the last to marry. Gray was deeply religious and involved in Sunday school and Bible class teaching in St Mary's Church. She married Dr James Manson Craig, an ordained Church of Scotland Minister from Crail in 1911. They joined the Missionary Society and went to India: her husband died the following year. Around 1920, she re-married Captain Arthur James Bentley and settled in Lytham St Annes. At the time of writing no children of Elizabeth Gray have been traced.

Jamesina, the youngest of Tom's grandchildren, married Tom Morrow, a close friend of her brother, who was a textile engineer in the jute industry. Tom Morrow worked for the large Titaghur company who had operations in Calcutta and Dundee. He also worked in Brazil where he married Jamesina on 8 April 1911 and when they returned to St Andrews, they lived in the old Morris family home at 6 Pilmour Links. Jamesina sadly died in 1919, leaving her young two sons and a daughter. Tom Morrow made a second marriage in 1944 with Jean Stewart, a nurse and head gamekeeper's daughter, with whom he had a third son.

Jamesina's elder son. Ian Thomas Morrow, Tom Morris's great grandson, became one of Britain's most eminent accountants and industrialists. He sat on the boards of many large, international public companies during a career which spanned six decades, including being deputy chairman and managing director of Rolls-Royce. A member of The Royal and Ancient Golf Club of St Andrews, his locker in the Big Room of the Clubhouse, a privilege reserved for members of long standing, was directly beneath the portrait in oils by Sir George Reid of his great grandfather. A Freeman of the City of London, he was knighted by the Queen in 1973 for his services to industry. Tom Morris would undoubtedly have been very proud of the achievements of his great grandson. Sir Ian Morrow died in April 2006, aged 93.

After Tom's death, Bruce Hunter and Willie Rusack ran the Tom Morris business for a few years with guidance from David Anderson. David was one of Da's five sons who, with the exception of Jamie, are believed to have trained as club makers in the Forgan workshop. David and his brother Walter ran the successful business D. & W. Anderson, Club Makers in Ellice Place, St Andrews. David's son, another David, entered into partnership with Bruce Hunter after Willie and Agnes Rusack left for America. When Bruce and his wife Ellen died in the 1930s, their daughter, Doreen, continued the partnership with David Anderson and, after his death in 1970, with his son Morris Anderson who came to acquire the business outright. Today the amicable arrangement persists with Morris Anderson's son leasing the premises from Sheila Walker, a great-great-granddaughter of Tom Morris. Bryan Anderson, the managing director, still greets the golfing pilgrims at the shop door in the same way that Tom Morris did over a century ago.

Tom's business adapted to changing times. Forgan's did not. On 5 January 1963, Forgan's golf club factory closed and 41 club-makers found themselves unemployed. Forgan's had been acquired by the Spalding company, and the continuous modernisation that Robert Forgan and his sons had so prided themselves on, overtook and consumed them.

After Tom's death his grandchildren presented the Championship Belt to The Royal and Ancient. From the minutes of the General Meeting of the Club in September 1908, a letter from William Bruce Hunter reads:

> On behalf of my sisters and myself, I beg to ask the Royal and Ancient Golf Club to accept from us the Open Championship Belt which belonged to our late Grandfather, Tom Morris. The Belt was won outright by his son Tommy and he cherished it more than anything in his possession. In offering the Belt to the Club, we feel that we are only doing what our late Grandfather would have desired. We take this opportunity of thanking the Royal and Ancient Golf Club for the many kindnesses extended to our late Grandfather during his long connection with the Club.

The Meeting cordially resolved to accept the Belt and the Secretary was directed to forward a letter of thanks to the donors. Today, the Championship Belt is displayed in a cabinet in the Front Hall of the Clubhouse, beside the Claret Jug, the Open Championship Trophy, and the Amateur Championship Trophy which carries Tom's effigy.

The Links that Tom left has spread from three courses to six. The Eden course was built to a Harry Colt design in 1913. It was formed out of two fields that lay to the south of the railway line, across from the 16th fairway of the Old Course, together with three fields that bordered the 13th and 14th fairways and ran in a triangle from the railway yards (now the site of the Old Course Hotel) to the Eden estuary. When a sea of whins had been cleared from the side of the 12th fairway of the Old Course, the Eden Course came into being. It was immediately popular and hosted the Eden Tournament, at one time a major event in Scottish golf, which is still played today.

The Town's children had come to regard the Jubilee Course as their domain, and its post-war remodelling and upgrading left a vacuum for children and beginners. The Town Council filled this vacuum when it acquired 26 acres of land from Balgove Farm and constructed the 9-hole Balgove Course. It was opened in 1972 but did not have a long life for, with the remodelling of the Eden in 1990, the 'Royal Balgove', as it was affectionately known, ceased to be.

The Strathtyrum course came into being in July 1993 together with a new and improved Balgove. The Strathtyrum is a short course of 18 holes designed by Donald Steel and it was built to provide for young players who had outgrown the Balgove and for older players seeking a quiet and leisurely round. It has satisfied those groups and more competitive players with its subtle greens and tricky approaches. Donald Steel was also responsible for the brilliant redesign of the Jubilee in 1989 that turned a benign course into a challenging monster. The development of golf continues at St Andrews, with the opening, in summer 2008, of the Links Trust's seventh course, the magnificent Castle Course overlooking the Town.

Tom, with his youthful enthusiasm, would have relished and approved of it all. His 'Himalayas', the Ladies Short Course or putting green, flourishes still and is open to all. George Bruce's Embankment also carries a rather reduced putting green. The Caddies' Shelter, Caddy Master's Office and pavilion that Tom had overseen in construction opposite his shop on the Sandyhill above the 18th green, is now a shop owned and run by the Links Trust. The caddies were relocated to a new building beside the 1st tee in 1997.

Following the restructuring of Local Government in Scotland and the coming into being of Regional Councils, the St Andrews Links Act of 1974 authorised the Town Council to hand over the management of the courses to the St Andrews Links Trust and through it to the Management Committee. St Andrews Links are secure and remain within the combined control of The Royal and Ancient Golf Club and the townspeople, through the auspices of Fife Regional Council, in much the same way as in Tom's day with St Andrews Town Council.

Tom's name endures because of the indelible impression he left on golf. In St Andrews, his grave in the Cathedral burial ground has become a place of pilgrimage for people from all over the world. His effigy in bronze is set high on the wall of The Royal and Ancient Clubhouse overlooking the eighteenth green that today bears his name. In Holy Trinity Church, a plaque also commemorates his long service as an Elder and in the Cottage Hospital a similar memorial signifies where he died.

In July 2004, the Royal Bank of Scotland issued a £5 note commemorating the 250th anniversary of The Royal and Ancient Golf Club, and this bears an image of Tom Morris, the first time a golfer has appeared on a British banknote. It is also entirely fitting that his name lives on today in a very practical and tangible way. Tom Morris is the spiritual head and guiding force behind 'Keepers of The Green', a charity founded in 1995 and based in St Andrews, that provides powered wheelchairs to needy people, both young and old.

Few golf clubs in the world are without a picture of him on the wall. His features remain instantly recognisable to everyone who plays the game that he, more than anyone, made great.

Notes to Chapters

1 Roots in the Links

1. The earliest recorded antecedent of Tom Morris is George Morris whose son, Thomas, was born in 1649. Thomas married Susannah Flemyng and their second son, Alexander, was father to John Morris, born 1722, the great grandfather of Tom Morris. All the Morris families were of some substance in the Town, having their purchase of properties and title deeds registered in the Burgh records.

2. Until the Reformation in the middle of the sixteenth century, St Andrews was a prosperous and powerful place. Not only was it the religious capital of Scotland, but also the country's premier seat of learning. The University, founded in 1413, is the third oldest in the English-speaking world. Additionally, the Town was a thriving centre of trade and commerce.

3. The Robertson golf ball-making family derives from the marriage in 1640 of one David Robertson to Agnes, the daughter of Thomas Buddo, golf ball-maker in St Andrews. From David and Agnes came generations of golf ball-making Robertsons, ending with the great Allan Robertson and the era of the feathery ball and craftsmanship in ball-making.

4. One of the objects of this initiative of providing a Silver Club for competition was to promote and strengthen the position of St Andrews in the golfing firmament. In this, the 22 'Noblemen and Gentlemen' certainly succeeded, for St Andrews continued to be the 'Alma Mater' of golf, with all gentlemen golfers in the country aspiring to membership of the St Andrews Society and thereby becoming eligible to compete for it.

5. The following is an extract from *Reminiscences of St Andrews Bay* by George Bruce, 1884:

> Mr (Cathcart) Dempster, like his father, was a pompous, self-interested, opinionative official. His father, Charles Dempster, was at one time Provost, and about the year 1760 farmed the farm of St Nicholas . . . His son, this Cathcart, erected a factory near the foot of Abbey Street . . . and manufactured what was extensively known as 'Dempster's Duck', or

Dempster's canvas, for which he got a patent, and was recognised as one of the principal manufacturers of canvas, in Scotland, for the British Navy. But he lost both his reputation and his trade by one fatal mistake, viz., allowing the yarn to lie too long exposed on the East Bents, or St Nicholas, before it was converted into 'duck' or canvas; it was, to use a Scotch phrase, 'fusionless', partly rotten. Two men-of-war were supplied with it, and the first gale of wind blew the sails from the spars to ribbons, which also blew away his patent, and closed his factory.

6. Feu is a Scottish legal term for tenure of the right to the use of land, houses etc., in perpetuity, for a stipulated annual payment.

3 The Kirk, the School and the Apprenticeship

1. The given names 'Thomas' and 'Mitchell' are anomalies, for neither had been used in the Morris family for nearly two hundred years. Tom may have been named after friends of their parents in the Town and whilst there are two such possibilities, it is most likely that he was named after a weaver living close to the Morris home in North Street. Like Tom's father John, this Thomas Mitchell was a stalwart of the Weavers Trade Guild, being Deacon at the same time as John was Boxmaster (Treasurer). That the two men were close in friendship as well as in their craft can be deduced from their stances and agreements on every issue in the guild. They appeared to form a triumvirate with another Thomas Morris, who was also an office-bearer in the craft guild and of like mind on every issue. Tom was most probably named after both of these close family friends.

2. Dr Buist was a golfer, although his name has come down to us because of his fierce support of the established Church of Scotland and his vociferous attacks upon the reformers of the breakaway Free Church. The 'Wee Frees', led by Robert Chalmers of Anstruther, sought the abolition of patronage in the Church. In St Andrews the leading 'Wee Free' was Professor Brewster, one of the most distinguished men of learning in Scotland. Buist conducted a relentless, intellectual hounding exercise against Brewster, calling for his resignation from the University Court, which persisted until Brewster left to become the Principal of Edinburgh University. John Morris and his family were staunch Established Church, as his forefathers had been for centuries and as his family would be for years to come.

3. W. W. Tulloch, author of *The Life of Tom Morris*, published in 1908, states that Tom Morris attended Madras College. This could only be correct if Tom's schooling had extended beyond the normal age of ten or eleven as Madras College was not opened until 1 October 1833. The first pupils of Madras were from the English School where Tom would have gone, (so named because no Latin was taught), followed a year later by those of the (Latin) Grammar School. Other pupils from the numerous private schools in St Andrews also no doubt were sent

to Madras College. It was initially endowed by a bequest of £60,000 from Dr. Andrew Bell, the founder of the Madras monitorial system of education, and was greatly supported by the indefatigable Hugh Lyon Playfair. It is written in 1861 that 'a first-rate elementary education may be obtained for a shilling a quarter' and that a higher grade cost two shillings a quarter.

4. Robert Chambers first rented a house before substantially rebuilding and renovating Abbey Park around 1830, turning it into a fine building at the end of Abbey Street. It was in Abbey Park, unbeknown to the rest of the world, that Robert Chambers wrote his *Vestiges of the Natural History of Creation.* Published anonymously in London in 1844, this was the first popular and easily accessible work to question the origin of life on earth and in particular the origin of man. It was a Victorian sensation that fired and inspired the great debate on evolution that came to its height with the later publication of Darwin's *Origin of Species* in 1859.

Chambers maintained a deep affection for St Andrews, where he took up golf and, despite obvious business disadvantages, made his permanent home in the Town after the death of his first wife and marriage to his second. In Abbey Park and subsequently in the house that he built on The Scores, Robert Chambers did most of his greatest work. After his death he found a permanent resting place within the ruined chapel of St Rule in the Cathedral burial ground.

5. With the 1839 report of Allan Robertson winning the 'inputs', and that of Tom Morris doing so two years later, we have the first public notices of the two most important historical figures in golf, each winning the only 'professional' competition in existence at the time.

Golf did not warrant a routine mention in the newspapers of the day. The results of the Autumn Meeting of The Royal and Ancient were recorded, together with listings of the gentry present. In addition there was a full report given of the great social event of the year, the Club Ball in the Town Hall. These events were reported in the newspapers because they were of interest to the gentry. It was only when the big money matches came about in the 1850s and '60s that golf caught the public imagination and the outcome of events was regularly reported.

4 'A Kind of King Amongst Them'

1. Allan was a short, stocky man with reddish whiskers and an open, alert countenance. He wore a red coat and an almost perpetual smile when playing. He appears to have been quick-witted, expressing a droll sense of humour with a characteristic pawky way of address. The word 'pawky' is very expressive to those who have been brought up with it. It implies innate geniality with diplomacy and clever charm. A 'pawky' person is immediately likeable and enjoyed by all. If a golfer were to choose a playing partner, he would be well-advised to choose a skilled and pawky one; skilled to partner him through the game and pawky to support, encourage and companionably entertain.

2. Hugh Philp obtained William Fairful's lease for the links end of a feu at Pilmuir, by this time spelled Pilmour. Fairful had built a cart shed and stable on this plot overlooking the 18th hole soon after the Council's sale of the land in 1820. It was Fairful's very modest shed that would evolve, firstly into Hugh Philp's workshop, and ultimately the Tom Morris shop which stands by the Home Green of the Old Course to this day.

Hugh Philp was one of three master joiners at the time running well-established workshops in St Andrews and employing a number of men. He was said to be 'a lad o' pairts', in other words, a very talented man. His early training was as a wright, the doyens of the craft guilds. The Wrights Guild comprised carpenters, wheelwrights, joiners, cabinet makers and the early architects. It is from the wrights that all of the great Scots architects emerged, notably the Adams family. In St Andrews, George Rae, the City Architect who designed The Royal and Ancient Clubhouse in 1853 and Jesse Hall who succeeded him, started out as wrights. Machine-makers, the inventors who drove the Industrial Revolution with their originality, were in the main wrights by training. As a crafts guild, they were the most fiercely protective of their standards and qualifications for membership.

Little is known of Philp's success as a joiner, carpenter, wheelwright or cabinet maker and, in different places and at different times he was referred to as one or other of these. He and his workmen, however, must have had a good reputation, for he was awarded the contract for the woodwork in Mr Cheape's grand new house at Strathtyrum and he had been responsible for work on the Union Club's Parlour, at that time accommodating The Royal and Ancient Golf Club. Hugh Philp was also becoming recognised as a maker of very fine golf clubs.

3. The Piries were regarded as the best players of their day in St Andrews. When David Pirie died in March 1854 his obituary read:

> [He] was one of the 'old guard' of St. Andrews golfers, and upheld the celebrity of the Links some twenty or twenty-five years ago. The family of Pirie has contributed a respectable quota to the ranks and renown of St. Andrews professionals, and David was, we believe, the first who made the name famous in a generation now past or passing away. He and his brothers were the 'crack' men of our Links before Allan Robertson and the modern race of notables were known, or at least had acquired repute. The Piries figured frequently in grand matches during their period, against the heroes of the golfing grounds, singly as well as in 'foursomes' with amateurs.
>
> The story is told of Tom Alexander of Musselburgh, in the early 1830s, on 'a fly-away' and unexpected visit to this cold, grey town [St Andrews]. There were no regular professionals at that time and most players had some trade or other. The only man considered capable of tackling the formidable Alexander was Sandy Pirie, the wabster (weaver) and he was away working in the harvest-field! However, they sent for

him post-haste; and he came into St. Andrews on pony-back, beat his man and went back to work!

To emphasize their superiority, Sandy and Davie Pirie defeated Robert Oliphant and Tom Alexander by 7 holes over 2 rounds of the St Andrews Green in September 1835. The Pirie brothers were undoubtedly the leading players of their day before the emergence of Allan Robertson.

4. This conclusion is contradicted by Thomas Hodge, an artist, doyen of the St Andrews Links and The Royal and Ancient from the early 1850s until the 1890s. Hodge was adamant that Allan was not responsible for the general increase in the use of iron clubs. In his own presentation copy from the publishers of *The Badminton Library, Golf* of 1890, he annotated the references to Allan's increased use of irons in the following terms: 'Quite incorrect! Allan never played an iron through the green', scoring out the relevant sentences with 'Not correct'. There is, however, evidence from the private manuscript notes of H.S.C. Everard relating a conversation he had with Robert Clark, the author and golf historian, in the Big Room of The Royal and Ancient in 1893. In these notes, Everard writes that Clark recalled watching Allan playing in a match that included Col. Playfair. Allan's ball had come to rest near the Scholars Bunker, the last bunker on the left before the Road Bunker in front of the 17th green. Allan lofted his ball over the Road Bunker to within a yard of the hole. When Playfair said, 'a fine shot Allan – you won't do that again', Allan replied, 'bet ye a ba' I do it three times; mind ye, I'll no say that I'll be so close, but I'll stay on the green'. Playfair took the bet and Allan dropped three balls and did it every time. Clearly, Allan was playing with a lofting iron and Hodge was referring to iron clubs in general that were becoming increasingly commonplace in general play.

5. Allan's personal clubs came out of Hugh Philp's shop until James Wilson left Philp in 1852 to set up on his own account as a club-maker. After this time, Allan would appear to have played with clubs made mainly by Wilson. He invariably had the heads of his clubs stamped 'ALLAN' below that of the club-maker.

6. Although no better or worse educated than others of his class in the Town, Allan doubtless saw himself as a 'cut above' most, constantly alert to self-improvement and perhaps even self-promotion. He certainly relished signing his name and address on his possessions wherever possible. In his personal copy of *The History of the Robertsons* (i.e. the Clan Robertson) he signed his name no less than 4 times. The case containing his gold and pearl tie-pin is signed and inscribed, 'Allan Robertson, Links, St. Andrews, 1832'. This design, of two crossed golf clubs and a pearl hanging between them representing a golf ball, would appear to have been adopted by Allan as his emblem, and it is perpetuated in stone on the obelisk over his grave in the Cathedral burial ground.

When he bequeathed an unusual penknife in the shape of a hare to his brother David in Australia, by way of a codicil to his will dated 9th Dec. 1852, he attached a label proclaiming: 'A knife that belonged to Peter Robertson Golf Ball Maker

North Street St Andrews in the year 1800 Grandfather to Allan Robertson, Links, St Andrews'. Additionally his snuffbox is emblazoned with the Coat of Arms of the Clan Robertson. Allan was clearly aware of his own importance and certainly proud of his heritage.

If he was conscious of his family's historical connections with golf and St Andrews, he was equally aware of the importance of learning and education. Allan was 17 years old in 1832 when William and Robert Chambers first published the *Chambers' Edinburgh Journal.* This was a weekly publication of interesting and diverse articles, being the first national attempt to bring affordable literature to the masses. Allan was clearly an early subscriber for, in December 1843, he had 49 of the weekly editions bound into book-form, the earliest dated October 1832. Each contained articles that interested him, of which only three related to golf, one of them being a flattering reference to himself. The others covered broad and diverse subjects, showing that his interests extended far beyond the Links. He numbered each page of the volume and wrote an index of these 57 articles at the front, as well as signing, with his address and date, Dec 11 1843, both internal back and front covers. It is, however, in the 5 August 1843 edition that he gives us a poignant reminder of the sadness and heartache he himself was experiencing at that time. In this, Allan outlined in ink a poem entitled 'Separation', a sad and melancholy elegy on the parting of a loved one. The poem must have struck a chord in him, for his wife, Helen, was at the time gravely ill and within a few weeks she was dead.

In May 1854, Allan also compiled a scrapbook of newspaper cuttings, scorecards, photographs and other material, dating from 1835, which he continued until his death in 1859. The large leather-bound volume is inscribed in gilt lettering, 'Allan Robertson's Golf Album', and contains newspaper reports of the meetings of The Royal and Ancient Golf Club and of his own and his contemporaries' important matches, together with other articles that captured his attention. Most of the items are annotated and dated in his hand. Not only do they provide us with a picture of golfing life in St Andrews during his lifetime, but they also permit a glimpse into the character of the man himself. This scrapbook was later donated by Allan's second wife to The Royal and Ancient Golf Club and is today one of its most prized possessions.

The personalising of these belongings illustrates the importance that Allan attached to them. It is somewhat difficult today to comprehend how few possessions people had in those days and, of those that they did have, the value they attached to them. Allan's book, *The History of the Robertsons,* his heraldic snuff box, and his grandfather's ornate and unusual knife, would be of the utmost value and attachment to him. The gold and pearl stick-pin (tie or cravat-pin) was a treasure far beyond the wildest dreams of the ordinary man, and particularly of the youth who acquired it at the early age of 17 years.

7. All previous attempts at renovating the infrastructure of St Andrews had foundered for lack of both money and commitment. Hugh Lyon Playfair certainly had

the commitment and also the will to raise the necessary funds. His nephew, Lyon, Lord Playfair, noted: 'He laboured with the will and authority of an autocrat, and forced money by subscription with the audacity of a highwayman. Naturally he constantly gave offence, but as his reforms were always justified by their good results, the Major's tyrannies were condoned.'

Playfair's renovations were only made possible, however, by the Police Act of 1833, which was passed by the first Whig Government of Earl Grey. This Act enabled towns to levy rates (local taxes) to improve street lighting and paving as well as water and sewage systems. St Andrews adopted the Act in three stages between 1833 and 1861, ultimately giving the Town Council the right to make householders responsible for pavements outside their properties and removing projections into the streets. Playfair would appear to have enforced this Act with rather more zeal than the Provosts of nearby boroughs. St Andrews' rates were 11 pence in the £1 in 1861, by which time the Gas Company had been established (1835) and the water supply improved. Despite the unsanitary state of the Town, there was much opposition to the rates increase in 1849 when the sewage system was renovated. Indeed, Playfair was forced to fight for every penny he could raise from the Town's rates even although they were low compared to many burghs of similar size.

5   Foundations for the Popularity of the Game

1. An excerpt from *Golfiana*, by George Fullerton Carnegie, 1842, illustrates the esteem in which Davie and Allan Robertson were held:

> Great Davie Robertson, the eldest cad,
> In whom the good was stronger than the bad;
> He sleeps in death! and with him sleeps a skill
> Which Davie, statesmanlike, would wield at will!
> Sound be his slumbers ! yet if he should wake
> In worlds where golf is play'd , himself he'd stake
> And look about and tell each young beginner,
> 'I'll gie half-ane . . . nae mair, as I'm a sinner.'
> He leaves a son, and Allan is his name.
> In golfing far beyond his fathers fame.

2. This was a much-used derogatory expression describing small land-owning farmers (lairds) with social pretensions. They wore flat caps (bonnets) and, despite their debts, they maintained dovecotes on their land, as did the land-owning gentry, for purposes of sports shooting.

3. The process of making a feather ball had not changed in hundreds of years. As is well known, three pieces of leather cut to the correct size were sewn together to form a hollow sphere. This was then turned inside out so that the stitching was on the inside and stuffed to compaction with damp feathers using a brogue that fitted to the ball-maker's chest. The outer covering of leather was drawn taut,

with the hole through which the feathers were inserted finally sewn up. When the feathers expanded and the leather contracted as they dried out, the ball became hard. There are several accounts of making feathery balls, but only one record is known to exist of the process given by someone who actually made a ball. This is contained in a letter dated Sept 22nd 1903 from Tom Morris to a Captain Wade in response to the Captain's question about the process. From this letter we learn that 'the feathers in the Ball are mostly Hens, but they were all chopped down very small before they were stuffed in the Ball . . . The Leather is Boars Hide and had to be soaked in water for a time before using. The Balls were all sewn together, and the mark you see in the Ball is the end of the thread, which was very strong, and which I well know required some hard pulling to draw close.'

Estimates of the number that a skilled man could make in a day vary between four and ten.

6 The Gutta Affair

1. Until the late nineteenth century, match play, either singles or foursomes, was by far the dominant form of golf and 'odds' or 'handicaps' were negotiated either privately between the contestants, or were fixed by others, usually professionals or club secretaries. This handicapping would, in match play, be either 'holes-up', in other words a number of holes start given to one competitor, or at certain holes a competitor would be given a stroke.

For stroke play events there were initially no handicaps. Later, competitors were sometimes divided into different classes, each class being given strokes according to ability and in some instances separate prizes were awarded for each class. In the last few decades of the nineteenth century, with the increasing popularity of strokeplay, the concept of individual players receiving their own stroke allowance was introduced at some clubs, but each club selected its own method of allotting handicaps.

There was no such concept as fixed personal handicaps that were transportable to different courses, nor were handicaps given in stroke play used to calculate handicaps in match play. The 'Handicapper' fixed the 'odds' for that particular day, conditions of the weather and current form of the players. Often in stroke play the golfer did not know what handicap had been allotted to him until he had finished.

As the game expanded and the railways enabled more golfers to play on different courses, the pressure increased for a more equitable and universal method of arriving at handicaps for amateur players. In 1924 a meeting of the British Golf Unions took place at York to evolve such a uniform system, which eventually, after many years and changes, resulted in the position we have today in the United Kingdom.

2. Allan and Tom both took an active part in the social activities of the Club. Allan was elected Captain in 1854 and whilst he did play in the Club's main medal

competitions during his year of office, he did not play as a competitor. Since the time of the Club's inception, both Allan and Tom regularly donated balls as prizes in the main events and Tom continued to donate balls, even during his years at Prestwick. They also made a contribution to the Club's social evenings. Allan was obviously something of an orator, for newspaper accounts show that he frequently acted as croupier (master of ceremonies) at Club dinners.

3. Samuel Messieux, a young Swiss modern languages master at the Madras College and a member of The Royal and Ancient Golf Club, is reputed in 1836 to have driven a feathery ball 361 yards. This mighty drive was the entire length of the Elysian Fields of what is now the 14th hole of the Old Course. Mr Messieux's big strike was under the most favourable conditions with a dry, hard, running fairway and a wind off Lucklaw Hill from behind. Interestingly, this drive was much longer than the longest hit ever recorded with a gutty ball, which rendered the feathery obsolete, until it was deposed itself by the rubber-cored ball around 1902. In wet conditions with a waterlogged ball it is doubtful if the feathery would have flown 100 yards.

4. The story has oft been repeated of how the celebrated maker of feather balls, John Gourlay of Musselburgh, foresaw the end of his business and dispatched every ball on the premises to fulfil all outstanding orders. This is a colourful story but untrue, as witnessed by the accounts drawn up at his death in 1869, showing that he was still selling feather balls three years after the introduction of the gutta.

5. An article appeared in *The World* on 25 September 1894 which confirmed that Tom's personal relationship with Allan was not impaired over the gutta ball incident: 'Allan Robertson was particularly sore at the innovation [of the gutta ball], and his prejudice led to a rupture in the business relations of Tom and himself, though it never interfered with their friendship'. The whole article was clearly written with Tom's co-operation.

6. Tom Morris is the only craftsmen from whom we have today examples of both feather balls and clubs which were unequivocally made by him. There are in existence a small number of feather balls stamped 'T. Morris', as well as long-headed clubs, similarly stamped, made by him about this time.

When the gutta ball was introduced in 1846, the skill needed to make the new ball was very much less than that required to produce the feathery, and gutta percha could even be fashioned into golf balls by the players themselves. It is not surprising that many club-makers turned their hand to producing and marketing the gutta balls, as well as clubs.

7. It is interesting that the marriage banns of Allan and Tom were called within days of each other from the Holy Trinity pulpit and are juxtaposed in the church register.

7 Marriage and Movement

1. Agnes was the daughter of Alexander Bayne and his wife Helen Brodie. In 1817 when her sister Ann was born, Alexander was described as a labourer in the baptismal records of Dairsie Parish Kirk. In 1818, at the baptism of Agnes, he was giving his occupation as handloom weaver.

2. The national and established Church was disrupted in 1843 when some two hundred parish ministers formed the Free Church of Scotland. This was a result of the long-festering resentment in many parts of the Church against patronage, mainly the right of the local landowner to select the minister for the parish. St Andrews was a hot bed of resentment at the time when Professor Brewster, Principal of the University and one of the ground-breaking thinkers of the age, was a leading figure in the disruption. Hostile confrontations occurred in the newspapers between supporters and proponents of the Free Church. In St Andrews it came to a head with the building of the new Martyrs Free Church in North Street, defiantly and directly opposite the ancient chapel of St Salvators.

Some thirty years later, when passions had cooled and reason returned, the Unitarian Church movement built its church, Hope Park, at the corner of Hope Street and St Mary's Place. As the Town grew, a second Established Church was built in St Mary's Place and a further one, St Leonards, in Hepburn Gardens. It was not until 1924 that the Churches would come together again as the Church of Scotland.

3. When Allan Robertson's father, David, died in 1836, the Rev. Dr Ferrie owed the deceased £4 17s 6d, a sum which was more than three times more than any other debtor. The debt, however, was 'considered good' by the administrator of the estate.

4. In the census of 1851 Tom is recorded as Tomas Morris and no correction is made. He gives his age as 29 and Agnes gives hers as 32, both correct, although Agnes had given an incorrect age to the census in 1841. The census also shows that Agnes's unmarried sister Margaret Bayne, aged 27, lived with them in the house at 4 Pilmour Links and was listed as a domestic servant. The fact that the census was taken in April, and Tommy, their second child, was not born until May, possibly explains her presence in the household. Their neighbour at No. 5 was Bob Kirk, then giving his occupation as a shoemaker. Hugh Philp and his family were living in No. 6, the house that the Morris family would eventually come to own and where they would spend the rest of their lives. Philp gave his occupation as a wright, as did the club-maker James Wilson round the corner in Golf Place. Only Tom and Allan designated 'golfball maker' as their occupations in the census.

5. Both George and Agnes were employed as domestic servants by Robert Chambers at his home, Abbey Park, St Andrews.

8 Sowing Seeds in the West

1. In the development of golf, the coming of the railway was just as important as the invention of the gutta ball. The new 'Permanent Way' made the links land courses of Scotland more accessible and, together with the new gutta ball, brought about a great expansion. These two technological developments, which coincidentally came about around the same time, were the driving factors in the popularization and development of golf.

2. The prospect of a railway connection to St Andrews as a branch line from Leuchars was first raised in 1849 when the St Andrews Railway Company was formed. It was not until November 1850, however, that the Fifeshire Journal reported that application had been made to Parliament for authorization to construct a railway from Leuchars to St Andrews.

With Provost Playfair in the chair, the Town Council held a meeting with all interested parties to encourage local subscription for the £21,000 capital required. With three-quarters of the sum raised within a week, the St Andrews Railway Company Act was promoted in Parliament, passed in both Houses without objections and received Royal Assent in July 1851.

Construction work began in early September 1851 under the direction of Mr Thomas Bouch who later came to national renown as the engineer responsible for the construction of the ill-fated Tay Bridge. Traversing flat land with only two wooden bridges required to span the River Eden and the Motray Water, and little in the way of banking or cuttings work needed, construction progressed quickly. With only four sidings and a station terminus at St Andrews to construct, the St Andrews Railway was not a major undertaking when compared to railway endeavors in other parts of the country. Sidings were sited at Haig's whisky distillery, the Guardbridge dock wharf on the Eden's estuary, and the brick and tile works at Guardbridge and Kincaple. Only the siting of the station at St Andrews was controversial. Initial planning for this located it at the Balgove farm sheep park, roughly where the driving range is today. Local opinion was that it should be sited closer to the Town beside the lifeboat shed where today the Links Road curves to its junction with Gibson Place. This, however, would have meant the loss of that part of the golfing ground that today forms the 17th green and the 18th tee. A compromise was reached and the station was built on what is today the site of the Old Course Hotel.

It is perhaps not well known that the famous road that is such a telling and decisive hazard behind the 17th green, the green of the Road Hole, is in fact called Station Road. Throughout the second half of the nineteenth century it was one of the busiest thoroughfares in the Town.

The first train traveled from Leuchers to St Andrews on 22 June 1852 and the official opening ceremony was held on Tuesday, 29 June. On the following day some 50 members of the general public enjoyed a cheap day excursion to Dunfermline. But before the end of July, excursions into the Town already greatly exceeded those out of it. One excursion train from Glasgow was described as a 'monster' in the local newspaper. St Andrews would never be quite the same again.

9 A New Beginning as an Era Ends

1. At Musselburgh in 1850, the Honourable Company had appointed John Gourlay, the ball-maker, to alter and improve the existing course. Willie Dunn had been likewise charged a year later with the task of doing what he could to improve the Blackheath course in London. Neither Gourlay nor Dunn had the good terrain, or the near-absolute authority that Tom enjoyed at Prestwick. Their efforts at both venues went unheralded.

2. While *The Golfer's Year Book for 1866* was clearly intended by Howie Smith to be an annual publication, it could not have met with a great deal of success for it never appeared again. Today this book is one of the rarest and most coveted in golfing literature.

3. John Gray (1824–1904) was a blacksmith whose forge was sited only yards along the Main Street from the Cross and the Red Lion in Prestwick, in the side street that today bears his name. John was the third generation Gray to work the forge. Soon after the arrival of Tom Morris and the founding of the Mechanics Golf Club, he turned his hand to making iron club heads, which Tom would shaft.

He became an extremely proficient cleekmaking craftsman. All his club heads were hand-forged and such was the demand for his work that he turned to cleekmaking full time. For many years he was the only iron club-head maker in the West of Scotland, but even in St Andrews there was a demand for his clubs that were much prized. Gray's clubs are today considered to be the best examples of the early cleekmaker's art.

John Gray was a highly respected person in the Prestwick community, becoming a Freeman of the Burgh and Captain of the Prestwick St Nicholas Club.

10 The 'Honest Toun' Park

1. The Blackheath Minute Book of 8 April 1854 records that 'It was proposed and carried that James Dunn be taken into the service of the Club – 7s per week'. It is possible that Jamie went to work for his twin brother at Blackheath a year earlier and was subsequently officially employed by the Club as evidenced by this minute. They were both sacked by Blackheath for inappropriate behaviour, Willie in 1864 and Jamie probably a year or two earlier.

2. According to Willie Park Jnr., his father's ball-making business started in Musselburgh in 1853. He is recorded as a club-maker in North Berwick 1873–75 and as a club and ball-maker in Musselburgh, employing a number of men in his workshop, shortly afterwards. The quality of the long-headed wooden clubs that

have come down to us bearing Wm. Park's name is comparable with the work of Hugh Philp, the McEwans and Johnnie Jackson. Very few of his clubs and balls are known to exist today, which suggests that his output was not large.

3. Rev. John Kerr, in his *Golf Book of East Lothian*, quotes Dr Argyle Robertson describing how he saw Willie Park on the St Andrews Links: 'I think, in the spring of 1854', but the editor of the *Fifeshire Journal*, H.B. Farnie, reported that Park's first visit to St Andrews was at the Autumn Meeting of that year.

4. Tom Morris and his son Tommy were to dominate the Open Championship with eight wins between 1861 and 1872. The Park family, however, was only one victory behind them. Willie gained golfing immortality by winning the inaugural event in 1860 and went on to record a further three victories, the last in 1875. But the Park family had talent in depth. Willie's younger brother, Mungo, won the Open in 1874 and Willie's son, Willie junior, carried off the Claret Jug in 1887 and 1889.

11   Genesis of Tournament Golf

1. The Manchester Golf Club (now the Old Manchester Golf Club), whose members were mainly Scots living in Lancashire, were apparently not invited to send a team and consequently held a long-term grudge against The Royal and Ancient and presumably also Prestwick! The conditions of the event were that 'All Golf Clubs shall have the right of competing, on payment of £4', and one can only assume that the problem with Manchester reflected poor communications and publicity.

2. The Blackheath members were so delighted at their victory that not only did they make the two heroes, George Glennie and Lieutenant J.C.Stewart, Honorary Members, but they also produced an elaborate coloured lithograph, recording full details of their victorious matches in the tournament. The lithograph also carried photographs of Glennie and Stewart, together with the result of the final, boldly stating that 'The Royal Blackheath Golf Club beat the Royal and Ancient St Andrews Golf Club by seven holes and won the Prize'.

3. Taken by Thomas Rodger of St Andrews, this photograph is the earliest one of a golfing subject that can be accurately dated. It was taken between 29 and 31 July 1857, and from the shadows cast from the west was executed in the late afternoon or early evening after play on one of these days. Ord Campbell, the missing member of the North Berwick team on the first day, is included. As the condition of the Committee for giving a bye into the second round to North Berwick was that he should turn up at St Andrews sometime on that first day, it is nearly certain that the photograph was taken in the afternoon, after play, on 29 July, 1857. This is further corroborated by the fact that an original photographic print is included in Allan Robertson's scrapbook, annotated in his own hand with the date 'July 29 1857' and the names of the men depicted.

4. The clubs specifically invited by Prestwick were: St Andrews, Musselburgh, Bruntsfield, Leven, Carnoustie Panmure, Montrose, Perth, Blackheath, Dirleton Castle, North Berwick, Aberdeen.

5. This 13-stroke victory stood as a record win margin for any Major Championship until the year 2000, when Tiger Woods won the US Open at Pebble Beach in California by 15 strokes.

6. Gambling had long been at the core of club dinners before the seasonal meetings. Club betting books of the eighteenth and nineteenth centuries attest to the entertainment enjoyed as the croupier and the secretary drew matches and recorded the bets as they were called.

12 'Cast in the Very Mould of a Golfer'

1. An Act of 1672 made the parishes responsible for the destitute. Few parishes made assessments and levied a local tax for relief of the poor. St Andrews, for instance did not, relying entirely upon church collections and charitable endowments. The Board of Supervision was established in 1845 to administer the Poor Law and from that date the parish of Monkton and Prestwick had an assessment system and levied a tax, the proceeds of which were applied to the relief of the poor in their community.

13 The Apostles of Golf

1. George Gosset emigrated to New Zealand in 1883. Like his father, he was an avid and proficient golfer who won the New Zealand Championship in 1885. He was also a diarist who religiously recorded his play and the significant events in the golf of his time. It is through him and his descendants in New Zealand, that we are fortunate in having access to the Reverend Isaac Gosset's records, for they provide a unique insight into early golf in England and Westward Ho! in particular.

2. Some inkling may be gained of what was behind Whyte-Melville's opposition by considering the position that Andrew Strath had held in St Andrews at the time. For almost six years Strath had largely filled the void on St Andrews Links left by the death of Allan Robertson.

Employed as a club-maker by James Wilson in Golf Place, Andrew was on hand to partner the gentlemen players and from newspaper accounts of matches played, he was clearly favoured. Not only did he replace Allan Robertson as Sir Thomas Moncrieffe's playing partner in his ongoing matches with James Fairlie and Tom Morris, but he was also the regular playing partner of both John Whyte-Melville and his son George. Andrew also took Allan's place as Tom's foursomes partner, but unlike Allan, he was prepared to take on the Parks from Musselburgh – with more success than failure. Andrew Strath may have had expectations in St Andrews and the Whyte-Melvilles could well have encouraged him in this respect.

Any hopes Andrew had of improving his position were, however, dashed when Tom was appointed as Custodian of St Andrews Links. His ambitions also took a knock when, as a result of the members ballot at Prestwick, Charlie Hunter was appointed Tom's successor. It is hard to avoid the conclusion that Andrew Strath was encouraged in his expectations and harboured resentment about the situation he found himself in, for, hard upon Tom's arrival back in St Andrews, he left for Musselburgh.

Although it has not been possible to establish in what capacity or with whom he was employed in Musselburgh, he was certainly golfing. In January 1865, the *Fifeshire Journal* happily reported that, after being 'chaffed' by Willie Park, Andrew agreed to a match for £5 that he duly won. Andrew Strath and his family lived in Musselburgh until May 1865 when Prestwick finally called on his services.

14 Home to Roost

1. The St Andrews property valuation roll shows that John Ramsey, a labourer, owned the property that Tom and Nancy moved into in Golf Place. The term 'labourer' was used at that time to describe any general workman or builder who was self-employed. James Wilson, the club-maker who had rented this property for twenty years, had done so again for that year, but his name had been scored out in pencil by the Town Clerk and that of Thomas Morris, club-maker, again in pencil, substituted. James Wilson moved into the premises that had housed the Union Club before The Royal and Ancient Clubhouse was built, a few yards down the road to be nearer, 'the lug o' the law', as he put it. Wilson's new property was valued at £19 10s per annum, a ten-fold increase over that which he had vacated and the one Tom Morris came to rent.

Robert Kirk, caddie and golf ball-maker, was next door to Tom on the north side; on the other, was the house and yard of James Conacher who farmed twenty acres. Next to him, at the corner of Golf Place and Pilmour Links, was the yard of James Kirk, the stonemason, who had made the obelisk headstone on Allan Robertson's grave. The Auchterlonie family would come to own the Kirk property and establish their golf shop on it. On the other side of the road a straggle of properties ran from what had been the Union Club to Mr Leslie's newly opened Golf Inn.

2. The Strath family in St Andrews originated from Alexander Strath who died, aged 94, in 1878. He came from Old Deer in Aberdeenshire as a dancing master and married Margaret Anderson of St Andrews in 1810 when his eldest son Alexander was born, and it was from his marriage to Susan Reid that the golfing Straths derive.

John Strath was born in 1837 and worked as a plasterer with his father before he died unmarried in 1869.

Andrew Strath, born in 1838, was a club-maker in St Andrews when he married Euphemia Johnstone. They had four children, one of whom died in 1862. His winning the Open Championship in 1865 was his only success as he did not significantly distinguish himself in any other golf competition. Andrew died in Prestwick in 1868 with his brother, George from Glasgow, present at his death.

William Strath was born in 1842. He married Catherine Fisher from Leuchars, Fife, in 1867, when he gave his occupation as a gardener, Jamie Anderson witnessing the nuptuals. He played in the Perth Tournament in 1864 and contested the Championship Belt in 1864 and '65, but without any monetary success. Willie was, however, a problem in the Town; over a thirty-year period he had numerous cases brought against him for assault and theft. His criminal career started in 1860 when he was accused of assaulting William Mason by 'repeatedly striking him over the legs with a golf club outside the shop of James Wilson the club maker'. It comes as no surprise to discover Willie Strath's death recorded in the Marine Deaths Register. He died in a ship off the Island of Mull in 1891; the cause of death was a 'blow to the back of the head sustained by a fall or a blow by a club'. Willie, a sometime caddy and professional player, lived by the club and probably died by the club.

George Strath, the fourth son, was born in 1844. He gave his occupation as a ship's carpenter when he married Christina Ronald, the daughter of a barley miller in St Andrews. He moved to Glasgow, becoming the first professional at the resurrected Glasgow Golf Club, firstly at South Side Park and later at Alexandra Park and entered the Open Championship lists five times between 1878 and 1886, without distinguishing himself. In November 1884, George moved to Troon where he worked for three years and considerably improved the course there. In January 1887 he and his family emigrated to America, one of the first Scots professional golfers to do so. He was the professional and greenkeeper at Dyker Golf Club, Brooklyn, New York, a 9-hole course that he had laid out. George died there on 21 January 1919 and was buried in Greenwood Cemetery.

Euphemia Strath was born in 1846. She was bridesmaid at all of her brothers' weddings but there is no record of her own marriage. She died in St Andrews in 1873.

David Strath was born in 1848 and died in Melbourne, Australia, in January 1879. The youngest of the Strath golfing brothers, he was two years older than Tommy Morris and became his firm friend, as well as rival, in St Andrews. Their battles on the Links attracted the attention of the national press and thousands flocked to see their encounters, raising the profile and popularity of the game to unprecedented levels.

James Strath was born in 1852 and died in Partick, Glasgow in 1872. His brother, George, was present at his death.

3. The Register of Sasines for Fife has two pertinent entries for 1866. The first is the registration of a bond for £400 from Thomas Milton to Thomas Morris. The security of this bond was the title to the property at Pilmour Links as well as an insurance certificate on Tom's life for £100 payable in the event of his death. Tom had taken out this policy with the Globe Insurance Company of London some years earlier when in Prestwick. The second is the property purchase registration of

6 Pilmour Links by Thomas Morris from Richard Bartholomew Child of Henley-on-Thames, Oxfordshire.

4. Tom's property was assessed at £17 for the house and £5 for the shop in terms of rates value in the 1866 Valuation Roll. In 1867 improvements that were made took it to a combined value of £27 which Tom contested and had reduced to £25. This annual sum was paid to the Town Council for the upkeep of civic amenities, such as roads and street lighting and was based upon a property's rental value. The growth of the Town and the costs of the developments that Sir Hugh Playfair had started, and Thomas Milton was continuing, meant that rates were higher in St Andrews than in towns of comparable size elsewhere in Scotland at that time.

16   A Champion in the Making

1. Alexandra Park was public land used by the inhabitants of Glasgow for recreational purposes. In the early 1870s Glasgow Golf Club obtained permission from the City Council to lay out some golf holes.

2. William Doleman won the Montrose event and, although an amateur, took the £6 first prize. He was recorded in the press at that time as 'a milkman carter in Glasgow'; the first prize would have been equivalent to half a year's income.

3. Baxter reported that Bennet Lang had a fine reputation for making golf clubs. A speciality was apparently being able accurately to copy any club to his customers' requirements. He must have learnt the art of club-making well in Tom's workshop. It was also said that he was a good violin maker.

17   The Finest Rounds Ever Played

1. The results and individual scores of the 1868 and 1869 Open Championships have been previously wrongly recorded in both the *R & A Championship Records, 1860-1980* and *Prestwick Golf Club, Birthplace of the Open*, published in 1989.

2. In 1870 the Course was essentially a strip of holes, the outgoing and incoming in the main sharing the same fairways and greens, with the total width averaging about 140 yards. The greens serving two holes had two hole positions cut, with different coloured flags defining the 'out' and 'in'. Apart from the 1st hole, there were no designated teeing-grounds, the ball being teed not less than six club lengths and not more than eight from the previous hole. The fairways of what today are the 2nd to the 7th holes did not exist and even the narrow, shared fairways of 1870 would be barely recognisable now. Furthermore, a horse-drawn mower could only cope with level ground, so the humps and hollows remained rough. The greens themselves had much improved since before Tom Morris arrived in 1864. He embarked upon a general renovation of them and this, together with his dictum of 'mair saun' (more sand), and the newly introduced man-pulled lawnmower

and heavy roller, had not only enlarged them but had also greatly added to their smoothness and texture. Holes were referred to by names that changed with the times; some suffixed with 'out' and 'in', for example, the 'Cartgate Out' and 'Cartgate In'. Names that were in common use for the holes in 1870 have, in the main, persisted to modern times.

3. It was at Hoylake that Tommy enjoyed himself most, for there was a special atmosphere and vigour about the place. The members of the Liverpool Golf Club worked hard and played hard. It was a place where the men who were at the forefront of trade and industry in Liverpool came for their golf and there were fewer concerns about class distinctions than at the other leading clubs.

Tommy first played the Hoylake course in his travels in 1870 when it comprised only nine holes. In the year that the Club gained royal patronage, he was back again in 1871 with Bob Ferguson from Musselburgh, to represent Scotland in what was referred to as the first International Golf Match by newspapers in Liverpool. The event was held at the opening of Hoylake's 18 holes. Jack Morris had nursed the Royal Liverpool course into a full 18 holes and it was opened in some style. Tommy and Bob, representing Scotland, were matched against Johnny Allan from Westward Ho! and Bob Kirk from Blackheath, representing England. That Johnny and Bob were as Scottish as they came was incidental and they doubtless put up as good a fight as they could for England, as well as the pot, but it was not good enough, because Tommy and Bob won comfortably. Tommy was at Hoylake again in 1872 for a Grand Tournament that attracted the biggest field of amateurs and professionals hitherto assembled south of the border. Tommy won his biggest purse at this event, £15, which was £7 more than he received for winning the Open that same year, as well as a handsome medal that he never took the trouble to have inscribed. The members of the Club generously subscribed £102 for the prize-list and full expenses for the professionals. Heaven knows what the conservative Scots thought of that largesse.

Mr James Muir Dowie of St Andrews and West Kirby was the principal promoter of golf at Hoylake, being the first Captain of the Club. Mr Dowie's wife was Robert Chambers's daughter, brought up in the family home at Abbey Park, St Andrews where George Morris, Tom's brother, was in service. It is most probably through this connection that George Morris was asked to lay out the first nine holes on the racecourse at Hoylake, in which task he was assisted by Robert Chambers himself.

George's son, Jack, was a character and much appreciated by the distinguished player and golf writer, Bernard Darwin, who tells the story of how Jack found himself in charge at Hoylake. When George Morris was invited to lay out the course in 1869, he took Jack with him on the long journey to Liverpool. George executed his task and left Jack, then aged 22, at Hoylake with the job of looking after the course and the members. His first 'shop' was in the stabling behind the Royal Hotel, which then acted as the clubhouse. Jack prospered and remained at the Royal Liverpool Golf Club for the next sixty years as greenkeeper and professional, being made an Honorary Life Member of the Club on his retirement.

Jack Morris was born at St Andrews in 1847. He attended school at Carnoustie before entering employment in the office of William Thomson, a corn merchant in Dundee. He was introduced to golf on the links of Monifieth and Carnoustie where his father was the professional.

During his long stay at the Liverpool club, Jack was instrumental in the emergence of many notable players. Harold Hilton and Jack Graham were two who early on made an impression, but Jack was most closely associated with the Ball family, who ran the nearby Royal Hotel. The Royal acted as the clubhouse and Jack Morris enjoyed play with two generations of Balls at Hoylake. John Ball Senior learned to play golf in his forties and is said to have become a scratch player within a year of taking up the game. While he and Jack enjoyed regular matches against Captain Molesworth and Johnny Allan from Westward Ho!, he was, however, closer to his son, John Ball junior, who became the outstanding player. Young Ball grew up on the links with Jack, for he did not go away to school or University. As a player, he was supreme in his generation, winning the Amateur Championship eight times after 1888, and the Open in 1890. Jack Morris played in the Open in 1873 and again in 1878 without distinguishing himself. It was as a club professional and teacher that he was lauded in his day, none more so than by John Ball and Bernard Darwin.

18   Renovations in Making the Play

1. Spoil from excavating the foundations of Alexandra Place in the Town was first dumped on the Sandyhill in May 1867. The ground was levelled and the hollow across the Links filled and smoothed. By July, The Royal and Ancient had added palings to stop encroachment on the newly seeded areas. Not unexpectedly, in the council chamber, George Bruce objected to the fencing being put up without Council consent but he was immediately overruled. More spoil from the foundations of Major Bethune's property at Abbotsford Crescent was dumped on both sides of the Burn throughout the winter months of 1867 and in the spring and summer of 1868 seeding of these areas continued apace.

Seeding of the newly-prepared ground was not completely successful, for in March 1869, turf laying from the Sandyhill down to the road was begun. Turf was obtained from a grass park beside the railway station and it was carted and laid by Andrew Strath, the eldest of the redoubtable golfing brothers and the winner of the Open in 1865, and his men. They completed the job by May 1869 but not without a scare, for in the spring of that year it did not rain for six weeks and the turf would have been lost but for the Town fire brigade, who dammed the Swilken Burn and regularly hosed the whole area.

2. Banking and controlling the course of the Swilken Burn took place in phases that can be clearly seen in the stonework and the materials used along its length.

The process started at its highest reaches when a bridge was built for the new Station Road in 1850. This banking progressed in stages down the Burn to the Swilken Bridge from 1867 to 1870 and beyond, past the site of the green to where another wooden bridge was built over to the present day 2nd tee. Below this, the Burn remained largely untamed and it was not until 1889 that its modern day course was finally set.

That same year, building work on the Strathtyrum estate produced spoil that was dumped on the northern side of the Burn – on the Cheape property, it should be noted – which altered its course to double back onto the Town's land, the present day 1st fairway. Some saw this as a Cheape attempt at a land grab and protest was made to the estate. With no response forthcoming, Mr Fernie, a member of The Royal and Ancient, took it upon himself and at his own expense, to hire a workforce to put matters to right and restore the Burn to what he understood to be its original course. It is said that this was completed overnight but whether this was the case or not, Mr Cheape served a writ on Mr Fernie and action in the courts was only averted with a public apology and a payment of £30 compensation to the estate. The revised course of the Burn was allowed to remain, however, and its course has stayed fixed to this day.

19 An Unlikely Match

1. Archery at the time was an elitist leisure pursuit of the nobility and landed gentry. The use of bow and arrow as a weapon of war had ceased several centuries before, but The Royal Company of Archers in Edinburgh continued to act as the Sovereign's Bodyguard in Scotland, a tradition maintained today. Wolfe Murray, a member of this august body, was clearly sufficiently skilled in the art of shooting arrows with bows that he felt able to challenge Tommy Morris's prowess with clubs and ball. There are several other similar contests recorded in the nineteenth century with different contestants.

2. It may be happenstance that Margaret Drinnen was employed as a ladies' maid in St Andrews some time after 1871. Tommy and Margaret may have met in a number of ways in the Town; after church on a Sunday evening or perhaps at Mr McPherson's dancing classes. Certainly, if Margaret did not attend the Rose Club Ball held in the Town Hall in January 1872, she would have heard all about it, for it dwarfed in scale and grandeur even the annual Autumn Ball of the The Royal and Ancient.

3. Margaret Drinnen was the daughter of Walter Drinnen and Helen Donald. Walter was born in Tarbolton in Ayrshire in 1812. Helen, born in 1817, was from Strathairn in Lanarkshire where they met and married in 1836. Their eldest son, George, was born there in the same year. In 1838 Walter was in Carluke, where Agnes and William were born, and Lesmahagow in 1840, when Helen gave birth to John, the second son. They were back in Carluke in 1841 when Margaret was

born and were still there when baby Helen appeared in 1844. By 1846 they were settled in 5 Crofthead Road, Whitburn, where William was born.

4. William, the second son, died in 1851 just before Mary, who was destined to become a domestic servant, was born. Walter was born in 1853 and he was followed by Robert in 1855 and finally by Catherine in 1859. By the time Catherine was born, George, Agnes and Margaret had left home. John Drinnen continued to live there. He was a pillar and first captain of the Greenburn Cricket Club. John left to set up his own home when he married Marion Giff in 1867. Watty and John had a reputation for their pit-bull fighting dogs.

20 A Tied Match in West Lothian

1. The location of Playfair Place has long been something of a mystery. The only record of their home address is to be found on Margaret's death certificate, and that address remains a puzzle. Playfair Place does not exist today. The only records of it having existed as a street are to be found in the 1871 census and the Town's Property Valuation Roll. A close inspection of the census reveals the location of Playfair Place to be the extension of North Street at its then west end. It was named in honour of Provost Playfair soon after his death in 1861.

The Boyd family owned the two-storey house together with the larger three-storey one next door. John Leslie, vintner and proprietor of the Golf Inn across the road at the top of Golf Place, rented the larger of the two houses in 1874 and the smaller property had already been rented when Tommy secured the lease late in the year. The name of Mrs James Gillespie has been crossed out, and that of Thomas Morris, 'golf ball maker', is overwritten in pencil in the Valuation Roll for 1874. The two houses together comprised what then existed of Playfair Place. This little street was re-named Albany Place in honour of Prince Leopold, who was created Duke of Albany in 1881, by which time the much grander Playfair Terrace on the other side of the street had been built.

22 Recognition and National Acclaim

1. While David Park was overshadowed by his famous brother Willie, he nevertheless was a formidable golfer. His role and ability has been somewhat overlooked, but his professional career spanned nearly twenty years. Davie's most notable success was in 1866, when he was runner-up to his elder brother, Willie, in the Open Championship.

2. The reminiscences of an old Carnoustie man, who had been the coachman of the town's four-in-hand and a caddy as a young boy, recalled: 'A great professional tournament came to town . . . And I remember us lining up at the station to look for Young Tom Morris, David Strath and Jimmy Anderson, as if we were to welcome three kings. It may interest readers to know that Young Tom met his

match that day and the tournament was won by Davie Strath. Davie was a boy at heart all his days and ever ready for any fun or nonsense.'

23 The Beginning of the End

1. Tom Morris started to keep a scrapbook of newspaper cuttings soon after his arrival in Prestwick. The scrapbook is an out-of-date Glasgow, Paisley, Kilmarnock and Ayr Railway Company record book of *Return of Daily Traffic* at Prestwick Station.

Tom's first entry is a *Fifeshire Journal* account of Col. Fairlie's installation as Captain of The Royal and Ancient Golf Club of St Andrews, dated October 1850. The scrapbook is made up of 138 newspaper articles pasted onto 29 sheets of the *Daily Return*, covering matches, club meetings and notices at St Andrews, Westward Ho! and Prestwick. Touchingly, the last entry, dated September 6th 1875, is *The Scotsman's* account of the professional meeting at North Berwick, which included the notice of Tommy's wife's death.

24 The Ultimate Tragedy

1. While the regular edition of Clark's *Golf: a Royal & Ancient Game* was published in 1875, the Large Paper Edition (50 copies) and a few special presentation copies contain the Tommy Morris obituary written by James G. Denham in January 1876. These two editions must therefore have been published in that year.

It was Denham who proposed the toast to Tommy in the Golf Inn on his triumphal return to St Andrews in September 1870 after making the Challenge Belt his own. He was also a trustee of James Hunter's will, and as such was central to the administration of the estate of Tom's son-in-law following his death in Alabama in 1886.

2. We have consulted Emeritus Professor Sir Roddy MacSween, Britain's most distinguished pathologist, who, on the available evidence, gave rupture of an aneurysm of a large artery, with fatal bleeding into the right chest cavity, as a high possibility of cause of death.

26 Heartache

1. Although the second Royal Captain of the Club, Prince Leopold was the first to 'drive-in' and actually come to the Club. He was only the second member of the English Royal Family to visit St Andrews, the other being Charles II some two centuries before. While the Prince of Wales (later King Edward VII) was elected the first Royal Captain in 1863, he did not play himself in as Captain.

Prince Leopold, who was a haemophiliac, was urged by his doctors to take part in non-contact sports. He took up golf and a course was laid out for him in the grounds at Windsor. He became a reasonable player and was encouraged in the game by William Skene, a close friend at Christ Church, Oxford. Skene was from an old landowning St Andrews family, a keen golfer, and Captain of The Royal and Ancient in 1873.

2. This report from the *Fifeshire Journal* implies that Tom Morris had made the club especially for the occasion.

26 An Unmarked Grave in Australia

1. David Strath's grave remained unmarked and forgotten for 127 years until Noel Terry, Historian of Royal Melbourne Golf Club, discovered, after much research, its location, and the circumstances of his death. On 29 January 2006, in a moving ceremony with a representative from St Andrews and a piper present, a memorial stone was unveiled to mark his final resting place. The Golf Clubs of St Andrews and the Golf Society of Australia, together with some individuals, raised the funds for this memorial which marks the grave of Davie Strath, the great friend and golfing rival of Tommy Morris.
 The inscription reads:

DAVID STRATH
CHAMPION GOLFER
BORN ST ANDREWS, SCOTLAND 1849
DIED MELBOURNE, AUSTRALIA 1879

ERECTED BY SUBSCRIPTION FROM THE MEMBERS
OF THE GOLF CLUBS OF ST ANDREWS, SCOTLAND
& THE GOLF SOCIETY OF AUSTRALIA

 One week later, a dinner to celebrate his life was held in the clubhouse of Royal Melbourne Golf Club. It was attended by over 140 people. David Strath had finally received the recognition and acclaim he so richly deserved.

27 'Generous with His Time and Spirit'

1. Miss Phelps has proved difficult to identify. She performed the unveiling of Tommy's memorial plaque in the Cathedral graveyard and we can find no obvious reason why she should have been afforded this honour. Phelps is not a common Scots name; there are no Phelps recorded as friends or relatives of the Morris family and no one in the Scottish census of 1871 could be found fitting. In the 1871 Georgia census, however, a Phelps family was living in Savannah where John Phelps, the head of the family, was described as a floor cloth merchant, exactly the same as had appeared in the Scottish census in Edinburgh ten years earlier. The Edinburgh family had emigrated to the United States sometime before 1870 and

it is possible that Lizzie had befriended the family during her stay in Darien. The eldest of the three Phelps daughters was the same age as Lizzie and she is the most likely candidate to have performed the ceremony. It is not unlikely that Miss Catherine Phelps had accompanied James to visit Lizzie in St Andrews at that time.

28 The Road War

1. Mr MacGregor, a house painter who was the founder of the still thriving auctioneers which bears his name, with Mr Bain of the Royal Bank of Scotland behind him, was the leading speculator. Like Mr MacGregor, Mr Harris and George Bruce were town councillors who also purchased Pilmour Links cottages and sub-divided the feu before selling the properties on at handsome profits. But the Council was also made up of men of independent means who clearly resented the blatant opportunism in this speculation on land and, more importantly, the abuse of the privileges of the councillors.

In 1876, the Hon. Charles Carnegie, another town councillor and a member of The Royal and Ancient, completed a fine house for himself facing the Links halfway between Sandyhill at the corner of Golf Place and Grannie Clark's Wynd. Others soon followed. Mr Harris completed a house next door, designed by the same architect, and a terrace was started. General Moncrieff rented this house and with the completion of a third house by Captain Allen, it was impossible to arrest further development. It would take less than ten years for the terrace to spread up the hill to Tom's shop.

Bain and Macgregor, who had purchased many of the northern ends of the fues, were clearly men of foresight, and Carnegie, Moncrieff and Allen were men of influence. With Macgregor, Carnegie, Harris and Bruce on the Town Council and Carnegie and Moncrieff on the Committee of Management of The Royal and Ancient, they formed a powerful and ultimately invincible cabal.

2. Extract from the cross-examination of Tom Morris in the Links Road legal case:

> (Q.) Did Mr Paterson tell you anything to this effect, that the stopping of the road would be the first step to getting back the ground on the west of the Swilkin Burn? (A.) *Yes; I quite admit that. I object to the town having given that away to the Dempsters in the beginning of the century, and I would sacrifice anything to get it back. I have said I would give the roof off my house to get it back.* (Q.) Is your objection to this road a step towards getting back the Links to the west of the Town? (A.) *I hope so. If I got back those Links I would be quite content to leave the road as it is. It was Mr Paterson who put the idea into my head about getting back the Links to the west of the town.* (Q.) And you say the objection to this road was not his idea? (A.) *No; I object stoutly to a road as a hazard for golf* (Shown No. 62.) *I signed that paper. That was before I changed my mind.* (Q.) And everything you did before that goes for nothing? (A.) *Just that.*

I don't recollect a special committee of the Club being appointed in March 1878 to consider the question of this road. I have no recollection of such a committee consulting me on the subject, as to whether the road would do any harm to the green. That may have happened. I don't recollect expressing any opinion to Major Boothby about it at that time. (Q.) Do you recollect that they in consultation with you were unanimously of opinion that the road should be formed? (A.) *No. My opinion in 1878 was not that a road should be formed, but I wanted a bank formed to keep the water from this disputed ground from going over the green. That would be done by raising a turf verge, and sending the water down the terrace.*

3. These leading members of The Royal and Ancient included Leslie Balfour, Major Bethune, Major Boothby, the Hon. Charles Carnegie, George Mitchell Innes, Captain Randle Jackson, Sir Alexander Kinloch, Dr George Lees and John Whyte-Melville.

31 Characterising the Game

1. Douglas Rolland was clearly annoyed by an article in the weekly magazine *Golf* of 3 August 1894 which reported that 'Rolland, for reasons which need not be stated here, cannot go to Scotland'. He wrote a letter of complaint informing them 'that there is no truth in this statement, and that I am able and willing with the sanction of my present employers, to go to Scotland at any time'. *Golf* duly apologized.

While the Union of the Crowns of England and Scotland in 1603 united England and Scotland under one Sovereign, it was not until 1707 that the Act of Union was ratified. This created the United Kingdom of Great Britain uniting the two countries under one flag (the Union Jack) and one Parliament (in London) but embodying the Scottish national identity by preserving as inviolate the Presbyterian Church and the Scottish Legal System. Thus a civil Scottish writ could not be enforced in England, and hence Rolland was beyond the jurisdiction of the Scottish courts for as long as he did not set foot in Scotland.

32 Death in Alabama

1. Archibald Downie was engaged to redesign an upper storey to be built over the shop. The local newspaper described him as a 'rising young townsman'. He was certainly an outstanding young golfer and the sons who followed him were equally good. The builder and contractor appointed was William Ness. Mr Alex McPherson, another good golfer, was engaged to do the concrete work.

The right-of-way to the Links Road from 6 Pilmour Links at the Town end of the property was enclosed in the building operation and a doorway built from this passageway onto the road.

2. The fact that James Hunter donated club shafts as prizes might suggest that he

was involved in the hickory trade from America. Donors of prizes invariably presented their own wares and club shafts had never been presented before, or since.

33 Family Affairs

1. Major Robert Bethune and Alexander Keiller-Bruce signed Deeds of Assumption as trustees on 3 April 1886 in a solicitor's office in Ayr when Charlie Hunter resigned his trusteeship of James Hunter's estate. His resignation went into the Books of the Lords of Council on 7 June. We do not know why Charlie resigned trusteeship of his cousin's estate but there was no animosity involved. Tom and Charlie remained close and loyal friends for the rest of their days. It is most probably the case that Charlie was satisfied with the Quorum of Trustees in St Andrews and, with Robert Hunter being granted administrative rights of James's estate in America, he felt that everything was satisfactorily in place.

2. Cheques for £3,092 were received on 28 September 1891 and a further £5,000 on 5 March 1891. £1,470 arrived on 1 July 1891, £1,882 in December 1891 and £1,308 in May 1892 in settlement of the cash due from the American estate to the trustees.

Mr Stuart Grace, Secretary of The Royal and Ancient Golf Club and a solicitor in St Andrews wrote to Robert Hunter and the Probate Court of Mobile County concluding the estate and its administration. Robert had served Lizzie and her family well. The accounts he kept as Administrator of her late husband's estate in America were meticulous.

36 New Facilities on the Links

1. George Bruce was an outstanding man of Victorian St Andrews in an age of outstanding men. Born in 1826, he was the son of a local surgeon and attended the Madras College with some academic distinction. He was destined for the University but before he could sit the scholarship and bursary examinations, both his parents died leaving him and his brother, Alexander, aged 15 and 14 respectively, to support the family. George's plans for higher education were abandoned and both brothers were apprenticed to tradesmen in the Town. His interests, however, remained scholarly and he wrote lengthily and on a wide range of subjects, publishing *The Birds of St Andrews Bay, Reminiscences of the Wrecks of St Andrews Bay* and *Destiny and Other Poems*. He was of independent thought and nursed a barbed and biting wit that was the scourge of the council chamber. The private museum that became his daughter's sitting room in Market Street was remembered by townspeople long after his death.

2. This sewer causes problems to this today, for it passes diagonally across the 1st and 18th fairways of the Old Course and from time to time requires attention when the ground caves in on it.

39 The Old Order Changes

1. Jamie Anderson's brothers had established a club-making business which flourished under the management of David, 'the wee Da', Jamie's younger brother, who continued as an Open Championship player for some years without any noteworthy measure of success. Old Da' Anderson had five sons who all entered the club making business after apprenticeship with the Forgans. David and his younger brothers prospered while Jamie, the eldest of 'Da's tribe', and a three times Open Champion, did not. Jamie's nephew, David's son, would however play a significant role in the future of Tom Morris's business.

40 A Constant Benefactor

1. John Kirkaldy, the eldest, was the first of the brothers to enter the Open lists at St Andrews in 1882 and again at Prestwick in 1884. Hugh joined him in the field at St Andrews in 1885 and at Prestwick in 1887. All three brothers played in 1888 at St Andrews by which time his younger brothers were already eclipsing him.

2. David Herd went to Littlestow, Fred to Knebworth, Sandy ultimately to Fixby at Huddersfield and James and John to Chicago.

42 In Testimony

1. Lyon Playfair, 1st Baron Playfair of St Andrews, was the nephew of Sir Hugh Lyon Playfair. He was born in India in 1818 where his father was with the East India Company and at the age of two was sent home to St Andrews where he was educated at the grammar school and the University. He enjoyed a remarkable and distinguished career in science before entering politics where he became Post Master General, Chairman of the Ways and Means Committee and Deputy Speaker of the House of Commons and a Cabinet Minister. He was an earnest supporter of Prince Albert's proposal for the Great Exhibition of 1851 and for his work as chairman of the awards committee, for his services to Parliament as a Liberal MP and to science as a distinguished chemist, Queen Victoria rewarded him with a peerage. He was also a Lord-in-Waiting to Her Majesty.

2. The stationmaster's house is now the Jigger Inn attached to the Old Course Hotel that occupies the site of the first St Andrews Railway Station.

44 The Evangelist and a Place of Pilgrimage

1. James Foulis (pronounced Fowls) was one of three men and a boy employed in the Tom Morris workshop in 1870. He was born in 1841 at St Andrews where he lived for the rest of his life and became an outstanding player in the Operatives, St Andrews and The Rose Golf Clubs. His brother Robert, born in 1843, was a

cabinetmaker who turned his hand to club-making in Robert Forgan's workshop sometime after 1871. James was a millwright by training who became a club-maker with Tom Morris soon after he acquired G.D. Brown's premises at the Links in 1867. James was Tom's first employee and the shop foreman for over 40 years.

2. Robert Forgan was three years younger than Tom. According to his obituary, he joined his uncle, Hugh Philp, in his club-making business in 1840 and inherited it as a one-man undertaking from him in 1856. When Robert died in 1900 he was employing 50 clubmakers as well as office and labouring staff.

Two of Robert Forgan's sons, James and David, worked in banks in St Andrews before emigrating to America in the 1880s. Both enjoyed phenomenal success in American banking. James succeeded Mr Lyman Gage in the management of the First National Bank, Chicago, when Gage was appointed to President McKinley's Cabinet in 1896. David, meanwhile, rose to become President of the Union National Bank, Chicago, in 1898. In May 1900, when both brothers were back in St Andrews on holiday, they planned an amalgamation of their respective banks and resolved to put a proposal before their directors. This plan was adopted and the banks combined, adopting the name of the larger partner, the First National Bank, and in doing so made it one of the most influential banking institutions in the US. James became President of the new unified bank and David assumed the role of Vice-President.

Bibliography

PRIMARY SOURCES

The Minute Books and records of:

The Royal and Ancient Golf Club and the Union Club
Crail Golf Club
Earlsferry Thistle Golf Club
Irvine Golf Club
Prestwick Golf Club
Prestwick St Nicholas Golf Club
Shinnecock Hills Golf Club
St Andrews Golf Club
St Andrews Thistle Golf Club
The New Golf Club, St Andrews

Documents held by:

The National Archives of Scotland
The National Library of Scotland
The Scottish Record Office
The British Library
The Mitchell Library, Glasgow
The Ida Hilton Public Library, Darien, Georgia
The Probate Court and Library, Mobile, Alabama
The University of South Alabama
St Andrews Preservation Trust
St Andrews University Library Archive
The West Lothian Local History Library
The Morris, Morrow and Rusack families
The Baird family
The Playfair family
The late Joseph Tiscornia Collection
Various private collections

Periodicals and magazines

The Field
Golfing Annual, Vol. I (1887/1888) to Vol. XXIII (1909/1910)
Golf, 1890-1899
Golf Illustrated, 1899-1912
Golfing, 1895-1910
The Golfer, 1894-1898

Newspapers

Ayr Advertiser
Ayr Express
Bell's Life in London and Sporting Chronicle

Dundee Advertiser
Dundee Evening News
Fife Herald
Fifeshire Journal
Glasgow Herald
Northern Echo
St Andrews Citizen
St Andrews Gazette
The Edinburgh News
The Scotsman

Scrapbooks compiled by:

Morris, Tom, *Selected newspaper cuttings, Oct. 1850–6 Sept. 1875,* 1875.

Robertson, Allan, *Book of selected Chamber's Edinburgh Journals, Oct 13 1832–Dec 2 1843,* 1843.
    Book of selected newspaper cuttings 1835–1869, started May 1864.

SECONDARY SOURCES

Adams, John, *The Parks of Musselburgh,* 1991.

Adamson, Alistair Beaton, *Allan Robertson, Golfer – His Life and Times,* 1985.
    In the Wind's Eye, North Berwick Golf Club, 1980.

Aikman, George, *A Round of the Links: Views of the Golf Greens of Scotland,* 1893.

Balfour, Arthur J., *Defence of Philosophical Doubt,* 1879.

Balfour, James, *Reminiscences of Golf on St Andrews Links,* 1887.

Baxter, Peter, *Golf in Perth and Perthshire: Traditional, Historical and Modern,* 1899.

Behrend, John, *The Amateur, The Story of The Amateur Golf Championship, 1885–1995,* 1995.

Behrend, John and Lewis, Peter N., *Challenges and Champions, The Royal and Ancient Golf Club, 1754–1883,* 1998.

Behrend, John, Lewis, Peter N. and Mackie, Keith, *Champions and Guardians, The Royal and Ancient Golf Club, 1884–1939,* 2001.

Behrend, John and Graham, John, *Golf at Hoylake,* 1990.

Bennett, Andrew, *The Book of St Andrews Links,* 1898.
    The St Andrews Golf Club Centenary 1843–1943, n.d.

Boyd, A. K. H., *Twenty Five Years of St Andrews,* 1892.

Bruce, George, *Destiny and other Poems,* 1876

Browning, Robert H. K., *A History of Golf: The Royal and Ancient Game,* 1955.

Burnet, Bobby, *The St Andrews Opens,* 1990.

Carnegie, George Fullerton, *Golfiana, or, Niceties Connected with the Game of Golf,* 1833 and 1842.

Cant, R. G., *St Andrews in 1793 and 1838: The First and Second Statistical Accounts,* 1991.

Chambers, Charles E. S., *Golfing: A Handbook to the Royal and Ancient Game,* 1887.

Chambers, Robert, *Vestiges of the Natural History of Creation,* 1844.

Clapcott, C. B., *The History of Handicapping,* n.d. [1924].
    The Rules of the Ten Oldest Golf Clubs from 1754–1848, 1935.

Clark, Eric D., *The 150 years: A History of the St Andrews Golf Club 1843–1993,* 1993.

Clark, Robert, *Golf: A Royal and Ancient Game,* Large Paper Edition, 1876.

Cockburn, Lord Henry, *Circuit Journeys,* 1888.

Colville, George, *Five Open Champions and the Musselburgh Golf Story,* 1980.

Colville, James, *The Glasgow Golf Club, 1787–1907,* 1907.

Cousins, Geoffrey and Scott, Tom, *A Century of Opens,* 1971.

Dalrymple, W., *Golfer's Guide to the Game and Greens of Scotland,* 1894.

Darwin, Bernard, *The Golf Courses of the British Isles,* 1910.
   A History of Golf in Britain, 1952.

Dow, James Gordon, *The Crail Golfing Society, 1786–1936,* 1936.

Everard, Harry S. C., *A History of the Royal and Ancient Golf Club, St Andrews from 1754–1900,* 1907.

Farnie, Henry Brougham [A Keen Hand], *The Golfer's Manual,* 1857.
   Handy Book of St Andrews, 1859 and 1865.

Farrar, Guy B., *The Royal Liverpool Golf Club: A History, 1869–1932,* 1933.

Fleming, D. Hay, *Historical Notes and Extracts concerning the Links of St Andrews, 1552–1893,* 1893.

Galbraith, William, *Prestwick St. Nicholas Golf Club,* 1950.

Geddes, Olive M., *A Swing Through Time, Golf in Scotland 1457–1744,* 2007.

Gillon, Stair A., *The Honourable Company of Edinburgh Golfers at Muirfield, 1891–1914,* 1946.

Goodban, J. W. D., *The Royal North Devon Golf Club, A Centenary Anthology,* 1964.

Grierson, James, *Delineations of St Andrews,* 1807 and 1838.

Hackney, Stewart, *Bygone Days on the Old Course,* 1989.
   Carnoustie Links: Courses and Players, 1988.

Hamilton, David, *Golf – Scotland's Game,* 1998.

Henderson, Ian T., and Stirk, David I., *Golf in the Making,* 1979.
   Royal Blackheath, 1981.

Henderson, J. Lindsay, *The Records of The Panmure Golf Club,* 1926.

Herd, Alexander (Sandy), *My Golfing Life,* 1923.

Howie Smith, Robert, *The Golfer's Year Book for 1866,* 1867.

Hughes, W. E., *Chronicles of Blackheath Golfers,* 1897.

Hutchinson, Horace G., *The Book of Golf and Golfers,* 1899.
   Famous Golf Links, 1891.
   Fifty Years of Golf, 1919.
   Golf: The Badminton Library, 1890.

Information – *Golfers of St Andrews against Charles Dempster etc., 1805, Edinburgh.*

Information – *Charles Dempster against Hugh Cleghorn etc., 1805, Edinburgh*

Jarrett, Tom, *St Andrews Golf Links, The First 600 Years,* 1995.

Johnston, Alastair J., *The Clapcott Papers,* 1985.

Johnston, Alastair J. and Johnston, James F., *The Chronicles of Golf: 1457 to 1857,* 1998.

Ker, William Lee, *Kilwinning,* 1900.

Kerr, John, *The Golf Book of East Lothian,* 1896.

Kirkaldy, Andrew, *Fifty Years of Golf: My Memories,* 1921.

Kroeger, Robert, *The Golf Courses of Old Tom Morris,* 1995.

Lamont-Brown, Raymond, *St Andrews, City by the Northern Sea,* 2006.

Lang, Andrew, *The Book of Monifieth Golf Links Bazaar,* 1899.

Langton, Harry, *Thomas Hodge – The Golf Artist of St Andrews,* 2000.

Leach, Henry, *Great Golfers in the Making,* 1907.

Leman, G. E., *A Short History of the Origin of Golf at Northam and the Foundation of the Present Royal North Devon Golf Club*, n.d. [1926].

Lewis, Peter N., *The Dawn of Professional Golf*, 1995.

Lewis, Peter N., Grieve, Fiona C. and Mackie, Keith, *Art and Architecture of the Royal and Ancient Golf Club*, 1997.

Lewis, Peter N. and Howe, Angela D., *The Golfers – The Story behind the Painting*, n.d. *The Royal and Ancient Golf Club of St Andrews: celebrating 250 years*, 2004.

Lewis, Peter N. and Morrison, Angela D., *Good Men Remembered – A Tale of Golf, Empire and St Andrews*, 2000.

A Grand Man and a Golfer: The Novelist George Whyte-Melville and his Memorials, n.d.

Lewis, Peter N., McDougall, Fiona and Morrison, Angela D., *A Focus on Golf: St Andrews and Photography 1845–1859*, 2001.

Low, John L., *F. G. Tait, A Record, Being his Life, Letters and Golfing Diary*, n.d. [1900].

Louden, David, *Biographical Sketch of the late Lieutenant-Colonel Sir Hugh Lyon Playfair*, 1874.

MacArthur, Charles, *The Golfer's Annual for 1869–70*, 1870.

Macdonald, Charles Blair, *Scotland's Gift, Golf*, 1928.

Mackie, Keith, and Harper, Chic, *One Hundred Years New, A History of the New Golf Club, St Andrews*, 2003.

Maughan, William Charles, *Picturesque Musselburgh and its Golf Links*, n.d. [1906].

McCartney, Keith, *Tom Morris of St Andrews – 'The Grand Old Man of Golf'*, 1998.

McDougall, Fiona and Howe, Angela D., *A Memorial on the Links – The Life and Legacy of Lyon, 1st Baron Playfair of St Andrews*, 2002.

McEwan, Peter J. M., *Dictionary of Scottish Art & Architecture*, 1994.

McLaren, R. M., *The Honourable Company of Edinburgh Golfers, 1744–1944*, 1944.

McPherson, J. Gordon, *Golf and Golfers, Past and Present*, 1891.

Miller, T. D., *The History of the Royal Perth Golfing Society*, 1935.

Mortimer, Charles G., and Pignon, Fred, *The Story of the Open Championship 1860–1950*, 1952.

Orr, J., *The History of the Kennedys*, 1854.

Park, William, *The Art of Putting*, 1920. *The Game of Golf*, 1896.

Peter, H. Thomas, *Reminiscences of Golf and Golfers*, n.d. (1890).

Pilley, Phil, *Golfing Art*, 1988

Playfair, Hugh, *The Playfair Family*, 1999.

Playfair, Sir Hugh Lyon, *Memoirs*, 1861.

Reid, William, *Golfing Reminiscences: The Growth of the Game, 1887–1925*, n.d. [1925].

Robb, George [A Golfer], *Historical Gossip About Golf and Golfers*, 1863.

'Rockwood', *Reminiscences of West Country Golf*, 1904.

Ryde, Peter, *Royal and Ancient Championship Records 1860–1980*, 1981.

Salmond, D. S., *Reminiscences of Arbroath and St Andrews*, 1905.

Salmond, J. B., *The Story of The R. & A.*, 1956.

Shaw, James E., *Prestwick Golf Club, A History and Some Records*, 1938.

Simpson, Sir W. G., Bart., *The Art of Golf*, 1887.

Smail, David Cameron, *Prestwick Golf Club*, 1989.

Smith, Charles, *The Aberdeen Golfers: Records & Reminiscences*, 1909.

Tulloch, W. W., *The Life of Tom Morris, with Glimpses of St Andrews and its Golfing Celebrities*, 1908.

Index